**Mrs. Smithson, Principal.**

*"The Four Communities Classroom brings out the best in children and there is considerable carry-over."*

**Mrs. Dubray, Vice Principal and grade 4/5 Teacher.**

*"I've seen the benefit - it pays dividends all year."*

**Mrs. Dubray again.**

*"The energy you are able to give to your children in terms of teaching curriculum is so much greater. There is significantly less stress, and it seems that children take on much more responsibility and carry on with their tasks. The Four Communities Classroom allows children to develop their abilities and blossom at their own level in a way that they feel safe."*

**Ms. Gaudet, Grade 3 Teacher.**

*"The Four Communities Classroom is a very user friendly system."*

*"Parents reported that the Four Communities Classroom made their children more manageable."*

**Ms. Eva, Education Assistant.**

*"I noticed that all the children had really high self esteem, they learned what was important and were applying that to their lives and learning."*

**Ms. Tibbs, Internship Education Student.**

*"I think that any of the teaching interns could have been nominated for the Bates Award for excellence if they had used this system."*

*"My internship supervisor from the College of Education was really impressed with my class."*

*"The Four Communities Classroom helped me to put into effect the philosphical thinking learned in university teacher-education classes."*

**Danny, Grade 7 Student.**

*"It helped you to make friends. We knew everyone in the class very well."*

## Bullying Sidelined

It is important for children to feel the strength, power and efficacy of communities and communication, founded upon an experiential understanding of autonomy (of self), integration (with others) and the importance of mutual regard.

Thus children can take joy in being valued and in valuing others. All are celebrated members in an environment of infinite potential. This is a place where each child can feel emotionally safe, move forward with greater confidence in self and be excited about learning. This is what we strive for and live, in our Four Communities Classroom. (p. 3)

---

Children learn how to understand and communicate difference as a vital part of life, rather than a source of unrest or basis for bullying. This is a powerful process to engage in troubled classrooms.

# MY DAUGHTER CAN'T WAIT FOR MONDAY MORNING

## Child-driven Responsibility For Sustainable Education In Happy And Productive Classrooms - Bullying Sidelined

The Sterling System for Ecologically-based Sustainable Classrooms

## Martin J. Sterling

Edited by Heather Sterling

> A sustainable future begins with children.
> The most influential person in the world today
> is the person who spends time with our children.

Cover design by Christian Jensen

My Daughter Can't Wait For Monday Morning; Child-driven Responsibility For Sustainable Education In Happy And Productive Classrooms - Bullying Sidelined

The Sterling System for Ecologically-based Sustainable Classrooms

Copyright 2013 Martin Sterling - author

Edited by Heather Sterling

Cover design by Christian Jensen

All rights reserved. Except for pages marked with 'can be photocopied', no part of this publication may be produced, stored in a retrieval system, or transmitted, in any form or by any means, electronic, mechanical, photocopying, recording, or otherwise, without the written prior permission of the author.

This book is catalogued at Library and Archives Canada.

ISBN 978-0-9881379-0-5

Printed by CreateSpace, a book print-on-demand division of Amazon.

Order this book on line at www.amazon.ca

and other retailers www.createspace.com/3928729

Frazer/Sterling Publications

martinjsterling.com

To my wife Heather, and sons Simon and Robin, for our happy family life,
my parents Victor and Dorothy Sterling for my happy childhood,
to the teachers and principals who invited me into their schools,
and to the many children whose company I have enjoyed in the classroom.

# The Four Communities Of
# 'My Daughter Can't Wait for Monday Morning'

The Sterling System for Ecologically-based Sustainable Classrooms organizes children into four communities - one community in each corner of the classroom, where children work towards a culture of mutual regard, becoming ever more skilled in being thoughtful, effective people, not only within their own community but in the classroom community as a whole.

This means that learning opportunities throughout the year are capitalized upon with increasing effectiveness, whether it be in interpersonal relationships or taking ownership for learning and curriculum.

For teacher and children, the school year becomes interesting, enjoyable and effective. Curriculum learning, therefore, is also poised to be seen by children as interesting, enjoyable and an effective process.

---

## THE FOUR COMMUNITIES MISSION STATEMENT
### Transitioning To Mutual Regard

All children in the Four Communities Classroom are engaged in the development of:

- considered thinking processes in relationship with others.

- awareness, at an emotional level, of the importance of reciprocation.

- understanding that difference in thinking is an expression of the individuality of us all.

- understanding that learning is often enhanced through interpersonal communication.

- understanding that our own and others' feelings are part of our communication process as we grow and learn.

# Acknowledgments

Following a career teaching in elementary school, high school and university, and giving workshops to teachers throughout Saskatchewan, Canada during professional development days, I had no plan to write a book on teaching.

Only after being invited into classrooms to demonstrate the Four Communities Classroom system I had developed with children in my own classroom and being asked if I had some written material on this, did the idea take hold to write a book.

I have principals and teachers of the Saskatoon Public School Board, Saskatchewan, Canada, to thank for welcoming me into their schools and classrooms. I would like to particularly recognize teachers Ingrid Benning, Shannon Rak, Marie Gaudet, and Elaine Dubray for their contribution to the book.

Special thanks goes to the late Dr. Douglas Hicks, Superintendent of the Saskatoon Public School Board, for his support and faith in me from the earliest days to the beginnings of my writing, and also to Professor Don Cochrane, Educational Foundations, University of Saskatchewan and Dr. Alan Ryan, College of Education, University of Saskatchewan.

I would also like to recognize Dr. Dudley Plunket and Dr. Peter Figueroa of Southampton University, England, Dr. David Selby, who I first met at York University, England, and my brother Dr. Stephen Sterling, Professor of Sustainability Education at Plymouth University, England.

I owe a debt of gratitude to Christian Jensen, friend and award-winning graphic designer who unstintingly gave of his time and considerable artistic talents to design my book and trouble-shoot along the way as I worked on layout.

Most importantly, I want to give a huge thank-you to my wife Heather for her encouragement and words of wisdom throughout our many thought-provoking discussions and for applying her considerable editing ability to this book.

# Foreword

By Dr. Edmund O'Sullivan

*Dr. O'Sullivan, professor emeritus at OISIE (Ontario Institute for Studies in Education) at the University of Toronto, Canada, is the author of 'Transformative Learning: Building Educational Vision for the Twenty First Century', published by ZED Press. His work centres on "ecological issues that emphasize a global-planetary vision combining ecological literacy, social justice, and human rights concerns, and diversity education …"*

Searching for a meaningful vision for education in the twenty first century: This is the challenge for educators. We are living in a period of the earth's history that is incredibly turbulent and we are slowly coming to an understanding, in some quarters, that we have a deep responsibility for the present state of the world. We have to acknowledge, in Al Gore's words, that we are not only creatures of nature, we have become potent 'forces of nature'. As humans, we have to take complete responsibility for this power that we have been both blessed and cursed with. On this account alone, it is indeed appropriate to consider the role of educational institutions in creating a sustainable way forward; one which makes the fundamental task of our times a choice for a sustainable planetary habitat of interdependence. In our present historical moment, we are in need of new visions for education that will deal with the new demands of our sustainable survival.

Martin Sterling's book entitled 'My Daughter Can't Wait for Monday Morning'; Child-Driven Responsibility For Sustainable Education In Happy and Productive Classrooms - Bullying Sidelined' is a work that addresses these challenges.

Martin Sterling is a seasoned educational practitioner who has taken on for himself the formidable challenges that educators face in our time. The book that he has penned is both practical and visionary. With a wealth of practical wisdom and experience, he invites us to think 'outside the box' of conventional wisdom as we move into a new way of delivering education for sustainable, vibrant living.

Can our goal for our classrooms be the creation of a habitat where children are so engaged that they can't wait for Monday morning? Is this a realistic outcome? Can we expect our students to be happy and doing serious and productive work at the same time? In Sterling's view, a quality education must be embedded into the deeper values of vibrant joyous living. The deep relational possibilities of living fully and growing into full proportions with a solid enduring sense of self, requires a holistic and integral education, fostering deep connections to the largesse of the "web of life".

At the outset, Sterling outlines the current worldview of modernism, initiated by Descartes. He invites the reader to consider the fragmentation produced by the worldview of atomistic mechanism and its deleterious effects on modern educational theory and practice.

He then moves the reader into perspectives of holism and integration theory. He refers to this foundational theory as the theory of living systems, offering the busy teacher an overview of the philosophy and function of the book, so that he/she can, if preferred, move directly and swiftly to the 'How To' chapters, begin classroom change and later visit, at leisure the more in-depth foundations of this system in the appendices. Here, Sterling references the collective work of such scientists as Fritjof Capra, Candace Pert, Carl Sagan, Ann Druyan, John Briggs and F. David Peat, gathering and bringing to the fore revolutionary concepts to illustrate the theory of living systems. It is his contention that the theory of living systems, embedded in the synergy of these theorists is relevant and applicable to children's education. He makes this parallel because he considers the children are, after all, living systems as they go about the tasks of their learning journeys. Therefore, Sterling contends, in understanding the theory of living systems that sheds light on our ecological core and, in colloquial parlance, what makes us tick, an environment can be created for children conducive to growth, learning and joy.

The 'How To' in the ecological classroom is the hands-on section for the teacher, which Sterling lets us know can be initiated without the theoretical background

I would suggest if this direction is taken first that the teacher ultimately go to the foundational work in the appendices to round out and fully stabilize the new worldview orientation that informs Sterling's suggestions for classroom practices. What is important for the teacher, using Sterling's suggestions, is that he/she gets his or her own footing in the suggested practices being offered.

This is a refreshing book by a teacher and educational practitioner with a wealth of classroom experience. It is an ambitious and imaginative book; a groundbreaking work that offers, both at the level of theory and practice, a powerful ecological vision, providing a way to develop whole human beings in the context of sustainable education that befits the emergent needs of this century.

# Introduction

Over the past decade, I have worked extensively with teachers, helping them establish enabling environments for their children.

Our collective experience, engaging in ecological-classroom action research, gives me the confidence that this book will provide a useful guide for teachers and children. Fundamentally, the Sterling System for Ecologically-based Sustainable Classrooms facilitates constructive inner dialogue within children, empowering them to live more sustainably with each other and positioning them to explore their potential and to be happy and productive within their classroom environment. So evolved 'My Daughter Can't Wait for Monday Morning: Child-driven Responsibility For Sustainable Education In Happy And Productive Classrooms - Bullying Sidelined'. My work has been informed by the discovery of what I see as important links between my own study, observation, and experience, and the cumulative work of a number of scientists over the twentieth century. Since I am not a scientist, their collective work has served me well. The synergistic writing of Fritjof Capra, Carl Sagan, Ann Druyan, John Briggs and F. David Peat, and Candace Pert, put forth concepts that discuss the interconnectedness of all things. This seems to be very applicable to teaching, and how children think and learn in an environment of sharing, connecting and working together in an atmosphere of mutual regard.

The premise of my system is simple. Go back to who we are. Instead of seeking damage control and exerting zero tolerance, we can create classroom environments that go to the root of human response - right to our ecological core.

Sadly, problems in our schools abound, are rebounding on society, and are not going away - bullying, negative peer pressure, disruptive behaviour, inattention, disinterest, teacher burn out, failure to reach potential and diminished outcomes. We need immediate solutions with staying power. We need to create a classroom environment that resonates with children and makes the classroom a happy and satisfying place to be.

When you take children, in their formative, explorative years, into a classroom adventure for life that is exciting and makes sense of their world, they respond. Given children's strong and innate sense of fairness and what is right and logical, you and they have the basis for a winning team. Nothing is more right and logical than the ecology of the natural world. It is a pattern for life that, in our 'sophistication' we have lost and one that can be reclaimed as our birthright.

You can build on this to create the class, and the teaching experience, of your dreams. It works. I've done it. My teaching colleagues have done it in their classrooms.

Those of you struggling with student behavioural problems gain a better understanding of children and their behavioural choices. Bullying is brought under control by the collective empowerment of the class. You will find, as I have, that parents consistently report that their children are happier, look forward to school, and come home eagerly with daily reports on classroom life.

When a parent of a grade five child tells me, "My daughter can't wait for Monday morning"; when a Vice Principal and grade 4/5 teacher reports, "This class has had the fewest discipline problems I've ever had in my teaching career and some of these kids have histories of discipline problems" when Brittany, a grade seven student, says, "It's the best thing we've ever done!"; and when children love school and love learning, we have sustainable education.

Will moving towards an ecologically aware classroom require wholesale alteration of educational systems? No! Does curriculum have to be altered, and yet more room found in an overcrowded timetable? No. The success of the ecologically sustainable classroom system is contained in the breathing of new awareness into classroom life that embraces children and teacher seamlessly throughout the day.

This book outlines both a philosophy for change and, most importantly, a detailed action plan to make it happen.

Welcome to the fun and adventure of 'My Daughter Can't Wait for Monday Morning'.

- ***Ecology*** - *the study of relationships between living organisms and their environment.* The Collins English Dictionary

> Capra, '83, p. 266
> "Every organism - from the smallest bacterium through the wide range of plants and animals to humans - is an integrated whole and thus a living system. Cells are living systems, and so are the various tissues and organs of the body, the human brain being the most complex example."
>
> Capra, '96, p. 170
> "The new concept of cognition, the process of knowing, is thus much broader than that of thinking. It involves perception, emotion, and action - the entire process of life. In the human realm cognition also includes language, conceptual thinking, and all other attributes of human consciousness."

## The Four Communities Classroom - an expression of ecological living system dynamics

We cannot separate how a child feels from how a child learns. Nor can we separate quality of relationship, environment and the child's emotional comfort from how the child learns. This is what I explore in 'My Daughter Can't Wait For Monday Morning'.

We all share the roots and foundation of ecological heritage. Without the ecology, we would not exist, nor would we have sustenance. The entire community of life takes its place in, and rests upon, the ecological expression of living system dynamics - an inseparable web of relationships. We, however, are not central to this plan. Without us, ecological expression of living system dynamics would still function. The world would still turn. The environment, alongside all creatures great and small, would carry on. All human constructs of community, formed from cultural and individual perspectives, are adjuncts. Thus, regardless of world view, whether it be founded upon technology, science, politics, religion, ideology, economics, or some combination thereof, all are dependent on the ecology for being, all subject to living system dynamics.

But it is equally important to note that our ability to create perspective arises from the human's ecologically-endowed sophisticated intelligence, which gives us powers of reasoning above those of other species. However, to pursue any perspective, without regard for our ecological roots represents, at best, a narrow use of that intelligence, and also represents failure to understand the significance of mutuality and the connectedness of all things. We must never forget that, as intelligent humans, we have within our power the ability to build or destroy.

The onus is on us to ensure that ecologically-sound, mutuality processes are part of our understanding of community relationship processes. Communities need to communicate. Mutual-regard communication is key.

Foundationally, the ecology creates the sustaining context for all communities. Happily, it supplies the blueprint that we can take into the classroom so that children can most effectively live, learn and have their being in a world of communities and communication.

It is important for children to feel the strength, power and efficacy of communities and communication, founded upon an experiential understanding of autonomy (of self), integration (with others) and the importance of mutual regard.

Thus children can take joy in being valued and in valuing others. All are celebrated members in an environment of infinite potential. This is a place where each child can feel emotionally safe, move forward with greater confidence in self and be excited about learning. This is what we strive for and live, in our Four Communities Classroom.

"We can never speak about nature without,
at the same time,
speaking about ourselves."

Fritjof Capra, '83, p. 87

# Contents

| | | |
|---|---|---|
| **Chapter One** | Change | 8 |
| **Chapter Two** | The How-To of the Four Communities Classroom | 22 |

- **Preliminaries, concepts and practicalities** — 23

    Preparations, prior to children's arrival in the fall, that will help create the environment for becoming and belonging in the habitat of your classroom — 23

    The concepts of becoming and belonging as guiding principles in the classroom — 25

    Inviting and engaging children in the creation of their classroom environment — 25

    Groupings, arrangement of classroom space, desks and other furniture — 26

    The Four Communities Classroom Quick-Look Check List — 32

- **Section One - Developing the Four Communities Classroom:**
    **the teacher's role, the children's role and sharing development** — 33

    1. Creating four groups — 33
    2. Asking THE foundational question — 33
    3. Towards good teaching and learning — 35
    4. Talking about why we have groups. Group formation, friends and group membership changes — 36
    5. Talking about how we have classroom areas for each group to care for, use, organize, and decorate for classroom life and learning — 40
    6. Explaining the point system; its planning, process and integration into classroom life — 41
    7. Explaining class and group discussion and communication. The talking stick - learning to share and listen — 51
        A. Introducing the class to the idea of discussing and communicating — 52
        B. Discussion and communication for the class and groups - some guiding principles — 54
        C. Creating primary-experience life learning with class discussion process as the focus — 57
    8. Choosing group names — 61
    9. Explaining group jobs — 65
    10. Numbering students, use of in/out trays and work record keeping — 66 - 70

    ---

    The teacher as a group member — 40
    Problems or opportunities in the Four Communities Classroom — 46
    Living systems, and links to the teacher's role in discussion process — 56

    ---

- **Section Two - Developing the Four Communities Classroom - discussion forums** — 71

    11. Classroom rights (and responsibility for self and others) — 71
        A. The rights balloon activity — 72
        B. Human rights activity — 82
            - Group discussion on human rights/needs — 83
            - Group prioritization of human rights/needs arising from group discussion — 85
            - Part one - Class discussion to refine and rationalize the listed outcomes from group discussion — 87

**Chapter Two, section two cont.**
    C. The classroom rights activity    92
       - Group discussion on classroom rights    92
       - Part two - Class discussion to refine and rationalize the listed outcomes from group discussion    95
  12. Using classroom rights (responsibility for self and others)    107
  13. Learning the importance of difference    110
  14. Self-correction    113
  15. Listening-to-others- [and the teacher] awareness activity    118 and 132

---

  Introduction to the freedom/task concept for children (an avenue for primary learning experience)    75

  What if you get resistance from children, at this or any point, in developing the Four Communities Classroom?    80

  Talking stick protocols and development of responsibility    85

  The teachers freedom/task process - thinking on your feet while dealing with the unexpected    88

  The imposed directive    92

  The power of nuance    93

  Allowing time for process    101

  The voting process    102

  Thoughts on child participation    105

  Additional outcomes from discussion process    106

---

**Mid-Year Introduction:**
- **of The Four Communities Classroom**
- **of The Four Communities Classroom when seeking remedy for behavioural problems**    119

  What to do about current wall displays    123

---

**Activities for The Four Communities Classroom**    125

  More ways groups can be used in class organization and learning process    135

  The Four Communities Classroom teacher's mindset and presentation    137

---

**Chapter Three**   Teaching children how to do jot notes: furthering children's capacity and ownership for learning    140

**Chapter Four**   Group dynamics within the four communities classroom, and beyond    168

  1. General grouping concepts, and Four Communities Classroom grouping    168
    Autonomy and integration dynamics    170
    Acceptance, becoming and belonging and the exercise of identity in the group setting    171

  2. The dynamics of group integration    172
    The power seeking child in class-size setting and smaller groups    175

- **Additional thoughts on grouping children**    176
    1. Group rights: Guiding groups to more effective function    176
    2. Opportunities for children to visit other groups    177

    3. Your role as a member of each group      177
        The pre-arranged single group meetings with the teacher      178
        The impromptu single group meeting with the teacher      178 and 218

## Chapter Five     The Four Communities Classroom: accommodating different age groups     180

     Grade 2 and 3      180
     The grade 2 and 3 balloon ride photocopy page      190
     The grade 2 and 3 classroom rights balloon page      191
     Grade 4 and 5      187
     Grade 6, 7, and 8      187
     Some thoughts on High School      189

## Chapter Six     Children in action - classroom case studies     192

---

     Canadian test of basic skills (CTBS) results - a Four Communities Classroom grade 5 class      222

     Letter for photocopying for Parents or Guardians      224

     A guide to relationship dynamics in the Four Communities Classroom (diagrammatic illustration)      226

---

## Appendices     225
## Content pages     228 - 230

    (i) **Processes of change, difference and potentiality - foundations of existence and of living systems**     232

    (ii) **Ecological foundations for productive, happy learning**     248

    (iii) **Difference, commonality and the importance of emotion: connections to productive, happy classrooms**     260

    (iv) **Living systems and self-descriptors: constructive inner dialogue and the joy and succcess of life in the classroom**     282

    (v) **Communication and behaviour in the classroom: the containment influence of attractors alongside nuance, discernment, and learning**     292

     Central thoughts for teachers of the Four Communities Classroom - creating the happy, productive classroom environment
(an interconnected list for classroom life)     306

     Interactive entities of the Four Communities Classroom that engage living system dynamics (diagrammatic illustration)     307

## Glossary     308
## Index     310

# CHAPTER ONE

## CHANGE

*Busy teachers eager to move on to the 'How To' of chapter 2 can gain, in this overview chapter, insight into the direction, intent and philosophy of the Four Communities Classroom.*

*When you have the time and inclination to learn more about the ecological science of living systems that informs this teaching and learning approach, you will find it in the appendices starting on page 225.*

### Education rooted in scientific history

Imagine for one moment, spending each day of your working life sitting in a roomful of people in rows, facing the back of someone's head, with an authority figure telling you what to do and what to think. If we would not want it for ourselves, why would we think children would enjoy this environment?

However, when one looks back on the history of education, it is not surprising that we see children sitting in symmetrical rows, faces trained on the teacher, unquestionably the authority and last word on all things academic. A perfect child in this classroom listened carefully, assimilated knowledge, produced neat homework and studied avidly for exams. Order was extolled. Learning was divided into manageable modules – each subject in its own compartment. The three R's – reading, writing and arithmetic - often taught with much dedication, provided every child with a foundation for success. The teacher taught. The child listened and learned. This rather linear approach, appearing to promise an almost mechanical process of certainty, was borrowed, historically, by academia from the scientists of the seventeenth and eighteenth century and is one which has, foundationally, received little scrutiny until recently. The experts had spoken and why would one question them?

Briggs and Peat, '90, p. 175.
*"But linear models are notoriously unreliable as predicators, which is their usual function. Forecasts don't work out. … attempts to make predictions suffer a chaotic fate. The predictions fail because the models can't take in the whole of how the elements in sensitive dynamical systems interact."*

It was Rene Descartes (1596 – 1650) and Sir Isaac Newton (1642 – 1727) who collectively inspired the idea that the world and the universe could be better understood from a mechanistic perspective; a reduction into its constituent and measurable parts. Known as classical science, this reductionist and linear vision, built upon the assumption of the certainty of mathematics, created the idea that the compartmentalization of knowledge was the route to the analysis and mastery of knowledge and the understanding of existence. The advances in science and technology that followed appeared to prove the worth of this reductionist approach as a true and logical way to understand reality and encouraged the notion of separateness as part of this reality.

With life perceived in this way, one can understand how the study and understanding of nature extended to the human body and mind, and social function, with all incorporated into an exercise in analytical separation and compartmentalization. So a mechanistic worldview evolved that tended to separate and compartmentalize every aspect of life, learning, and endeavour, while marginalizing people's need to integrate knowledge with experience, intuition and feeling. People became experts in each of the many 'parts' that make up the 'whole' of human existence and focused on their particular expertise. Expertise became synonymous with certainty; certainty became a podium on which authority could stand and deliver. And, very significantly, these perceptions had a huge influence on the decisions taken on how to educate children.

With education and acculturation processes founded upon Cartesian/Newtonian/Classical science for around 300 years, and hierarchical sociological assumptions for likely thousands of years, this influence has continued to pervade and indeed been embraced by those who feel they have succeeded within its structure. Even those who feel less fulfilled will likely have been sufficiently acculturated to defer, with little question, to the authority of the status quo and be resigned to not being able to 'succeed' within the classical frame of reference. And so the classical frame has become the dominant measure for self.

Capra, '83, p. 101.
*"(The) Cartesian (Descartes) world view and the principles of Newtonian physics maintained their strong influence on Western scientific thinking."*

So it follows that, with the best of intentions, in the education of our young, our classical science assumptions continue to influence. There is the tendency to believe that preferred outcomes are realized through the teacher taking responsibility for children's behaviour and learning and that this is achieved through hierarchical control.

Thus, while this Cartesian approach has often been very useful for scientists, it has also limited our understanding of ourselves.

## A glimpse into the classically driven classroom

Within the classically driven classroom we are often missing the opportunity to see, touch, experience, connect with and build upon our holistic, emotional, intuitive and feeling selves, in relation to learning. When education is influenced by the Cartesian reductionist view and the 'learn things by taking them apart' approach of classical science, education can find itself, as classical scientists did, with little facility to accommodate unwanted variables or as Briggs and Peat explain, *"take in the whole of how the elements in sensitive dynamical systems interact."*

The classically-driven classroom does not welcome behaviours (the unwanted variables) that cut into the effective transmission of curriculum to classes of children. Emotionally-driven student behaviour signifying irresponsibility, bullying, disrespect, discipline problems, inattention, lack of motivation, dislike of school, dislike of a subject or a teacher, all hamper efficiency. Having to teach, simultaneously, children with wide-ranging abilities and/or interest, as well as children with learning and/or emotional and/or psychological problems, all present problems, with a friction potential that can cut into the efficient transmission of knowledge. These 'variables' are major stumbling blocks, when the assumption that too often drives educational endeavour is that learning means learning the curriculum and the acquisition of knowledge. The variables, often expressed through discipline problems, force schools into accommodation.

While much is done in schools to look after and encourage individual children (although often limited by time and resource constraints), the underlying assumption of the primacy of curriculum and the need to get through it still remains. Teachers will do their best for children, within the constraints of time, budget, and the curriculum. Many agree that a broader vision of education is nice if one has the time (and patience), but broader visions are sometimes seen as presenting peripherals to the 'essential' knowledge and curriculum transmission. The assumption at work here appears to be that if contextual factors and relationship building are given precedence, it may well be at the unacceptable cost of reduced knowledge transmission.

However, many schools do develop initiatives that accommodate needs beyond the curriculum. The case for integrating some special needs children into regular classrooms is one example. This approach enables socialization to occur between children of different needs and, according to the special needs of the child, a varied range of other benefits. But it is a case of new initiatives occurring within old parameters of functioning. Benefits realized arise within the knowledge-based underpinnings of classical science that still informs the teacher and forms the basis of expectations (especially for the teaching of children with no 'special needs'). This, inevitably, makes teaching more demanding for the teacher primarily charged with curriculum completion, and represents somewhat of a contradiction for a system that prefers to minimize the impact of variables upon curriculum transmission.

Teachers, of course, deal with variables that affect teaching daily, and know that variables affecting efficient transmission of knowledge cannot be avoided. They understand that emotions and sense of well-being or otherwise, are triggered by putting people together and are, therefore, inevitably, part of the school context. Relationship dynamics are part of being human. Feelings, like it or not, are part of the educational context. And herein lies the dilemma. The response of 'we must get through the curriculum at all costs and struggle with the fallout as best we can' will not necessarily present happy solutions.

How many of us feel that the more exhausted we are at the end of the workday, the more we have proven our worth? But it doesn't have to be that way. We need to dispel, as myth, the notion that struggle is part and parcel of achievement. This can be difficult when we've been conditioned since the early days of Descartes and Newton to believe that 'order' is to be sought after, no matter how tough and elusive it appears to be.

Why did we not realize, long ago, that a mechanistic, knowledge-driven approach to education is not necessarily efficient or viable for every child? It is, of course, western history's impact upon the present. It is the modus operandi that has been woven into the fabric of everyday lives for centuries. Though the mechanistic approach established by early scientists in an attempt to understand and create order was flawed, especially in its application to human interaction, it was also deeply entrenched. Given that established norms of society tend to pass seamlessly and unquestioned from the conscious to the unconscious, the vestiges of outmoded beliefs tend to prevail. And so, despite many educational initiatives, the actual foundation of mechanistic education - a product of classical science — has remained largely beyond question. Moreover, with a lot of hard work, the mechanistic approach has produced results for many students in the classroom. Teacher and student may not always find it a joyful experience, but when was school supposed to be always fun? And those who fail are seen as simply not measuring up. The system did its best, but the student, unfortunately, was not up to the task.

## From the classical science of mechanistic certainty to the new science of dynamic potentiality (see appendices for more)

In recent times, new science has shifted the mechanistic idea of existence being formed from irreducible and determinant building blocks of life (as atoms were once thought to be) to an understanding of connections and potentiality between electron particles (which also manifest as waves) as the basis of subatomic reality. New science shows us that all living things have a dynamic quality that man-made, classically-based mechanisms do not possess. New science also shows us that the dynamism of go-with-the flow survival with all its varieties within the ecology is key to infinite potential; an exciting prospect for teacher and child. Moreover, the revelations of new science (the basis for systems theory science) are further illuminated by its quantum physics foundations [appendix (i)], providing a window on a world of relational equilibrium and non-equilibrium probability, full of variables.

What this new science means for us is captured in the words of physicist Fritjof Capra who says in his book The Web of Life, '96, p. 37:-

*"Ultimately — as quantum physics showed so dramatically — there are no parts at all. What we call a part is merely a pattern in an inseparable web of relationships. … For the systems thinker, the relationships are primary."*

So, from the subatomic level to the over-arching context of ecology, of which we are part and parcel, the top-ranking element of connection and relationship appears to be, after all, the stuff of life or, as Capra calls it The Web of Life. This is a living system and ecological worldview of connection and relationship with profound implications for how we see children, their development processes, and their education.

This connection and relationship form the foundation upon which my teaching system is based; that the life of the classroom is, at its very core, an interconnective, ever-changing and unquantifiable process; a process of life that, in classrooms, needs accommodating, facilitating, and enabling; a process of living systems in action.

I outline, in layman's terms [appendices (i) to (v)] the theory of living systems, and its associated theories (systems theory) to ground an approach that recognizes how education, in theory and practice, fits into the ecological context of existence.

The science, discussed in physical, chemical, biological, and ecological terms, is used as a window to shed light on children and their learning patterns. In the Four Communities Classroom we see living systems dynamics at work and the ways in which we can engage discernment in children to maximize learning in the classroom.

Interestingly, when teachers choose to adopt this Four Communities Classroom teaching system they find they are not entering foreign territory at all. In fact, they find that their own intuition and belief in the interconnectedness of all things, which is at the ecological core of each one of us, is only too happy to guide and direct them in this new adventure. Children, (who are not asked to understand the science) likewise, respond with an innate understanding and enjoyment that engenders happy and productive classrooms.

Although my system is grounded in living system science, which of itself is fascinating, it is not actually necessary to have a deep and thorough knowledge of the science to adopt the Four Communities Classroom system as your own. Just as one learns to drive a car by driving it, you will increase your understanding of the Four Communities Classroom through practice. You do not have to begin as an expert. You invite children into the adventure and explore it together. It is your job as guide to make this a fun adventure. My 'How To' chapter (p. 22) is a detailed handbook that will serve as co-pilot on your journey. You begin with effective tools and passengers full of potential.

### Systems theory science applied to the classroom

As Capra says, (The Turning Point, '83, p. 77),
*"In contrast to the mechanistic Cartesian view of the world, the world view emerging from modern physics can be characterized by words like organic, holistic, and ecological. It might also be called a system view, in the sense of general systems theory. The universe is no longer seen as a machine, made up of a multitude of objects, but has to be pictured as one indivisible, dynamic whole whose parts are essentially interrelated and can be understood only as patterns of cosmic process."*

Systems theory science offers an exciting concept that can take children into an ebb and flow of classroom life that encourages the innate dynamism of young minds to flourish and learn with joy and excitement. And you will find that when your classroom environment offers children this opportunity, behavioural problems will diminish and curriculum assimilation will flow. Your classroom will be a happier place where children love school.

The path to this classroom environment is far from an elusive one. System theory science leads the way, and links and connections can be made with of learning and relationship. (See 'A Guide (a diagrammatic illustration) to the Relationship Dynamics In The Four Communities Classroom', on p. 226). The nature of child-created variables, properly accommodated, are no longer stumbling blocks that impede knowledge acquisition, but opportunities for growth, learning and harmonious connection. It's fun and it's fascinating. It's ecological education at its best and most productive. Curriculum acquisition becomes more closely aligned with life process, following the natural flow of delight in learning to reach for one's full potential.

All learning is experienced within an environment of autonomy (sense of self) and integration (relationship with ecological/social environment). In an ideal environment there is mutual respect between each individual child, as well as child and teacher, facilitating the integration of the classroom group into one mutually dynamic whole of autonomy and integration in balance. The key to achieving this ecological classroom lies in understanding what makes us tick. Children long to be understood. We all have that need. We are all complex beings, full of variables. Appreciating that variables can be an expression of classroom diversity can enable happy learning in all children – even beyond what the curriculum requires.

Let's take a closer look at emotional elements (positive and negative) that are, in fact, an integral part of our ecological makeup.

Remember 'Thomas the Tank Engine', the little engine that could; the little engine that surpassed all expectations by learning to say, "I think I can. I think I can." For decades, children have delighted in this story of empowerment, although they may not know what empowerment means. But they know the feelings that Thomas had, very well.

## Problems within educational process?

But how often does a child feel less than empowered when he or she is clearly identified as less than others, in terms of measurable knowledge acquisition. Sadly, this can be an unfortunate and inadvertent outcome of an education process that ranks knowledge above all, at the expense of feelings. Low self-esteem can be high on the list of outcomes for some. For too many, education can become a process (especially in the higher grades) of discovering the degree to which you are lacking knowledge, perhaps unable to match those who aren't lacking and are able to get close to 100% in the measurement tables. So the little engine says, "I think I can't. I think I can't" and from there it can mean diminished outcomes if not a downward spiral. The highlighting and recognition of curriculum attainment, through posted results, honour roles and (publicized) award programmes compound the feeling of exclusion and the belief of inadequacy. Therefore, such selected recognition processes can not only define the 'successful' child or school, but can also, for the majority, engender self-perceptions of shortcomings. Since only a few, perhaps even just one, can win an award, striving may seem futile for the majority. To compete, 'successfully' can now mean an ever tighter concentration and focus upon, perhaps, a single goal, and at what cost to the well-rounded education?

This is not to say that measurement of progress and knowledge acquisition is not important, but that it must not be the only recognition of a child's abilities and worth in school. The whole child has a great contribution to make to his or her learning, to his or her peers, to his or her teacher and to the life of the classroom in general. For the child who lives in a classroom environment that affirms every aspect of learning and emotional response, constructive outcomes can be realised - a child who genuinely feels, right to the bottom of their soul, "I think I can. I think I can." And you know what? They can. It's living systems theory in full flow in the classroom. It's the ecological classroom doing its mighty work. And it is not the teacher making everything happen. The teacher is the facilitator and guide. Making the ecological classroom system work is everybody's job.

## Towards the ecologically sensitive classroom

The science and dynamics of living systems show that all life exists in very complex patterns of connection, in community with other life. For example, from the limbs and organs of the body to the anthill factory, to the beehive, every individual part has a job to do that is essential to the health and wellbeing of the whole. It is representative of the process of autonomy (of self) and integration (with others) in balance. These elements of connection are fundamental to expressions of ecological existence and, therefore, also human existence. We are ecological beings. It follows, therefore, that, through interconnectedness within the classroom environment, every individual has a job to do that is essential to the health and wellbeing of the whole - the classroom and everyone in it.

Thus, when children, through experiential learning, are guided towards a classroom ethic that values the importance of difference, the importance of a balance of caring for the needs of both self and others and the value of mutual regard, children are empowered to contribute in constructive, positive ways to their own and others' development.

- **Seeking to make sense of the world**

From early childhood, in everything we do, we strive to make sense of our world. Before a child can talk, the baby seeks signals of response in the mother's face. Growing and developing, the child gains a greater sense of self and awareness of relationships with those around, establishing a place in the world of the family. Seeking to make sense of the world is a process that continues as the child ventures into the wider world of school. So how does a child make sense of an ecological, interconnective and contextual world (of which we are all derivatives), in an education system that functions largely in a de-contextualized, compartmentalized and primarily measurable-only environment? Confusion can ensue. Some children adapt and accept. Some do not. Problems loom. While a preparation-for-the-economy approach to education is laudable, is it a sufficient basis for the discovery of self and others, identity, human potential, one's fit in the world, and the shaping of a preferred future for self and society? The classical scientific model has served us well in many respects – striving for a quantifiable foundation of certainty. But is it enough? Will it provide an environment where the child can develop happily into a whole and well-balanced person with the tools to make sense of the world and his place in it? A re-work of classically-based education in terms of a broader contextual vision and ecological connectivity may, in fact, prove useful by taking all that is good and placing it alongside a recognition of variables and the impact of emotion on learning.

- **Towards emotional maturity**

Integrated into every fibre of the ecological classroom is a recognition that the child's emotional response can range from the most evident to the most subtle. Just as life-forms of the natural world follow their preordained patterns of behaviour (their ecological niche), so children, as thinking emotionally motivated humans, seek and find comfort and affirmation in life patterns and responses that make sense to them. Recognition of children's drive to seek comfort, affirmation and sense has huge implications for understanding where children are in their thinking and chosen behaviours, and also in working towards the goal of a happy and productive classroom. This is a quest that children and teacher undertake together as partners co-existing in the world of the classroom. The science of living systems can help the teacher through an experiential approach to learning, to be the wise and caring guide who lights the way on the never-ending path to each child's infinite potential. The term, 'the sky's the limit'; it's true.

Poet and playwright William Butler Yeats (1865-1939) said, "Education is not the filling of a pail, but the lighting of a fire."

And indeed, throughout the history of education, there have been many initiatives and many dedicated teachers who have inspired their students to aim for the stars. What is key in the science of living systems is the greater ease with which wonderful outcomes can be realized. It introduces the all-embracing, ecological view of one cohesive whole into the classroom. It creates a comfort level that children choose in order to make sense of their world. It affirms them. They gain confidence in their ability. And so it becomes their preferred way of being. They choose mutual regard. They recognize and value difference. They gain a building sense of self and an appreciation of others; a healthy balance of autonomy of self and integration with others and surroundings. They find themselves happy in their classroom environment and excited about learning. That is why many potential problems are averted and that is why problems which do arise can often be addressed by the classroom as a whole.

The children have the tools to do it.

The observation of Ms. Eva, an Education Assistant and signer for a hearing impaired child offered an interesting example of this when she noticed the behaviour of some children in a grade eight class that had, in grade five, been in a Four Communities Classroom. There seemed to be a legacy effect from that experience, she said, so strong that she jokingly nicknamed them 'the implant children'; children who seemed to have something extra about them.

*"I noticed that all the 'implant' children had really high self esteem, not necessarily leaders but definitely not followers. They were not afraid to be themselves, and not concerned about being cool, fitting in or being popular. Without working at it they were cool and popular because of being themselves, strong characters with a sense of humour - just nice kids to be around. The children seemed to have learned to pick and choose what was important and what was not, and were applying that to their lives and learning."*

The process that Ms. Eva jokingly referred to as 'an implant' was, in fact, a reflection of allowing and nurturing that which is in all children.

Ms. Eva went on to say, to my continued delight and amazement -
*"Some of the other children in the class who displayed behaviour problems, didn't take academics seriously and gave school a low priority, started watching the 'implant' children and appeared to be thinking - 'well it looks like it might be better to be like them, and get attention that way.' The types that thought it was cool to be tough started to adapt. It's as though the implant children were bringing them up - not consciously - just in the way that they were."*

It seems there is even a beneficial knock-on effect for children who had not experienced the Four Communities Classroom. Is that possible? In terms of the living systems interactions of autonomy (self) and integration (surrounding environment) it is - qualities emerging in self (allowed and nurtured) through environment and relationship. In other words, the 'implant' children created a positive integrative environment for other children's autonomy of self - one that enabled benefits to flow. Thus, a beneficial environment constructively affected other children's autonomy.

So let's take a closer look at the approach to classroom life, based on the science of living systems.

### The dynamics of ecological living systems; a guidepost to productive, happy classrooms

Interestingly, the classical scientists' ongoing search for certainty led, eventually, and, rather paradoxically, to the discovery of quantum mechanics, paralleling the theory of living systems that, instead of certainty, reveals a dynamic changing reality.

We begin to lay the foundations for the creation of productive and happy classrooms by first recognizing that the quest for absolute certainty cannot avoid being an authority-imposed state where dynamism tends to go unrecognized rather than harnessed. Within any group of individuals, there are no absolutes, but rather a dynamic changing reality; a reality that, in your classroom, is as natural and inevitable as the changing tides; natural as life itself. Absolute certainty and order is, therefore, not a state to be sought or prized. Unfolding alongside the classroom structure there may be minor (or even major) 'disruptions' to the smooth running of your classroom. Rather than being viewed as problems, these provide, instead, opportunities for all to contribute to a resolution, while learning about the ups and downs of life in a safe, accepting environment. The classroom is, in fact, a microcosm of the complex world where we coexist alongside all living things. Let us take a look at those dynamic elements of living systems theory, our place within the ecological context, and how this relates to classroom life.

We have observed that the communities of life in nature self-organize in their relationship to habitat context. We see bees working together, each one sure of its place in the big scheme of things, each adapting to variables for the optimum success of the hive. Likewise, anthills have a beautifully orchestrated group of workers, each ant with a job to do - surmounting obstacles, but none straying from its appointed task. In a dynamic work environment balance is achieved. It is a self-organizing ability. This self-organizing ability in relationship to context has relevance also for the organization of human communities and processes of interaction and learning.

In other words, ecologically, everything evolves and changes in response to an environment that is a reflection of its constituents; the dynamics of autonomy (of self) and integration (with surroundings) at play. This makes the ecology a dynamic, interactive process. We, and all of life, are an expression of this ecological process.

What I have discovered in my action research with children and in classrooms is that by recognizing our ecological foundations, we can build an ecologically sound environment where children can flourish, be happy and make sense of their world - a place where they can gain a healthy balance of self-esteem and mutual regard. The striving towards balance of autonomy (of self) and integration (with surroundings), so vital to the natural world, can be brought into the child's world and the life of the classroom. This is a world full of dynamic variables that are accepted and welcomed as opportunities for learning.

Ms. Gaudet, grade three teacher.
*"Children get to know kids that they would, as a rule, probably not talk to - they have to communicate with their small group and it bonds them - therefore, there are few discipline problems"*

Everyone has a job to do. Everyone is responsible for the wellbeing of the whole. Children, through guided experiential learning, acquire the tools for making this happen. The teacher is no longer alone and assuming responsibility for classroom success. The happiness and success of classroom life is a shared endeavour. Children enjoy this newfound regard for their thoughts, contribution and feelings. They enjoy assuming responsibility for understanding and recognizing the thoughts and feelings of others and most soon decide that this path to a happy, productive learning environment is the preferred one. Important for the success of the Four Communities Classroom, these processes represent part of the legitimizing of constructive inner dialogue in children.

Attention-getting behaviour, frowned upon by the children, becomes a less attractive option. Children working together and looking out for each other are not isolated and, therefore, less easy targets for bullying. Would-be bullies, who are given a voice and choices, are more able to choose to earn the acceptance of the group, rather than disrupt the classroom and all its stakeholders. (See 'Moving forward with bullies - The Story of Jason' - case study p. 195.)

As children learn the importance of difference (p.110), they begin to appreciate difference in each other. Teacher and children begin to enjoy and embrace the variables that each day brings and work around obstacles to reach their goals of happiness, harmony, good teaching and good learning. That's what they are there for and, children agree, nothing less will do. Academic success is a happy byproduct of happy days.

You may be thinking, that perhaps this is too good to be possible. It isn't. We have the self-organizing ability of our ecological core resource; the laws of nature to guide us.

Ms. Gaudet, grade three teacher.
*"The Four Communities Classroom is a very user friendly system"*

## Making four communities in your classroom

Your class is built on a foundation of four communities. Children are divided into four groups, with desks arranged in open circles or horseshoe shapes. The children work together with three complementary goals - for individual success, the success of their group and the success of the entire class. Thus the four groups compete with each other, yet support each other. It's a fun and inspiring platform for autonomy and integration in action, as well as mutual regard. Each individual attends to his/her task, while striving for the good of the whole, surmounting obstacles to achieve learning harmony. The Four Communities Classroom structure and methodology create an enjoyable and challenging environment with infinite potential. Most importantly, the components of this system are not add-ons to a 'classical' classroom. This is a living, breathing system that is an integral part of classroom life. Each facet is woven seamlessly into the tenor of the day to create a classroom culture unto itself, where children begin to naturally assume responsibility for learning, accept and respect each other, listen and learn from each other and consider each other's ideas and opinions. It is a culture that does not seek certainty or absolutes, but rather aspires to the striving towards balance of autonomy (of self) and integration (with others).

What this all comes down to is a focus on relationships. Every child is a highly complex, thinking, feeling, reacting individual. Every nuance of both yours and each child's behaviour will have an impact on the whole. As guide, everything you do and say and how you do and say it will have an emotional impact on each child. Children will learn from your example. In a safe, accepting environment, where variables are to be expected, they will learn from each other.

Since the emphasis of the Four Communities Classroom is on constructive relationships and connection let's now take a closer look at the dynamics of relationship.

## The dynamics of relationship

In general, the quality of responsibility felt by two people towards each other is closely linked to the quality of the relationship.

- Quality of responsibility affects quality of relationship.

Inversely, the quality of the relationship is determined by the quality of responsibility each person feels towards the relationship.

- Quality of relationship affects quality of responsibility.

So it could be said that good relationships are maintained through responsible behaviour, and that responsible behaviour generates good relationships.

However, the potential for a positive relationship can be diminished when one person attempts to assume control over the other. Responsibility assumed by one over another makes it difficult for either side to nurture a constructive relationship. The imposed upon person's sense of responsibility to the arrangement is compromised, and likely diminished. The relationship is not as good as it could be. Just as this is true of individuals, it also applies to groups, peoples, institutions, countries and classrooms.

We've had ample evidence of compromised relationships in societies based on hierarchical foundations, where there is the assumption of the right to take responsibility and control of others. This is rarely a mutually agreed upon arrangement, but it is often assumed to be the logical way to proceed. Assuming authority and control, even with the best of intentions, often results in dominating relationships whereby the dominating party hopes that uncertainties and variables will be minimized; direction will be more easily established and lead to more precise outcomes. However, when the variables are people and their decision-making involvement in the relationship is rendered less meaningful, the relationship is unlikely to be a happy one. Feeling marginalized tends to dampen one's desire to cooperate.

And this is a pattern we tend to find in the classical classroom, where the teacher assumes authority, with the best of intentions. After all, she/he believes, that use of authority and discipline is the principle way to ward off any potential for poor behaviour. The children have to know who is boss and, hopefully, that will minimize the uncertainties and variables of unacceptable behaviour. Children have to learn to respond in a 'responsible' and 'intelligent' way.

But sadly, the sought-after cooperation is not always forthcoming. This lack of cooperation is then seen as 'irresponsible', simply underlining and demonstrating the need for stronger discipline and more control. What we end up with is, on the one hand, co-option (responsibility assumed by the teacher) and on the other, marginalization of the child, perhaps creating a diminished desire to invest effort in constructive contribution. The efficiencies envisaged by the controlling teacher may then not be realized, perhaps due to resentment on the part of the child. Moreover, any further initiatives to correct subsequent problem behaviour may appear to the now marginalized child, to be imposed dictates. This type of relationship is rarely constructive. Teacher and child are not happy.

Children need, rather, an engagement within the classroom that enables them to practice sensitive relationships with empowered, professional teachers, so that the constructive, open-to-life learning mind-set, so often displayed by children in early grades, is built upon, encouraged, and enabled to continue. This, in fact, means the enabling and continued use of children's ecologically endowed innate capacities. Let's look at how this can be achieved.

## Creating the classroom with emphasis on constructive relationship

In all types of relationships, where there is a high level of mutual regard, there is a greater recognition of alternative views, values and desires. There is a need for compromise and a striving for integration of preferred outcomes. The process will generally require some effort. It is going to take perhaps lengthy transactions - some constructive, others not - to accommodate the imprecision and unpredictability that is a part of every interaction. However, since imprecision and unpredictability are a part of life, engaging children in this process would, it seems, be a vital part of their education and learning.

A Four Communities Classroom environment based on mutual regard and accommodating the variables is a far cry from the classroom where the teacher feels a need to control a situation by assuming responsibility for all parties involved and deciding on a course of action that must be unquestioned – everyone falling into line and 'behaving themselves'.

Some children, as they grow older, may not fall happily into the assumption of unquestioning deference to authority. Even the little child wants to ask "Why?" Nature has primed them to seek answers. When deciding their own responses to situations and influences around them, children do not necessarily assume acculturated perspectives of the adult world. Perhaps they have not yet been sufficiently acculturated to make Cartesian-based assumptions, and don't know the 'rules' (yet). Children do, however, have at their disposal the influence of their ecological core – their innate sense of what is right. Having to put their feelings, responses, opinions, decision-making and autonomy on hold for six hours a day doesn't feel right. Having the teacher, no matter how kind and helpful, assume responsibility for everything they do, thereby offering little opportunity for them to make considered, responsible decisions, and then asking them to behave responsibly, doesn't feel right. It doesn't feel right not to have adequate opportunity, throughout the day, to experience the striving towards balance of autonomy of self and integration with others and surroundings, found in relationships of mutual regard. Though a child could likely not express or define these feelings, every child, nevertheless, has a finely tuned sense of what is right and fair. When their world is not in tune, children can tend to either withdraw or show resentment through bad behaviour. The teacher is left feeling confused and upset when classroom life is disrupted by 'problem' children and is less than rewarding when some children withdraw and show little interest in learning.

It doesn't have to be that way. It's time to shift some of that responsibility over to where it belongs. It's time to create a classroom environment where everyone takes responsibility for good teaching and good learning. The Four Communities Classroom creates the enabling environment for the eager young minds in your class.

- **Children assuming responsibility**

In deciding to allow children to assume responsibility for their behaviour and learning, you should not immediately envisage a free for all - far from it. Constructive relationships do not arise from free-for-alls. Just as there is structure in nature, which accommodates variables that, in turn, create strength and order, so it is in the Four Communities Classroom. Just as trees are rooted in the earth, live and grow within that structure and yet individually, produce a variety of leaves in endless shapes and shades, so children grow within the structure of the Four Communities Classroom and produce a variety of thoughts and responses in endless shapes and shades. The classroom community operates on a discussion-based approach, developing in each child a sense of reciprocation and mutual regard. This structure affords everyone dignity; constructive relationships in action. In the How-To chapters, I offer suggestions on how to facilitate (rather than lead) discussion, alongside some experiential learning activities.

Building a sense of reciprocation, mutual regard, dignity and constructive relationship seems to exhibit beneficial effects beyond the classroom.

Ms. Gaudet, grade three teacher.
*"Parents reported that the Four Communities Classroom made their children more manageable."*

- **Good teaching and good learning**

The ultimate foundation of this classroom is about good teaching and good learning. This is the starting point, established at the outset. You ask the children "What are we here for?" Discussion ensues. It's interesting to ask the question, "What would your parents say if we sent a letter home to say that we're not interested in good teaching and good learning?" They can all see that wouldn't fly. There are never two discussions alike, but, invariably, children, of their own volition, decide that they are here for good teaching and good learning and that it is a good and worthwhile goal. We decide together that, from now on, everything has to meet those criteria. We all get to accept good teaching and good learning as the foundation of our classroom. There is structure established in a common mindset that we have arrived at through an all-inclusive process.

From now on, no child can avoid confronting problems with the foundational question: "How does taking someone's pen help with good teaching and good learning?" How does coming back late after recess help with good teaching and good learning?" How does bullying another child help with good teaching and good learning? Soon you will find that it's not only you asking the question. You've got a team of watchdogs. Right now, if you want to see some turnaround stories, take a look through the case study chapter (p. 192).

- **Classroom rights**

Your classroom agenda also includes the discussion of classroom rights. This fits well into the classroom atmosphere you are building – one of dignity, constructive relationships, reciprocation and good teaching and good learning. This is why, at this point, children come up with useful rights, such as the right to be listened to, the right to our own space, the right to learn, the right to be different. You'll find you won't have to feed the discussion. Good rights will come. In my experience, every class comes up with different rights, their own version of what they want for themselves and for each other, but always with the same foundational points. (see pp . 71 and 92.)

- **Respecting differences**

Creating a classroom where everyone respects each other and gets along does not mean that everyone has to be best friends. Some children think differently from others and have different views and perspectives. But they do learn to respect and have regard for each other. They learn to appreciate difference and agree to differ. That is an end in itself. In the environment that you create, good connections naturally evolve and grow between children. But that is theirs to do and relationship outcomes usually have little to do with you as a teacher. They get there on their own. Hence they take ownership for their classroom environment and the relationships they create.

Niki - grade 7 talking of grade 5.
*"You organized the group, but we organized ourselves. You gave us the group and we then decided who did what."*

Danny - grade 7 talking of grade 5.
*"The Four Communities Classroom helped us to make friends. We knew everyone in the class very well."*

Megan - grade 7 talking of grade 5.
*"Learning of others ideas and thoughts and how to incorporate them with your own was valuable."*

- **Primary and secondary experience**

The children's quotes indicate their experiences as being primary, as opposed to secondary. The primary experience is a foundational element of nature and also of the Four Communities Classroom. When you tell children, unequivocally, what to think and do, it is a secondary experience. When you guide them through discussion or observation, they make their own decisions on how to respond and how to think about their thinking. This is a primary experience. The key difference is that a secondary experience touches only the mind. The primary experience engages the heart and the mind – the whole being. It is experiential learning. Learning that sticks. It's the learning that children take ownership for.

Mrs. Dubray, Vice Principal and grade 4/5 teacher.
*"The real strength of the Four Communities Classroom is the kids take ownership for it."*

Charlie - grade 7 talking of grade 5.
*"We were really proud of being in the Four Communities Classroom."*

- **Feelings, contribution and shared responsibility**

Children become the proprietors of good teaching and good learning; proprietors of themselves and their environment. It's the expression of what is innately ecologically within. <u>It feels right</u>.

Michael - grade 7 talking of grade 5.
*"Even if you couldn't contribute to the class, you could contribute still to your group at all times. That made you feel good. Then you would want to contribute more to the class."*

The Four Communities Classroom is grounded in feeling. Very quickly you will find positive feelings with positive interactions and feedback are beginning to naturally grow and flourish in you classroom; (the growth varies, of course, from one child to the next).

I cannot stress enough the importance of feelings. More important than attention to curriculum content, is attention to children's feelings. When children feel happy and engaged they are more open to learning and hence curriculum acquisition. Thus, the Four Communities Classroom teacher not only cares for each individual child in his/her classroom, but also hones skills in knowing how to care for children generally from a shared responsibility basis and for each group as a whole. By following the How-To guide, he/she guides children towards their potential, with the wisdom of living systems theory in practice. Knowing why children do what they do makes relationship building so much easier. When the teacher role-models respect for children, she enables them to appreciate the importance of respect for each other.

The teacher has a 'sensitivity antenna' a mile high, making sure that every child is valued for being there, listened to and, if they choose to contribute to discussion, respected for voicing their thoughts to the class or their community group.

Megan -
*"Having different skills and sharing makes a good community."*

No child feels diminished or marginalized. No child need feel alone or fearful.

Niki -
*"Voting makes us feel important. It gives us a say - makes us feel we can do stuff ourselves."*

Josh - grade 7 talking of grade 5.
*"Responsibility for myself makes me feel more mature."*

There is an ongoing sharing of thoughts and feelings that engenders trust and open dialogue.

Laura - grade 7 talking of grade 5.
*"When you are with people a lot more in the groups you get more comfortable and feel like you could be more open."*

Mrs. Smithson, Principal.
*"The Four Communities Classroom brings out the best in children and there is considerable carry-over."*

Children learn to take care of each other. Needless to say, bullying does not do well in this environment.

Essentially, the children re-learn what, in their short lives, may have been lost along the way. Our natural state is one of joy and laughing. Little children have that, and sometimes social conditioning and the classroom experience can take it away. How often are people told to "be serious"? How often are children told to "simmer down"? How often do disenfranchised children strike out by being difficult in the classroom or by being mean to each other? What happens from the time a child first goes to school and the time, in later grades, when behavioural problems may arise?

Most young children look forward to going to school, especially if they have older siblings who do this grown up thing every day. So on the first day of school, in a grade one class, the teacher generally looks out on a sea of open, eager little faces, filled with anticipation. These are children with energy to spare, on a quest for fun activities. I remember that my eldest son was so keen that he was sure he would be able to read by the end of his first day in grade one. This is a little group of minds ready to learn; to soak up new experiences and adventures like so many little sponges. It's a lovely image and one that should remain throughout a child's entire school experience and throughout life.

Every moment cannot be a good or happy one, but this is where the teacher's sensitivity to the feelings of each child can turn a problem into an opportunity for learning and defuse an otherwise negative experience that could have left a child feeling angry, upset, and/or confused. When children feel they are not understood or listened to, they can respond with negative behaviour. Children who feel they are respected and listened to, children who do not feel powerless, children who feel that they are understood, look forward to being in this environment every day because, right to the depths of their ecological core, they feel safe. They can relax and have fun learning, because they know this is a good place to be. What you are giving them is an environment in which they can transcend and shine, using every faculty bestowed upon them by nature.

A precious endowment of every amazing human being is the power of reasoning. This highly sophisticated and complex faculty sets us apart from other species. It is a gift, but it is also a huge responsibility. It gives us the power to choose our way through life, from the smallest decision to the most monumental.

Meanwhile, each individual is interacting and integrating with other human beings with the same powers. And alongside this highly developed faculty of reason is the often more powerful element - that of emotion. The "How does it make you feel?" is, more often than not, the deciding factor in human response and behaviour.

So when you, as a teacher, respond to and interact with children, the key question cannot be "How can I make them learn?" but "How can I enable them to feel good, open and responsive so that they will want to learn?" And the answer is there in the theory of living systems – by striving towards establishing a balance of autonomy of self and integration between teacher and child and between children and each other.

### Understanding the science of living systems or developing the four communities classroom - what comes first?

It's your choice.

You will find, in the appendices, p. 225, thoughts that are foundational to the Four Communities Classroom. However, for those who wish to embark on their own Four Communities Classroom experience without delay, the information in the appendices can wait for another day. Teachers have done just that and have been very successful.

Now that you have read this chapter, if you wish, begin right away to explore the Four Communities Classroom process with your class. I suggest that you be open with the children. Tell the class that you have discovered a new way of learning in the classroom and you thought that you could explore it together. Thus, you may want to say something like this - "Let's try this and see where it takes us." By saying this you invite children to participate in an adventure (and one that is safe, because you too are involved). With the spirit of adventure, comes the spirit of anticipation and open minds. This is a great way to start something new. Let the exploration begin.

Teacher notes throughout the 'How To' will give you a ready reference that you can see at a glance as you introduce and practice with children, day by day, the elements of the Four Communities Classroom.

When you have the time and inclination to learn more about the work that informs this teaching and learning approach, you will further be able to discover throughout the science of living systems the parallels between the classroom environment and the natural world. It's a study that reveals the wonderfully orchestrated dynamics that create the endless, ever-changing, evolving symphony of communication, learning and limitless potential.

Regardless of your starting point, the Four Communities Classroom teacher's job is to help children feel at ease in this dynamic process. Through following the 'How-To' chapters you begin to enable children to be anticipatory and confident in the pursuit of their potential. They will begin to naturally appreciate the strength and beauty of mutual regard for each other. Together, you and the children will be creating an environment conducive to living classroom life more fully, learning and loving every minute of the great adventure. All those lovely little minds are there to be guided towards this greatest gift we can ever have. What a privilege for every teacher. The 'How To' will take you and your wonderful companions, step by step, on this amazing journey.

**Happy children.**
**Happy classrooms.**

# CHAPTER TWO

## THE 'HOW-TO' OF THE FOUR COMMUNITIES CLASSROOM

*This 'hands on' approach to building an effective learning atmosphere using living system dynamics was developed over a number of years. It has been observed in action in grade three to eight classrooms, both in my own teaching and assuming a facilitative role with teachers who wished to adopt the Four Communities Classroom system. In addition to the classes that experienced the evolutionary development process of the Four Communities Classroom system for the entire school year, there were a number of classroom contacts occasioned by disciplinary difficulties that I was asked to address in classrooms in both Canada and England. I found I was able, with the Four Communities Classroom approach to fairly readily 'turn these classes around', showing how to break the cycle of unsatisfactory relationship processes that were contributing towards behavioural and discipline problems and, of course, to unsatisfactory learning environments. The Four Communities Classroom learning process proved an effective restorative tool for classes in difficulty, as it resonated with children's ecological core.*

*Children and teachers expressed relief and thanks.*

**The Four Communities Classroom is:**

- always a process of exploration and discovery.

**The ecological process is:**

- the teacher participating as the facilitator and guide - the children being given the means to participate and contribute.
- the teacher sharing responsibility - the children being given the means to assume responsibility for themselves, collectively and individually.
- an evolving, growing process throughout the school year, creating the life of the classroom and a mode of operation in which curriculum teaching is immersed.

For the foundations that inform the Four Communities Classroom see p. 225 - Appendices

My Daughter *Can't Wait* for Monday Morning!

| The ecological process is not: |
|---|
| - a 'bolt-on' to regular classroom approaches.
- 'covered' as rapidly as possible so that a week later it's 'business as usual'.
- something you do when you haven't got more pressing demands.
- something you do when you have only 'good' kids.
- something just for the kids to learn in order to make them easier to handle. |

## Preliminaries, Concepts And Practicalities

Journeys of discovery involve structure, planning, and parameters to guide and focus the exploration. This chapter describes the collaborative creation of these guides.

We look at the thoughts and ideas that build effective environments; how children begin and continue to develop a classroom life of learning how to learn; how they become effective and constructive architects of their own persons. In short, how children learn to take responsibility for themselves and those around them. This chapter weaves into one picture the hands-on directions for building the Four Communities Classroom, detailing everything from furniture placement to methods that facilitate the inclusion of children's thoughts as they learn.

Initially there are five considerations for the teacher:

1. Preparations, prior to children's arrival in the fall, that will help create the environment for becoming and belonging in the habitat of your classroom.
2. The concepts of becoming and belonging as guiding principles in the classroom.
3. Inviting and engaging children in the creation of their classroom environment.
4. My space my place.
5. Groupings, arrangement of classroom space, desks and other furniture.

## 1. Preparations, prior to children's arrival in the fall, that will help create the environment for becoming and belonging in the habitat of your classroom

*If you are introducing the Four Communities Classroom part way through the school year see p. 119 for further information.*

In your classroom, wall-space will serve as a medium for a primary learning experience and the abundant sense of ownership that it can generate; the beginnings of becoming and belonging for children in your classroom. However, prior to the children's arrival in the fall, many teachers spend considerable time decorating the classroom and 'use up' this wall space.

With four large walls staring blankly and uninvitingly, coloured paper, scissors, tape and glue seem important. Teachers prefer to greet children with a warm inviting room rather than empty walls. Of course, as the year progresses, children's art work is added to the decor, but the teacher has been the initial and primary decorator. This seemingly welcoming action creates a problem that mitigates against the process of children 'becoming and belonging'.

To illustrate, consider the preparations taken in our homes before welcoming guests - cleaning, tidying, and vacuuming to present furniture, décor and pictures, indeed the entire home, attractively. Guests, upon arrival, do not re-arrange the furniture, or hang their own pictures. A gracious guest accepts and appreciates your style and the mark you have put on your personal space. Regardless of the comfort level you provide, the pleasing nature of your home environment, or the level of your friendship, your guests will feel no ownership for your choices; nor should they. A host may provide a wonderful environment, but guests are not part of its provision, or integral to it, other than influencing the social atmosphere during the visit. Generally, I think, it is fair to say that good guests adjust to the host's environment; it is a relationship of provision on the one hand, and fitting in on the other.

This presents an important question for the classroom relationship.

*Are children to be seen as visitors to the classroom or as an integral part of the classroom environment? 'Fitting-inners' or providers?*

This question has implications for the role and expectations we have of children in the classroom.

If children are seen as having a visitor role, are they then expected to maintain responsible 'guest attitudes' for an entire year?

Alternatively, if children are seen as providers, is the feeling of freedom and certainty experienced by home owners in the development of living space and environment transferred to children, enabling them to constructively create their classroom environment? Do children, indeed, feel ownership for their learning environment?

I think that most would agree that, though it's wonderful to be a guest for a short period, neither guest or host would welcome a year-long visit.

Pleasant though it is, guests, in the role of 'fitting in', engage in a secondary experience and, since the experience is supplied by the provider, is essentially one imposed upon the guests. Providers, on the other hand, as creators of environment, are essentially engaged in their own experience. It is, therefore, for the provider, a non-imposed primary experience.

These two experiences -
1. guests' secondary experience, and
2. the providers' primary experience,
engage two important differences in being that affect senses of becoming and belonging.

1. <u>The guests' secondary experience and his/her sense of being when integrated into an imposed secondary-environment.</u>

Imposed environments, necessarily, are secondary experiences; you accept what is, you move in and out of the environment with little or no say, your feelings are essentially irrelevant to the situation. (However pleasant, imposed environments provide secondary experiences - you exercise little control and carry little influence. In order to seek a sense of becoming and belonging on your terms you will have to go elsewhere).

2. <u>The providers' primary experience and the sense of being when involved in the primary experience of creating environment.</u>

Adults engage in primary experiences when, for example, they consider and purchase a home. This primary experience involves excitement in the planning, anticipation, and consideration of alternatives. Questions arise. How would we organise our new home? How would we decorate it? What feel would we like? In short, the individual has a say and can express and explore feelings. These are all higher-order thought processes; the advanced ecological capacity of becoming and belonging, in part, through our brain's frontal cortex (p. 270), which evolves and flourishes through use.

Two possible choices for children's sense of being emerge for teachers to consider:

1. A sense of being arising from integration into a secondary and imposed environment - *fitting-inners*.

2. A sense of being arising from the primary experience of creating environment. - *providers*.

At the start of the new year, the sense of 'being' that the child will experience is chosen by the teacher. This decision impacts preparations and affects the use of classroom space and attitude to the children.

Thus:

1. Will space in the classroom be used to give children an imposed secondary experience, with the teacher as the host and children as guests? Will this arrangement mean children will also be supplied with a list of expected behaviours and perhaps consequences?

OR

2. Will space in the classroom be used to engage children in a primary experience?

The second option is full of positive possibilities.

- The classroom experience becomes an exploratory one, with freedom to plan, think, share, evaluate, and refine in consultation with others, with the teacher as facilitator.
- The classroom becomes a place where what is thought and the decisions that are made shape environment and engage ongoing learning experiences.
- Children are immediately and relevantly engaged with feelings in this process, providing both an opportunity to accept responsibility and to exercise it.
- The classroom becomes an environment in which responsibility is difficult to avoid since even doing nothing can have the consequence of developing unsatisfying feelings that, in turn, can impel action.
- A sense of ownership can take root along with feelings of becoming and belonging.
- Children are enabled to build a sense of responsibility and ownership to help create good learning foundations for the classroom.

Much can be obtained by allowing classrooms to be primary-experience based. However, balance is key to good teaching and good learning. Classroom foundations should still include secondary experiences with the teacher as provider. Fundamental teacher-provided secondary experience includes structure for learning opportunity to cover curriculum.

It is the balancing of secondary experience alongside giving children the opportunity to be the creators of their primary experience, that enables an environment to evolve in harmony with the ecology of the developing human mind; a learning environment in step with the learning mind. Primary and secondary experiences are essential to an ecologically based classroom. Using only one or the other can cause difficulty in learning. Balance is key.

Also, children's ability to respond to primary experience and to constructively contribute to the learning environment, it should be noted, reflects developmental progress and provides an important observation point in the process of becoming for both children and teacher.

Development is most often visible through a growing sense of self and self-confidence. It is a process that is exciting and rewarding to be part of.

For more on primary and secondary experience see pp. 19, 175 and 278. Also see p. 197 for an anti-bullying approach using the primary and secondary experience perspective.

## 2. The concepts of becoming and belonging as guiding principles in the classroom

*(From p. 254) 'It is conceptually important, say Prigogine and Capra, to move from the idea of set states of being, to ones that are in a constant process of becoming. It can be said that life is a process of becoming.'*

Children are in a constant state of becoming. Recognition of the concept of becoming in children, especially when combined with a sense of belonging, can prove constructive to the learning process, important to the establishment of an ecological classroom environment, and in the building of relationships.

In the ecological classroom 'becoming and belonging' are guiding principles. Since, life has its ups and downs, these principles do not always offer a smooth process, but creation of the classroom environment under the becoming and belonging imperative is a $powerfully constructive process that encourages learning from experience; our own and each other's. Reflection and self-analysis become valuable and appreciated tools for children, and especially so when such nuance enhances their relationship with the teacher and other children.

(For further reference see index under 'becoming and belonging', and 'process of becoming'.)

## 3. Inviting and engaging children in the creation of their classroom environment

Let's go back to the question of preparation in the fall and the blank classroom walls. We want the children to be the creative force in this classroom; creators of their environment. The walls, instead of being a decorating job for the teacher, now become an opportunity for the class in the process of becoming and belonging; a canvas for children and a primary experience. The children will walk into the blank-walls canvas of your classroom on the first day, and after the first four elements of the Four Communities Classroom, outlined on pages 33 to 36, have been explained, you will announce to the children their role in making the walls of the classroom a reflection of their creative talents. See element five, 'Talking about how we have classroom areas for each group to care for, use, organize, and decorate for classroom life and learning' on p. 40. By the way, the teacher will, of course, reserve wall space for his/her needs in relationship to the class, to dispense general information, and for classroom-wide initiatives.

When you engage children in 'decorating for classroom life and learning', the first thing to keep in mind is that you are encouraging children to participate in creating their own unique environment. Therefore, please DO NOT be tempted to neaten up children's creations, (outside of appropriate taste of course) or to suggest ideas (except ideas of the most general nature to kick-start creativity for those who appear to need it) or you will instantly undermine children's fledgling sense of ownership, as they look over their shoulders for teacher approval. Also, do not concern yourself with other adults' possible opinions of your classroom walls, which would constitute, incidentally, submission to secondary experience. Wall-space will become, for your class, an avenue to developing a sense of ownership and experiencing primary learning.

## 4. My space my place

"My space my place." This is the thought most likely to arise in the child's mind, given the tools, the space, permission and encouragement.

When the 'my space my place' thought takes root, self-organising principles emerge from which arise positive primary experiences; ownership, feeling in control, wanting to try out ideas, leading to creativity, contribution, belonging; all constructive affirming processes of becoming.

One group I worked with, of its own volition, hung on its pin board, a sign that announced, 'Home Of' and listed the names of the people in their group. "Nice idea", I confided to the group upon its display.
Sterling, S., 2001, p. 54.
*"... the ecological paradigm emphasizes the value of 'capacity building' and innovation, that is, facilitating and nurturing self-organization in the individual and community as a necessary basis for 'systems health' and sustainability."*

## 5. Groupings, arrangement of classroom space, desks and other furniture

The number of children in your class may require the formation of groups with uneven numbers. As illustrated in the diagram on p. 28 groups 2 and 4 have eight children, while seven children are in groups 1 and 3 for a total of 30 children. Arrange children between groups to make numbers as even as possible. However, uneven numbers do not compromise the functioning of the Four Communities Classroom.

Avoid creating groups only by gender, or grade if you have a split grade. A winners and losers mentality can sometimes form, with the accompanying negativity in feelings and emotions. This is, of course, not helpful when trying to establish a constructive learning environment.

- The desks in each group are arranged in an open circle (allowing a space for you to walk into, and for the caretaker to more easily clean).

- To enable children to see the board without having to turn too much in their seat the open part of each circle is oriented towards the chalk board. There may be one or two children who choose to go to the work table when you are teaching from the chalk board.

- Besides children choosing group names, (explained in element eight) groups are numbered 1, 2, 3, and 4 and are given some responsibilities for their corner of the room (explained in element 5).

- Groups are well separated. This is important in the building of a sense of belonging in each group (group-ness). For example, conversation, when appropriate, is encouraged to occur within groups rather than between groups. A general homogenization of groups (groups in too close contact), will defeat the concept of housing four distinct communities within the classroom community, and also impact the creation of harmony within the Four Communities Classroom.

- Don't let the physical layout of your classroom be a hindrance. Creative layout provides each group with a separate 'home' area. Work around the position of the door, windows, fixed shelves, cupboards, chalk boards and bulletin boards. Various devices can be sought to assist in creation of four areas in the room, e.g. anything moveable, perhaps on wheels, at approximately desk height that can be seen over, such as shelving, cupboards, low partitions, or anything else that would serve as a divider and perhaps double as a pin board (added bonus). While it can be helpful, none of this dividing 'furniture' is essential, but as a minimum requirement, physical distance between groups is essential.

- You may be able to position your desk and perhaps a work table in places that help separate the groups and create group home areas.

- Home areas and a sense of group-ness can be enhanced in a number of other ways. Carpet or area 'rugs', perhaps cut from discarded pieces after a re-carpeting at home and brought to school, can be placed in the centre of each group's circle of desks. This space is used for group discussion purposes, and when sitting cross-legged on the floor, the carpet, of course, is more inviting than the bare floor. (More ideas for building a sense of group-ness are outlined in elements 5 and 8)

- Space is opened up in the centre of the classroom. This space can be used for:-

1. extra space for a group/groups that may need some 'elbow' room for a project
2. a gathering-around spot for viewing/discussing a demonstration/illustration/display.
3. a table to work individually with children, or to work with a gathering of children collected from each of the groups, etc. or a practical arts table.

Children in the habitat of your Four Communities Classroom will interact primarily with their group, as well as the class as a whole. Together you will explore ways, outlined in this chapter, to ensure smooth group process and enhance individual learning. Some incentive to work cooperatively is provided through a point system ('token currency') which the children are invited to advise upon. (See p. 41)

Also in this chapter, in two sections, are the various elements for developing the guides, parameters and structures of the Four Communities Classroom from the first moment of contact with your new class in the fall.

If you are introducing the Four Communities Classroom part way through the year, all the elements are the same with the exception of:

(1) 'Creating four groups', and

(3) 'Explaining and exploring what we are about to embark upon: the rationale for the Four Communities Classroom approach to classroom life, and good teaching and learning'.

Please go to p. 120 for notes on these two exceptions.

Before you is a journey for your class on which, together, you will come across many exciting and wondrous discoveries. That is my expectation and wish for you.

## **Externality**

'Externality' is an inclusive term I use to describe the surroundings/habitat/environment, collectively created by teachers and children in the classroom.

## **Teacher thought boxes**

 **Referencing these 'teacher thought' boxes in chapter two, and also in the appendices, will help in understanding the processes and dynamics you are engaging in the classroom.**

# DESK ARRANGEMENT

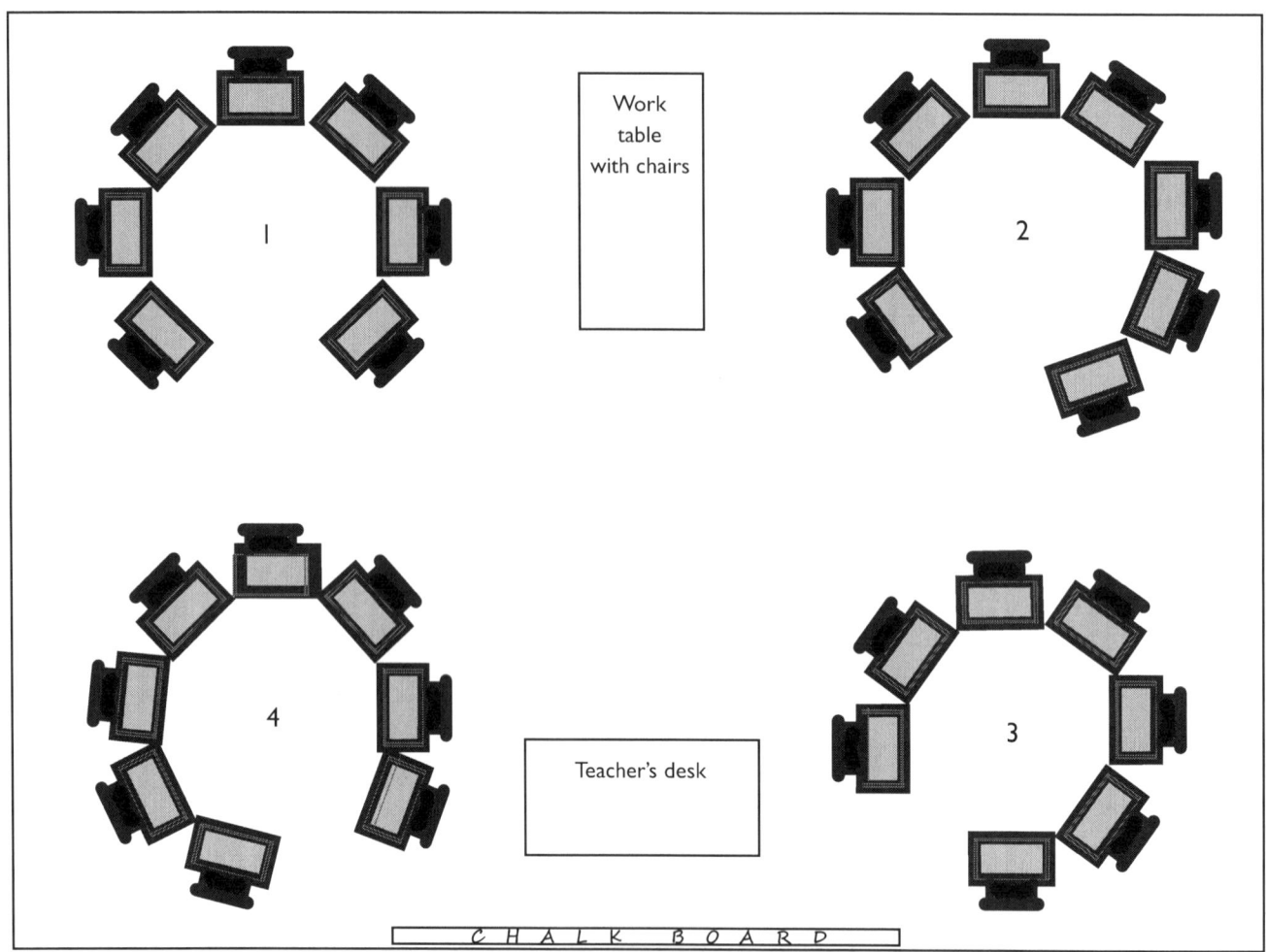

### TEACHING JOT NOTES    Chapter Three, p. 140

I found the jot note concept (capturing pertinent facts) is easily understood by children and embraced from the first day of introducing the Four Communities Classroom. Very soon, children from grade four and up, build a sophisticated capacity to quickly capture and document information. Some teachers prefer to introduce jot notes later. That's fine. Establishing the ethos of the community classroom does not require mastery of jot note taking. However, acquiring the skill does complement the Four Communities Classroom philosophy that seeks to develop children's capacity to take ownership for their learning. Therefore, teaching jot note taking is recommended.

| GROUP PROJECTS     from p. 136 |
|---|
| A class-wide topic can be divided between the four groups. For example, a study of ocean life may engage group one in researching deep sea fish, group two close-to-the-surface fish, group three arctic waters, and group four researching coral reefs. Each group's work is further subdivided amongst individual children. Pictures, diagrams, maps and written work can be displayed on each group's wall space for other groups to see. Presentations of the material that children have researched can then be made by groups to the other groups. This approach to research can, of course, be applied to other subject matter. |

| A LISTENING-TO-OTHERS [and the teacher] AWARENESS ACTIVITY     see p. 132 |
|---|
| If your children have difficulty paying attention to you or to other children, this activity can form an important step in enabling children to diminish or dispel these learning impediments. Listening-to-the-teacher skills are also developed when teaching jot notes - see p. 141 for a summary. |

Most children feel more comfortable sharing their thoughts and ideas in a small group.

# The start of the new school year and the children that are coming your way

*If you are introducing the Four Communities Classroom part way through the year see p. 119 for further information.*

This is it, the beginning of the school year. You may never have seen your children before - you know nothing about them, other than perhaps information on certain "difficult" children. You are about to embark on a relationship-building life process. I suggest you not have this brand new event (a primary experience for you and the children) influenced by another teacher's relationship and behaviour synopsis of children, (a secondary experience). Let this be a fresh start. Assume the best from all, and that all want the best.

We know that some children build dossiers that perhaps indicate troubling conduct. Awareness of, or access to, this history may, in some instances, be important in learning how to handle this child. However, I feel, that, in many cases, it is not necessarily constructive, in terms of guidance for you, in moving children forward in their development. Fresh starts with new people can often have a more powerful effect in overcoming baggage. However, I suggest you do draw upon history when you feel or are informed that background knowledge may help you better help the child. But try not to let a child's history colour your perceptions or responses. Expectations, positive and negative, can impact the shape of relationship building. It is important that you not be drawn into perpetuation of a child's negative self image. It can happen. We are all emotionally motivated humans beings. At its best, that is the power and strength of relationship building.

The mantra to put front and centre is, 'worthiness'. Worthiness is within us all, although in some it is more apparent than in others. But don't be discouraged. Assume it and it will carry you and the children far.

The 'How To' of this chapter is not offered as a script. Scripted dialogue (outside of drama) creates stilted communication. In the classroom, you need to know where you are headed, of course, but by responding to the immediacy of the moment and the children, and choosing your words accordingly, you are going to build a genuine relationship. You will only know exactly what to say as you speak.

At the outset, when encountering newly formed groups in the Four Communities Classroom, the sudden transformation to group status can sometimes cause excitement as children contemplate their new condition.

Other children may feel that they have little in common with those around them. But when grouping initiatives such as responsibilities for their surrounding area are outlined, and children begin to build familiarity through working as a group in the earning of points, a sense of groupness starts to form. (See 'Talking about why we have groups', p. 36)

> **A mix of direction, suggestions and commentary**
>
> Throughout, I alternate between direction, suggestions and commentary to facilitate both establishment of the Four Communities Classroom and interpretation of the process. Together, you and your class should find yourselves on a dynamic, thoughtful, exciting journey of discovery, safe and free in the comfort of your classroom habitat. The Four Communities process is one where you can learn as you go - a journey of discovery.
>
> Over time, and with your growing familiarity with the tenets of ecologically sound practice, you may also wish to put your own ecological stamp on classroom life and learning.

# The Four Communities Classroom
## Quick-Look Check List

### Section One (p.33)

To be completed within the first two days
(More time will be required for grades 2 and 3 - see chap. 5)

1. Creating four groups. 33

2. Asking THE foundational question. "Why do you think we are here?" "Why do you think that we come to school?" 33

3. Towards good teaching and learning. 35

4. Talking about why we have groups (easier communication). Group formation, friends and membership changes. 36

5. Talking about how we have classroom areas for each group to care for, use, organize, and decorate for classroom life and learning. 40

6. Explaining the Point System; its planning, process and integration into classroom life. 41

7. Explaining class and group discussion and communication. The talking stick - learning to share and listen. Sections A, B, and C. 51

8. Choosing group names. 61

9. Explaining group jobs. 65

10. Numbering students, work in/out trays, and work record keeping. 66

### Section Two (p.71)

To be completed within the first two weeks
(More time will be required for grades 2 and 3, and with modification - see chap. 5)

**Discussion forums:**

11. Classroom Rights (responsibility for self and others): 71

    a. The Rights Balloon Activity 72
       - Individual ranking 72
       - Ranking in pairs 74
       - Ranking with two pairs 74
       - Plenary discussion 76

    b. Human Rights Activity 82
       - Reading the true story of hardship 82
       - Group discussion on rights 83
       - Group prioritization of rights 85
       - Plenary - listing of group decisions 86
       - Part one - Class discussion to refine and rationalize the listed outcomes from group discussion 87
       - U.N Declaration on the Rights of the Child 90

    c. Classroom Rights Activity 92
       - Group discussion on classroom rights 92
       - Part two - Class discussion to refine and rationalize the listed outcomes from group discussion 95

**All of the above lead the way to:**

12. Using classroom rights (resp. for self and others). 107

13. Learning the importance of difference. 110

14. Self-correction. 113

*It is through their use that foundational tools 12, 13, and 14 become better understood and internalized by children, pp.107-113.*

---

**Section one and two are important for teachers and children in the evolution of a constructive community learning habitat. The emphasis is on an 'evolutionary process', since it is the continuous use, practice and involvement of these elements that creates and builds the Four Communities Classroom habitat.**

*My Daughter Can't Wait for Monday Morning!*

You may photocopy this page for ready reference.

**Section One**

# Developing the Four Communities Classroom:
# The teacher's role, the children's role, and sharing development

Section one is usually completed over a two day period - interspersed with curriculum work.

### 1. Creating four groups

Assuming you do not know the children who will be in your class, it is impossible to know which combinations of children will work well together. Yet you immediately need groups. Don't worry.

(a) Form a line of girls in the hallway, (or in the classroom), and the boys along the other side. If you have a split grade class, create more lines of boys and girls from each grade. Count along each line, giving each child a number, 1, 2, 3, or 4. These numbers correspond to group numbers, and serve to create groups with a balanced mix of girls, boys and grades.

Emphasize - "Remember your number!"

(b) Ask all the children with number one go to one circle of desks, all the children with number two to go to this circle of desks, etc.. I have always made it the children's choice as to where they decide to sit in the group; I seldom intervene. That's it. You have your students in groups, seated in a way they may never have been before, and they are wondering, and speculating; not a bad way to start minds working. Of course, some of that wondering will be about you. First impressions are important. But do not tell them the year is going to be great. Some may be 'inspired' to challenge that. As the term unfolds children will form their own impressions; impressions formed through actions observed, not superlative statements.

(c) Focus the children's minds through speculation - that's always good. Now you are ready to frame the foundational question. Pose it with a nuanced tone; one that maintains speculation. Everyone is in a speculative frame of mind. You've created the stimulus for speculation, now you build upon that.

### 2. Asking THE foundational question

This question is foundational because its answer will be the basis for your journey into the Four Communities Classroom environment.

"What are we here for?" "What is the reason that we come to school?"

But stop. Where is the speculative nuance in these questions? Where is the message that you like the idea of building constructive relationships, and would welcome the thoughts of wondering minds?

TEACHING NOTES

**Why do you think we come to school?**

Sometimes a slight change in word use can make a big difference in conveying nuance. You could ask instead, "What do you think we are here for?" "Why do you think your parents send you to school?" I underline 'you think' to draw attention to the addition of these words, rather than to suggest they be emphasized. This change of wording conveys an implicit message - that you are interested in someone's thoughts. Thus the question goes one step further, validating each child's thought process.

But if you do emphasize the underlined words, the question changes, implying a message not contained in actual words, but lending an aggressive tone to the question. A negative nuance could change a child's state of mind from one of constructive speculation to wariness.

Thus, along with word use, tone of voice is important to nuance. To invite children's thoughts, choosing the words "What do you think ............?", along with an interested tone and nuance indicates your interest in connecting. Connectivity is part of constructive relationship.

> 💡 **The use of constructive nuance is constructive to relationship building.**

Moreover, your interest in the children's thoughts, conveyed by your nuanced tone of voice and language use, will often generate thoughtful answers. And it won't be long before you'll be hearing children telling you that school is a place for learning.

> 💡 **Respect children's mind processes.**

**Is learning easier if you get good teaching ?**

Ask ancillary questions, such as, "How do we learn?" "Is learning easier if you get good teaching?", and constructive discussion has begun. You are connecting, and the children are already taking ownership for the shape of things to come.

Now you need to work towards the spot where you can summarize the children's thoughts, perhaps with a question. "So you are saying school is a place where we need good teaching and good learning?" And/or. "I agree, school is a place where we need good teaching and good learning." Summaries in question form can add power to consensus when they elicit a yes answer.

**All agree:**
- **good teaching and learning is our foundation.**
- **everything we do is shaped by that understanding.**

Having established, through consensus, the reason for all of us being here, we are now in a position where we can agree that good teaching and learning is our foundation and that everything we do in our classroom is shaped by that understanding.

**TEACHING NOTES**

Children will now have had their first experience in Four Communities Classroom communication, in which their thoughts have been valued; they have been affirmed as individuals and have made connections. It is this connection that you will continue to build upon; a cornerstone of the Four Communities Classroom.

> 💡 **Thoughts valued and individuals affirmed are the beginnings of building constructive mind/brain connections with children.**

Little time has passed, but much has transpired - every moment has been significant.

### 3. Towards good teaching and learning

As in all good teaching, you take children to new places by building upon previously established understanding. Now you can reaffirm and take things a step further. "If what we want is good teaching and learning, we need to ask ourselves, 'How can we get that?' 'What do we need to do?' " This is rhetorical, of course, but children will be wondering, and wondering is good.

**How do we get good teaching and learning?**

**What do we need to do?**

> 💡 **Wondering maintains an open mind, and alerts the mind to possibilities - potentiality.**

Your job is to put out signposts, not answers to help answer that question. So you could say, "Over the next few days, we are going to be thinking about what makes good teaching and learning and at the same time find out why we are sitting in four groups. There's a lot to learn and, as each day goes by, we will discover more about how this classroom works."

**As each day goes by we will learn more about how this classroom works.**

Wondering is maintained, and some focus is offered.

Adding positive thoughts at certain junctures can sometimes be useful. Now we could say, ..."We are going to be together in this room for a year, so finding out how we can make it as good a time as possible is really important. That is what this classroom is all about. We want good teaching and good learning. But we also want to enjoy our year together."

**Since we are together, teaching and learning for a year, we want to make it as good a time as possible.**

Enthusiasm, happiness and learning should go together in the classroom.

*Erica, grade 8, recalling grade 5.*

## "It was a happy time."

As Charles Kingsley said,

*"All we need to make us really happy is something to be enthusiastic about."*

## 4. Talking about why we have groups. Group formation, friends and membership changes

The following is a group rationale idea you may like to offer children and can use, change, or adapt for grade level. This idea is a mini story, providing a mind picture for children to relate to. Storytelling can open up teaching possibilities and adds colour and relevance to information.

**Why are groups in circles or semi-circles?**

> When talking to children, look for things that they can relate to.

"When you go out for recess this morning, perhaps you will get together and ask each other, what do you think of our classroom so far?" "Do you think you'll be standing in a line, when you are talking to each other in the playground one behind the other, facing each other's backs as you talk?"

**Will you be talking to each other in rows when you go out for recess?**

(Small children, especially, would probably appreciate it if you could arrange a mini demonstration, for just a moment, of 2 or 3 people standing in a row, one behind the other, having a conversation). It, of course, looks ridiculous. The children laugh.

Then you ask the class, "Are you going to talk to each other like that?"

"If you saw children talking like that, would you wonder what's the matter with them?"

> Enable children to make sense off their world. Lay the groundwork that will encourage children to explore their sense-making.

"But, do you know, I used to do exactly that in my classroom - put everyone in rows, so all that children could see were the backs of heads."

**It's better to talk to each other facing each other.**

"But then I thought, when people want to talk to each other they get together in circles, so why not do the same in the classroom and put everyone in circles. Then, I thought, we will be able to come up with some good ideas about how we can work towards some good teaching and learning this year."

According to grade level, variations on this idea of circles being a more natural way for people to group can be offered to children.

### Group Members and Group Changes

**Good teaching and good learning means that we want groups that can function well.**

Four well functioning group habitats make one well-functioning classroom habitat. Therefore, when creating group membership, the aim is to create groups of children who function well with each other. As we have said, not knowing the class makes determining this a trial and error process.

My Daughter *Can't Wait* for Monday Morning!

> **TEACHING NOTES**

But that's O.K.– read on.

Counting off children with numbers 1, 2, 3, and 4 for group placement just gets things started. Usually, sooner than later, you know that certain children do not do well when sitting together. It would be better if these children were in different groups.

Also, as there will be point-earning (p. 41) - competitive interaction between groups - it is not helpful to class function if one group of children includes too many struggling souls, while another has too many high-flyers. You may need to mix children in different combinations. Through observation, make as many changes and as frequently as necessary to take all the groups through a refining process, working towards creating an environment for the best teaching and learning. Explain at the outset that some children might get moved in a few minutes, or this afternoon, next week or next month. Make it clear it's not punishment, or picking on anyone, it's just that in this class anything we can do to make things better for everyone is what we do. "Changes will be experienced from time to time."

(I have found every class inherently contains many workable grouping combinations. You may find, after one or two initial adjustments, that only occasional changes need to occur as the year progresses).

Like all life in the Four Communities Classroom, it is practice that forms the habitat of your classroom. In the life process of the class we create the opportunities to learn about the value of intelligent thinking and action. Implicit is the idea that working towards improved environments can be a shared and empowering experience.

Teachers who introduce the Four Communities Classroom part way through the year know their children better and can be further advanced in this refining process before they start. However, I don't recommend delaying the Four Communities Classroom introduction for this reason. There are different dynamics at play with mid-year starts (see p. 119) and it is a time when an awareness of likely group combinations becomes more important.

An important factor in group make-up is maintaining, as much as your enrolment allows, an equal number of boys and girls. (And, if applicable, an equal number of each grade).

### Friends

You can say to the children, "If you are with a friend, that's great. You will be able to stay with your friend, provided that you make it work, and we have good teaching and learning. If you want to talk to your friend at times when it would be disruptive for your group or the class then we don't get good teaching and learning and then, of course, it's best if one person is moved. So whether you get to stay with your friend is up to you."

**Friends can stay together as long as you are able to make good teaching and learning happen.**

TEACHING NOTES

> **Create conditions for children to exercise and assume responsibility.**

**What does community mean?**

Introduce, at some point, the idea of the groups being communities. Perhaps ask what 'community' means. Ask for examples of communities. A town, village, city, province, state, country, family, church, school, classroom, etc..

Explain how, "Communities come in many different sizes, and all are groups of people. Right now you are sitting with a group of people, and we could call each of our groups a community. We have then, in these four groups, four communities. Four communities in the one larger community of our classroom. In fact, this type of classroom is called the Four Communities Classroom. You are part of a community group in the Four Communities Classroom."

At this point, you can talk about the formation logistics of group members.

"If you have ideas about who you would like in your group, then you can tell me your thoughts/wishes. It may be possible to make changes, if not now then perhaps at some later date. But there can be no guarantees. It's impossible to make up groups according to everyone's wishes. If you have one or two friends in your group that is good. Grouping changes will be made from time to time, and it is possible that, at these times, you could find yourself with other friends."

> **Children should feel that they have both recognition and responsiveness to their concerns, while at the same time learning that wider considerations are also part of their reality.**

You may wish to completely change groups each term. I have used the end of term to announce that changes will occur, and find children enjoy the anticipation of new grouping possibilities for the new term. Knowing the children makes re-grouping an interesting, but not always easier, process. I find the best way is to take a class list and cut it up into individual names, and try different combinations of children within the four groups. I try to balance requests, and gender make-up, with the goal of improving our good teaching and good learning environment.

I put thought to group combinations considering:

- Even distribution of children with behavioural problems.
- Even distribution of children with learning difficulties.

**TEACHING NOTES**

- Placement of at least one child in each group, who seems to have a solid sense of self identity.
- Placement of at least one child, in each group, who is academically strong.
- Separation of children who can be disruptive when together.
- Other considerations relevant to your situation.

However, despite the thought and care you put into groupings, it is not uncommon to find groups that have to work through compromise, towards harmony. Compromise for the good of self and others proves a valuable learning experience. See p. 218 - 219 for a case study. Groupings in the adult work-world may contain friends, people that you don't particularly like, and some you really don't have any connection with. I tell children that you can't always have all your friends together, and that learning how to get along with others is also an important part of learning in school. Children, of course, are not left to their own devices. The Four Communities Classroom process includes creating a sound environment for learning, relationship, and mutual regard. Grouping processes are part of the life of the community classroom.

**Classrooms are also about learning how to get along with others.**

Mark, grade 8.
**"Putting us in groups is a better way to get to know each other and also to discuss and have ideas and to get kids talking and thinking."**

---

Hilary, Christine and Christopher, in grade 8, recalling grade 5.

**Christine:** "It was a year for making friends - new friends."

**Hilary:** "We've now got a wider circle of friends."

**Christopher:** "Even if we don't hang out with them, you can go and talk with them anytime."

**A safe and happy learning environment.**

> ### The teacher as a group member
>
> (See also 'Your role as a member of each group' - chap. 4, p. 177.)
>
> At some point you may choose to explain to the children that you are actually a member of each of their groups. There will be times when you will come over to a group and talk over ideas that they are working on - to give them feedback and help if needed. Examples of the need for this interaction may include the decision making process on the name a group is choosing for itself, or decorating ideas for a group's display board.
>
> It is very important, however, that you fill the role of informed group member engaged in the discussion, rather than the provider of answers and direction. If you are met with silence it could be your teacher role is showing too much and deterring children from making further group contributions. It can be a fine line of interaction between yourself and children. Decide whether children are being advanced by your presence. Is their sense of identity and self esteem, for example, building? Are children likely engaged in constructive inner dialogue? Do you and they feel equally comfortable and has your arrival enhanced the discussion process?
>
> If you feel that you can answer 'Yes' to these questions, you are also likely being very effective in your classroom generally throughout the day.

### 5. Talking about how we have classroom areas for each group to care for, use, organize, and decorate for classroom life and learning

**Groups are in charge of their area.**

I tell each group that they are in charge of their corner of the room. No student from another group, I tell them, is allowed there unless they give permission. They think this is great. They can hardly believe their ears. Their faces tell it all.

*Mrs. Dubray, Vice Principal and grade 4/5 teacher.*

**"I've watched children take charge. For example, when Mark is trying to work and someone comes over to his group, he will take leadership and say, 'I'm trying to work and would you go back to your spot.' I don't have to say a word. The children see this as their area to work in and if people interfere, they take it upon themselves to correct others. Correction is taken so much better from a peer. 'Oh! Mark's telling me he wants to work. I'd better go back to my desk and my group'."**

Now it's time to talk to the class about logistics again.

"Of course, group three, (that occupies the place by the lockers, let's say), won't stop you getting to your lockers before class starts, but after that they won't want to be disturbed. It's the same with the group by the door. No problem getting in and out of the classroom, except, once class begins, they won't want to be disturbed. So each group has their own area of the room that they are in charge of. It is your area and no one else's."

> **TEACHING NOTES**
>
> **Groups in charge of their bulletin board.**

"Each group also has its own bulletin board. You can (provided it's teacher accepted), decorate it as you wish. Each group member can put up their own artwork, or you may, as a group, decide on a display theme. Also group project work can be displayed from time to time, showing perhaps maps, pictures, pieces of writing."

Children, always show lots of enthusiasm for the bulletin board opportunity, and in their expressions you can see ideas already taking shape. It seems that in most classrooms it is possible to arrange a bulletin board near each group. However, I once had a setting where the teacher was obliged to divide up the one bulletin board into four, necessitating individuals from different groups to cross the room. The use of a portable board, sometimes available in schools, can often be used to advantage in awkward room layouts.

If the room allows, I also try to organize a shelf area beside each group, so that each group of children can organize that space between them for book, paper and bag storage. Low shelf units, (and/or tables) also serve well as definers of space between groups.

In fact, in addition to each group's primary use of their space, all group-specific arrangements have the effect of defining group space, and therefore, creating greater group definition and identity. Group-ness and sense of belonging (to a group) is enabled by defining group space.

General appearance of each corner is the responsibility of each group. Each child's relationship-building process within the group will be a learning experience, and development will be reflected in, amongst other things, the appearance the group creates for its corner, artistically and/or in tidiness. This will involve some individual and group self-organization. Observe from a distance. As a catalyst, the occasional comment may help.

## 6. Explaining the point system; its planning, process and integration into classroom life.

(For a discussion on the merits of token economies (points) from an ecological perspective please see p. 50 )

Using the point system, individual children can earn points for their group, and children can earn points as a group. These points are counted up during the day and added, usually the next morning, to an accumulating score. I found entering daily points on a dated page of a points book an easy way to proceed. I simply drew, each day, small charts with numbered columns.

(See the following page)

TEACHING NOTES

**Points chart**

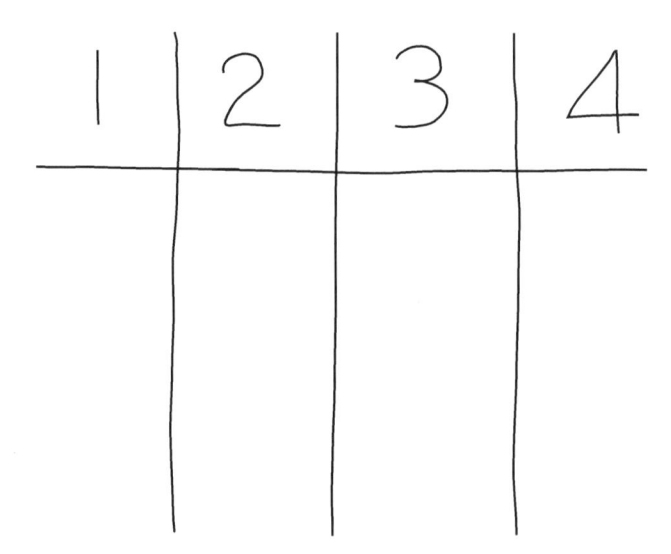

```
  1  |  2  |  3  |  4
_____|_____|_____|_____
     |     |     |
     |     |     |
     |     |     |
     |     |     |
```

You may choose a points currency where earning one, two or three points is the norm and five points 'amazing'. Some teachers of grades 2, 3, and 4, find that younger children are more impressed by big numbers and, therefore, pick a currency system that awards five or ten points at a time. I found myself giving, for grade five and up, points in the one to five range. But, I suggest you stay consistent with your chosen set of point values. This also means maintaining consistency in what behaviours earn what points.

It is important to keep the awarding of points a fairly even process between the groups. If a group decides that it is 'impossibly' behind they may give up. This will devalue the whole process and can cause disruptive influences to arise in the group that is tailing badly. Children, as we all do, have to feel that there is reason for hope.

After a period of time (say two or three weeks), the group with the most points wins a prize. This has been done in various ways and over various time spans. I'd advise that more than three weeks would be too long for children to wait and to carry anticipation. In my experience, by far the most popular prize offered has been a chocolate bar for each group member (be aware of nut allergies), although it's been reported that stationary, plastic animals, pens, and bouncing balls have also been well received.

I've had teachers use the following approaches in point recognition. You may want to try one of their ideas:

- The group with the most points by 'prize day' (the date previously announced, of course), wins.

OR

- First group to achieve a certain number of points wins, the group with the next highest score wins a lesser prize. Or, continue on down the groups with some recognition for every effort.

OR

My Daughter *Can't Wait* for Monday Morning!

**TEACHING NOTES**

- When the sum of all the groups points reaches a certain target it triggers a class prize, (perhaps a field trip/outing, swimming, rental of a movie, class party, free class time to play board games, etc.). The group with the highest points gets to choose/suggest the activity.

OR

- A group qualifies and receives a prize upon reaching a certain number of points, then their score returns to zero. All groups win eventually, but some, through working better, earn prizes with greater frequency. The faster a group can reach the qualifying score the more prizes it wins.

The number of points that trigger a prize, I suggest, should take, on average, about two or three weeks of effort. Times should be adjusted to your class circumstances - prizes should be reasonably achievable.

> **Look for ways to create situations in the classroom where ecological dynamics can find positive expression. In this instance - self-organization.**

With details of your point system chosen, explanations to the class can continue on these lines.

"With the point system you can earn points for many different things. I give **points to groups:**

- **who are ready first for a lesson.** Ready means you have made preparations that will enable full attention to be paid, such as, everything cleared off desks, books open, pencil and paper ready, including **everyone** **in the group being quiet and looking to the teacher, waiting for the beginning of the lesson.** The first group to be ready earns five points, second group ready - four points, third ready three points, and the last group to be ready gets only one point."

(You'll be amazed at how fast a state of readiness can be achieved. A getting-ready process, that was, perhaps, in the past agonizingly slow, may now be achieved in as little as 10 seconds!)

**Points go to groups who:**
- are quiet, prepared and ready for lesson.
- clean up at the end of the day.

- **who clean up at the end of the day.** The first group to have cleaned up their part of the room, with books, paper and pencils put away, and no mess on the floor, sitting quietly ready to go home, gets five points, the second group ready gets four points, the third gets three points and the last group gets one point."

(You'll be amazed at how fast clean-up can be achieved! One or two minutes and it's done properly. You will not, of course, recognize a group for points until it has, indeed, cleaned up properly).

What is happening here is that unproductive downtime is now virtually non existent.

### Self-organizing in response to externalities

"With organizing yourself you didn't want to let your group down, so you always had everything at hand - so when you said, we have math next, everyone took books out as fast as they could. If they couldn't find their stuff, they would ruin it for the rest of the group. You'd have to do the best you could do - so as not to let the rest of them down."

*Mitch, grade 7, recalling grade 5.*

*Mitch's explanation of how children self-organized while referencing themselves with externalities - their group.*

**Points encourage good use of time, and help good teaching and good learning to happen.**

Points are important, I tell students, as they help make good use of time, and good use of time contributes to good teaching and good learning. I usually mention that if we all have to wait five minutes for those people who, it seems, can never find their books or pencils, it means that, adding up 30 children times 5 minutes we have lost 150 minutes of learning time. If we go through getting ready four times a day, lost time adds up to 600 minutes every day. (I often ask them to do the math, and the answer shocks them). I sometimes add, "We really don't want to be held up like that, do we?" Very soon, peer group pressure to be ready develops, and some groups assist those children with poor desk organization skills so that they all can be ready quickly. Often this assistance will be offered after a few failed attempts at being ready first. It is an example of individuals and groups constructively self-organizing in response to externalities. (for further information on externalities see pp. 27, 250, 308.)

- **Occasionally you may want to give points for the group with the tidiest corner.** Let the children know that, without warning, you may give points for tidiness. The incentive is, of course, to keep a tidy corner. Suddenly giving a group five points for tidiness, has an amazing effect upon the other groups.

Children like being involved in the development of point use, and you may decide to invite their ideas.

To illustrate, I give the class the following example of a class problem, and how the class reached a solution based on points.

**An example of how children used points to solve a class problem.**

### The problem of the latecomers

"I once had a class with a few children who, after morning recess, and afternoon recess, always came in late. And when school started at 9.00 and at 1.00, again they would come into the classroom late. Often they were five minutes late. Everyone would be waiting for them."

"Now, being late four times a day for five minutes (4x5 minutes) meant that twenty minutes was wasted every day by these slow people. Twenty minutes a day for five days a week = 100 minutes wasted, or one

*My Daughter Can't Wait for Monday Morning!*

> TEACHING NOTES

hour twenty minutes a week. Multiply that number by four weeks, and each month five hours forty minutes (say six hours) were wasted. That's like losing more than one day a month at school just waiting for a few students. If this continued, by the end of the school year, everyone would have spent more than two weeks (half a month!) just sitting in school waiting for a few children. I asked the class, "Is that fair? What shall we do?"

"Children put their hands up, and had many ideas. We had a class discussion, and the children decided that the solution lay in points. People coming in late should lose points for their group. The amount to deduct became the question, and through a vote the class decided to deduct two points from a group if one of their number was late. Done! But then someone, offering examples, asked, what if there is good reason for being late? Mmm. They thought about this for a while, and children thought each case should be decided by the teacher on its merits. That, they thought, should look after the continual lateness problem. You see - points were used by the class to look after the problem."

Note:

All the children, including those who were the cause of the problem, were involved in the discussion. All were able to hear other children's points of view and listen to how people felt about the problem. The latecomers were not cajoled, but were free to enter the debate without even being specifically singled out (though, of course, everyone knew who they were). The latecomers had a lot to think about, and opportunity to work on changing attitudes. But turning their backs on the problem was not an easy option, as it meant turning their backs upon their group. There was, therefore, a lot of incentive to try harder and make improvements that would not only benefit themselves, but also their fellow classmates.

Does this provide a 'foolproof solution'? No, nothing is foolproof. But it takes most classes far in learning about self and others, and in the value of discussed democratic solution. For the rare out and out intransigent, other solutions for helping children develop a better sense of themselves in relationship with others are available. See p. 172 'The Story of Ryan' and his 'Visiting Rights', p. 173.

The lateness story usually resonates with the class. (See also 'Grade Six Class introduction/discussion on the point system', p. 211)

## Problems or Opportunities IN THE FOUR COMMUNITIES CLASSROOM

Problems can arise in all classrooms. However, in the Four Communities Classroom problems are used by teachers and children to build more understanding of relationship process.

In the example of the latecomers, responsibility for the problem of tardiness is not assumed by the teacher alone, but by teacher and children together. There is no remedy sought through the teacher employing appeal devices, or systems of rewards and punishment.

In a teacher-assumes-responsibility approach, success relies, to some considerable extent, upon each child's willingness to conform to the demand (in this case, to be on time). Some children may challenge and cause friction. Thus, right or wrong, the risk of more problems occurring is a possibility. This is not good for relationship building.

It's up to the teacher to not put him/herself (and the class) into this adverse situation. Children need to be steered through a course that avoids potential for upset, and instead turns problems into productive learning experiences.

A focus of the Four Communities Classroom philosophy is one of shared life process. Therefore, when class problems arise, they are everyone's problems, for everyone's consideration. The question is always, What are we going to do about it? The assumption is we have a shared responsibility for our lives together, and a shared responsibility to search for a remedy. Adverse situations, then, rather than presenting risk to effective class function, become instead opportunities to learn and exercise ownership for self while recognizing the effect of our actions upon others. The book explores a number of 'Problem or Opportunity?' situations.

---

**Ecological pattern - relationship, and autonomy and integration**

The 'Lateness Story'

As further explained in appendix (i), order (in the classroom) was brought to a degree of chaos (in this instance - disruption of learning time) by children being late. This brought about a need for change. The need for change brought the situation to a point of bifurcation (a fork in the road) [p.237] and eventually to a new order (options discussed, decisions made). In going through bifurcation, learning occurred.

As explained in appendices (ii) and (iii), children had the opportunity (in a process of constructive relationship with the teacher) to exercise communication and response-ability capacities to work towards balance - a striving for autonomy (self) and integration (with others) in balance. Thus, this was an opportunity to learn, not just for the tardy children who needed help in developing better self-correction skills, but for all children. All the children learned about the nature of their externalities (the classroom and others within it) and themselves in relationship with externalities; minds engaged in constructive inner dialogue.

| TEACHING NOTES | You may wish to continue your points discussion with the class -

Here are some examples that you may like to use with your class.

1. <u>How are points lost?</u>

"I don't take points away if someone doesn't know an answer to a question. That's O.K. We can't know everything. That's why we are in school - to learn. But if the person doesn't know what the question is, then I take away points. Not knowing the question means that they were not listening. I take two points away from people who don't even know what the question is."

**Points lost for not knowing the question.**

Groups, of course, are not pleased with the loss of points. Individual group members don't like to be the cause of points being lost. And so you tend, much more, to find classes tuned in and attentive, helping build an atmosphere of interest, and, of course, in learning generally.

**Points for good ideas.**

2. <u>Can the class find other uses for points?</u>

When I first started developing the Four Communities Classroom, one group asked if they could make a poster displaying their group name. Yes, I said. The other groups thought that this was a good idea too, and wanted to follow suit. Immediately a problem arose. The first group objected stating it was their idea, and not to be copied. The rest of the class objected to being told they couldn't make a group name poster.

### Problem or Opportunity?

I had, as I saw it, two options:

**Option 1**    Teacher assumption of responsibility.

**Option 2**    Shared responsibility.

With a teacher assumption of responsibility, I could either:

a. announce that we will drop the idea of displaying group names.

OR

b. announce that all groups can copy the idea.

By weight of my authority, and riding on assumptions that teacher knows best, I could have enforced either announcement. But what message would I have sent out to the class, and to what effect?

With the enforcement of either decision, the 'idea' group would likely feel upset and annoyed. While the other three groups may express triumph with the decision (b), as it is in their favour. Decision (a) would garner no approval from any group. But with either of these options a message would

**TEACHING NOTES**

be clear - immediately to the first group and likely shortly thereafter to the others - that it's no use having ideas and original thinking around here, so, in future, why bother. This approach would carry yet another message, that this classroom, if 'necessary', will resort to polarized unhelpful competition, with the teacher as arbitrator of disputes.

What children would have learned from this experience is that individual child responsibility for relationship resolution ultimately has to defer to authoritative ruling; that when it comes to the crunch, teacher knows best (secondary experience) and there is no room or time for student discussion, negotiation and problem solving (primary experience).

To gain some vestige of power in this dictatorial environment, children can quickly realize that the game is on - we create the problems, teacher creates solutions. And, of course, every dispute that needs a ruling means less time teaching, and learning opportunities lost.

With decision (a) or (b) I would, in a moment, have weakened children's desire to be creative and lessened their willingness to contribute towards the class and their own learning. Teaching and learning would have become more difficult.

### Shared responsibility, (option 2)

**We have a class problem - what are WE going to do about it?**

The Four Communities Classroom teacher response: We have a class problem. What are we going to do about it?

I asked children, what are we going to do about it? The question started to elicit ideas and hands went up. The first group, however, immediately 'saw' through the question, and stated that it wasn't a class problem, and they weren't interested in any discussion. They just wanted to keep their idea, thank you. So I said, yes, but what if next time there is an idea from another group that your group would like to copy? Perhaps we need to decide what we are going to do when other groups have ideas that you would like to use. They hadn't thought of that. The first group changed its attitude and the whole class proceeded to discuss the issue.

Discussion revolved around resolution through the use of points. The class voted that groups could copy other group's ideas by transferring 10 points to them for the use of their idea. Copied ideas could earn a group ten points! Now we had healthy competition between groups. And, guess how much the creativity incentive was boosted in the class?

Sometimes, to illustrate how classes can use points, I tell the 'payment of ten points' story. I say, "It's a solution that suited that class. You don't have to do the same thing, unless you decide that it would work for you."

Interestingly, I've never had another class take up this idea, but it has demonstrated to classes that creating solutions for problems is encouraged,

**TEACHING NOTES**

and illustrates that points aren't necessarily confined to uses that I offer. (Maybe not taking up this idea is an indication of children already wanting to exercise their own creativity and not to jump onto other classes' ideas)

**Using points positively**

**Points for groups that do well.**

Rather than taking points away from a group that is noisy, or one that perhaps is not getting down to work properly, I'll award five points to the other three groups for working well. In this circumstance, my recognition of the other groups is really motivated by the need to get one group working better. Suddenly that group realizes that it could be doing better and the children begin to apply themselves, often as well as the other groups. They don't get rewarded for this though. The unspoken message is that groups who work well, without reminders, get ahead. You may not be losing points but you do fall behind. This awarding of points makes class management much less demanding in time and energy.

*Vanessa, grade 8, recalling grade 5.*

**"You would reward us by giving points, which would help us to recognize that we were doing well."**

> **Ecological pattern - relationship, externality, and self-regulation**
>
> The awarding of points to other groups becomes the motivating externality (see pp. 27, 250, 308) for the less on-task group to apply self-regulation, to their actions.
>
> Response to feedback from an externality can generate self-regulating behaviours. (p. 241)
>
> Since the group can only respond adequately if all its members cooperate, self-regulation dynamics are also a factor in the relationship between an individual child and the group he/she is part of.

*Andrea, grade three.*

**"Points help you work together a bit more because you have to work together to get points."**

> **For the Four Communities Classroom teacher, class management becomes a lighter touch**
>
> Instead of constantly working to maintain 25 - 30 children's attention you'll find that six, seven or eight children in a group tend to self-regulate, requiring only occasional light reminders. It has the effect, in terms of class management, of being a bit like organizing the teaching and learning of just four children rather than twenty-five or thirty. Thus, much of the regulation of classroom life and much of its learning process starts to be assumed by the children. This, of course, means that teacher energies can be poured into producing good teaching and good learning opportunities.

*In conversation with grade 8 students recalling grade 5.*

**Erica:** "If someone lost us points they heard about it. That helped with classroom control because you didn't want to lose that five points for your group."

**Me:** "Was it better to hear from each other rather than me?"

**Shauna:** "It was better in a way, but in a way not, because it's worse to hear from friends."

**Erica:** "Yes, but it makes you learn better."

**Hilary:** "If your friends start getting mad at you, you know for sure you had better smarten up, because usually friends encourage you."

---

*Mrs. Dubray, Vice Principal and grade 4/5 teacher.*

**"In the fall you may wonder if you are spending too much time on developing the Four Communities Classroom but it is always very worthwhile. I would never want to rush the process. I've seen the benefit - it pays dividends all year."**

---

### The 'token economy' debate

There has been much debate on the merits of token economies in the classroom. In brief, the concern, it seems, is that children's application to school work which should be motivated by the joy/excitement of learning, is instead motivated by the awards of the token economy, i.e. earning points.

In ecological terms the anti-token economy argument seems, at first glance, to be valid. Learning is a life process imperative and, therefore, innate to life forms, with high expression in humans. Preschoolers, who have learned much before they arrive on the school doorstep, demonstrate their innate learning capacity. So why should one not be able to maintain this innate learning capacity in school?

One can, but the complexity of the ecology, its impact, and meaning cannot, of course, be revealed and comprehended through isolating and referencing one innate attribute - learning.

As appendix (i) outlines, learning occurs through very complex processes, involving the interrelated elements of order/chaos, bifurcation, feedback mechanisms, etc.. All these elements are foundational to ecological change and development process and, therefore, foundational to processes of referencing externalities. Thus we can also say that ecological change and development occurs through referencing externalities using the processes of learning. In other words, in ecological terms, learning always occurs in reference to externalities.

Thus if there is to be joy or excitement in learning, it will depend upon externalities - the habitat. Joy or excitement in learning will not arise in isolation, or be the product of some higher sophisticated process of the mind, especially if the four walls of a classroom are not perceived favourably by the child. Joy and excitement are emotions, and as described in appendix (iii), emotions are part of ecological endowment.

> The 'token economy' debate - continued.
>
> Children (product of the ecology, and users of its endowment and emotions) love points. Points give children a sense of achievement; something to strive for; a benchmark that rewards effort. I find points are embraced as a positive habitat externality by children. Innate life endowments are encouraged and constructively engaged. Constructive learning process is enhanced. Joy of learning is enhanced.
>
> It is interesting to note that the point-earning prize of, for example, a chocolate bar, striven for with such zeal, could be effortlessly purchased by many children. It's the sense of achievement and recognition that is being worked for.
>
> It is also interesting to ponder how many of us would feel valued and take joy in our work if there were not a measure of our worth in concrete terms.

## 7. Explaining class and group discussion and communication. The talking stick - learning to share and listen.

> **The discussion process is an invitation to constructive dialogue. It indicates to children that trial and error in exploring ideas is O.K; their thoughts are considered valid. It is important that children feel welcome in contributing to the life of the classroom; everyone recognized.**

Capra, '96, p. 279.
"...communication is esentiallly a coordination of behaviour."

Discussion and communication form a cornerstone of the Four Communities Classroom, and are considered in three parts.

A. Introducing the class to the idea of discussing and communicating

B. Discussion and communication for the class and groups - some guiding principles

C. Creating primary experience life learning with class discussion process as the focus.

> <u>Ecological pattern</u> - the communication imperative
>
> Communication is important to all life. Life cannot function without communication between communities of various life entities. Communication even occurs between cells in our bodies. Our need to communicate is an extension of the ecological communicative process of life.
> (pp. 242, 289)

TEACHING NOTES

## A. Introducing the class to the idea of discussing and communicating

Although you have already engaged your class in some discussion, this section will expand children's use and understanding of discussion in the Four Communities Classroom.

Use the chalk board to show connection between these words,

community<br>communication

**Community and communication.**

Ask children what communication means.

Then you might say, "Communities of people talk, and talking is how we communicate with other people. What sort of things might you communicate to other people?"

Of course, answers are endless, so I suggest that you field a few, and when you feel the point has been made and understood, summarize - perhaps something like this.

"That's right we tell people:

**Communication of ideas, thoughts, feelings.**

- our ideas,
- what we feel about things, or
- what we feel/think about what others have said."

**People get to know us and we get to know them.**

"This gives the community of people around us some understanding of us, and of course, we need to listen to other people when they want to tell us about themselves."

"So, with the people in your community (your group), you will be communicating; communicating to discuss ideas. For example, you will probably want to talk to each other about how you are going to use your bulletin board. Or you might have other ideas that you may think will make your group work better for good teaching and good learning, and to earn points."

So you will be:

**Explaining, trying things out, and finding out what works in your group.**

- explaining ideas to each other,
- trying things out,
- finding out what works and what doesn't.

"You or your group might let me know of an idea that you think would be good for the whole class. If your idea will help in good teaching and good learning we might be able to use it."

> **Ecological pattern**
> Communication/feedback is an innate and ecological imperative. (appendices)

"Now I would like to tell you about group discussion. Group discussion is one of the ways you can share your ideas with your group and tell each other what you think. You will be communicating in

*My Daughter Can't Wait for Monday Morning!*

| TEACHING NOTES |

**Talk quietly in groups so that other groups can't overhear your groups ideas.**

**group discussion circles**, everyone sits cross-legged in the space in the middle of your circle of desks. Sitting close together helps the group to talk quietly, so that other groups can't hear, especially if you have ideas that are yours and you don't want other groups to hear and copy."

This invites constructive dialogue. Giving children the opportunity for open discussion is saying that trial and error in exploring ideas is O.K and that children's thoughts are considered valid.

Thus children are invited to feel welcome in contributing to the life of the classroom; everyone is recognized.

A teacher of a grade 2/3 split, found that during group discussion very young children benefited from a structured routine. Children were required to sit on the floor, with their knees touching, in the same order as they sat in their desks. The routine prevented time wasted in children jumping up to sit elsewhere in the circle and even outside the circle. For information specific to grades 2 and 3 see Chapter Five, 'Accommodating Different Age Groups', p. 180.

"Another important thing to remember," you say, "is that group discussion doesn't work very well if more than one person talks at a time."

A small demonstration is useful. If you are able to arrange to have another adult with you for a moment, ask the children to listen carefully while both of you speak simultaneously for a minute or so. Watch the children as their eyes move back and forth between the two speakers. It becomes immediately clear that it is not possible to listen to two people at the same time and get full understanding.

---

**Ecological pattern - primary experience** (p. 278)

Acting out a situation can be used to engage children at an experiential level, making the learning experience a primary one. Primary learning experiences enable children to internalize and make their own sense of information.

Being told, "It's hard to listen to two people talking at once," is a secondary learning experience that will have less effect on children's minds than if they experience it firsthand.

Considered and internalized understanding by children puts them, and you, considerably ahead in the teaching and learning process.

---

**Different people's ideas are difficult to follow if more than one person talks at the same time.**

**The talking stick leader helps groups to have only one person speaking at a time.**

Reinforce the children's thoughts by saying, "More than one person talking can be very confusing", and add, "so it's important in your group discussions that only one person talks at a time." "To help with this, each group will have a talking stick leader. The talking stick leader, by giving the talking stick to the person who wants to talk, makes sure that everyone has a chance to talk and they will be listened to. Only you can talk when you are holding the talking stick. This is important to good communication and good discussion. It is something a group has to learn to do well, and I give points to groups who can do it well."

**TEACHING NOTES**

**Group responsibility shared:**

- **Important job for the talking stick leader - to give everyone an opportunity to speak.**

- **Important job for group members - to raise their hands to get the talking stick.**

Often children enjoy bringing something distinctive from home to be the talking stick, for instance a stuffed toy. The object doesn't have to be a stick.

I tell children that although the talking stick leader has an important job to do in helping group discussion, that everyone has an important job too. The job of everyone else, is to put up their hands and wait to be given the talking stick. The talking stick leader will have to work hard at making sure that everyone talks in the order in which they put up their hands. Being good at group discussion is a shared responsibility.

I tell students, "In class discussions everyone knows to put up their hand and wait their turn. And everyone knows that they will have a chance to speak. I will be looking for people who put up their hands to speak in group discussions."

"There are going to be a number of jobs for people in our groups, and first we need to choose someone in each group to be the talking stick leader."

This process is probably best done with children in their desks. A coin toss, by the teacher, at each group, is fun and quickly settles the issue. Make a record of who will do this job.

At this point children are aware of class and group discussion, its need and some framework for procedure. There is, however, much to learn. The children will acquire communication and discussion skills through practice and, especially in the wider arena of class discussions, your role modelling and guidance.

### B. Discussion and communication for the class and groups - some guiding principles

The discussion process is something children, at any age, have to practice. To a large extent it's learning to listen to what another child is saying, and making an effort to understand and give consideration to the words being spoken.

In the beginning children sometimes display impatience, and are quick to categorize another's thoughts as being inadequate, i.e. offering put-down summaries such as, 'that's stupid.' You respond by explaining that put-downs do not help our classroom and do not help good teaching and learning.

Put-downs can either be the start of argument, or the shutting down of children who feel they would have been better off not to have spoken. In either case, children witnessing the put down will reassess their willingness to join discussion. Such thoughts can have long-term affects that might cause some to take a back seat in organized discussion, perhaps for years. What children experience now is important in building capacity to make intelligent contributions to their surrounding society; from groups to classroom to beyond. Children build capacity for mutual regard when establishing Classroom Rights (p. 92).

There are a number of strategies that can be used to help develop good discussion skills in children. The most important, perhaps, is the ongoing

> **TEACHING NOTES**

example provided by your facilitation of class discussion. There is a direct parallel between what you are asking the talking stick leader to do in group discussions and what you do during class discussions. The purpose, in both roles, is to make sure that everyone speaks, as far as possible, in the order their hands go up. This parallel can be explained to the children so that they see you as an example and also recognize that the talking stick leader has an important job. (I had one teacher give the role of talking stick leader to a different child in each group each day).

In early forays into the discussion process you will probably require that children practice using the talking stick properly. I find that such formalizing of the discussion process provides a foundation from which a group can work. However, I don't insist on continuing close adherence to the use of talking sticks. Essentially, what I look for is a group where children are being courteous in listening to each other, and where discussion is progressing constructively. I announce, from time to time, that I'm going to give points to groups who are discussing well. But whenever children have difficulties, the talking stick process is a default position that you can ask children to return to.

There is a second significant parallel between class discussions and group discussions. It is one that you may not necessarily want to draw attention to specifically, but nevertheless, through ongoing demonstration, make it part of the predominant atmosphere of the classroom. It is the role modelling of mutual regard; the adoption of the appropriate attitude to each other. I'm referring to giving regard to children as they speak. Everyone needs to feel good for having thought up what they wanted to say and then putting it into spoken sentences to make themselves understood. Everyone is thanked for their contribution, even if thoughts don't appear particularly useful to the discussion. Children need to feel that their endeavour was worthwhile, and that contributing is something they would like to try again.

As group and class discussion becomes an integral part of day-to-day classroom life, you will see an atmosphere of mutual regard evolving naturally.

Children, as we all do, assess and sort through the usefulness of what they have said. It is a self-organizing process in response to externalities. However, in your class discussions, children have the opportunity to practice and gain strength in this self-organizing process in a safe and caring environment, further building a sense of self. It is, therefore, important to evaluate whether any comment you may wish to offer the child on what they have said could complicate or assist in this sorting process. Beyond a 'thank you', safe non-judgmental comments may include a summary or clarifying summary of what you have heard. Always ask the child whether your account reflects the intended message. Give children the opportunity to explain further if they so desire.

Of course, in addition to the thoughts they voice, children will also have unspoken thoughts of their inner dialogue. What is important is the learning

> **TEACHING NOTES**

occasioned through this interactive process between children. Your job becomes that of provider of a positive constructive atmosphere for interactive communication. I use class discussion to teach children how to listen to each other and intelligently respond to what they hear. Unlike the secondary experience, in an objectives-based lesson, the discussion process takes children into situations where primary experience learning is likely to occur. Together you will, in fact, be engaging life processes; in this instance, communicative life processes. Your job is also to create opportunities that elicit thoughts that lead to the points you want children to consider. Section C of class discussion process on the following page offers, in part, ideas on how this can be done.

### Living systems, and links to the teacher's role in discussion process

Discussion is a process of communication, and includes a process of feedback on thoughts and perceptions. Feedback can affect individual sense of self in relationship to externalities.

Briggs and Peat, '90, p. 165.
*"It appears that the greater an organism's autonomy (sense of self), the more feedback loops required both within the system and in its relationship to the environment".* (my bracketed words)

If we want to enable constructive development of a child's autonomy (sense of self), it is best done through a feedback system contained within a constructive externality. In other words, the quality of the communication environment in the classroom impacts the constructive autonomy of the child. The communicative environment is the integrative element, and the child brings his/her self (autonomy) to the discussion. Through feedback, dynamics of autonomy of self and integration with others are engaged.

Briggs and Peat, '90, p. 154, remind us that autonomy and integration feedback process has an emotional component.
*"…our most private thoughts and feelings arise out of a constant feedback and flow-through of the thoughts and feelings of others who have influenced us. Our individuality is decidedly a part of a collective movement. That movement has feedback at its root".*

The teacher facilitates class discussion as a process of autonomy and integration for the child. Thoughts and feelings are paramount. Therefore, let's consider the teacher's role in the discussion process.

- Never criticize or dismiss a child's contribution to discussion, not if you want to hear from this child again, or, in the near future, from many of the children who are observing.

- Occasional summary feedback oils the wheels of expression and communication. Always ask if your summary is what a child means, and allow for further clarification if the need is felt.

- Encouragement is essential and wonderfully powerful. It enables a child to consider trying, to consider experimentation, to consider risking him/herself to uncertainties, to consider approaching a bifurcation point (a fork in the road), where learning and development can take place.

- All discussion is a shared event. All must feel free and welcome to contribute, including the teacher.

- The teacher is both contributor and facilitator of process, fairness, and focus. Focus is gently applied, allowing for different ideas to be expressed by inquiring minds, while steering towards resolution and understanding, and perhaps a voting question.

> Living Systems Science, and Links to the Teachers Role in Discussion Process - continued.
>
> The teacher shows care and interest in all children and all contributions. Judgments are suspended, nothing is labelled as wrong, but the teacher prompts for clarifying statements when needed, and/or provides summary, and possibly other ideas for consideration - but no dictates. Dictates can undermine communication process and autonomy and integration balance - the ecological processes you are trying to nurture.
>
> What you are seeking to encourage and engage is sound communication, and free flowing mind processes, so contributions must be accompanied with reasons. How and why, does that contribute to the question? Does that help us to understand what is being discussed? Ask gently. Don't dwell on contributions which fall short on rationale. Don't invite the possibility of embarrassment or resentment.

### C. Creating primary-experience life learning with class discussion process as the focus.

OR -

How to create and build constructive discussion and communication process between children

As you focus on the primary experience of communicative processes, you will need to engage children in shared communication that both offers ideas and listens to ideas. But shared communicative process needs a stimulus to get minds to focus on constructive thoughts and ideas. Stimulus can be found in the speculative question.

To engage children in offering thoughts and opinions in class, phrase a question with a, 'What do you think of …?', or perhaps, 'What do you think will happen if …?' Any grade-appropriate issue or subject will serve.

Hands go up. Let's say that the first three hands that you point to for comment are those of **John, Susan and Bill.**

John makes a statement. Hands go up. He has said something that's caused some to have other ideas. You, as the teacher, also have a response to what John has said, but since you are facilitating children's dialogue and thought interaction, you wait to see if your thoughts will be echoed by a child. Look around, try to choose a raised hand of someone who may offer some useful dimension to John's contribution. This will be easier if you know the children well, but at this early juncture that's unlikely, and, in any case, useful contributions are never guaranteed. Don't worry. Allow children to continue to offer their thoughts. Whatever number of contributions it takes - go with the flow. You point to Susan. She says something that is somewhat in line with your thoughts, and that appear to undermine John's statement. Ask Bill (his hand still up), 'What do you think?'

Bill, having listened to the discussion, offers an opinion that appears to build upon and reinforce what Susan has said. You go back to John and say, 'What do you think John, do you agree with what you've just heard, because it is different from what you said, or do you want to stay with your opinion?' Tone of voice (nuance), is vital here. Your tone of voice should imply that if John wants to stay

> **TEACHING NOTES**

with his statement, then that's just fine, and if he wants to modify it, having heard other points of view that's perfectly understandable. It's extremely important that your voice does not carry, or imply, any judgment. John must judge his statement in the light of words he heard from the children, not upon perceptions of expectation carried in your voice. He must feel completely free to voice his studied opinion.

This is important for a number of reasons:

- John must not be discouraged from further contribution. If he is made to feel foolish he will feel hurt, maybe resentful. This is not good for relationship building between you and he. John, as we all do, will go through many thought processes and changes in life. Allow him to experience this in the emotionally secure environment of your classroom.

- All the children will observe whether contributing to discussion is risky or not. If perceived as risky, many may decide that they don't want to invite the possibility of being made vulnerable. Such a lesson learned, diminishes future learning outcomes. Wariness is not conducive to either learning or building relationships.

John, (because he's in grade 5 and young enough to have an open mind) without a problem or any show of awkwardness, says yes, he agrees with Susan and Bill. Great! But you still don't state your opinion, or show that you are pleased that he has changed his mind. You simply acknowledge John, and say 'O.K.'

What are John and all his classmates learning? They are learning that:
- it's O.K to voice your opinion.
- it's O.K to listen to others.
- it's O.K to consider what others say.
- it's O.K to change your thinking in response to externalities if it makes sense to you.
- it's O.K to be engaged in these processes with, and in front of, other people.
- it's O.K to take charge of your own thoughts.
- it feels really good to look for things that make sense.

Communication has been opened up and seen as positive.

Through your positive orchestration of a series of moments, children are becoming aware of a lot of O.K's to move forward and enrich your Four Communities Classroom habitat.

But we do, nevertheless, have a situation where John might feel that what he said was shown not to be well thought out. Negative fallout is still possible.

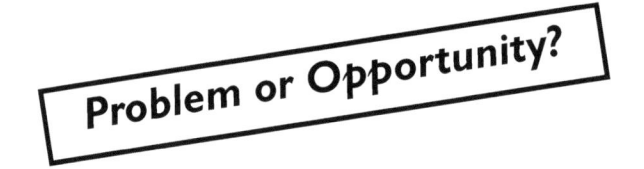

**Problem or Opportunity?**

*My Daughter Can't Wait for Monday Morning!*

**TEACHING NOTES**

You can turn the problem into an opportunity.

Ask the class, "Who do we have to thank for what we found out in the discussion?" Some will say Susan, for first bringing us towards a good conclusion. Others may say Bill for actually bringing us to conclusion. John - he's being left out of the thanks, until you say, "But I wonder if Susan would have thought of her ideas if not prompted by John's statement. Would Bill have been able to have said what he did without hearing Susan's ideas?"

These questions engage children in an enlightening thought; a primary experience showing that discussion can be a powerful process with every thought valid. It is an interaction of minds expressing and sharing ideas to reach consensus. Children are quickly brought to the realization that if John had not started the discussion, we likely wouldn't have benefited from Susan and Bill's thinking. Therefore, we have all three to thank, but especially John who got the ball rolling.

Now what have the children learned? And how does John feel?

John feels great. He's reassessed his statement. It was O.K. He's reassessed his feelings towards himself. He's O.K. He will certainly be more than willing to continue making his contribution to class discussion. Importantly, John's mind is advantageously positioned to go from strength to strength in developing sense of self in relationship to his externalities.

The class has witnessed this whole process. Many could be thinking, 'Yes, I like this. I could speak out too and perhaps good ideas will build, because of my contribution. When I think of something, I'm going to try this'. The whole class is advantageously positioned, in each of their minds, to go from strength to strength, in their sense of self and relationship to people around them.

## Discussion process and more

John and the entire class have been engaged in a life process, with a particular focus on communication. It is an engagement that cannot, however, be objectively conceptualized into a package of attainment. What we can say is the children have been introduced to avenues of understanding that facilitate constructive discussion but since practice is essential, we cannot say children know how to discuss. Instead of making the claim 'most of us now have discussion skills', or 'we have covered discussion skills', rather we need to recognize that, for all children in that classroom, an opening has been created to a broader range of benefits.

In appendix (i) elements of living systems are referred to as being linked and dependent on each other. So also life process in the Four Communities Classroom has dependent elements.

Life processes, in the classroom and within the groups, can be advanced simultaneously on a number of fronts; developing communication skills, building self esteem, self-identity, relationships, responding to feedback processes and responding to externalities, with all the accompanying dynamics of chaos/order, bifurcation, etc.. [see appendix (i), 'Processes of change, difference and potentiality'.

Since emotion also speaks to everything we do and think, teacher sensitivity to children's emotions is vital.

**TEACHING NOTES**

Let us return now to the class's discussion and communication journey, and consider what individual children's journey may look like.

Children who are outgoing (the children most likely to have their hands up), are, through your encouragement, reinforced in their desire to discuss, and will be joined by more who feel they too can speak. Quieter children, wanting to further observe the ins and outs of discussion in this class, will put themselves on notice that, perhaps sooner than later, they will give this a try. Others may still take a back seat when it comes to contributing, but not a back seat to being a listener.

Listeners are thinkers of inner thoughts, so whether thoughts are vocalized or not, all children are participating, all are learning. The quiet ones will speak when their minds are ready, and when their internal learning process feels prepared.

*Said Craig in grade 8, who had seldom spoken in grade 5 class discussion, and went on to be an honours student in high school,*

## "What I loved most in grade 5 was the class discussions."

I suggest caution against intruding into the private internal learning process of children. For example, if during class discussion, you say to Mary, the listener, 'What do you think Mary?', Mary may not be ready to contribute and feel awkward and embarrassed. When not feeling pressure to contribute, one can allow thoughts to process and gel. Your well intentioned inquiry may fluster and set back a mind that was close to contributing. For a sense of Mary's developing readiness to contribute to class discussion, look to her group interactions. For many children, group discussion process becomes a 'training ground' for class discussion.

However, should you be dealing with Mary the window gazer, asking for her thoughts could be sufficiently uncomfortable for her to decide to pay better attention to class discussions.

There are many occasions in class discussion where building on each other's thoughts (similar to John's, Susan's and Bill's), arise. Early in class discussion, look for an opportunity to take children through a review of their discussion process, outlining how ideas build from one to another. It is important that the John-type situation is acknowledged, in order to bring to children's attention the importance of listening to each other and the value of intelligent response.

Being aware of the value of listening and in the offering of intelligent responses contributes to the building of an ecological foundation in the Four Communities Classroom - communication.

*My Daughter Can't Wait for Monday Morning!*

TEACHING NOTES

## 8. Choosing group names

Choosing group names is a group-ness device, i.e. it helps children build a sense of belonging to a group, while it also helps define group space.

However, the choosing of a name, by children who may not yet, necessarily feel a sense of togetherness, may feel like a fairly empty exercise. This is best done when the children have spent a week or so together and feel comfortable enough to share ideas of this import. When feeling more established, choosing a name is something children like to do. The process of choosing is also an opportunity for children, sitting cross-legged in the space surrounded by their desks, to have a group discussion and practice speaking using the talking stick, quietly, one child at a time.

Offer gentle direction and expectation by saying, "If there is one person speaking in each group, and we have four groups, how many people will be talking at one time in the classroom?"

**If one person is speaking in each group, how many people will be talking in the classroom?**

Also, "You are choosing a group name, so you had better speak very quietly, or another group may hear and copy your idea."

**Speak very quietly, or another group may hear and copy your idea.**

"I will be giving points to groups who can discuss well together."

Since you have created a situation where children will want to take ownership for this process (keeping their group ideas to themselves) children will sit quietly discussing their ideas. Perhaps small reminders like, "I can hear what group three is saying from over here", will be all that is needed to bring about quick self-correction in the group.

The idea, the atmosphere, the culture of quiet group discussion is being laid, not because you say so, but because the children can see the relevance. Positive contribution to this understanding is what is also being rewarded by your giving of points. (Again it's a demonstration of the effectiveness and relevancy of the primary experience that you are creating, rather than a secondary experience - of instructing children to discuss quietly.)

Thus, children are not just engaged in choosing a group name, but in a process involving discussion, recognition and regard for other children, earning of points, and the creation of a functioning class culture. The Four Communities Classroom in practice. Whatever moment the class happens to be engaged in (this time choosing group names) should build community classroom practice.

Walk among the groups - listen in, chat, offer not-too-intrusive guidance. "When you are ready," you say, maintaining at all times, a gentle guiding hand at the wheel, "you will need to get my approval for your group name idea."

---

I once had a grade five group that couldn't decide between two name possibilities that had been suggested in their group - 'The Green Diamonds' or 'The Green Dominators'. (Green was the group colour) Naturally, I was concerned about a group in the Four Communities Classroom naming themselves 'The Dominators'. I decided to try and steer them towards the name diamond by explaining that there is another precious stone, which is green coloured, called the emerald. The group seemed to like the idea of calling themselves 'The Emeralds', but they wanted to vote first. Then one child suddenly asked me what dominator meant. I had assumed they knew of what they spoke. I explained that a dominator always wants their way and may even be mean to others to get their way. The children looked shocked - "We don't want that! " They named themselves 'The Emeralds'.

Children sometimes, of course, hear words without understanding meaning. But perhaps if heard in a 'cool' context the word is now associated with cool and perceived as attractive. It seems the moral of the story is do not assume that children always understand everything they appear to. Children do not, especially in your classroom, have to be unwitting purveyors of questionable social mores.

---

Many names have been chosen over the years. For example, animal names such as, The Cougars, The Monkeys, The Wild Cougars, or The Red Hot Monkeys, names of sport teams, or names made from the first initial of each child in the group. But there is usually no need to offer any suggestions or spur thoughts, as children seem to have no shortage of ideas.

You will likely find names are chosen within a few minutes; certainly within 5 to 10 minutes. To the undecided, you say, "Groups that haven't decided can let me know tomorrow.' Then get on with whatever is next on your agenda for that day.

Sometimes groups fall short of time, perhaps through wasting it, perhaps through difficulty in coming to agreement, or perhaps working with an ambitious idea. Do not inconvenience the rest of the class, or compromise the day, by waiting. Inform the group that they should work things out in found time, i.e. recess, or time available when they have finished other class work, etc. and carry on with the day's work/lessons/curriculum.

Thus the classroom environment carries unspoken messages, or understandings:

- We don't hang around waiting indefinitely.
- The onus belongs with each group for assuming responsibility for its situation.

It is important to move on to the next stage before children's enthusiasm wanes. So within a short time, perhaps that afternoon or the next day, arrange an art period(s) to create hangings for group names. The following ideas may be used or used to stimulate other ideas. Provide each group with a plastic hoola-hoop, like those found in school gyms. These can be hung from the ceiling, centred over each circle of desks, and decorated by the group to announce their group name. This has been done in various ways, from collages to the hanging of each child's individual art work. Fire retardant paper is available, to satisfy fire safety concerns.

If you have groups incorporate their group numbers in their artwork, they identify with both name and number which means you can readily refer to groups by their number or name. Point out the efficiency of being able to use their number when directing activities.

If your classroom does not lend itself to hanging group name displays from the ceiling, bulletin boards can be used. See p. 29 and the next page.

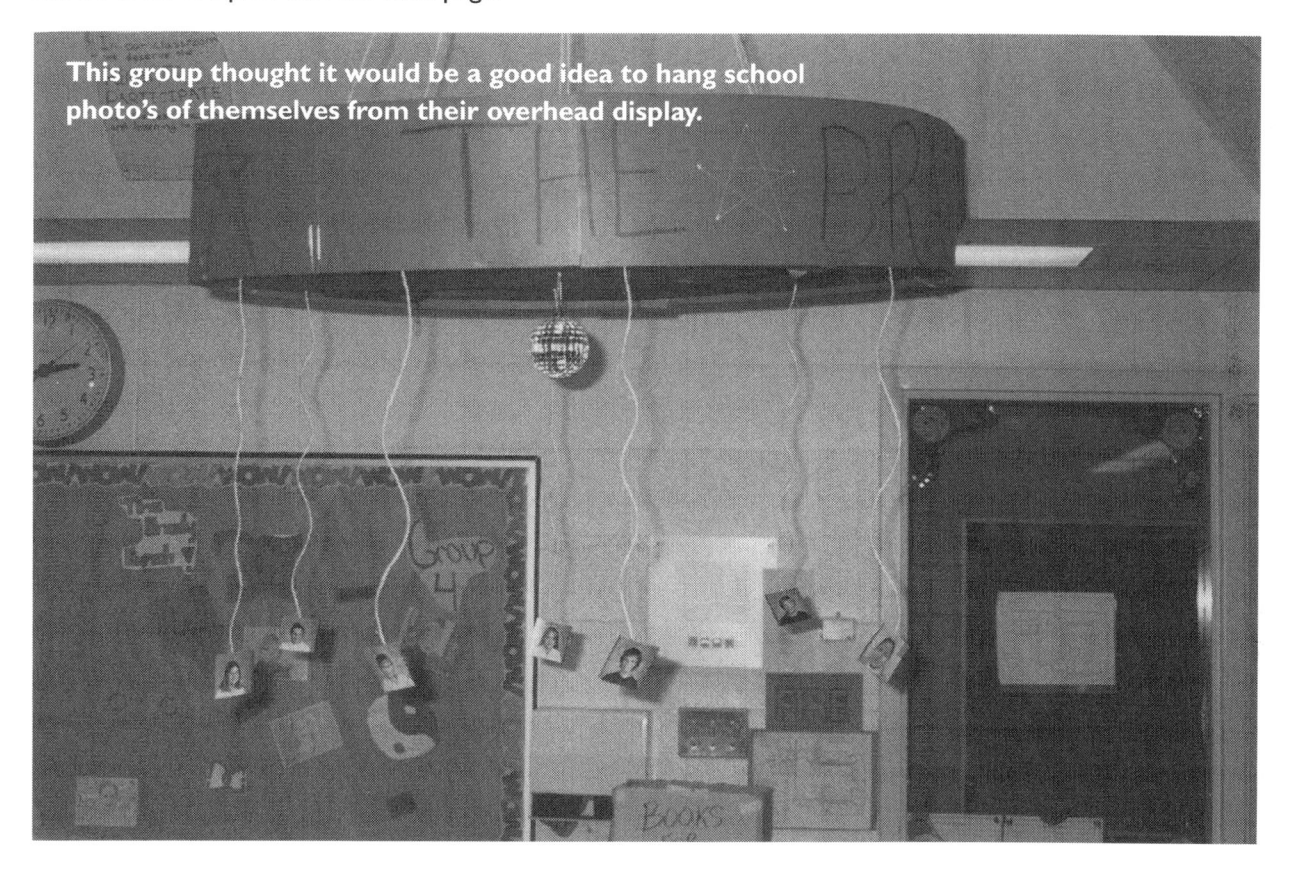

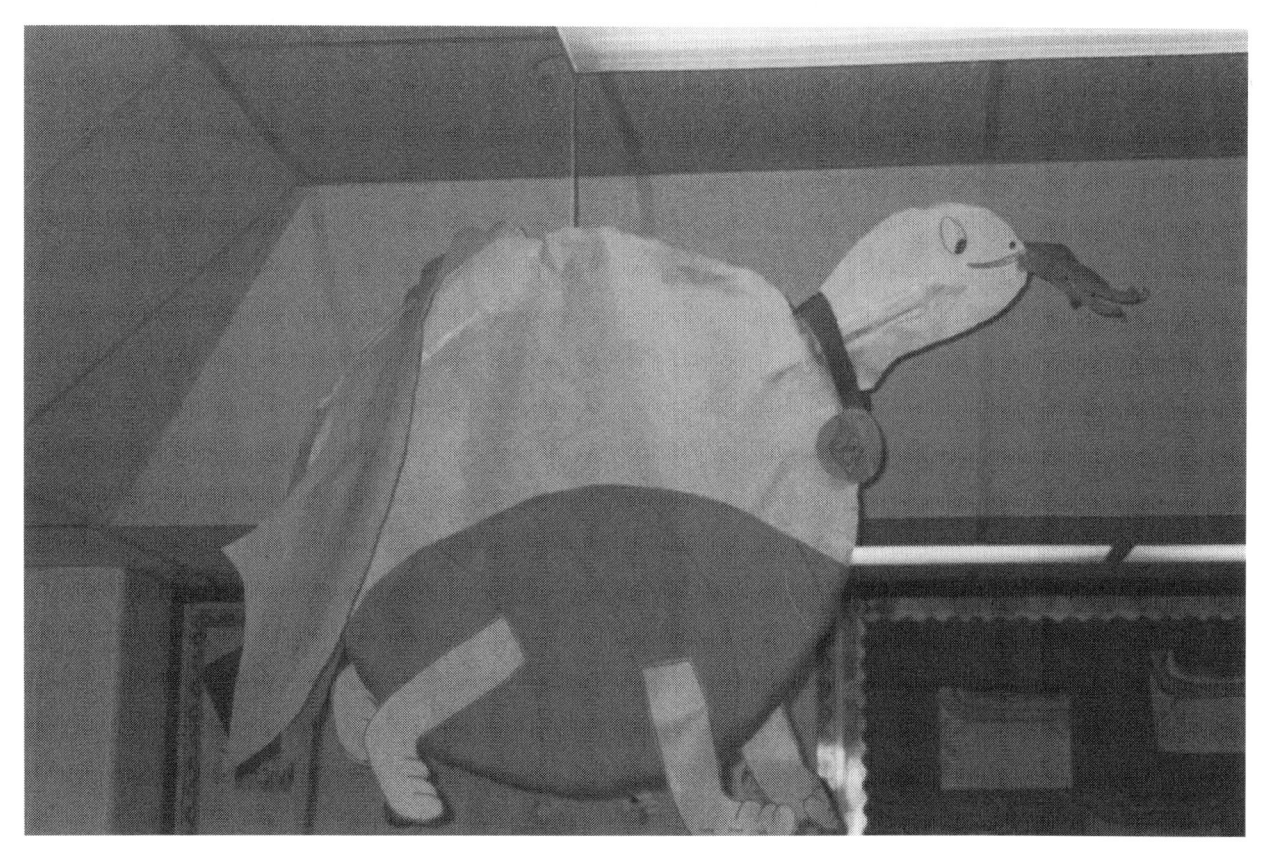

**This group thought it would be a good idea to hang school photo's of themselves from their overhead display.**

63  My Daughter *Can't Wait* for Monday Morning!

The children in Group Four have used both an overhead display and a bulletin board to announce their group. The portable bulletin board also doubles as a divider between the group circle and the classroom lockers.

My Daughter *Can't Wait* for Monday Morning!  64

**TEACHING NOTES**

One advantage of having individual art work in a group's name sign is that, if group membership changes, art can be easily moved and replaced. New members can readily add their work to the group sign. Children, seeing their work as part of the display, quickly feel part of the group.

One group chose to display their name in a collage of art and hung small photos of each group member from coloured ribbons.

## 9. Explaining group jobs

Children in elementary school love jobs and love the responsibility that comes with them. Essentially, jobs represent opportunities for recognition, and it is this that they enjoy. The Four Communities Classroom provides much opportunity for job sharing. I try to find a job for each child in each group, by designating small responsibilities that contribute to the smooth running of the classroom. Thus each group has for example, a talking stick leader.

Other jobs that I have found a need for are:

- Recorder. The recorder takes notes during group discussions. For example, he/she may write down a list of ideas offered by children for the group name, or keep track of ideas and thoughts presented on issues. The recorder is often the one who reports on the group's thinking in plenary sessions to the class as a whole, although all group members are always invited to amend or add if they wish.

- Book Collector. The book collector is your quick access to individual children's work that needs to be marked. Book collectors collect work from children in their group, in alphabetical and numerical order (see p.66), and present it to you for marking, and indicate that work has been handed in on a form provided for the purpose (see p. 69). You are able to see at a glance, at any time, each child's record of handing in work. The book collector also quickly hands back children's work, or hands out letters home, work sheets, or anything else that needs distributing.

- Band leader. This is not what it sounds. But it does make playing of another sort go more smoothly. This is your quick route to the organization of gym and sport game activities (see p. 135). Each group has a colour. You may decide on red, blue, green and yellow. Request the help of parents to make coloured gym bands for each group member. I've had children, at the end of the year, ask to keep these as mementos. If, however, you still have them, they, of course, can be re-used. The band leader is in charge of:

    - keeping these bands in a safe place in their group corner (i.e. they don't get lost),
    - handing them to his/her group at the beginning of activities, and,
    - collecting them in at the end of activities.

TEACHING NOTES

- <u>Gym helper</u>. The gym helpers (one from each group), get equipment out and ready for use, and also put equipment away. If you decide to allow gym helpers to be assisted by other children in putting equipment away, the gym helpers are the ones who assume responsibility and make sure that everything is done properly.

- <u>Reminders</u>. The reminder's job is to remind you, for example, to hand out letters to parents at the end of the day. I found there were many 'housekeeping' details, that, in a busy day, I thought I might overlook. Whenever needed to I'd just alert my reminders of such matters. You may not need this assistance, but with four people as reminders, it helps. By the way, this could be a point earning job.

- <u>Gardener</u>. Gardener is the rather grandiose title I give the plant waterers. This is a job delegation that I found really useful when engaging the class in growing and studying plants. I had each group grow a number of vegetables using the bottom halves of pop bottles to hold the soil. The clear plastic containers allowed observation of root growth.

These are jobs that I have given children. I rotate responsibilities from time to time, making sure that everyone has a job at some time or other. You may find, in your class, other job opportunities, suitable for children.

## 10. Numbering students, use of in/out trays, and work record keeping

<u>Numbers</u>

It sounds a bit regimented to give each child a number, but I found it useful in a number of instances (also outlined on p. 135, subheading 2).

First, the numbering process. In each group, list the children in alphabetical order, and number each child down the list. Against each number add the group number. Thus the first person on the list, in group one, would be numbered 1,1. The second person on the list in group one would have the number 1,2. The third 1,3, and so on.

In group two, the first child listed alphabetically would be numbered 2,1. The second child would be numbered 2,2, etc.

When this listing is completed for each group, there will be four children who from four groups are numbered one, and four children numbered two and so on. Please refer to pp. 135, 136 for examples of how the numbering system is used to facilitate some learning activities. **The 'Mark Sheet' on the next page can be photocopied,** and used to keep a record, group by group, of children's assignments and marks.

| Class number | MARK SHEET<br>Date<br>SUBJECT/TOPIC<br><br>NAME | **ASSIGNMENTS** | | | | | | | | |
|---|---|---|---|---|---|---|---|---|---|---|
| **GROUP ONE** | | | | | | | | | | |
| 1.1 | | | | | | | | | | |
| 1.2 | | | | | | | | | | |
| 1.4 | | | | | | | | | | |
| 1.4 | | | | | | | | | | |
| 1.5 | | | | | | | | | | |
| 1.6 | | | | | | | | | | |
| 1.7 | | | | | | | | | | |
| 1.8 | | | | | | | | | | |
| **GROUP TWO** | | | | | | | | | | |
| 2.1 | | | | | | | | | | |
| 2.2 | | | | | | | | | | |
| 2.3 | | | | | | | | | | |
| 2.4 | | | | | | | | | | |
| 2.6 | | | | | | | | | | |
| 2.7 | | | | | | | | | | |
| 2.8 | | | | | | | | | | |
| **GROUP THREE** | | | | | | | | | | |
| 3.1 | | | | | | | | | | |
| 3.2 | | | | | | | | | | |
| 3.3 | | | | | | | | | | |
| 3.4 | | | | | | | | | | |
| 3.5 | | | | | | | | | | |
| 3.6 | | | | | | | | | | |
| 3.7 | | | | | | | | | | |
| 3.8 | | | | | | | | | | |
| **GROUP FOUR** | | | | | | | | | | |
| 4.1 | | | | | | | | | | |
| 4.2 | | | | | | | | | | |
| 4.3 | | | | | | | | | | |
| 4.4 | | | | | | | | | | |
| 4.5 | | | | | | | | | | |
| 4.6 | | | | | | | | | | |
| 4.7 | | | | | | | | | | |

*Example of how to use 'Mark Sheets'*

| Class number | SUBJECT/TOPIC MATH  NAME | Multiplication | Long division | Fractions | | | | | | | |
|---|---|---|---|---|---|---|---|---|---|---|---|
| \multicolumn{12}{l}{**MARK SHEET** — ASSIGNMENTS — Date November — 10th 11th 12th} |
| \multicolumn{12}{l}{**GROUP ONE**} |
| 1.1 | BROWN, JILL | 10/10 | 9/10 | 11/12 | | | | | | | |
| 1.2 | COOK, BETTY | 7/10 | 6/10 | 8/12 | | | | | | | |
| 1.3 | JONES, MICHAEL | 4/10 | 3/10 | 3/12 | | | | | | | |
| 1.4 | HARRIS, TOM | 5/10 | 4/10 | 6/12 | | | | | | | |
| 1.5 | PARK, JOHN | 8/10 | 7/10 | 9/12 | | | | | | | |
| \multicolumn{12}{l}{**GROUP TWO**} |
| 2.1 | ADAMS, JIM | 5/10 | 4/10 | 5/12 | | | | | | | |
| 2.2 | CARR, SARAH | 7/10 | 7/10 | 9/12 | | | | | | | |
| 2.3 | MANN, BILL | 8/10 | 9/10 | 11/12 | | | | | | | |
| 2.4 | RICHARDS, BEN | 7/10 | 8/10 | 10/12 | | | | | | | |

*Record of Work forms (or how to keep track of children's work)*

Next to each in-tray (see below) place a clip board with a 'Record of Work' form clipped to it with the group names listed in alphabetical order. **The 'Record of Work' form at the top of p. 69 can be photocopied.**

Record of work forms are individualy made for each group. The example on the bottom of p. 69 lists (for example) the children's names from group one.

Fill in the top of an empty column with date and assignment. The book collector simply places a check mark against each child's name who has handed in that assignment. If it is work done during the day, but is unfinished and, therefore, has to be finished at home, the book collector can mark H.W for homework. Then you know, and the book collector knows, to look for this work the next day. Through this process the book collectors keep you informed as to whether everyone in their group is up to date, or not, with their work.

*In/out trays*

I suggest you provide an in-tray and an out-tray clearly labelled for each group and positioned within easy reach of your desk. The in-tray is where the book collectors (p. 65) place work that the children in their group have handed in to them, and the out-tray is the place where the book collectors pick up work to be handed back to the group members. It works well, as everyone remains seated, while just four book collectors bring in and return work.

You ask the book collectors to collect the work in alphabetical order from their group. Then when you take work home to mark, it is all in alphabetical order, per group, making it easy to fill in your mark sheets that correspond to the group lists.

*My Daughter Can't Wait for Monday Morning!*

Record of Work form (form for keeping track of children's work)

| RECORD OF WORK | | A S S I G N M E N T S | | | | | | | | |
|---|---|---|---|---|---|---|---|---|---|---|
| **DATE** | | | | | | | | | | |
| | | | | | | | | | | |
| **GROUP** | | | | | | | | | | |
| | | | | | | | | | | |
| | | | | | | | | | | |
| | | | | | | | | | | |
| | | | | | | | | | | |
| | | | | | | | | | | |
| | | | | | | | | | | |
| | | | | | | | | | | |

Example of how to use the Record of Work form

| RECORD OF WORK | | A S S I G N M E N T S | | | | | | | | |
|---|---|---|---|---|---|---|---|---|---|---|
| **DATE** September | | 10th | 10th | 11th | 12th | 14th | 15th | 18th | 20th | 20th |
| | | Jot notes | Journals | Spelling test | Math Problem Solving sheet | Permission slips signed by parents and returned | Oceans report | Multiplication | Story | Social studies |
| **GROUP** One | | | | | | | | | | |
| 1.1 | Brown, Jill | ✓ | ✓ | ✓ | ✓ | a | ✓ | ✓ | ✓ | ✓ |
| 1.2 | Cook, Betty | ✓ | ✓ | ✓ | ✓ | ✓ | ✓ | ✓ | a | ✓ |
| 1.3 | Jones, Michael | ✓ | ✓ | a | HW ✓ | ✓ | ✓ | ✓ | HW | ✓ |
| 1.4 | Harris, Tom | ✓ | ✓ | ✓ | ✓ | ✓ | ✓ | HW ✓ | ✓ | |
| 1.5 | Park, John | ✓ | ✓ | ✓ | ✓ | ✓ | ✓ | ✓ | ✓ | |
| 1.6 | Smith, Mary | ✓ | ✓ | ✓ | HW | ✓ | ✓ | HW | HW | HW |
| 1.7 | Williams, Ron | ✓ | ✓ | ✓ | ✓ | ✓ | ✓ | ✓ | ✓ | |
| 1.8 | Young, Sally | ✓ | ✓ | ✓ | a | ✓ | ✓ | ✓ | ✓ | |

Analysis of group one's Record of Work form

| RECORD OF WORK | ASSIGNMENTS | | | | | | | | |
|---|---|---|---|---|---|---|---|---|---|
| DATE September | 10th | 10th | 11th | 12th | 14th | 15th | 18th | 20th | 20th |
| | Jot notes | Journals | Spelling test | Math Problem Solving sheet | Permission slips signed by parents and returned | Oceans report | Multiplication | Story | Social studies |
| **GROUP One** | | | | | | | | | |
| 1.1 Brown, Jill | ✓ | ✓ | ✓ | ✓ | a | ✓ | ✓ | ✓ | ✓ |
| 1.2 Cook, Betty | ✓ | ✓ | ✓ | ✓ | ✓ | ✓ | ✓ | a | ✓ |
| 1.3 Jones, Michael | ✓ | ✓ | a | HW ✓ | ✓ | ✓ | ✓ | ✓ | HW ✓ |
| 1.4 Harris, Tom | ✓ | ✓ | ✓ | ✓ | ✓ | ✓ | ✓ | HW ✓ | ✓ |
| 1.5 Park, John | ✓ | ✓ | ✓ | ✓ | ✓ | ✓ | ✓ | ✓ | |
| 1.6 Smith, Mary | ✓ | ✓ | ✓ | HW | ✓ | | HW | HW | HW |
| 1.7 Williams, Ron | ✓ | ✓ | ✓ | ✓ | ✓ | ✓ | ✓ | ✓ | |
| 1.8 Young, Sally | ✓ | ✓ | ✓ | a | ✓ | ✓ | ✓ | ✓ | ✓ |

Group one's 'Record of Work' form for September documents a number of pieces of information that can be noticed at a glance by the teacher.

- Jill Brown was absent the day that the permission slips were handed in. She will need to be followed up on that if she is not to miss the field trip.

- Michael Jones is sometimes not completing work in school and is having to complete work at home. Since he hands his work in the next day he is doing it at home, but is he making good use of his time in the classroom? Or is it a case of him needing extra help?

- There is an obvious problem with Mary Smith. There are four occasions where work has not been handed in at school, neither has it been completed as homework and handed in the next morning. This 'Record of Work' form acts as a clear demonstration to Mary that she has a problem that is growing. It's also clear that others are doing their work in her group. You and she can then decide how Mary is going to correct this problem. Perhaps she needs extra help. Mary also discovers how easy it is for the teacher to quickly see that her work is not being completed. Being 'lost in the crowd' and, thereby, avoiding work-completion and making an effort, won't work for her.

NOTE:
The 'Record of Work' form and the 'Mark Sheet' form are very similar in appearance.
The intention is to make it very easy to keep track of work being done on a daily basis and then transferring marks you give children to the Mark Sheet.

# Section Two  (usually completed within the first two weeks - interspersed with curriculum work)

## Developing the Four Communities Classroom - Discussion Forums

*Brittany, grade 7.*

*"The Four Communities Classroom, over the days, was unfolding as we went - it wasn't just heaped on us. We gradually got used to it. It wasn't so sudden that you were saying, oh, oh, what do we do?"*

### 11. Classroom rights (and responsibility for self and others)

The establishment of classroom rights and responsibility for self and others is a major undertaking, and represents the single greatest effort that you will make with your class, not in difficulty, but in time commitment and energy. The activities on the following pages - **(A) Rights Balloon Activity** and **(B) Human Rights/Needs Activity,** that form the background for **(C) Classroom Rights Activity** - should be conducted over a number of days, preferably first thing in the morning when children are most alert. It is important that the length of each segment of time spent on classroom rights activities is dictated by the needs and attention capacity of the children. Spend whatever time is required to reach successful conclusion, stage by stage, while choosing steps that do not strain children's attention spans. The time needed varies from class to class and grade to grade. It is time consuming.

The entire process is, however, very good use of time. Four Communities Classroom learning carries much 'in tow'. In this instance, reaching consensus on classroom rights engages every aspect of the dynamics of learning, as described in the appendices starting on p. 225, and covering aspects of learning as described in appendix (iii), all founded upon an emotional base. It will represent, regardless of ability, a mental workout for children, opening a door to both a greater capacity to learn and an increased assumption of responsibility to learn. Every child, whether delayed or advanced, can feel a sense of belonging (a foundational emotional need) and is thus enabled to develop and grow.

**Many parents reported to me that past responses of, "Oh nothing", or "The usual", to questions of, "What did you do in school today?", were replaced with lots to say every evening without being asked.**

The dividends you reap from children's engagement in the activities and the production of classroom rights more than pay back time invested. You will find children achieving much and learning much in the year ahead. The enjoyment quotient of your year together, for you and the children, will be enhanced.

*Parent of a grade five child.*

### "My daughter can't wait for Monday morning."

> TEACHING NOTES

## A. The Rights Balloon Activity

This activity is courtesy of David Selby and Graham Pike from their book Global Teacher, Global learner, and is a three part ranking activity involving ten considerations. Each ranking activity asks children to imagine riding in a hot-air balloon with ten rights to consider. Please see pages 125 to 128 for the details and the ten considerations that can be photocopied (figures 1 and 2).

In brief the activity engages children in decision making in three different circumstances.

1. <u>Individual ranking with no right answers</u>. First, children, individually, make decisions on the order of importance of ten considerations. It is made clear that there are no correct answers. Children are free to make their own choices.

2. <u>Ranking in pairs.</u> Secondly, children form pairs to discuss and come to agreement/compromise on ranking the same ten considerations. Again, there are no right answers. The pair can come to any decision that they feel comfortable with.

3. <u>Ranking with two pairs</u>. Finally, two pairs of children come together, to compare notes and ideas, to discuss and argue their views to create a ranking that now entails the thinking of four people.

**Individual ranking with no right answers.**

### 1. <u>Individual ranking with no right answers</u> (The first balloon ride)

The purpose of the individual ranking activity, in addition to other benefits (see below), is to introduce children to the idea of independent thinking. This helps prepare children for their contribution to the establishment of the mutual regard process of classroom rights. This exercise is, therefore, an important precursor to the creation of classroom rights.

Children do their ranking in silence. Talking and comparing ranks will obviously colour children's thinking and choices. In free choice ranking children are thrown on their own resources, and are, in effect, obliged to think for themselves.

Such obligation can cause some internal wheels to turn. Many children have grown accustomed to evaluating themselves in terms of how 'correctly' they can do their work, and that, ultimately, validation comes from an external authority. Children being the sole evaluator of their thinking can represent a significant departure for them in their school experience. If we wish to encourage independent thinking, children need the opportunity to explore their own nuanced thoughts.

**No one will tell you that you are wrong.**

Thus, for many children, it is a unique experience to be told that they are free to form opinions, with no one to tell them that they are wrong. This represents, beyond an eventual paper product, a mental freedom and turning point; opening up to children the idea that their thoughts can have legitimacy.

> **TEACHING NOTES**

This process is a primary experience for children, and is one where they start to discover a route from an old order of thinking to a new order.

In this case the old order is one where the teacher validates children's thinking - an external one-way reference of what is right or wrong. By contrast, the new order opens up the concept of thinking for oneself. This a passage through change representing a bifurcation process for the mind. See bifurcation (the fork in the road - passage through change) appendix (i).

However, don't worry. Children realize that you are enabling an expanded frontier of thought, rather than negating the need to integrate with externalities - in this case you the teacher. They appreciate your respect for their opinions and do not see this as an invitation to devalue the teacher's assessment process.

A child accustomed to being told what to think may find a different way of learning unsettling. The question for the child is, 'Will this feel alright?' 'Will I be able to (emotionally) handle the process and likely outcomes?' For many children, a journey into unexplored territory can be seen as chancy. They fear looking foolish. They may think that they will not be able to supply the 'right' answer.

Children who are being required to consider something that will lead them towards change are better able to move forward if they feel safe. They are less likely to be resist change. Therefore, children's comfort level (emotional state) is important to keep in mind, especially when engaging a primary experience change process. Your job, at this point is to watch and facilitate.

You will likely observe some children struggling with the ranking. This doesn't matter, as the ranking product is not as important as the process that they are engaged in. It is this living-through-a-new-experience, that sometimes slows children down. You don't need to know their reason. You just need to know that children are, importantly, having their minds opened to possibility. Nevertheless, if need be, perhaps ask individual children some questions to help guide them through the ranking process, such as, what do you think is more important - this or that? They will, after all, want to complete the exercise, (like everyone else is doing).

**You may need to guide individual children by asking them, 'What do you think is the most important right?'**

The objective, as understood by the children, is to rank the considerations. If they do that, they will have met your request. Most children will want to concur. And all children will be feeling the freedom of being asked to think for themselves. In the classroom setting this may be a new experience. This is an introduction to primary thinking as part of the norm for their learning in your classroom environment.

The mental processes you are engaging are not to be measured. This is a stepping stone towards further exercising a primary experience in the next two activities, and in your classroom generally.

> **TEACHING NOTES**
>
> **Ranking in pairs. Ask children to find partners.**

## 2. <u>Ranking in Pairs</u> (The second balloon ride)

Ask children to find partners. Explain that the partner can be anyone from the classroom, not necessarily just from their community group.

You say, "Find a place where you can sit on the floor or at a desk, and take a balloon ride together. Now I want both of you to decide together how to rank the ten considerations."

- "Each will have to explain to the other why you made your choices."

- "You may want to try to persuade your partner to make the same choices as you, and he/she may also try and persuade you to agree with their choices."

- "To do this you are going to have to listen to each other, and decide between you what your new set of choices will be."

- "Number your shared choices in the second column."

Now you are taking children to another point of bifurcation, as they now have to integrate their thinking with another person. This takes listening, asking for clarification, even discovering the need to ask for clarification in order to make sense of an idea, justifying their own thought processes and formulating them into a persuasive case. It is a process of reciprocal interaction, and compromise. These processes, from pair to pair, will have many expressions, but even children who may appear 'unmatched' in strength of will, will be in a learning process. The meek and the aggressive have got to start somewhere on the road to mutual regard.

I have had children be surprised that other children hold alternate views, and that they can't always be persuaded to change. For many it's an eye opener that other perceptions can exist. This awareness of diversity of opinion is, in itself, an important learning experience, and an important realization, not only generally, but also for life in groups and the Four Communities Classroom.

Now you move to the next level.

> **Ranking with two pairs. Ask children to find another pair to take a balloon ride with.**

## 3. <u>Ranking with two pairs</u> (The third balloon ride)

You say, "Find another pair to take a balloon ride, and again find a spot to sit. Now you will need to do a lot of talking and listening as you decide how you are going to do this ranking, not with just two people but four on the balloon ride."

This may be another unique experience. The teacher is saying that children are going to need to talk to each other in their balloon groups. Incidentally, if your class numbers result in one group consisting of three pairs, that's O.K. Some children will experience the perspective of six-person negotiation.

*My Daughter Can't Wait for Monday Morning!*

> **TEACHING NOTES**

The integrative processes of ranking in pairs is now considerably more complex, as there are two pairs (or more) trying to merge thinking. Now there is the possibility that various combinations of temporary alliances could arise. This often helps children discover that the more people there are involved in a discussion, the greater the need to consider carefully all opinions. They find more effort is required to reach some form of consensus, and that consensus often means compromise. From group to group, the consensus process will be expressed differently and, therefore, each child's experience will be different.

---

### Introduction to the freedom/task concept for children (an avenue for primary learning experience)

The freedom to think for self in a group causes children to transfer their focus from the familiar teacher/child interaction to a self and other children interaction. Yet alongside this freedom of thought and decision making there is the teacher expectation that the ranking of rights will be carried out. This is a freedom/task process. In the larger grouping this can create, for some children, an additional emotional aspect to deal with. Is this a freedom where I can get away with being inattentive to the task? Perhaps the link between freedom of thought and a one step removal from teacher supervision means that I don't really have to apply myself; I can be silly and fractured in my effort. The teacher, of course, knows that freedom is being given to children to conduct themselves as they see fit in the completion of a task, but completion of the task is expected.

But, since this freedom/task process is a new experience for most children, responses can vary from a diligent effort to a silliness that distracts from the task at hand. Whereas your presence moving around the room has a 'keep-to-task' effect, and is strengthened by some helpful thoughts to groups, the real learning is contained in the handling of the freedom/task process, and in the handling of your helpful suggestions in the absence of you giving children orders. The children are in the early stages of the freedom/task process; some groups will function better than others; some may have real difficulty focusing effectively. Outside of a group having a disruptive effect upon the whole class and, therefore, requiring your attention to correct, let the 'silly' group fail. For children in a freedom/task process it is not the teacher's responsibility to see that the group works to completion. It is theirs. They have to fail on their own terms in order to begin learning how to be successful in freedom/task processes. Therefore, the teacher has to allow the failure to occur. For children who fail it is likely that some will engage in an inner dialogue of thoughts on better ways of handling freedom/task situations. This may start to occur during the plenary discussion. (See the next page.)

---

See page 88, 'The teacher's freedom/task process: Going with the flow of discussion while staying focused - or - Thinking on your feet while dealing with the unexpected.'

| TEACHING NOTES | **The Plenary Discussion** |

**The plenary discussion. Each group chooses a child to report the group's experience.**

It is important that each child is aware of the variety of experiences that occurred in the room, and that their's was one of many. To impart this, you engage in a plenary session. Ask each group to choose a child to report the group's experience. Others can add to this. The plenary discussion makes children aware of the diversity of group process and of the likelihood that they will need to adapt when they find themselves in other groupings.

For the plenary, number the balloon groups for easy reference. Take mental or written notes on what is being reported, so that you can make summarizing comments on the discussion/agreement process that you are witnessing. Be very, very clear to the children that you do not need to know the order of group choices. "What is important," you say, "is to know how you went about deciding which rights/weights to throw out." "If I had been sitting quietly in the corner of the basket on your balloon ride, what sort of things would I have heard?

**Be very, very clear that you, the teacher, do not need to know the order of group choices.**

**'I want to know HOW you went about deciding which rights/weights to throw out.**

**'If I had been sitting in a corner of your basket, what would I have heard?'**

1. Would I have heard you getting upset with, perhaps, always the same person blocking agreement?
2. Would I have heard one pair against the other pair making agreement difficult/ Or,
3. Would I have seen everyone being given a chance to talk before taking a vote? Or
4. Perhaps one person taking charge and telling everyone what to do?"

It can be quite amusing to see little nods and glances being made.

I find that mentioning possible scenarios, like these, helps children understand the sort of information wanted.

1. "Anyone can speak for the group, and anyone in the group can add their comments."
2. "Which group would like to be the first to tell us what happened on their balloon ride?"

Invitation invites children to think about involvement. I have yet to have a class where I've had to tell a group to contribute. There is always, it seems, one child in one of the groups who wants to tell what happened. Always ask children if they agree with what has just been said by their group member. Especially ask the child who may have been identified as a problem in reaching agreement. You may find various opinions exist. Whatever is said, accept it, without judgment, with a thank you. This exercise is partly an unspoken realization that the diversity of life also produces diversity of opinion. Passing judgment would be counter productive.

**Always ask children if they agree with what their group member has said.**

When the teacher shows interest in the children's thoughts and ideas in the plenary process, and when thoughts arrived at through the groups' process are accepted without judgment or the hurting of feelings, the

> **TEACHING NOTES**

children are encouraged to continue, seeing that this is a safe environment in which to voice their feelings and ideas. Other groups, observing this, can also feel safe and, therefore, more comfortable in making their contribution. And so it grows. Constructive bifurcation (change) process is more likely to occur if emotions are being cared for. Everything you do with the children is an opportunity to reassure them and make them feel comfortable with community classroom process.

'Next group. Who would like to tell us about their balloon ride?'

Opportunity exists in most interactions in the classroom, so view whatever occurs, during ranking or the plenary session, as a step forward towards creating a primary learning experience environment. Go with whatever happens.

During the ranking process, do not be alarmed if one group is not appearing to do well - perhaps acting flippantly. If a comment to keep them on task has only a temporary effect, this will only highlight for the rest of the class that lack of application means little is accomplished. The problem arising from too little being accomplished is a problem the members of the group have brought upon themselves, and they will, of course, eventually have to face this, likely during the plenary session when they are required to report on their process. This will not be without some discomfort; another primary experience. Again, you are non-judgmental. This is their problem, do not allow it to be yours or the class's. They put themselves into this situation.

Some and perhaps all children in this group of low accomplishment will have something to think about. It's an opportunity that they have given themselves to consider better self-correction in relationship to their environment. In other words, the whole exercise, while you maintain a positive atmosphere, also highlights that ownership for choice of conduct cannot be dodged. They have provided themselves and the entire class with a demonstration that responsibility for self can be a preferable experience. This doesn't have to be articulated. For most it will be felt.

---

**Ecological pattern - the self-correction endowment** (pp. 113 and 283.)

For some children, self-correction can get a little 'lost', and rediscovery can be a long road. It becomes apparent who needs more 'help' in self-correction. It is, of course, your call as to how much help different individuals will need. I find, however, that giving the benefit of the doubt, and opportunity to self-correct, (that may include expressions of puzzlement from you) can go a long way in enabling children to make better choices.

---

You will likely find yourself listening to a cross section of accounts from the groups who made a genuine attempt at ranking. Some groups may have

**TEACHING NOTES**

tried to use a fair voting system. Other groups may have adopted a less considered approach. There may be groups who just allowed someone to take the lead. Some may have had no trouble readily agreeing. Others may have been bossed by one or two members. These are examples of various self-organization processes that groups may have used. All self-organization processes are acceptable at this stage - offer no judgements. Thank everyone, and start your summary of the self-organization processes that occurred in each balloon group, and engage each group, one by one, in conversation.

You say,

"O.K. it seems that balloon group one organized themselves in this way ………..Would you agree balloon group one?" (You can ask this either at this point or during the plenary reporting.)

"What did it feel like to be on your balloon ride?"

"Did you mind having decisions made for you by others in your group?" (if that was the case)

- If the answer is 'Yes, we did mind having others make our decisions', ask, Why? What did you try do about others making decisions for you? Why didn't your efforts work?
- If the answer is 'No', ask, Why? etc.

Then move on to the next balloon group and go through a similar process of conversation.

From the experiences relayed to you, and the class, and after your summary of group processes and discussion, you may, in conclusion, be able to make a number of points:

1. If you don't speak up, decisions may be made that you don't like or agree with.
2. If you don't speak up, you only have yourself to blame if you don't like what's happening.
3. If you don't take into consideration the thoughts and opinions of others, they may become hard to work with.
4. If you don't listen to everyone, you may miss out on some good ideas and thoughts of others.
5. The groups who voted fairly made the best progress.

"In your community groups, you will be making decisions in the future. Use what you have learned today, about group discussion and decisions, to make your community group the best that you can, and earn the most points."

The experience of these activities and your summary and conclusions have placed the children on a learning curve that they have to make sense of. You have provided an externality with which the children have to find their way forward, based on their experience and thinking.

**Five important group discussion points.**

**TEACHING NOTES**

All this is a lot to take in. But children can take note, - as they know others will have done - that this has been a constructive experience, and that different ways of interaction have been considered.

Thus, through the three parts of the balloon rights activity, each child has now been exposed to thinking about:

- the freedom/task process (p. 75)

- the opportunity to apply, unchallenged, their own thinking to a situation.

- experiencing a shared solution with another child, who may have presented a challenge with his/her thoughts.

- the bigger challenge of exercising, in a larger group, consideration, consensus-building and compromise to reach solution.

- recognition of the validity of self and that of others.

- the need to work at finding a consensus process that fairly considers everyone.

- the effectiveness of their behaviour, and their opinions in relationship to others.

Children have been engaged in a passage through bifurcation (p. 237) bringing about changes in perception (a new order of awareness). This is more tiring and demanding than acquisition of facts. This is why it is best to learn Four Communities Classroom process in the morning.

Stop at this point, recognize that children will need to 'sleep on this', so that their minds will have a chance to internalize and make sense, not only of the experience, but of the emotions that they felt today, as they launched into new territory of thought. Continue the day now with more familiar curriculum items such as reading, writing, mathematics, gym, etc..

But, keep in mind, a new order of awareness will speak to every aspect of your classroom community life; a classroom life that builds on the process of becoming in each child.

Through the rights balloon activity, you have, in effect, supplied an avenue for the legitimization of children's thinking including the expansion of perception through a primary experience. The freedom/task process is part of that primary learning experience. It is important that this expansion is used and that now you've 'done' the exercise, you don't let things return to 'normal'. Children will feel confused if you offer a mixed message, i.e. balloon rights (primary experience) game followed by only secondary curriculum experience learning. Creating relevance and reinforcement for these perceptions is now something that should start to occur in classroom interactions. In other words, be sure to provide children with more freedom/task processes so that they are able to develop

**TEACHING NOTES**

and hone these skills, both in group decision-making, individual work and, when you feel ready, in freedom/task processes in curriculum areas. Thus, curriculum learning can become, for your children, a mix of primary and secondary experiences.

Integration of primary thinking and secondary learning experience is a mix and match process that, like all learning, should proceed at a pace that remains comfortable with the learner. For further discussion on primary and secondary experience learning see pages 19, 24-25, 175, 278. Use of the opportunities created in today's passage through bifurcation processes will become more a matter of course as time goes on.

(Note - You may wish to take your class through an optional Rights Balloon Activity. See pp. 127 to 128).

The next day, a new day with every child fresh, you should continue to develop understanding of Four Communities Classroom elements. This brings you to the human rights activity.

But first, thoughts on helping children who do not seem ready for change.

## What if you get resistance from children, at this or at any point, in developing the Four Communities Classroom?

You may experience resistance in children who believe that this new approach is not a lot different from business-as-usual classical, secondary experience teaching. These children will be looking for and may even try to elicit a standard censorship 'correction-response' from you, thereby 'proving' things are no different. This 'proof' will allow, in their minds, continuation of their 'tried and true' ways of 'surviving' in the classroom. They have, after all, a number of years invested in devices to counter the teacher's authority, and a reputation to maintain amongst peers. So, although it may be tempting for you to abandon the discusssion approach in favour of "do it because I say so", it is usually better not to resort to 'business as usual' 'classical' teacher censorship with such children, as you could be in danger of 'proving' their point. (I am not saying, however, that it never has its place). There are exceptions or modifications. See chap. 6, p. 215 for a discussion - 'Dignity and the story Brent and the story of Bill'.

I think it is reasonable to say that resorting to classical teaching approaches within the Four Communities Classroom can, in effect, ask the child to consider two dissimilar externalities.

On one hand:
1. Classical teaching discipline, and on the other hand,
2. Community classroom teaching,

while at the same time implying that only the Four Communities Classroom is valid. Well, if it's so valid, children may wonder, why the need to abandon it in favour of classical teaching techniques?

Thus, being asked to conform, under threat of punishment, in a classroom where independent thought is encouraged is a contradiction. The contradiction can confuse a child who may ask him/herself, "What am I being asked to consider?"

**What if you get resistance from children, at this or at any point, in developing the Four Communities Classroom? - continued**

Inner processes of the mind are always functioning in some form, be it constructive or negative. Censorship tends evoke a negative response, perhaps voiced and/or demonstrated through disruptive behaviour. ("I don't want to be told what to do and think.") When the child feels his/her only available behaviour option appears to be geared toward satisfying the integrative demand of the teacher, the child's options for making constructive autonomous choices become diminished. At this point positive behaviour choices may appear to be just signs of giving in to the integrative demand, which does not satisfy the human mind's need to experience autonomous process. Some children's sense of self won't allow them to 'throw in the towel' to this extent. Thus negative autonomous actions may become the only autonomous actions available and the child may build on them. Children with low self esteem may feel that maintaining resistance to an integrative demand is the one thing they still have. When this level of frustration is reached, even the most reasonable integrative demands are not always helpful to the child's inner struggle towards constructive autonomy.

The trick is to harness the strength of the 'paddle your own canoe' resolve that the child may exhibit, in a way that is constructive for him/her (their autonomy), and constructive for those around (integration). This is done through using the fundamental message of the Four Communities Classroom - that of inclusion. Ask, "What do you think?", "Why do you think that?", "How does what you are saying help with good teaching and learning?" By taking this approach, you have not let the child manipulate you into reinforcing his/her prejudices by your reverting to the use of integrative control mechanisms, thereby reducing your capacity to be an external constructive guide in the child's internal (autonomous) journey - the point of the what, why, how questions.

Children are more likely to consider their fit in your classroom if you consistently maintain the Four Communities Classroom environment.

If you are still faced with behavioural challenges see, 'Moving forward with bullies - the story of Jason', p. 195; a story that offers some guidance.

Also, for more on resistance and thoughts on ways to enable children to transcend their blocks to constructive learning, see chap. 6, p. 192, 'Children in action - classroom case studies'.

| TEACHING NOTES | **B. Human Rights/Needs Activity**

The Human Rights/Needs Activity will reinforce children's primary learning experiences, gained from the Balloon Rights Activities and enable them to advance from whatever position they attained the day before. All children, whether finding the newness of these processes challenging or not, will find, in the human rights activity, a further engagement with the process along with an increasing familiarity and comfort with the new order. Don't assess their progress. Assess only your provision of a nurturing environment. The children's job is to adapt, and they will, each at their own pace. Have fun!

There are six parts to the Human Rights/Needs Activity:

1. Read a true story of impoverishment to the class to form a basis for discussion on rights. (I suggest the book 'Families of the World' - see below.)
2. Group discussion on human rights/needs.
3. Group prioritization of human rights/needs arising from group discussion.
4. Plenary session, and chalk board listing of group decisions.
5. Class discussion to refine and rationalize the listed outcome from group discussion (part one)
6. Compare rights with The U.N Declaration on the Rights of the Child.

### 1. The reading of a true story to the class

**Announce that you are going to read a true story.**

You make no link to the balloon rights activity. You simply announce that you are going to read a story that is true about how a family in another country lives.

I use books by Helene Tremblay, 'Families of the World', in two volumes, that were provided to all schools in Canada in, I believe, 1990, by the Canadian International Development Agency (CIDA). The books give 24-hour chronological accounts of Ms. Tremblay's observations while staying with typical families; typical for each country in terms of economic wellbeing, job opportunity, family means of living and, in many cases, plain survival. Families in the Americas and the Caribbean are covered in one book, while families of East Asia, Southeast Asia, and the Pacific countries are covered in the other. The books are written at an upper elementary to high school level. With younger children it is necessary to be familiar with the story you are going to use and paraphrase to suit.

Ms. Tremblay's books do not date in terms of the hardship and difficulty of many people's lives. Using Ms. Tremblay's books, I take children through a family's day and show the accompanying pictures of the family, inside and outside their (often shanty) home. It is a sobering experience for all children. The room becomes silent as you read.

My Daughter *Can't Wait* for Monday Morning!

TEACHING NOTES

## 2. Group discussion on human rights/needs

In preparation for group discussion, ask children a series of questions:

- What are these people missing in their lives?
- What should all people in the world have in order to live a life with needs met?
- What do people need to live properly?

> **Speculation focused on a problem.**
> Look for opportunities to invite children to focus on problems through speculation.

**The rights emphasis is on needs not wants.**

The emphasis is upon need, not want. Explain to children that you do not need, for example, a wide screen T.V., or a video game to live; these things are wants. Focus thoughts on what is needed to live. Wants/needs perspectives might need consideration, through class discussion, for a few minutes. (You may decide to revisit, at some time, the needs/wants debate. It is an important consideration for all).

**Discussion title - 'Human needs'**
**The talking stick leader helps with discussion, the recorder writes down what people say.**

You say, "I want the recorder to write at the top of a piece of paper the heading Human Needs." (Write the heading on the chalk board). Then say, "The talking stick leader will take the talking stick, and the recorder will take pencil and paper, and each group will sit in discussion position inside the circle in the centre of your desks. In your group, think of as many needs as you can that this family should have to live properly."

The family's plight usually motivates children, and they have little trouble in either thinking of contributions to the discussion or in offering their thoughts. Such motivation creates a good impetus for the group discussion; their first major one.

**Talk quietly so other groups can't hear your ideas.**

Prior to all group discussion, it doesn't hurt to remind children to speak quietly so that the other groups can't hear and copy. This has a number of effects:

- Contributes to sense of groupness; it's us working together.
- More quiet and focused discussion.
- A generally quieter classroom, that can help create a more serious mental attitude and approach to work.

You may find the awarding of points for discussion inappropriate when such important matters are to be aired. Therefore, only mention them if focus or process lags. If you award points to on-task groups, you will find off-task groups tend to rapidly reapply themselves and refocus.

Understanding the influence of externalities on learning   (For further information on the term 'externality' see p.p. 27 250, 308.)

1. Your class is now considering an externality; e.g the family's plight. This, at the moment, is the <u>No. 1 externality</u> for your children's thinking.

2. However, one group, may be overtaken by a more immediate externality where attention is diverted, perhaps, by a spontaneously-occurring disagreement between children (<u>No. 2 externality</u>). 'What is happening around me right now (integrative external influence) and how do I (autonomy of self) deal with it effectively?'

3. When such additional externalities impede progress, the teacher can award points to other on-task groups. The teacher awarding points to other groups now becomes for the off-task group an even more immediate externality (<u>No. 3 externality</u>) They will now be more likely to respond by reapplying themselves to the No. 1 externality.

> **Ecological pattern - constructive integrative externalities can arise where children help to create the classroom environment** (p. 250)
>
> Moments in the classroom can help build your own understanding of ecological process in action - learning environments evolving.
>
> There will always be a series of externalities occurring in children's lives within the classroom environment. Externalities are integrative influences affecting teaching and learning and a child's autonomy. Enabling children to shape a constructive externality for themselves contributes to their understanding of how to create constructive environments for everyone - classroom learning environments evolving constructively.

Beyond the externality at hand (the family's plight), let's consider how group discussion expands Four Communities Classroom learning for children:

- The children are discussing in their community groups. Since this is a different set of children from those of the Balloon Rights Activity, children will likely be comparing and contrasting the processes of the previous experience with what is happening now. This in itself is a learning process. Also, following yesterday's experiences, children will be more aware of their responses in relation to others, i.e. trying out modified/alternative approaches in interactions with others. All of this is a primary experience for children; engaging inner thoughts about self in relationship to what is going on around them (their externality), and all in the safety of your caring classroom environment (their externality)

- Mind processes are moved forward from considering the ranking of the given set of statements of the rights balloon activity, to now recalling, and responding to the complexities of lives foreign to them. They are debating with each other their recall of the same story; contextualizing their discussion in terms of what constitutes the fundamentals of living.

These are demanding tasks for children which take the mind through further perception bifurcation points; it represents a workout for the mind.

| TEACHING NOTES |

**Highlight/underline the five most important needs on your list.**

### 3. Group prioritization of human rights/needs arising from group discussion

A rise in noise levels will likely indicate that children appear to have exhausted ideas. At this point, ask each group to highlight/underline the five most important needs on their list. This will generally eliminate thoughts from the list that would probably fall into the 'wants' category.

Apart from this refining of lists, let's look at the Four Communities Classroom elements being experienced by children.

- Discerning what is most important and categorizing thoughts, from important to trivial.
- Listening and analysing other children's thoughts as they hear them support their contribution to the list.
- Experiencing a further opportunity for discussion and discernment.
- Experiencing other children's evaluations, rather than turning to the teacher for appraisal.

Gaining approval from the teacher is now expanding to include demonstrating capacity in the above elements. Mastery of these elements is not easily measured, nor should it be. What you will likely observe are children closely involved in the process of list making. But bear in mind that some children will still be in an observing stage. All, however, are learning. All minds will be engaged. This human rights/needs exercise is an introduction and invitation to children to practice considered contributions to learning in the classroom.

---

### Talking stick protocols and development of responsibility

You may find that talking stick protocols are being somewhat neglected. If, however, groups are making satisfactory progress in the tasks you have set, in this case, the discussions, the creation of lists, and the refinement of lists, then I suggest that you turn a blind eye. Talking stick protocols need only be maintained as a default requirement for groups that would seem to benefit. If challenged by, "Why us? That group isn't using the talking stick properly" Say something like, "Well if you could discuss as well as that group without the talking stick, then certainly I'd have no problem with you not using the talking stick." The group overhearing your comments also gets praised, incidentally, - and so encouraged. The emphasis has been placed on the group having to work to try and deal with their problems, rather than you, the teacher. This is a learning opportunity for children, not a problem for you to solve. The message; responsibility for you falls upon you.

---

When groups have had a reasonable time to discuss, you say, "Groups who have finished picking their five most important rights, can sit in their desks."

Thus when children are seated in their desks it announces to you, and other groups, that they are finished. An air of 'wrap up' hurries other groups to completion.

**TEACHING NOTES**

### 4. <u>Plenary session, and chalk board listing of group decisions</u>

**Each recorder tells us one of their highlighted rights/needs.**

Now, you say, "We shall go around the groups and ask each recorder to tell us one of their highlighted rights/needs. I will list the right on the chalk board, with the group's number next to it. When every group has given us one of their rights, then we will go around the room again and get the recorder to tell us another right that their group has chosen. We will keep doing this until all groups have told us all five of their most important rights."

"If you hear a group mention a right that you have on your list, then when I get to your group you can tell me about that and I will add your group number to that right. Then you can tell me about another right your group chose."

This maintains fairness, and avoids problems such as children shouting out that they thought of that too, or they thought of it first and that, therefore, they deserve the credit, or even accusations that the other group overheard and didn't think of it themselves.

**Add rights on the chalk board without comment, other than saying thank you, or asking for clarification.**

Do not make any comments as you add rights to the list on the chalk board, other than saying thank you, or asking for clarification. You may choose to ask, 'do you mean …..?' and/or, 'if I write it this way will that say what you mean?' Always go with the intended meaning of the children. Refining the list, stage 5, on the opposite page, will present the opportunity to take discussion further.

**Are there any other rights that you feel must be included?**

When all groups have their five choices of rights listed, ask the groups if they have any rights not mentioned, that they feel are important, and should be on the list. This will often produce three or four more good ideas. Again, add to the list of rights without comment. (Sometimes, groups, while in discussion, confide that they are having trouble confining their list to five. Tell them not to worry, they can add a sixth right to their list if they think it is important. Thanks, they will say).

If children start saying that some things on the list have the same meaning, say, "I think you could be right. We will take a look at that in a minute." With a questioning tone you ask, "Is that O.K?" Your short question recognizes the child's thinking and questioning, and values the individual as a participant in the process. This interchange, like much in the classroom, is short, small and passes quickly. A moment properly nuanced can make a huge difference in building the connection between you and the class: its importance should never be underestimated. Cumulatively, small events and moments, create the classroom and shape the ethos of its life.

> TEACHING NOTES

**Ask the children, "Is there any right/need listed that means the same as another?"**

## 5. Part one - Class discussion to refine and rationalize the listed outcomes from group discussion
(there is a further discussion of this process, part two, on p. 95)

When you are sure all useful contributions are listed, ask if anyone can see anything on the list that means the same as another.

Hands go up, suggestions and thoughts are offered. This is your opportunity to pose (not impose) your own thoughts for consideration. You are now positioned to enter into a class discussion of import. You will, through the process and practice of class discussion, involve children in furthering their understanding of discussion and communication.

> **The teacher's job is to role-model fairness and consideration for everyone's contribution.**

However, some children may have been forceful in their groups, dominated discussion, and left other group members feeling that they had limited say and influence. That group-discussion experience is now going to be compared by them and contrasted with what you are about to do with the class as a whole. You are going to be the role model and the guide to fairness and due consideration in the quest for consensus; mutual regard in action (observed by both the dominating child and the dominated).

> This refinement of the human rights list on the chalk board is similar to the process that will be carried out in the next activity - 'The Classroom Rights Activity'. However, since, importantly, the classroom rights are the rights the children will choose to live by, you will be applying more rigor (and time) to the refinement process in the classroom rights activity. The classroom rights activity section starts on p. 92 and enters into a more detailed account of discussion process in part two, (p. 95), 'The process of class discussion to refine and rationalize the listed outcomes from group discussion'.

Right now the refining process of the human rights list will, through discussion and consensus, combine and/or re-word children's contributions to the list of rights that children feel all people should have. You will be, as in every discussion with children, engaging the teacher's freedom/task process. You may find the next page helpful - 'The teacher's freedom/task process: going with the flow of discussion while staying focused - or - thinking on your feet while dealing with the unexpected.'

When no more thoughts are forthcoming and children appear to have finished refining the list, number the rights.

**When the refining of the list is complete, NUMBER THE RIGHTS!**

Part of every discussion with children is the teachers freedom/task process.

### THE TEACHER'S FREEDOM/TASK PROCESS: Going with the flow of discussion while staying focused - or - Thinking on your feet while dealing with the unexpected

When children are invited to discuss and offer their thoughts, you will be in receipt of many and varied responses. It is important to be prepared to interact with children and their thoughts, and deal with the unexpected, in order to constructively nurture good teaching and good learning experiences. It may seem easier at times to revert to secondary experience statements, such as, 'because in this class we expect people to cooperate.' Or, 'what you have just said doesn't help us in what we are discussing right now'. But such statements will not encourage the development of constructive primary thoughts in children and, therefore, will be counterproductive to constructive child development in the Four Communities Classroom. Carrying the thought in your mind, 'does this child present a problem or is he/she presenting me with an opportunity to advance learning in our classroom?' can help you to develop the right mindset.

**Example one:**

Children in a grade four/five class were doing the optional Rights Balloon Activity (p. 127) This is where each balloon-group's ranking of the rights are accumulated on an overhead to determine the entire class's overall ranking of the balloon rights.

Suddenly, and unexpectedly, a boy declares that he is in disagreement with the outcomes and the exercise is producing results that he not only does not agree with, but are wrong. He then proceeds to lecture everyone on why. This triggered a response from another child. A heated discussion is about to start. The outburst threatens the process I'm engaging the class in, and therefore, one's first response may be of secondary experience in nature - 'we are not going to discuss this now. It interrupts what we are doing'. That, of course, shuts down the problem, but certainly leaves everyone with a mixed message - 'can we have our own ideas or not?' With the problem 'shut down', the first boy's feelings will likely not be constructive - perhaps feeling cross with the class and with me. In these fledgling days of the school year, this will not be good for the good teaching and good learning interactions we are hoping for. So, instead, with 'opportunities for good teaching and learning in mind' and, 'is this an opportunity to advance learning?', I find myself saying, "Because we are all different we will have different views. What we are doing right now is finding out the views of the class as a whole. It will be interesting for everyone to see where they agree with the overall class view and where they differ. There is no right or wrong, just different points of view." "O.K.?", I ask the boy. He nods agreement.

Result? The first boy is happy; his views and dignity intact. Everyone has been reinforced in their perception of the class being one where ideas are encouraged. The whole class is now actually better prepared to view the class's overall position in relation to their own. And I've made a mental note that, by reminding children of the fact that we are all different and that opinions can also differ, I will have future classes better prepared for this exercise. Opportunity capitalized!

Other pluses? We have to be happy that both boys were so involved in class process that their emotions gave vent. My response gave the first boy an opportunity to learn how to both maintain or modify his views on the rights (his inner dialogue call) and to consider how to modify his perceptions of himself within the class for his own and others' benefit.

| The teacher's freedom/task process - continued |

**Example two:**

I once had a grade five boy who, during the class discussion on 'Rights of the Child' (p. 90), astutely made connections that were perhaps, without a redirection of class discussion, beyond the comprehension level of many in the class. My task, as the teacher, was to give due recognition to the boy's contribution by asking some questions and summarizing his thoughts in terms that could most readily be understood by everyone without advancing too much into the tangent. I thanked him. The boys contribution, in a sense, had to be confined to the category of 'icing on the cake', rather than part of the mix in reaching the discussion goal. But the boy seemed happy - probably because his contribution was not (conveniently for classroom 'efficiency') sidelined as being 'off topic' but regarded as useful.

However, I made a note to myself to recognize this nine year olds apparent greater sophistication of thought process while at the same time remembering that, emotionally, he is still a grade five boy. (Be careful not to confuse possibly well-developed intellectual capacity with emotional maturity). It is possible, in fact, that if his mind is quicker than those of his classmates, he may be emotionally challenged in his relationship with his peers. This may cause him difficulties and perhaps some confusion as he struggles to make sense of his place in the class. The inner dialogue of the child is always important. This boy's inner dialogue may be more sophisticated, but also possibly more vulnerable to emotional confusion and hence the road to maturity more challenging. (The boy, I was later told, came to the school for a 'fresh start', necessitated by a history of behavioural problems.)

Your discussion engagement with the class always has elements of the freedom/task process. As the teacher, you initiate the discussion with a goal in mind (in this case, refining the children's list of rights on the chalk board). Since you are inviting children to think, formulate thoughts into speech and contribute to the class discussion, it is important that you maintain their interest and comfort level by valuing what they have to offer. Children will need both affirmation and guidance. Thus the teacher is facilitating a number of processes.

- The topic on hand.
- The development of carefully considered mind processes in children.
- The listening to each other and the teacher, and weighing in their own minds what they are hearing.
- Affirmation and guidance of thought. (Equal to affirmation of the individual)
- Role-modeling how to go with the flow while staying focused.

These elements are handled and are part of every discussion process the teacher engages in with children, whether individually, in groups, or class-wide.

For many children, class discussion takes them into a higher order of thinking, beyond what they are used to; they are exercising their minds in ways that amount to an exploration.

Offerings from children can vary tremendously, and can be unpredictable. In engaging with their contributions, it is your job to consider what is being offered and lend coherence to each child's thoughts, in terms of the overall task. However, if you feel that a contribution is not relevant to the topic at hand, thank the child, as part of the mutual regard process, and say (according to the situation) something in line with:

- Could we look at that later?
- That is an important thought. Can we look at that later? (continued on next page)

> The teacher's freedom/task process - continued
>
> - Could you remember your thoughts on that so that we can talk about it later?
> - Yes, but I was looking for something else, maybe we could get back to that.
> - That is a good thought, but I would like to just talk about (whatever the topic is) right now if that's O.K?
>
> Thus, there has to be in the teacher's mind an openness and sense of freedom in facilitating discussion processes, while keeping children's thoughts and minds on topic; the teacher's freedom/task process. Thinking on your feet is supported with thoughts of:
> - Is this a problem or an opportunity?
> - Can I enable, in children's minds, a constructive primary experience with this situation?
>
> It is very important to maintain each child's dignity.

See p. 75 for the freedom/task concept for children (an avenue for primary learning experience)

### 6. The U.N Declaration on the Rights of the Child

Now ask if anyone has heard of the United Nations.

You can photocopy The U.N Declaration on the Rights of the Child (Courtesy of David Selby and Graham Pike from their book Global Teacher, Global Learner. See p. 129).

You will likely have to inject a mini-lesson on the U.N. (United Nations) regarding its formation, the fact that it was created with a view to helping ensure world peace after the Second World War and that, as of 2006, 192 nations belong to the organization. Explain that its function is to try and create a world where people can live better lives in peace. You can continue your explanation with, "So in 1959 the leaders of countries (nations) that belonged to the U.N. got together and created a list of all the rights that every child in the world should have; a bit like the list that we have made."

**Check the list, and see if the U.N have any of the rights that we thought were important.**

And add, "I thought it would be a good idea if I gave each of you a copy of the list of rights that the U.N. made in 1959, so that you can see how our list compares. Check the list, and see if the U.N have any of the rights that we thought were important. They may have some that we didn't think of, and we might have some rights that they didn't think of."

"If you see rights on the U.N list that we have, put the number of our right in the column next to their right, or more if you think that perhaps two of our rights match what a U.N right says."

As you hand out the U.N rights list to each child, say, "Check to see how many of our rights are the same as, or similar to the rights discussed and decided upon by those grown-ups in 1959."

The kids are focused and interested to 'compare notes'. It's not long before they find lots of matches between their list and the U.N.'s.

**Now it's congratulation time.** "See how clever everyone is, in this room. You have made a list that has got most of the rights on it that

My Daughter *Can't Wait* for Monday Morning!

> TEACHING NOTES

the grown-ups thought up for their list. Well done! I think you can all pat yourselves on the back. Well done everyone."

Your congratulations switch on a light in the mind of every child. In neon lights the message says, 'We can think. We can figure things out for ourselves. We can decide what is important, and our thoughts are valid.'

What wonderful thoughts to entertain about self. You have enabled children to demonstrate to themselves the validity of their own thinking. This is a bifurcation point of great significance, as it deals with faith in self. For more on faith in self, see p. 140. Suddenly, expanded thoughts of self could be playing in children's minds, perhaps around self identity that includes a growing awareness of their capacity to apply discernment to learning. 'Perhaps I can do this again, have thoughts and ideas and dare to contribute them.'

You may find that you are experiencing an atmosphere in your room that expresses this awakening sense of self.

Discernment, once engaged, is not easy to ignore when behaviour choices present themselves. It is with such powers that responsibility for self is enabled and enhanced.

And so Four Communities Classroom tenets build; responsibility to self receives a boost. However, like all learning opportunity, different children will engage in different ways and at different rates. But the positive influence is there in the room, and the 'hold outs' increasingly become the minority. This is each child's journey with a growing incentive to join those who seem to be enjoying themselves. If you have 25 children, you are facilitating 25 journeys. Be patient with those whose steps are sometimes more like stumbles, as many fly.

---

**The rights balloon activity and human rights/needs activity, just completed by your class, form the background for establishing the next stage - classroom rights**

With experience in considering the rights listed in the balloon ride, and in putting thought to human rights and needs, I find children are able to apply themselves to the question of classroom rights quite effectively. Do not be tempted to omit the balloon ride and human rights activities in order to save time. These are important building blocks. It is not productive to jump into the creation of classroom rights without this background of rights and the attendant practicing of discussion process. Without the preparation arising from these activities children will struggle, making adequate classroom rights outcomes difficult to achieve.

> TEACHING NOTES

## C. The Classroom Rights Activity

*David, grade seven.*

## "It's great! Imagine, the thought of your teacher caring about you enough to let you pick rights."

There are two parts to this activity:
1. Group discussion on classroom rights
2. Class discussion to refine and rationalize the listed outcomes from group discussion (part two, the continuation of part one from p. 87)

### 1. Group discussion on classroom rights

**I wonder if we ought to think about what rights we would like to have for ourselves in our classroom?**

The next day, go into the classroom and say to the class, 'After all the work you have done on rights that children should have, I wonder if we ought to think about what rights we would like to have for ourselves in our classroom?'

This is invitational. It immediately injects wonder. The words, 'I wonder', will have others thinking to themselves, 'I wonder too.' Wondering maintains an open mind, and alerts the mind. This is good for teaching and learning.

It's important to understand that the power of nuance and wonder, in engaging the human mind, is greater than the imposed directive. Or to put it another way, the power of the invitation to primary experience is greater than the invitation to secondary experience. Discovery is more enticing than the instruction manual. It's not that the secondary or the instructive are not important; they obviously have a place in acquiring knowledge. However, it is, I believe, important that teachers maintain a quest for a balance, as a combination can often be the most effective approach for many learners.

---

### The imposed directive (usually involving a secondary experience)

Let us, for a moment, consider the effect on children, and you, in the use of the imposed directive; a more instructive approach. You come into the classroom and you simply instruct - 'We are going to look at rights for ourselves in the classroom.' Let's consider the scene that is now set? A number of thoughts arise:
1. The ball is in the teacher's court. "O.K.", the kids think, "so how are we going to do this?" Since little can proceed without further input and direction from you the directive offers little enticement or incentive to start thinking.
2. Children will wait for instruction on what you intend. As they can't know the shape of what's coming, they have to suspend judgment as to how much enthusiasm to generate. Perhaps this could be something that doesn't appeal. They'll work at what you give them to do, of course, but ownership and excitement for this effort may not materialize. (In the case of more familiar journeys, such as math, children already know, more or less, what to expect. Therefore, it perhaps could be argued, directives have a greater place and function in these more definitive pursuits.)

*My Daughter Can't Wait for Monday Morning!*

| The imposed directive - continued |
|---|

3. Children with uncertain ownership for a journey, may offer only uncertain contribution. Uncertain contribution can mean uncertain or diminished outcome - perhaps a group of unfocused, uncooperative participants that require discipline.

4. It's harder for everyone to feel enthused when there is diminished cooperation and contribution.

Obviously the possibility of setback is best avoided. Instead, try to create the conditions for positive experiences and growth in responsibility.

In 'good' classes - filled with compliance and obedience - the imposed directive can often be 'successful', i.e. lessons can proceed without discipline problems and disruption. But 'good' classes, some may say, are becoming more exceptional. Besides, should not children in good classes have an enhanced opportunity to realize their potential through more primary experience learning?

I was once asked by a (good) child, "How many rights are we supposed to think of?" It was important to her to have expectations clearly established - then she'd know what to do and what to focus upon (I want to fulfill your [secondary experience] expectations). I said that she could choose any number of rights that she thought were needed. Hmm, what do I do with that instruction? So I added, if I come round and your group has only thought of one right, I will ask why. If you are able to give me a good answer, that will be fine, but if you can't give me a good answer then I would expect you to think of more rights for your class. Whatever you decide, you should be able to give a reason. Is that O.K? She smiled and said yes. Her group then proceeded happily into a primary experience process.

## The power of nuance (usually involving primary experiences)

Often, in children's minds, engaging questions with wording such as 'what if?', 'what do you think?', can elicit interest, and can bring about huge differences in mindset and application to work; the stage set for primary learning experiences. With the speculative question, and minds invited to wonder, wondering begins, and you and the children are ready to explore. The thought let's go! jogs into place.

While the Four Communities Classroom is not articulated and understood by children in terms of ecologically based patterns, [appendix (ii) p. 248] children start to build a sense of how things work and how to conduct themselves in the environment that you are creating together.

Thus, the discussion on classroom rights is started with the speculative question, I wonder if we ought to think about what rights we would like to have for ourselves in our classroom? The speculative question sets the stage for wondering, but with parameters needing to be supplied. In the Human Rights Activity the rights needed for all children evolved through group and class discussion. The children may well be anticipating this process to be repeated in their consideration of classroom rights. They did, after all, do so well in this type of discussion. But before you shed light on that speculation, you must answer the bigger question that may be occurring in the minds around you. What is meant by classroom rights? This needs to be explained.

| TEACHING NOTES |

**Rights to make life better in the classroom - better teaching and learning**

**We need to choose rights that we can give each other.**

So you explain, "Just like yesterday when we chose rights that we thought would make life better for all children, we could, today, look for rights for ourselves that would make our life in the classroom better for all of us. We are always looking for ways to help us have better teaching and learning. So perhaps we could give ourselves rights that would give us better teaching and learning."

"But to make what we choose come true, we have to choose classroom rights that we can give someone and they can give us."

To help illustrate, I give an example of a right that children couldn't give each other, such as - "If it's a very hot day and we wished the classroom had air conditioning, could Michele go to Chris and demand that he provide air conditioning, saying, 'I have a right to air conditioning, so give it to me?' Could you provide Michele with the air conditioning Chris?"

Chris, obviously says no. "Therefore," you say, "it is no use including rights for our classroom that we can't give each other. Giving ourselves rights like that is not going to help us. We need rights that can help us AND that we can give to each other."

Another example, "We decide that we all have the right to a recess break that lasts twice as long as the other class's break. Can we give that to each other? Michele could you please give us that right?" Michele says she can't. "We would have to convince the principal, and all of your parents. Would we have much chance of doing that? So there is no point in looking at rights that we can't give ourselves."

**What sort of rights could we give ourselves?**

**What sort of rights would we want, to make life better in our classroom, and to make teaching and learning better?**

- But what sort of rights could we give ourselves?

- What sort of rights would we want, to make life better in our classroom, and to make teaching and learning better?

That's the question that I would like you to think about. That's the question that I want each group to think about."

Give children an example of a right they could give each other. "The balloon right not to be bossed around - could you give that right to someone else by not bossing them around?" The answer is, of course, yes. You say, "That, if you chose it, could be a classroom right. Choose rights that you can give each other."

"I want each group to go to their discussion positions, and I want the recorder to write down as many rights that the group can think of, that they would like to have in this classroom. Remember to only write down rights that you can actually give to another person. Think of things that you would like for yourself, that you could give others and they could give you." (Reciprocation).

After a minute or two, once group discussion is underway, wander around, listen in on discussion and take a look at each group's growing list of rights. Give groups feedback; reassurance that, yes, they are coming up

*My Daughter Can't Wait for Monday Morning!*

**TEACHING NOTES**

with some good ideas, and, when needed, guidance to keep them on track. You may need to say to a group or the class as a whole, "Make sure that you are choosing rights you can give each other." You may need to provide further examples, "Can you give Joe the right to have coloured pencils, can Joe demand that you give him coloured pencils?" The answer is, of course, no. "Well then that is not a classroom right, as it's not a right that you can give each other - to buy Joe coloured pencils will cost you money.

**Discuss quietly**

Remind children to discuss quietly so that others don't overhear their ideas. This is the second major group discussion for the children, so you will start to see, as children get more used to what is expected of them, a further settling and a better understanding of how to work together. Also of interest to them is that they are being given the opportunity to make decisions that could impact them in the classroom.

Groups are usually able to think of from 6 or 7 to perhaps 15 or 16 rights. Ideas will likely start to peter out after 10 to 15 minutes, at which time you repeat the announcement you made for the last discussion process. 'Highlight or underline the five most important rights on your list.'

**Highlight your five most important rights.**

The process you and the class are now engaged in is, of course, similar to the process used to discuss human rights, so you continue by going again through the following steps:

- If a group seeks permission, allow them to highlight six rights.
- Have group members return to their desks when they have completed the highlighting.
- Conduct a **'Plenary session and chalk board listing of group decisions'** (See p. 86, listing group contributions, one classroom right at a time.)
- Have a **class discussion to refine and rationalize the listed outcome from group discussion.** (As described on p. 87.)

This last item is especially important in building awareness of mutual regard, a cornerstone of classroom rights. So I now discuss this further.

2. <u>**Part two - Class discussion to refine and rationalize the listed outcomes from group discussion (the continuation of part one from p. 87)**</u>

Although mutual regard, as a concept, remains unarticulated, children are engaged in a process that elicits respect for the thoughts and feelings of each other. This comfortable and engaged environment, in turn, elicits emotions that tend to open minds. In their small groups the tendency is for each child to feel that their feelings are safe and they enjoy being asked to compare what is important to them. While recognizing these tendencies, we are, however, in a process where our goal is to enjoy safe comfort levels of mutual regard throughout the entire classroom.

TEACHING NOTES

With each group's rights listed on the board, the children are ready to experience the collective group process on a classroom-wide basis, as you role-model, once more, the discussion/communication process as a mutual regard process. Since children have had the opportunity to internalize the experience of the human rights discussion, alongside their personal interest in the outcomes of the current classroom rights discussion, you and the children are well positioned to consider classroom rights, and all this will mean for them.

Thus, while the obvious goal is the establishment of classroom rights, children will be engaged in the parallel process of a primary learning experience of human relationships, involving mutual regard and discernment. A visual documentation of this journey will eventually be displayed on a banner of classroom rights that you and the class create; rights that will become the class reference point in future journeys of learning. (See, Using Classroom Rights, p. 107.)

> **Establishment of classroom rights is the overt goal. The primary learning experiences of mutual regard, human relationship, and discernment run parallel.**

The following is intended as a guide in taking children along the route to establishing classroom rights.

At this point you will likely have a chalk board covered with all manner of rights, offered by the groups. Some will be useful and productive, some you see as problematic, contradictory or confusing, i.e. not necessarily conducive to producing a harmonious atmosphere for good teaching and learning.

Don't worry. The eventual, final list will be one that will promote harmony. Getting to that point will be a very important primary learning experience. Therefore, do not view the raw list as a barrier of work to be overcome, but as an opportunity to build children's powers of considered thought and discernment in reaching preferred goals. For that is what it is. You have brought children to this point for this purpose.

This arriving at a mutually agreed upon list of classroom rights (your stated goal) will expose children to a primary learning experience of mutual regard, as they practice and apply discernment.

> **The list of rights presents the opportunity to build children's powers of considered thought and discernment while reaching preferred goals.**

**"Is there any right on the list that means the same as another?"**

Start by saying, "Let's look at the list of rights and see if any idea on the list means the same as another?"

My Daughter *Can't Wait* for Monday Morning!   96

> **TEACHING NOTES**

Hands go up. Suggestions and thoughts come in. The opportunity to pose (not impose) your thoughts for consideration has arrived, but should be underplayed. The predominant feeling, both during discussion and with the final product, is that it is that of the children's. This is fundamental to the building of their capacity for discernment. Your role is one of a guide to promote thought, fairness, due consideration of others, and assist in the reaching of a preferred consensus; mutual regard in action.

There are a number of points to keep in mind during the refinement process:

1. Use a system of choosing raised hands, from group to group, so that everyone gets an equal opportunity to contribute.

2. Insist that everyone extends the courtesy of listening, i.e. "Everyone was courteous and quiet when you spoke, so we need you to do the same for Jamie. O.K?"

3. Encourage children to speak loudly enough so that everyone can hear. However, some children are pushing their personal barriers just to speak, so if speaking louder appears to stress them, don't push. Repeat what they said for children who couldn't hear the soft voice. Building confidence over a number of contributions, usually helps children get over the volume problem. Try not, however, to let low-volume contributions become 'accepted' habit.

4. Be patient with all children, regardless of how slow they may be in saying their piece.

5. Thank each child for his or her contribution, whether you agree with what is said or not.

6. Provide clarifying summaries, so that it is clear for you and everyone else what is understood by what has been said, again, regardless of whether you agree or not.

7. Always ask each child if your summary is the message intended. Use an open tone of voice so that the child doesn't feel intimidated into accepting your version, and will feel comfortable in offering their own clarification, if needed.

8. Encourage children to use each others names, e.g. 'When Tom said ……., I didn't agree, I think ….'

9. Ask Tom if he would like to respond, and ask if anyone else has any thoughts. (Asking for thoughts is more effective than asking if anyone has something to say, as everyone has thoughts, and such an invitation might prompt the speaking of them).

10. Keep children talking on one topic at a time. Sometimes, children want to speak on a classroom right that is not yet under discussion. Just say, "That sounds like a good idea, but if you wouldn't mind holding on to that thought, we will talk about that later. O.K?"

You will find that children are quite remarkable at seeing the sense in things. Children, like us all, try to make sense of the world, and will apply this desire to the rights discussion. This making sense of things will start

| TEACHING NOTES |

**When needed, be sure to interpret children's contributions so that others understand what is being said.**

**Introduce ideas that may prompt children into thoughts that could enable them to transcend an impass, or take them into considerations you see as important.**

**Truncating the process will truncate development of discernment.**

to play out in your discussion and you will find positions beginning to form around the current topic. However, depending upon the grade level and the group of children you have, there will be varying levels of sophistication in tackling issues. Of course, generally speaking, the higher the grade the greater the sophistication of thinking. Allow for this. Consider putting, verbally, into point form, the occasional contribution from a child that may seem beyond others in the room. Do this seamlessly, so that it is not apparent what you are doing. Children will be relieved that you have made another child's contribution understandable. You will maintain comfort levels, so that contributions keep on coming, while the level of debate may get a boost.

Important points for consideration, can, however, be missed. This is often a good time for you to broach thoughts that will prompt children into a range of thinking that may enable them to transcend an impasse, or take them into considerations you see as important. But, of course, make sure that your use of vocabulary and the level of sophistication of the concept you are offering is right for your class.

However, it can be very tempting for teachers, accustomed to directing children and keeping an eye on the clock, to make an exception to all of the above, and simply tell children that, in this instance, we will adopt my summary of the outcome. DON'T do this under any circumstances, as your unintended message will be a powerful one; there are limits to children's discernment capacity, and due consideration and mutual regard are conditional.

There are, of course, at any one moment, limits to a child's discernment capacity, but no limits to its development potential. It is this development that is in danger of being truncated if the process is truncated.

Also, the message - 'mutual regard can be subject to conditions' - does not help children in their understanding and use of mutual regard between each other. Mutual regard subjected to child-imposed conditions does not need reinforcement in the classroom.

> **Ecological pattern - infinite permutation and mutuality** (Appendices)
> Infinite permutation capacity, and mutual regard are the ecological factors involved in these considerations. They should not be hindered.

> **Allowing children full rein in thinking and discussion is important in the development of discernment and mutual regard.**

*Kristine, grade seven.*
**"If a group of people discuss things, you learn to form your own opinions, and learn to express them with the group."**

My Daughter *Can't Wait* for Monday Morning!

Allowing children full-rein in their thinking and discussion is very important to discernment development. It is essential to their assuming responsibility for mutual regard. However, I should make it clear that I am not saying that teacher directives are now a thing of the past. In the discussion process, for instance, your directives will be needed and expected to maintain fairness and consideration for others. In other words, you are as the training wheels on a bike. Gradually, as children's practice of fairness and consideration develops you will be able to 'let go'. Children's competence will grow and they will be able to carry themselves with increasing ability and confidence.

Thus the refining of the list of classroom rights will, through discussion and consensus, combine and/or rewrite children's contributions.

The order in which rights are discussed is, of course, a chance process, with children responding to the question "Look again at the rights on the chalk board and see if any more of the rights mean the same as another?" But that is O.K. Go with whatever happens.

As you go through the list of rights (each one accompanied by the contributing group's identifying number) you may need to ask a group, "What did you intend when you wrote that right?" Answers sometimes reveal quite a different intention, giving you the opportunity to share in a clarifying rewording - perhaps, although not necessarily, carrying a less problematic message.

'Problematic' rights need to be addressed through your engagement of student thought, not by teacher pronouncement. This can sometimes be achieved by contrasting rights. You ask, "If we kept these two rights, what effect would that have?" Without discarding a group's idea, a question like this poses, instead, a problem for children to consider. It is important that such considerations are not interpreted as 'teacher-approved' judgments upon group contributions. This is not an arena in which to determine winners and losers. The awarding of points, for example, is not part of this process. This is a forum for thinking and sharing together to decide what we want for ourselves in our classroom for the year.

You can help focus children's thoughts and sharpen their powers of discernment by asking, "Will this right create the effect that you want?" "Is this what you want for our classroom?" Sometimes it may be a problem of wording that needs to be worked on, at other times it may be something that is not going to work or is superfluous to another right.

I once had a grade 7/8 split class that was dealing with 'the right to freedom of expression'. In many ways this is a hard point to argue but, in the setting of the classroom, I could foresee problems. But the children had to be able to see the problems for themselves. So I offered a possible scenario. I questioned whether, if the right to freedom of expression was set alongside a

> TEACHING NOTES

right they had already agreed upon, the right to feel good about themselves, could these rights contradict? If, for example, Brad came into the room and insulted another child, claiming he had the right to freedom of expression, would that be O.K? Is that what you want for yourselves? I asked. Is that what you intend? (Mutual regard was at risk of being undermined)

I had some particularly articulate children in this class, who managed to maintain an argument in favour of the right to freedom of expression, but not able to overcome the downside of its possible effect on the right to feel good about ourselves in the classroom. Children spoke to both sides of the question, and minds got changed. When I felt that the downside had been thoroughly discussed and understood, I offered my summary of the question in preparation for the vote. The children voted to erase from the list the right to freedom of expression, favouring instead another right, the right to be listened to. (Thus, mutual regard would now not be subject to undermining.)

However, if the class had voted in favour of keeping the right to freedom of expression, I would have added a caveat. Since good teaching and good learning is our foundation, we would have to make sure that there would not be a damaging and compromising use of the right to freedom of expression. That would mean that changes would have to be made to ensure that good teaching and learning for everyone was maintained. Therefore, if the class could make this right work, ensuring that others were not adversely affected, then, under these conditions, we would keep the right. Importantly, children would have to assume the increased responsibility that comes with the right of freedom of expression, and this would become part of the understanding. But, ultimately, responsibility for all always resides with the teacher and, here, the logic for this position, and the need for children's increased levels of responsibility, would receive articulation.

Discussion of this right turned out to be time consuming, but formed, for this class, an extremely important opportunity for young minds in the development of discernment and mutual regard processes.

It is important that the teacher of the Four Communities Classroom see these events as opportunities rather than barriers that have to be overcome. Do not be tempted with thoughts of, "If I hadn't opened up this process I wouldn't now have to deal with this problem." "Maybe, in the interests of time-saving, I'll short-change the process and pronounce."

Life's process means, as we all know, having to deal with the unexpected. Therefore, not only does this discussion opportunity enable engagement with discernment and mutual regard process, but it also becomes an opportunity, in a safe environment, to enhance the validity of its process through consideration of the unexpected. The children's development, in this regard, is time well spent.

## Allowing time for process

The class discussion of classroom rights has a two-pronged goal:

1. The creation of a list of rights for children to use as a guide, throughout the year, in their class interactions - both a product and a process. The quality of the end product is affected by the quality of the process.
2. The creation of an atmosphere where children feel comfortable thinking, articulating and sharing their thoughts as they work towards creating their list of rights; the process.

I once had a class of grade five children who were discussing 'the right/need to be yourself' and whether they wanted this right/need to be included among the rights that they were choosing to keep. It soon became apparent that this was considered important to them, and I, therefore, could have taken this right to the voting stage early in the discussion, and moved quickly on to the next right to be discussed. However, I did not do this as the discussion (the process) was proving to be a very beneficial. The articulation of carefully considered thought regarding the importance of self and the futility of trying to be someone else, with thoughts on the impact upon friendships, the difficulties of resisting unconstructive peer pressure, and being true to yourself were a wonder to listen to. Children were nuanced in their contributions, using examples from their own understanding of life and relationship. There were many contributors, and all were listening. Powerful, even wise, messages were coming from children. Why take the question to a vote when so much was being learned?

The journey to the end product was a rich one that day. And to think it was only a few days since we took our first cautious steps into the discussion process. Minds had been given the space to open, and they did!

(Note. Every class is, of course, different. My main message here is to **allow time for process. It's a valuable use of time.** I've had as many different experiences as I have had classes, as you will too.

So, with these experiences, children in the Four Communities Classroom become ever more skilled in being thoughtful, effective people. This means that learning opportunities throughout the year are capitalized upon with increasing effectiveness, whether it be in interpersonal relationships or taking ownership for learning and curriculum. In short, the year, for teacher and children, becomes interesting, enjoyable and effective. Curriculum learning, therefore, is also poised to become an interesting, enjoyable and effective process.

You do not have to try to create opportunity for your class. It will always come, in one form or another. Opportunity often arrives, in the life of the classroom, not necessarily through a major event, but sometimes in a series of smaller occurrences. All are learning opportunities.

However, the classroom rights discussion is a process that will certainly present opportunity for discernment and mutual regard. Be prepared to allot the time it requires, likely interspersed over two, three or four days, taking breaks before children get tired, and while they are still enthused. Do not carry on with discussion when other things need attending to. Tell children that we will get back to the classroom rights discussion tomorrow.

> **TEACHING NOTES**

When re-engaging with children, after a break, remind children what the class is doing. This is a process whereby they, the students, are deciding what rights they would like for themselves in order to make the year together the best it can be, so that good teaching and learning can occur.

The list evolves as rights are discussed and rationalized. You will, through discussion, be making amendments, deletions and additions. Some rights will be combined, with some rewording. All changes are reached through consensus.

**All changes to the list of rights are reached through consensus.**

### The Voting Process

After views have been heard on a particular right, or perhaps a pair of rights, summarize and lay out the question to be voted upon. It may be a vote where the decision lies between two, three, or four possibilities. "All who think idea number one is the best put up your hands." you say, "All who think idea number two is the best put up your hands." etc. Always count hands around the room in a careful, deliberate, and clear way, group by group. This will have the effect of showing children that you are taking note of participation. Such attention encourages child participation through the voting process.

**Count raised hands around the room in a careful, deliberate, and clear way, group by group.**

> 💡 If a non-participant doesn't like the rights the class chooses it becomes the child's problem; an incentive to participate more thoughtfully; an opportunity for assumption of responsibility for self.

Back to the rights discussion process. Typically, classes of children will distil a list of twenty or more rights down to ten to sixteen. Many rights that children choose are informed by the balloon rights activity, e.g. the right not to be bossed around, and the right to be listened to. Other rights that often appear, in some form or other, are the right to privacy (in their desks), the right to concentrate, have fun, feel good about themselves, not be bullied or teased. (I've never had to seed these ideas - children always come up with rights that will work)

At times, the right to have friends is raised, which usually brings about the discussion that you cannot force someone be a friend, as that would be an empty gesture, and that one has to earn friendship by being a friend. That right usually gets deleted or modified, but the arguments made in discussion are always useful for children to air and listen to.

*My Daughter Can't Wait for Monday Morning!*

> TEACHING NOTES

The right to respect, or the right to be respected, offer similar opportunity for discussion. I ask, "How does one show respect?" The answer that children discover, through discussion is that one shows respect by using the rights that the class is choosing; rights that will make clear to everyone how to treat others and interact with them in ways that we all want. The rights they are creating for themselves spell out what is meant by respect and how to engage in it.

When the list of rights is completed - all discussion ended - ask the children to look closely at all the rights on the chalk board and to think whether these are the rights that they want. Each child has to ask her/him self, are these the rights I would want for myself. Not whether they think others may want them, but whether they would want them for themselves. Make it clear that if there is any right on the board that they would not want for themselves, they can say so. Silence ensues, as each child considers the rights from their own perspective. No hand goes up. All want what they see on the board for themselves. "Therefore", you say, "it seems everyone in this room wants the rights that are up on the board." Agreement is murmured.

**Each child has to ask her/himself, are these the rights I would want for myself?.**

"Who made up these rights?" you ask. 'We did', they say. "Right." "Did I put up any rights?" you ask. 'No', they reply.

**"Who made these rights?"**
**'We did,' children say.**
**"Right!"**
**"Did I put up any rights?"**
**'No,' they reply.**

**Thus it is clear, to one and all, that these are rights thought up and agreed upon by the children. This is an extremely important fact that has to be clearly understood and remembered by all in the classroom.**

"Who is responsible for making sure that you get these rights?" you ask.

**"Who is responsible for making sure that you get these rights?" you ask.**

Responses vary, of course, from class to class. Someone may suggest that you are responsible to ensure that every child gets their rights. But your class have just decided the rights they want for themselves; a process of assuming responsibility for themselves. You ask, "Could anyone else in the classroom take responsibility for the rights for everyone?" Eventually, through discussion, usually sooner than later, someone will say those magic words - 'We are all responsible for these rights'. "RIGHT!"

Reciprocation is a word you may not actually use in class, although it is vital to mutual regard. Here is the moment to underline to the class how each child has to rely on others to get the rights that they have chosen, and that every child in the room needs to be willing to give others their rights. In other words you give others their rights and they will give you your rights. That makes everyone important in the giving of rights. This two-way-street realization is an extremely important one for children to internalize.

It is also important for these rights to be prominently displayed. Artwork time. Each right should be hand printed and coloured/decorated on an approximately 11"x14" piece of paper (easily seen from across the room).

103  *My Daughter Can't Wait for Monday Morning!*

> **TEACHING NOTES**

Give each group a number of rights to be artistically drawn. The rights will then be arranged to form an eye-catching collage along the top of the classroom wall. A banner, affixed over the collage of rights proclaims 'In our classroom everyone has the right to:-'

Below the collage, a final banner will say, 'We are all responsible for these rights.'

Since these rights are used as a tool for good teaching and learning (Using Classroom Rights, p.107), I suggest that the collage of rights be up on the wall within a couple of days.

It is important that all the learning engaged in establishing the rights is validated by making rights a part of classroom life.

---

### The right to a good teacher

If the 'right to a good teacher' is presented by children for addition to the list of rights on the chalk board, include it and, as with all the rights that appear, deal with it during the rights refining discussion. I usually turn this 'right' back to the children and ask them if they think they have any control over whether a teacher is good or not, and whether it is a right that they can give each other. Often, in children's eyes, a good teacher is a nice teacher. I ask them, how do you make sure that your teacher is good to you? I ask more questions. If someone is behaving badly, how would that make your teacher feel? If the teacher is cross and angry, do you have a teacher on your hands who will be in a good mood with the class? 'No', is always the answer. How then do you make sure that you have a good teacher, and give the 'right to a good teacher' to others in the class - a teacher that you all like being with?

Help children's thought processes further by asking, 'Do you think that the teacher has a right to the rights? Would keeping the rights for the teacher, as well as for you, help keep the teacher in a good mood?'

This type of questioning is useful for children in helping them to shape their understanding of their constructive role in relationship with the teacher.

Once this is understood, it doesn't really serve to explain that the 'right to a good teacher' is a bit more subjective than that, and therefore, its inclusion has caveats. To expand to this detail is to invite confusion and to lose a good opportunity to shed light for children on their role in effective relationships with adults. Therefore, let the right to a good teacher stay as a classroom right.

# Thoughts on child participation

Participation by children, in discussion, doesn't always have to be verbal. As we know from 'Mary the listener', p. 60, not all children will feel comfortable speaking out. But in the Four Communities Classroom we do expect all children to put up their hands and vote. In order to vote intelligently, all children will need to listen to what is being said and decide whether they agree or not. Each child will have to make up his or her own mind. The right being discussed will, after all, have an effect on classroom life, so each child had better decide what they want for themselves. You may need to remind individual children of this reality, from time to time.

Thus, discussion process in the Four Communities Classroom should also become an avenue for opening up minds to responsibility for self. Children should be engaged in a process of assuming this responsibility.

You say, "If you don't like the rights the class chooses, and you don't think carefully and vote for what you want, then who are you going to blame? Listen carefully to what everyone is saying so that you are able to vote for what you want." These questions engage an inner dialogue that cannot be avoided. Even non-participation is a learning opportunity for the child if, at some point, he/she is confronted with the effects of opting out of opportunities offered.

Verbal participation in discussion, by all children, therefore, shouldn't necessarily be expected. Some children have to observe others participating, and be reminded of the importance and need. But that is O.K. See p. 102, 'The Voting Process'. Also see pp. 57 to 59 on the discussion between John, Susan and Bill, showing how children build their thinking through listening to others and weighing others' thoughts with their own. Sometimes, children may find that this process prompts thoughts that they may like to share, or perhaps alters their perspective. This is the business of inner dialogue, and a valid process. Children come to the realization that we are able to not only learn from the teacher, but from each other, and ourselves.

Although (immediately or eventually) each child will make the decision regarding participation, the need to participate is proposed by you in a tone that suggests that, of course, participation is what everyone wants.

However, beyond this encouragement, there should be no judgment of the child, specific or inferred. In this, as in other matters, judgment is a form of imposition. And imposition can generate problems of resistance. Inner thoughts of resistance can become the child's chosen option. Resistance is not, of course, helpful, as it can become an alternative basis for thought, perhaps resulting in non-cooperation or adoption of a challenging stance- what are you going to do about this? This can have the effect of removing, for the child, the need and desire to assume responsibility for him/herself.

A child's being should be built on a strong foundation of assuming responsibility for self. This is facilitated through enabling children's assessment of self in an environment of positive and constructive externalities. Teacher judgment tends to mitigate against this process. Therefore:

1. adopt a process in the classroom that encourages constructive inner dialogue that could lead towards participation and assumption of responsibility.
2. remind children, who may not be taking advantage of the classroom process, about the importance of participation. e.g. "listen carefully to what is being said so that you can vote for what you want."

All interaction between you and the class, as well as you and individual children, should be one of enabling journeys of constructive growth. Some children are ready to get going immediately, others need continuing help. Your classroom should be one that causes an inner dialogue towards thoughts of participation.

### Additional outcomes arising from the Four Communities Classroom discussion process

Engaging children in discussion can have 'additional' outcomes which are complementary to the prime stated purpose of enabling children to enjoy their education and enabling good teaching and good learning.

A sense of trust in the child's mind, although usually remaining unspoken, seems to come to the fore - a development of regard in children towards each other, and towards you as a teacher and adult. The sense of self-empowerment from the rights process, and the building of trust in you, form a favourable coupling in the child's mind.

The favourable inner dialogue of the mind builds through:
1. your invitation to children to give careful consideration to the establishment of classroom rights -
2. a process that children see as empowering, and
3. your non-judgmental responses, and
4. your encouragement of considered, but non-judgmental responses between children.

Trust-building can often be observed as children develop a growing willingness to share thoughts with others during class discussion. *"When you are with people a lot more in the groups you get more comfortable and feel like you could be more open."* Laura - grade 7 talking of grade 5.

Trust-building can extend to long-term effects. For example, before a taped interview for this book, one of a group of grade 9 students, former grade five children of mine, told me, "I'll come to talk to you, but I wouldn't for other teachers." He knew that he had a relationship with me where he could feel safe with his thoughts, and, importantly, wanted to help. This, of course, represents a sense of connection - an important aspect of constructive relationship. Relationships between child and teacher should be constructive for the child - mutual regard in action.

The development of a constructive relationship and mutual regard between yourself and the child requires sensitivity on your part, especially when contribution to discussion from children can occasionally include sensitive life experiences, offered, perhaps, to illustrate a point they are making. Since you cannot be in control of what children may put up their hand to say, your role in facilitating discussion, in such instances, has to be one where you respond with little comment beyond a 'thank you'. A regard that is not intrusive. Sometimes, however, you may gain an insight that may enable you to build a more empathetic understanding in the facilitation of the child's development.

For example, I had a child who once offered up a long-ago unhappy experience. She tended to make discussion contributions that were scattered in logic - tailing off, and then going again. She seemed confused and would confuse the class. It was embarrassing for her, but, wonderfully, she continued to try. There was, of course, nothing that I could do about her situation. That was not my role. My role was to help her gain confidence. My avenue was the classroom. Discussion process was a good tool. I engaged with her by 'reading between the lines', in a non-intrusive summary, asking her if that is what she was saying - thanking her for her thoughts. I became her empathetic outside reference for enabling her thought organization. This is an important role for you to play in your classroom.

<u>Summary of additional outcomes for teachers and children</u>

- building trust
- building mutual regard
- learning to be non-judgmental
- building constructive relationships

- the evolving of favourable inner dialogue
- development of sensitivity towards others
- development of the willingness to share thoughts
- development of self-empowerment and self-esteem

It is important to note that these constructive relationship elements cannot exist in isolation; each engenders each.

*All 8 of these elements mitigate bullying*

*My Daughter Can't Wait for Monday Morning!*

**TEACHING NOTES**

## 12. Using classroom rights (responsibility for self and others)

*Mich, grade seven.*

**When somebody was misbehaving, we just found a right that they were breaking. So instead of just telling them that they were disturbing people, we had something to turn to. This way kids had something to think about."**

As the architects, children absolutely own their classroom rights. Their classroom is now equipped with a powerful learning tool, created by themselves; a tool that enables respect to develop between children, and a tool that allows children to concentrate constructively on learning opportunities in the classroom. It is, therefore, important that all the learning engaged in establishing the rights is validated through their use in the life of the classroom.

Thus, when Johnny takes Jane's pencil without asking (and even perhaps, upon her request, is not inclined to return it), go to Johnny and ask him to look at the rights on the wall and decide which of Jane's rights he has taken away. He may say,

- I've taken her right to privacy by going into her desk, and
- the right to feel good about herself, because she's upset, and
- oh yes, the right to concentrate, because I have disturbed her when she was working.

What becomes apparent is that when one right is taken, other rights are simultaneously taken away. Having determined this, you say, "But I thought that you wanted these rights for yourself Johnny". 'I do'. "Well, what makes you think that Jane doesn't want these rights?" 'Sorry Jane'. Johnny has experienced the need to refer to the rights, and to think about whether his actions have taken away someone else's rights; the same rights that he wants for himself.

This is a powerful primary experience for a child. It prompts internal reflection within the context of an event involving another child. All this with the bannered classroom rights acting as a reminder of the mutual regard exercise that established the rights. Internal dialogues can be powerful and constructive learning processes. Violating rights is, for the children, going against their own decisions and their own thinking. Actively recognising the rights they have created has significance for all manner of events that could occur in the classroom, from non-cooperation, to disruptive behaviour, to teasing, to bullying. Though one internal reflection event will not in itself, of course, trigger a remedy for all behaviour problems, you, the child and the entire class do have a precedent-setting resolution process to refer to and to build upon. Importantly, an avenue is established for children to

> TEACHING NOTES

start assuming responsibility for themselves and the decisions they make; a reference and foundation that is always there for you and the children. Many children do not require the object lesson of being asked to refer to the classroom rights list. Some may need to experience this once. Others perhaps a number of times. Children who don't require prompting are usually appreciative that the rights list is there for others in the class to refer to.

*Craig, grade nine, recalling grade five.*

**"I think it's a really good idea that kids make their own rights and then post them. You have to be really stupid to break your own rules. You can point up and say that's a right that you made. Can you say why you are not following it?"**

What happens is that children begin to internalize thought process regarding behaviours that effect others. Children start to take responsibility for their actions, behaviours and relationship decisions. They become increasingly aware of the reciprocal nature of good relationships. Motivated children find that with a more solid frame of reference regarding behaviour, they can be less concerned about 'cool' kids who may mock. Rather than living with caution and feeling the need to be defensive in response to what someone may do or say, an air of greater calm and confidence in relationship building can free children to develop more meaningful relationships. Children start to feel happier and more content.

*Courtney, grade seven.*

**"Rights are better than rules for keeping order because there are always people who don't obey rules. Perhaps they break rules because they want attention. Rights cause people to think for themselves about what is best."**

Courtney refers to the fact that, for the classroom, when comparing rights to rules, there are different dynamics at work (although both engage inner dialogue).

1. Rights cause children to think for themselves (the inner dialogue), while

2. rule breaking can be a device used by attention seekers.

However, with rights, the rule-breaking, attention-seeking child is faced with a dilemma. To break the rights is to go against self and to make self look foolish in the eyes of classmates. This isn't the attention he is seeking. Rights, in effect, force the seeking of attention through positive means. (again the process of inner dialogue)

Both major and minor behavioural choices can be addressed through reference to the classroom rights. You and the children will, no doubt, be

> TEACHING NOTES

provided a number of opportunities to refer to the rights on different issues and events.

## Problem or Opportunity?

It is important that each event be seen as an opportunity to develop understanding of the rights and their meaning in the life of the classroom. As you guide them, children observe and learn, and start to feel the benefits of a more harmonious classroom. As this occurs, you will find that having to direct children's attention to rights is gradually taken over by children who will reference and adjust their own behaviours and, accordingly, the behaviours of each other. The rate at which this occurs, of course, varies from class to class, but it has been my experience that a critical mass of children, who like the rights and their constructive effect, fairly quickly become the dominant influence in the room, leaving 'hold-outs' in a distinct minority, with little or no influence. Without influence or audience, there is no fuel for negative behaviour, but space, instead, to consider joining the more constructive ambience of the room. Better still, attention seekers can become Four Communities Classroom leaders; a choice that many make.

Leadership roles, in fact, are adopted almost immediately by some children. I find, sometimes, that it is the independent thinker who rebels most in a regular classroom. In the Four Communities Classroom you can almost see the wheels turning as these children listen to how their thinking can have an outlet and be considered. These are the children who often become the most wonderful contributors to their group.

The teacher is also 'covered' by the rights; something that needs to be explained to the class. You too have the right to concentrate and feel good about yourself, etc. etc.. You can also point out that you have the right to be listened to. This, I find, is more effective than demanding attention, when teaching or speaking to the class. The children begin to see you as a person too, who also needs consideration. Day to day, both class and group discussion will be greatly helped by occasional reminders of the right to be listened to.

Human nature being what it is, you will find that a class, well adjusted to rights and their use, continues to need occasional reminders during the life of the classroom. Class harmony has become an interactive process.

Ms. Gaudet, grade three teacher.

**"Choosing rights was very, very effective. When I said to the class, 'We had all decided that everyone should have their turn', they couldn't argue with me because they had all come to common agreement that that was one of our rights. Little children's minds understood that. I was astonished."**

TEACHING NOTES

## 13. Learning the importance of difference

Understanding difference, and that each child exhibits difference, is important in accepting self and others. This has implications for mutual regard processes.

The right to be different is, as you know, a right that is part of the Balloon Rights Activity (see p. 126). The right to be different, sometimes chosen by children as a class right, is valuable to explore, and can become part of the importance-of-difference discussion. Difference and diversity are synonymous and fundamental to ecological sustainability.

Difference and diversity are certainly part of being human. Our different appearances reflect ecological diversity. As I say to children, "Look around and see how many people look exactly like you." But, of course, there is more to distinguish people than appearance, such as varying characteristics, personalities and likes and dislikes, which, as you may have to point out, distinguish identical (in appearance) twins.

Perhaps, a week after the rights collage has gone up on the wall and has been put into practice, when some progress has been made, start the importance of difference discussion one morning by asking, 'What would things be like if we all were the same?'

**'What would things be like if we were all the same?'**

The significance of this question rapidly becomes apparent as children put up their hands and offer thoughts. You'll get many interesting comments. A few that I've heard are, 'We'd all choose the same make, year and colour of car, and never be able to find it in the parking lot'. 'There would be no fun in sports or games. We would all win or all lose, and that's impossible'. And perhaps more sobering, 'We would all have the same thoughts, so there would be no need to communicate'. Among the many other realizations that I've heard, are, 'We'd all want the same thing and that would be boring. We'd all know the same thing and couldn't learn from, or teach, each other. We would all be bakers or firemen or police officers or farmers or doctors. We would all be the same age, and the same gender, and how would that work?' With gender being raised, we quickly realize that life itself cannot exist without gender difference. "Who", I ask, "are more important, boys or girls?" Expect boys to say boys and girls to say girls. But after the humour, it is clear that their importance to life is equal.

(To help monitor the discussion on the importance of difference you may find it useful to photocopy and use the chart 'Capturing the essence of your class discussion on the importance of difference' on p. 112.)

After summarizing the class discussion, it now doesn't take very much to bring children to the conclusion that difference is vital for life. "We cannot have life without difference. And because we are all different, that makes each of us very important. Being different makes each child very, very important and, therefore, very important to our class, and very important to each of our groups."

**Difference is vital for life.**
- We cannot have life without difference.
- Therefore, each child is important.
- Being different makes each child very, very important to our class, and to their group.

> TEACHING NOTES

**Bullies have no idea about difference and the importance of difference to life. No idea that your difference is important to life.**

Since, at times, some children find themselves wishing they were like someone else, or deriding those who are different, you can generally, at this point, hear a pin drop. What I say in this silent moment is, "People who tease others, or bully, are actually showing that they have no idea about difference and the importance of difference to life. Bullies try to make you think that you are not important. You can see how wrong they are. They have no idea how your difference is important to life. No idea at all. Your difference is important to life."

This is, of course, a very powerful message, and hugely underlines the importance of the rights the children have created. Perception of self, others and relationship is generally set on a different and more constructive course.

Give this new awareness a day or two to be internalized by the children, before introducing the self-correction activity on p. 113.

---

**Ecological pattern** - emotion, memory, learning and self-organization
Capra, '96, p. 25.
*"...understanding the pattern of self-organization is the key to understanding the essential nature of life."* (my underlining)

Positive moments of heightened emotional thought (such as learning the importance of difference) can give constructive power to children's inner dialogue and can trigger positive change.

The theory of living systems says that emotion (how we feel) is part of an internal peptide process of the body, [see appendix (iii), p. 263 'The role of emotions - the great motivators'] and linked to processes of memory, learning, and conscious self-organizing.

The peptide link between emotion, self-organizing, memory and learning makes the possession of constructive feelings very important for constructive learning processes in children.

---

**We can learn from each other. (Individual and group self-organization in process.)**

# Capturing the essence of your class discussion on the importance of difference

(This page can be photocopied)

Children's contributions during your class discussion on sameness will usually raise many questions and problems that would arise if everything in life was the same. Children's thoughts often align with one or more of the following statements:

Questions about self and identity
- Who are we?

Questions about feelings
- We would all feel the same thing at the same time
- Feelings wouldn't be private

Questions about life being impossible
- We'd all want the same thing
- We'd all like the same things
- All being winners or losers in sports would be impossible
- All being the same age
- All being the same gender

*You may wish to place a check mark against one or more of the discussion essences which seem to capture or reflect a child's contribution. It will be a matter of placing children's thoughts, if possible, into a category. Do not be concerned if, during the course of the discussion, you are unable to check everything. Children may, of course, offer thoughts other than those listed.*

Questions about pointlessness
- No creativity
- All the same thoughts would mean no need for communication of thoughts and ideas
- Competition in sports would not exist
- Make sports and games no fun
- Life would be boring

Questions about learning
- All knowing the same information means no one can learn anything from anyone else

Questions about obtaining things that people need to live
- All people just being farmers means that there would be food but no houses, or all being builders means houses but no food. (for example)

Questions about governance
- There could be no democracy since everyone thought the same

Questions about the ecology
- All animals all the same

As a result of the children's discussion, you will easily be able demonstrate that without difference life would be both pointless and actually impossible, enabling you make the extremely important point to the children that -

## difference is vital for life.

The checking of discussion essences can help you to keep track of the contributions, while, simultaneously building a summary of the main points made by children. This check list will help in the summation of your class's discussion and in your highlighting to the children the importance of difference to life.

## 14. Self-correction

*Brittany, grade seven.*

## "Self-correction is part of taking care of yourself."

*Lindsay, grade seven.*

## "Self-correction makes you feel nice, independent and grown up, and is linked with being equal because you don't feel stupider than anyone else when you correct yourself."

As discussed in appendix (iv) p. 282, self is a fundamental aspect of the ecology and life process. Self and the sense of self is not only important to individual children, but also to the life of the classroom. Self-correction is part of the story of self - part of a list of descriptors of self. For an account of self-correction and its link to other self-descriptors please refer to p. 283 'The self-descriptors'.

You are about to enter a discussion that awakens children to their inherent self-correction capacity, and encourages and enables its use in the life of the classroom. This will be a discussion where you will again be engaging children in primary learning and evoking in each child a perception-shifting inner dialogue. Because of this demand on the child's mind, and because of its implications for future learning in the classroom, I suggest that you choose a time slot first thing in the morning to take advantage of maximum alertness in the children.

One morning, come into the classroom and, without announcement or introduction, write the word, 'self-correction', on the chalk board, and then ask, **"Does anyone know the meaning of 'self-correction?'** "Does anyone know what this means?" With such an approach and with the time you spend writing 'self-correction', you will generally draw most children's attention.

OR, alternatively, try -

"Does anyone know the meaning of this?" and then start to write the word, 'self-correction', on the board. For a class that is slower to give attention, this approach is better, as children are often drawn to try and second-guess what the words are going to say. They will likely call out their guesses, but that's fine if everyone is now focused on what you are doing. Since this is a more connective way of proceeding than demanding full attention before you start, why not use it?

"Does anyone know what self-correction means?" One or two hands go up, and someone will usually tell you that it means correcting yourself. "Right."

**Are there any other ways that you could get corrected?** Then you ask, "Are there any other ways you could get corrected?" The answers usually come in fast, including perhaps, 'my mum and dad correct me', along with grandparents, coaches, teachers, etc. "Right." Start making a list under 'self correction' of the different types of correction children say they are in receipt of.

113    My Daughter *Can't Wait* for Monday Morning!

> **TEACHING NOTES**

For example:-
- Self-correction
- Parent-correction
- Teacher-correction
- Etc.
- Etc.

If no one mentions brothers and sisters, ask if anyone has a brother or a sister who corrects them. 'Yes', they will say. So you add brother and sister-correction to the list.

**Has anyone in the class been corrected by a friend?**

Ask, "Has anyone ever been corrected by a friend?" Yes. Add peer-correction to the list, making sure children know the meaning of peer.

Now you will have a list on the chalk board that may look something like this.
- Self-correction
- Parent-correction
- Teacher-correction
- Brother and sister-correction
- Peer-correction

You will find it is time consuming, and without added benefit, to produce a list with more than these main correction items. Therefore, try to confine the list to the above points.

Now ask this question for each correction category, discussing the issues raised as you build the list.

1. Who likes parent-correction?

**Place plus and/or minus signs against each category of corrections.**

Of course, no one likes it. But children will offer the pluses and minuses with, generally, the overall consensus, "although necessary and important, sometimes it doesn't seem fair."

On your list, mark this type of correction with a + and a -

2. Who likes teacher-correction?

Again you will hear the pluses and minuses, including comments on importance and fairness, and the difference between teacher correction of behaviour and teacher correction of work.

Mark this type of correction with a + and a -

3. Who likes brother or sister-correction?

Answers are usually less carefully weighed on this question. No! We don't like being corrected by our siblings.

Mark this type of correction with a -

*My Daughter Can't Wait for Monday Morning!*

> **TEACHING NOTES**

4. Who likes being corrected by our peers, such as other people in the class?

No! This isn't favoured either.

> Mark this type of correction with a -

5. Who likes self-correction?

You may receive a number of thoughts, but generally children are in favour self-correction.

> Mark this type of correction with a +

Then you say, "O.K. Out of all these corrections, which do you like the best?" Of course, the list of +'s and -'s gives the answer. But it is important that the children respond to the question directly. Children will say they like self-correction best. (You may like to have a vote with a show of hands to establish this).

Ask the children why they like self correction best. Answers usually come down to feelings. You feel better if someone isn't telling you what to do and putting you right.

**Ask the children why they like self-correction best.**

> **Feelings and emotions of children reflect a state of mind that influences their decisions, choices, and learning capacity.**

**How do you ensure that you feel good about things and reduce being corrected by others?**

You ask, "O.K. So how do you make sure that you feel good about things and reduce the number of times you get corrected by others?"

'By correcting yourself!' This may come as a chorus.

## "Right, the more you can correct yourself, the less correction you'll get from others."

Place this thought directly in the context of the classroom.

You ask, "What about the classroom? How do we feel about self-correction, teacher-correction, and peer-correction in the classroom?"

Peer correction is still turned down as not being very desirable. However, it is sometimes noted, 'that it can be nice to get help from friends'.

All still agree that teacher-correction is sometimes needed.

But it is now firmly established, "Yes, self correction is best."

Now you summarize.

**In the classroom how do you feel about:**
- **self-correction?**
- **teacher-correction?**
- **peer-correction?**

## "So could we say that in our classroom, for good teaching and good learning, self-correction is best?"

'Yes'

My Daughter *Can't Wait* for Monday Morning!

*Vanessa, grade nine, in discussion about grade five.*

**"I like self-correction because it gives some responsibility. Being allowed to self-correct is the same thing as saying I trust you"**

---

*Saud, grade six.*

**"If a teacher looks at you to encourage self-correction, you think this person is a good teacher."**

Now the time has come to make another banner for the wall, supplied by the artistic talents of the class, to remind us all that we think -

**'For good teaching and good learning, self correction is best.'**

Through this Four Communities Classroom discussion on correction you have facilitated, between children, an outer dialogue, and also involved each child's mind in an inner dialogue. This process of outer and inner dialogue is an innate human ecological capacity that you have enabled children to use constructively. In this discussion self-correction has been brought to consciousness. Self-descriptors, of which self-correction is just one (see below), are thought processes and processes of mind that often take the form of questions asked of ourselves to help develop understanding of self in relationship to surroundings and to shape our actions. Through consideration of self-correction, you have enabled a class of children to begin using their ecological endowment of self-descriptors constructively.

You have also established that self-correction occurs through reference to other people (externalities).

Appendix (iv), p. 282, describes self-correction and shows how it is part and parcel of the other self descriptors.

The self-descriptors include:

- Self-correction         (through reference to externalities)
- Self-regulation         (through reference to externalities)
- Self-monitoring         (through reference to externalities)
- Self-balancing          (through reference to externalities)
- Self-limiting           (through reference to externalities)
- Self-justification      (through reference to  externalities)
- Self-organizing         (through reference to externalities)
- Self-sustaining         (through reference to externalities)
- Self-reinforcing        (through reference to externalities)
- Self-assertion          (through reference to externalities)
- Self determination      (through reference to externalities)

**TEACHING NOTES**

## Summary of developing the Four Communities Classroom along with children

Children have been engaged in and establishing for themselves - four mutually-supportive and interlinked foundations for effective learning and relationship building.

The four foundational elements for the child and class are:

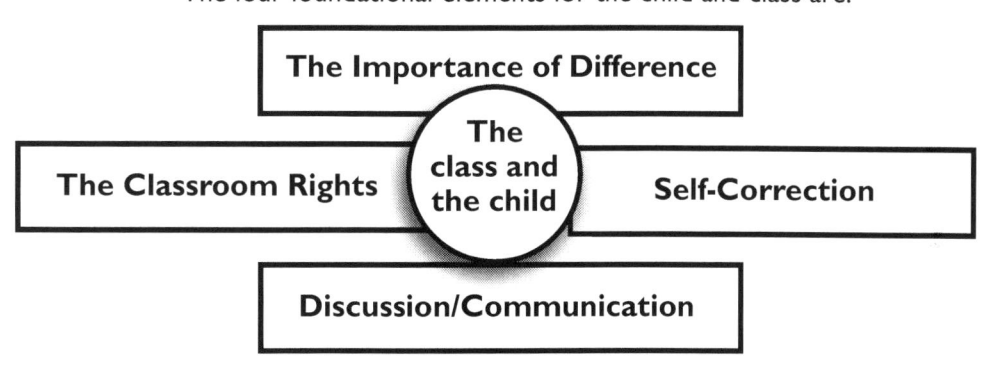

- **The Importance of Difference**
- **The Classroom Rights**
- **The class and the child**
- **Self-Correction**
- **Discussion/Communication**

- These ecologically-based foundations (described in the appendices,) though not articulated as such to children, are vital to an ecologically-sound classroom, in which your children, derivatives of the ecology, can develop their diversity and thrive.

But remember, for teacher and children to thrive and enable diversity, the journey is a reference-to-externalities-and-learn-as-you-journey process and, thanks to these foundations, not a blind free-for-all. Enjoy the ride. Every day spent with your class will reflect diversity. It will be evolving, new and different, as will experiences with other groups of children in subsequent years. Each Four Communities Classroom, with the four foundational elements, will create its own journey.

The following observations indicate children's appreciation of difference and, in combination with discussion/communication, self-correction and classroom rights; appreciation of the foundations of the Four Communities Classroom as valuable assets in their building of a constructive learning/relationship environment.

*Tanya, grade seven, talking about grade five.*
**"If someone broke the rights, we put things straight. It was self-correction."**

*Ms. Gaudet, grade three teacher.*
**"Rather than just saying sorry, in terms of rights, it's more significant for children to know and say why they are sorry."**

*Brittany, grade seven.*
**"I think that almost everything in the Four Communities Classroom is a route for self-correction. If you are hurting someone you've got to correct yourself to stop. If your work is wrong you have to try to correct it. If you don't like who you are sitting beside you try to make it work."**

TEACHING NOTES

## 15. Listening-to-others [and the teacher] awareness activity

The listening awareness activity is an optional activity. However, it is an activity that you may find very valuable if you have children in your class who have a hard time remembering to listen to others, and to you - communications disrupted. Children not listening in class can, of course, take many forms - gazing out the window, talking to neighbours, fiddling with books, papers, pencils etc. This reduction in focus by children in the classroom can be disruptive and get in the way of good teaching and learning; distracted children are less able to learn constructively than are focused children. The listening awareness activity is intended to give your class an advantage in dealing effectively with these problems.

With some children the experience of listening and communicating in the Four Communities Classroom is sufficient, and you may find that this targeted listening awareness activity is not required by your class.

However, the value in the listening awareness activity is that it enables children to feel what it is like not to be listened to properly, and to experience and become more aware of the difficulties in comprehension when distracted.

Thus, I have found it valuable to draw upon Pike and Selby's programme, and adapt it to a listening awareness activity. The activity is in two main parts, each with a plenary session.

For details please see 'Activities For The Four Communities Classroom', p. 132, Activity 4.

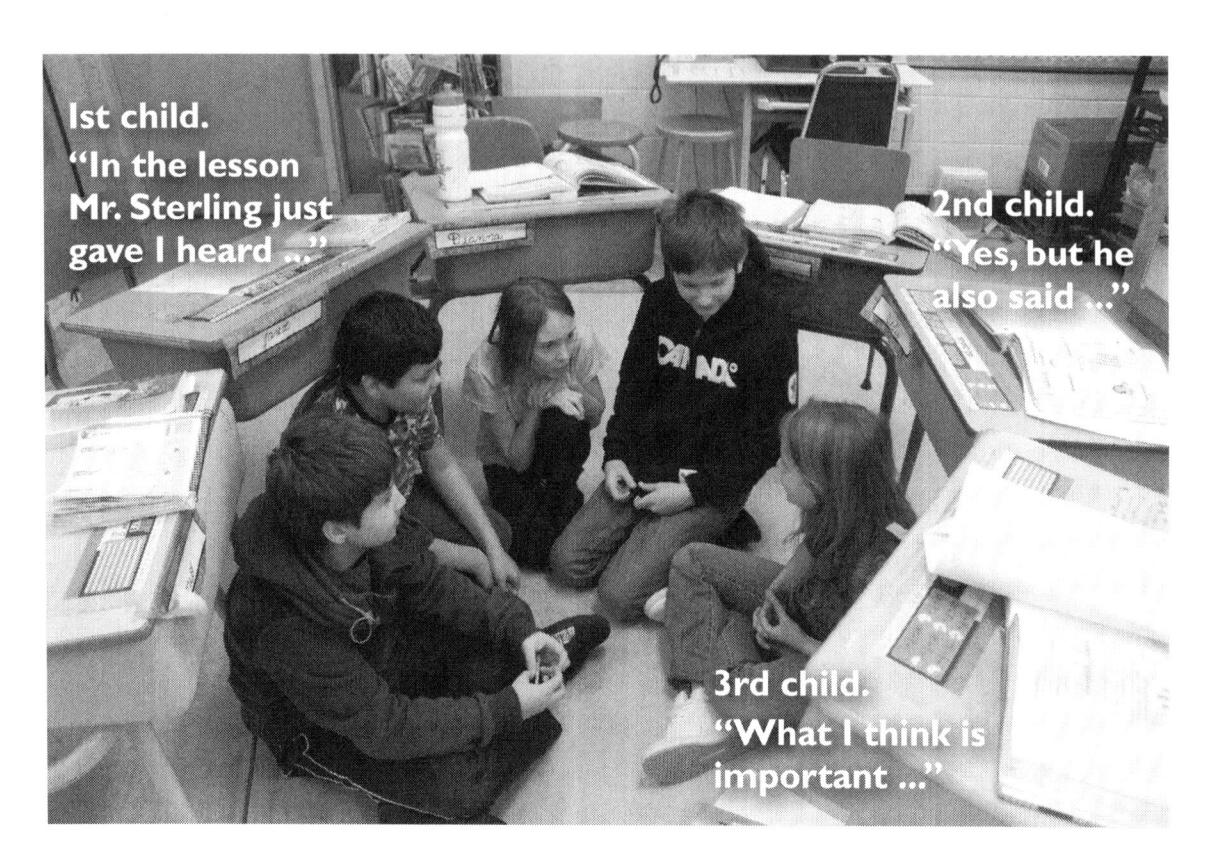

1st child. "In the lesson Mr. Sterling just gave I heard ..."

2nd child. "Yes, but he also said ..."

3rd child. "What I think is important ..."

# MID-YEAR INTRODUCTION:

- ## OF THE FOUR COMMUNITIES CLASSROOM

- ## OF THE FOUR COMMUNITIES CLASSROOM WHEN SEEKING REMEDY FOR BEHAVIOURAL PROBLEMS

It is usually preferable to start new processes at the beginning of the school year or at the beginnings of terms. However, the Four Communities Classroom can be introduced at any time through the year.

Teachers confronted with 'mid-year' problems, will find this offers a constructive way forward.

Sometimes you may feel that your class has some really nice kids and all would be fine if only circumstances were better. But the kids seem fractious, although usually less so when 'you-know-who' is absent. Things are not going as well as you would like and, although reasons for problems have been examined, solutions sought, and remedies tried, there may have been only marginal improvements, and you, and the children, remain frustrated. This is a need and incentive for change.

The teacher can see the need, but can the children? At the beginning of a new school year, people on both sides of the teacher's desk feel a sense of hope for new possibilities. It is this same condition, hope for new possibilities, that is most likely to produce constructive results now. Thus, importantly, with your seemingly intractable problems, the kids have to be on side in finding a solution.

When you decide to engage with the community classroom approach, you'll be moving from a teacher imposed environment to a facilitated discussion environment, where the new approach will not be viewed by children as 'another teacher device to keep us in line', but rather seen as moving forward together to enhance classroom life for both teacher and children.

If intransigence has become deeply entranched and the children do not see a need for change, or do not wish to engage in change, then the only changes will likely be further entrenchment, polarization, and lost opportunity. In that case, you had better hang in as well as you can and wait for that wonderful time for new beginnings - September. But, usually, children will be experiencing frustration too, and floundering in search of a solution; a discomfort sometimes hidden behind behavioural problems. Individually, most children are powerless to change negative classroom cultures, and welcome initiatives that collectively seek a solution. The children will likely be on side in finding this solution. In fact, the first productive step towards this interactive initiative is to assume you have allies.

**TEACHING NOTES**

When you are introducing the Four Communities Classroom part way through the year, all the elements are followed as outlined, (see p. 32) with the exception of element (1) and (3). A mid-year start necessitates a slightly different approach. Take children through element (3) first. However, there are changes to this element.

**(3)** 'Explaining and exploring what we are about to embark upon' is now changed to:

**(3)** 'How to get children to be with you in the quest for change (and solution).' The emphasis now becomes the recognition of the need/desire for change. This new heading transforms element (3) into a prequisite for element (1). If the class has been presenting behavioural problems you may wish to start by saying something like, "I think that we can all agree that things have not been going well recently. A number of people's work has been suffering. I have had to deal with discipline problems, you have had to deal with being kept in after school or being sent to the principal. Also, as we know, there are people who are not getting along well with others in the room."

"I have been reading about a different way of learning in the classroom that may make life more enjoyable for the rest of our year together. What I was wondering is, would you like it if we tried this out to see if it would work for us?"

You may have to field some questions that perhaps attempt to identify things that aren't running smoothly, but usually children answer yes!

Already, by stating the problem and asking the children if they would like to be part of the solution, you are at the beginning of a relationship change and a new way of functioning.

You may wish to choose the end of the school day or the end of the week to broach the question of change and then reach the point of agreement for change. Conclude by saying, "O.K. tomorrow morning, (or Monday morning, as the case may be), we'll start something new." This will help create anticipation. Anticipation is good for new beginnings.

'Something new' starts with element (1). Let us consider the changes needed for element **(1)** 'Creating four groups'.

Teachers who start the Four Communities Classroom part way through the year have the advantage of knowing their students. They are, therefore, better able to determine which group combinations of children would enable good teaching and good learning to evolve. Therefore, the numbering of children to create 4 groups, as described on p. 33, need not occur. When the children are known, I find that the best way to decide group membership is to take a class list, cut it into individual names, and try juggling different combinations of children within the four groups. This is a good opportunity to create a good mix of abilities and temperaments in each group.

> TEACHING NOTES

After the class decision to pursue change, and on the day that change is to start, children can either simply be told which group they will be in, or it can be discovered through an activity from Pike and Selby, called 'Going Dotty'. See p. 130 for instructions and a debriefing exercise. I prefer to use the 'Going Dotty' activity, as it tends to underline to the children that something new and different is really afoot; that the class is breaking ties with the old ways and moving into new territory. This is helpful in maintaining a sense of anticipation and wondering.

I offer the following as a guide to the beginning of the implementing-change-day. The children, at 9.00 a.m., come into the classroom and sit at their desks, as usual, except, as a result of the previous days discussion, everyone knows something different is going to happen, but are not sure what. Anticipation is in the air. Clear away the 'housekeeping' duties of registration, etc., and tell the class that today is the start of trying something new, and that, since we haven't tried it before, it will be an experiment that we will all have to work at. Together, we are going to see if we can discover a new way of being.

This is, in itself, an important change, as you are, in effect, announcing that you alone are not going to take responsibility for change and that, in fact, it will be a shared responsibility. In other words, the children will have to take responsibility, should it fail. Success or failure, it is a shared endeavour. Children should be able to recall, at some future point, 'Our teacher gave us a chance to turn our class around.'

Say to the class,

"We are going to start by pushing all our desks back to the wall, to leave a big space in the centre of the room. Push your desks back to the walls now." It's noisy, but the kids like this for a first move.

"I want everyone to stand in the centre of the room and form a circle." Space the kids out so the circle is evenly formed with no one standing behind another.

You are now ready for the 'Going Dotty' activity. (Go to p. 130, Pike and Selby.)

After the 'Going Dotty' activity, the children are debriefed and, sitting on the floor in four groups according to your pre-activity selection, are now identified with a coloured dot on their heads. After the debriefing, announce to the children that sitting in groups is one of the class changes, and their group is the one they are sitting with right now!

To reduce the likelihood of complaints about not wanting to sit with this or that person, and 'I want to sit with my friend', immediately say, "So I want all the people with red dots to get their desks and push them into a circle in this corner, and all the people with blue dots to take their desks to that corner, etc. You may wish to display, at this point, a large diagram clearly showing how each group arranges the desks in a horse-shoe shape and the position of each group in the room.

**TEACHING NOTES**

Let children do their own arranging of seating positions within each group. Groups and the pushing of desks into position is, again, noisy, but the kids like the activities so far. They are ready for more new events.

At this point you have completed, in the following sequence: element (3) 'How to get the kids to be with you in the quest for change', (Previously named 'What we are about to embark upon; rationale for this new approach to classroom life') and (1). 'Creating Four Groups.' You are now ready to bring more changes to classroom life by continuing to work through section one - 'Developing the Four Communities Classroom'.

In section one you may, according to your class needs, consider further re-arrangement of the order of the first ten elements. For instance, to continue a high level of interest in the changes you are introducing, you may decide to do next, number (5) 'How we have classroom areas for each group to care for, use, organize, and decorate for classroom life and learning', and then go to number (2) Asking THE Foundational Question - "What are we here for?" "Why do we come to school?"

Continue, in your preferred order, the other **Section One** elements yet to be covered (starting on p. 33).

1. Creating four groups. **(completed second)**

2. Asking THE foundational question. "Why do you think we are here?" "Why do you think that we come to school?"

3. 'How to get children to be with you in the quest for change and solution.' (Previously - Explaining and exploring what we are about to embark upon; the rationale for the Four Communities Classroom approach to classroom life. **(completed first)**

4. Talking about why we have groups (easier communication). Group formation, friends and membership changes.

5. Talking about how we have classroom areas for each group to care for, use, organize, and decorate for classroom life and learning.

6. Explaining the Point System; its planning, process and integration into classroom life.

7. Explaining class and group discussion and communication. Talking stick - learning to share and listen. Sections A, B, and C.

8. Choosing group names.

9. Explaining group jobs.

10. Numbering students, work in/out trays, work record keeping.

And then on to section two. **Section two** has no changes and is completed in the sequence as outlined starting on p. 71 - Developing the Four Communities Classroom - discussion forums.

My Daughter *Can't Wait* for Monday Morning!

> **TEACHING NOTES**

## What to do about current wall displays

We know from p. 23, that the classroom walls are viewed in the Four Communities Classroom as an opportunity for primary learning experiences.

Therefore, prior to children's arrival in the fall, you leave the walls undecorated; a blank canvas where the children, together create the environment for becoming and belonging in the habitat of your classroom. However, you likely have at this juncture part way through the year walls displaying perhaps posters, printed rules, children's work, and pictures.

With four sections of wall, one for each group, being needed for primary learning experience, you will have to decide what material can be removed immediately, what will be changed gradually through transition, and what will be kept.

First, since those of your secondary-experience wall displays have not, presumably, had the desired effect, I suggest you remove any commercially printed material that outlines responsible behaviour in the classroom, making way for a display of class-generated classroom rights.

'The Classroom Rights Activity' on p. 92 and, '(12) Using classroom rights', on p. 107, outline some of the behavioural benefits of having children choosing rights and assume responsibility for their own behaviour.

## The class in transition

The Four Communities Classroom seeks transition towards establishing an environment for children that will enable them to build confidence in self and understanding of others, in pursuit of learning and mental and emotional development. Some keys to this process and the type of environment in which this process can flourish are found in the mission statement on p. ii - 'The Four Communities Classroom, And, The Transition To Mutual Regard"

For further information on processes engaged by your class in transition. Please see Chap. 6, p. 192.
The child's perspective
- Positive curiosity
- Positiveness on hold
- Children's life experience
- Tentativeness precedes steps forward

Chap. 6, pages 195, 206, 214.
    Three mid-year class case studies.

---

Note. The time spent developing the Four Communities Classroom in subsequent years with, perhaps, largely the same class of children, reduces as children become more familiar with the process. However, time should be spent at the beginning of each year to refine and re-establish processes and to reach class consensus on rights, procedures and expectations. A re-visit reaffirms common understanding.

There are times to discuss, and there are times to quietly get on with your own work.

# ACTIVITIES FOR THE FOUR COMMUNITIES CLASSROOM
Adapted from 'Global Teacher, Global Learner' by kind permission of Graham Pike and David Selby

The rights balloon activity

The United Nations declaration on the rights of the child (1959)

Going dotty

A listening-to-others [and the teacher] awareness activity

### 1. The rights balloon activity (for pp. 72 to 80 and pp. 183 and 191)

Tell the children that you are about to tell them a story, and that you want them to sit quietly while they imagine they are part of the story.

**Students are asked to imagine that they are on their own, gently drifting in a hot-air balloon. On board are ten rights. Each weighs two kilos. Suddenly, their balloon begins to lose height. To stop their descent, the child must throw a right overboard to lighten the load. The balloon levels out for a while before beginning to lose height again. Another right has to be jettisoned. The process continues until they have only one right left.**

(I have added details when telling the story; that it is a nice sunny day and they are enjoying a wonderful ride in a hot-air balloon. They are over a large lake, with the wind taking them towards the shore, where they want to safely land.)

**The list of rights on the following page can be photocopied for each child in your class.** Ask the children to read the list carefully and think about which rights they are prepared to surrender and which they want to keep as long as possible. They then make their decisions - without discussing their decisions with any other children - by putting a 1 against the first right to be thrown overboard, a 2 against the second and so on. The right that remains at the end is numbered 10. This is each individual child's decision - there are no right or wrong answers. The child will use column 1 (see fig. 1) to rank the ride they take alone. Columns 2 and 3 will be used to rank subsequent balloon rides that they take with other children.

125  My Daughter *Can't Wait* for Monday Morning!

| NAME | BALLOON RIDES |||
|---|---|---|---|
| | First | Second | Third |
| The right to my own bedroom | | | |
| The right to clean air | | | |
| The right to an allowance | | | |
| The right to love and affection | | | |
| The right not to be bossed around | | | |
| The right to be different | | | |
| The right to holidays each year | | | |
| The right to food and water | | | |
| The right to time for play | | | |
| The right to be listened to | | | |

Fig.1

**1. The First Balloon Ride -** *Individual ranking with no right or wrong answers*

First provide each child with a photocopy of fig. 1 for recording, in the first column, the order in which they threw out their rights.

**2. The Second Balloon Ride -** *Ranking in pairs*

Secondly, ask the children to form pairs to discuss and come to agreement/compromise on ranking the same ten rights. Again, there are no right or wrong answers. The pair can come to any decision that they feel comfortable with. The children record their joint decisions in the second column - number 1 against the first right to be thrown overboard etc..

**3. The Third Balloon Ride -** *Ranking with two pairs*

Thirdly, two pairs of children come together, to compare ranking choices and ideas, to discuss and argue their views and to create a ranking that now entails the thinking of four people. The children record their two-pairs decisions in the third column. There are no right or wrong answers.

For a detailed description of how to proceed with balloon rides one, two, and three, see The Rights Balloon Activity pp. 72 to 75.

(On the reverse side of the rights list, you may wish to invite children who finish a balloon ride ahead of others to draw and colour their balloon, and/or, after the second and third ride, write the names of children who travelled with them.)

---

**The following 'Class Ranking' chart (fig. 2) can be photocopied and produced as an overhead. This is an <u>optional activity</u> used for determining the overall class ranking of the Balloon Ride Rights.**

|  | The right to my own bedroom | The right to clean air | The right to an allowance | The right to love and affection | The right not to be bossed around | The right to be different | The right to holidays each year | The right to food and water | The right to time for play | The right to be listened to |
|---|---|---|---|---|---|---|---|---|---|---|
| Balloon group 1 | | | | | | | | | | |
| Balloon group 2 | | | | | | | | | | |
| Balloon group 3 | | | | | | | | | | |
| Balloon group 4 | | | | | | | | | | |
| Balloon group 5 | | | | | | | | | | |
| Balloon group 6 | | | | | | | | | | |
| TOTAL | | | | | | | | | | |
| CLASS RANKING | | | | | | | | | | |

Fig. 2

**Class Ranking of Balloon Rights**
**How to use the chart on the previous page**

1. First establish one person from each balloon group to be the spokesperson for their group.

2. Ask the spokesperson to tell you what number their group gave the first right listed on the overhead, i.e. The right to my own bedroom.

3. Record their number on the overhead chart. Ask the same question of the second balloon group, and, of course, all of the balloon groups.

4. Ask the children to calculate the totals for each right as you proceed. This will enable you and the class to determine the ranking for the class as a whole.

Thus, the right with the lowest score would represent the right the class, as a whole, considers the least important and receives a one, and the highest score, being the most important, a ten. Children are then able to compare their choices, in all three of their balloon rides, in the context of what is, in effect, a class consensus. Remind children that this is an activity with no correct answers, and is, as we can see, a concrete example of how diversity of opinion is part of life.

You may have a group who dealt with the rights in a flippant way, perhaps according a ranking they cannot defend. They now find themselves at odds with the decision-making process and this may cause internal consideration involving their self-descriptors. It is their problem. They haven't disrupted process for others, and interestingly, the anomaly doesn't affect the class outcome significantly. The rights that are considered the least important and the most important usually still, more or less, appear in the expected order.

You may wish to point out that the things that many children complain about have been ranked by them as the lowest in importance, and those things they may take for granted are ranked the highest. This usually produces a moment of silence, as children ponder the significance of this thought.

## (2) The United Nations declaration on the rights of the child (1959)

**This table can be photocopied** (Use with instructions on p. 90)

| NAME | |
|---|---|
| **THE UNITED NATIONS DECLARATION ON THE RIGHTS OF THE CHILD (1959)** | |
| 1. The right to affection, love and understanding. | |
| 2. The right to adequate nutrition and medical care. | |
| 3. The right to free education. | |
| 4. The right to full opportunity for play and recreation. | |
| 5. The right to a name and a nationality. | |
| 6. The right to special care if handicapped. | |
| 7. The right to be among the first to receive relief in times of disaster. | |
| 8. The right to be a useful member of society and to develop individual abilities. | |
| 9. The right to be brought up in a spirit of peace and universal brotherhood. | |
| 10. The right to enjoy these rights, regardless of race, colour, gender, religion, national or social origin. | |

## 3. Going dotty (Referred to on p. 121)

If you know your class prior to introducing the Four Communities Classroom, this activity is a fun way for children to discover which group you have placed them in. Thus, before using the 'Going Dotty' activity, decide which children you are going to put together in each group, and choose a dot colour for each group.

**Resources to prepare**
- Purchase a packet of small, self-adhesive coloured dots, in four colours.
- Push desks back to the walls to open the classroom space so that students can move about freely.

### Procedure

(NOTE - be sure that mirrors and other reflective surfaces are covered or removed before doing this activity)

- **Students form a circle and close their eyes. You stick a coloured dot on each child's forehead.** (I usually position it just over the left eyebrow.)

To prepare children for this activity, I tell them they are going to be asked, in a minute, to close their eyes and not speak. And when everyone is ready with their eyes closed, I'm going to come round and stick a small dot on everyone's forehead. During this time, no one can speak or be tempted to peek. Those who do, will not spoil the activity for anyone, but they will spoil it for themselves. I tell the children that they must be patient for a few minutes, while everyone is getting a dot. I continue, "Once everyone has received a dot, I'll tell you to open your eyes, BUT, still no speaking is allowed, and I will tell you then what the next part of the activity is going to be."

- **Children then open their eyes and try to form groups of the same coloured dots without speaking.**

When children have received their dots, tell them to open their eyes and WITHOUT SPEAKING go and find people with the same coloured dot as they have. Children may be confused and wonder how can they do this when they can't see their own colour. Tell them, "See if you can figure it out." Usually, sooner than later, they start gathering in groups of the same coloured dots. Insist that there is no speaking. Don't be tempted to help children who may be having difficulty as, eventually, the children help each other to their group.

### Debriefing

Debriefing consists of inviting children to offer their thoughts and feelings, in response to a series of questions, such as:-

- While you were waiting for your coloured dot, what sort of things were you thinking and feeling?
- When I asked you to go and find someone with the same coloured dot, what did you think?
- When groups started to form, were you in a group, or still wondering which group you were in, and what were you feeling at that time?
- Did anyone help someone find their group? Did those who were helped, trust the person who was helping them to take them to the right group?
- Who was helped by someone to their group? What did you think while you were being helped?

Since children may not be experienced in discussion and sharing thoughts, don't worry if children's response is light, but be responsive to all children's offerings, and build upon them, where possible. You may hear that some children started to worry that they had been given a colour that no one else had and, therefore, would be left out. You may hear that children were relieved when they found their group. This can be built upon, by extending questions to thoughts on why is it, even in a game, that people feel anxious if they are outside a group? Some children may say they welcomed assistance, while others may indicate that they were uncomfortable being 'herded' by others. Thus you could comment on how we have things in common regarding being accepted in a group, but also differences in what we feel comfortable with.

When all has been offered by the children, you may wish to say:

"You can all look around the group you are with, all with the same coloured dot. But how do you know your dot is the right colour for that group? Maybe everyone is tricking you and you are sitting with the wrong group."

This, of course, causes a rapid weighing up of the likelihood of being in the wrong group. Some concern may be felt. Maybe they don't belong. It's not a comfortable feeling. You quickly dispel fears by saying, "Don't worry, everyone is in their proper group."

Thus, although the activity is to group children, you can take this opportunity to open their eyes to the feelings of people. Although not articulated, the experience that you have taken the children through can start to make children aware that they are not alone in concerns and desires. This is an important first message for children, as they embark upon the Four Community Classroom experience.

### 4. A listening-to-others [and the teacher] awareness activity (referenced on pp. 29, 118, 136, 142, 215)

This 'Listening-to-others- [and the teacher] awareness activity' is adapted from of Pike and Selby's programme. Since children are engaged in the ongoing practice of listening and communication in your Four Communities Classroom, you may find your class does not require this targeted listening experience.

However, if you find some of your children have difficulty paying attention to other children and to yourself and/or are sometimes disruptive, this activity can form an important step in enabling and empowering them to listen. It enables children to feel what it is like not to be listened to properly and to experience the difficulties in comprehension when distracted.

Lead the class, stage by stage, only explaining and providing intructions that go with each activity, rather than informing children ahead of what will be expected later in the activity.

It requires approximately 30 minutes of time.

The activity is in two main parts, each with a plenary session.

## Part One - Information received with no distractions

Part one is an exercise where you provide an environment with little or no distraction for the children. To ensure this, I suggest you go outside with children, preferably sitting on grass, where pairs of children can be far enough apart not to be distracted by other pairs of children, (the large open space provided by a gym will substitute in inclement weather).

1. Students work in pairs, sitting facing each other. One child is designated as A, the other B: (I ask children to choose who will be A and B)

    A is asked to talk to B for one minute on a specific topic (chosen by the teacher e.g. 'one thing I like about school is …')
    B then talks to A for one minute on same topic.
    Time both A children's and B children's one minute talks - announce when they are to start and stop.

2. Students find a different child to partner with and between them decide who will be person A and person B:

    A talks to B for one minute on a new topic (e.g. 'what I like about summer is …')
    B talks to A for one minute on the same new topic.
    Time both A children's and B children's one minute talks - announce when they are to start and stop.

3. Students return to their first partner (as in no.1). But children now switch roles to tell the other person's story from their first grouping as if it was their own. Thus:-

    A now becomes B, recounting what B had said, using 'I' the first person form.
    B becomes A, recounting what A had said, using 'I' the first person form.

Since children are recounting what they had originally heard from their first partner back to them, you may decide to leave children a little extra time. But again announce when the talks begin and end.

**Plenary session**

The whole class comes together to give feedback on their experience of the third activity.

Ask children how accurate the information was, coming back to them.

Ask children if it was difficult to remember, when they were unexpectedly asked to repeat what they had heard.

Many children report they were largely successful.

# Part Two - <u>Information received with distractions</u>

Part two is a similar exercise to part one except now children have to deal with distractions while attempting communication with their partner.

4. Children stay with their original partner from Part One, but this time students sit side-by-side and look directly in front of them, eyes do not meet. Both children have with them a binder and a pen or pencil.

   First, A talks to B for one minute on a different topic (e.g. 'what I dislike about winter is …') As A talks, B fiddles with his/her binder, perhaps drawing in the binder.

   Then secondly, B talks to A on a different topic (e.g. 'what I like about weekends …') Now, as B talks, 'A' fiddles with his/her binder, perhaps drawing in the binder.

5. - A questions B on what information he/she told B.
   - B questions A on what information he/she told A.

**Plenary session**

The whole class comes together to give feedback upon their experience from parts 4 and 5 of the activity.

- Ask children what it felt like to talk to someone while they were engaged in something else and not making eye contact.

   *Children often say that they found it difficult to concentrate on what they were saying, when someone didn't appear to be listening, and that speaking seemed like a waste of time, when someone didn't appear interested. It didn't feel good.*

- Ask children how well their partner answered questions on the information they had given.

   *Many children will report that questions couldn't always be answered properly.*

- Ask children if it was easy to concentrate on what their partner was telling them when they weren't making eye contact and instead were concentrating on their binder.

   *Many children will tell you that they had trouble paying attention to what was being said.*

**Now you summarize the activity for the class by asking questions**

So what you are telling me is:

- when you feel that you are not being listened to properly, you found it difficult to concentrate on what you were saying, and that people actually didn't know much of what you were saying? (Yes)
- when you were busy doing something else, you found it difficult to concentrate and answer questions? (Yes)
- when, in the first activity, you concentrated upon what was being said, you found you could remember, even when you didn't know you would be asked to remember? (Yes)

Yes, is, of course, the answer that children give to these questions. The children have experienced feelings associated with trying to concentrate with distraction, and concentrating without distractions.

Now it is time to extend children's now heightened awareness of listening and communication to the teaching/learning situation of the classroom, with some final questions: -

1. Would the teacher have the same feelings if she/he was talking to the class and someone is causing a distraction?
2. Would the teacher also have difficulty concentrating on what she/he was saying if there were distractions?
3. If the teacher was having difficulty in concentrating on what she/he was teaching, would that affect children in the room who were trying to learn from what the teacher was saying?

Children, of course, generally answer 'Yes'. And thus you have helped children to have a much finer understanding of the feelings that surround teaching/learning communication needs, both in their group and in the classroom generally.

The Listening-To-Others- [And the Teacher] Awareness Activity provides a demonstration and example of mutual regard in action.

## **Back in the classroom**

If, while teaching, children cause distractions in class, a quick reminder of that time outside on the grass, or in the gym, is often all it takes for a child to recall and understand feelings associated with communicating. Children who have been made aware of the thoughts and feelings of self and of others are better prepared to employ self-correction, when shaping constructive relationship behaviours in the classroom.

# MORE WAYS GROUPS CAN BE USED IN CLASS ORGANIZATION AND LEARNING PROCESS (AND THE BENEFITS IN NUMBERING CHILDREN)

> *Numbering children* (Repeated from p. 66)
>
> In each group, list the children in alphabetical order, and number each child down the list. Against each number add the group number. Thus the first person on the list, in group one, would be numbered 1,1. The second person on the list in group one would have the number 1,2. The third 1,3, and so on.
>
> In group two, the first child listed alphabetically would be numbered 2,1. The second child would be numbered 2,2, etc.
>
> When this listing is completed for each group, there will be four children in the classroom who are numbered one, and four children numbered two and so on.

Maintaining record keeping (see pp. 66-70) and class management can be made easier when children have their own number within their group. The book collector (see p. 65) both collects children's work from their group and distributes it. You appoint (or have each group appoint for themselves) a book collector. This is a job that children love to do and it saves time. Children's work is quickly and efficiently handled.

You, as the teacher, will get an up-to-the-minute record from the book collectors of the status of each child's work (completed or not) on the groups 'Record of Work Form' (see p. 69).

The following outline some additional ways that numbering can be used effectively. You will likely be able to expand upon this list.

## 1. Gym and sports activities

No longer will you, or the children, be faced with having to pick teams in your class. No longer will some children have to face being picked last - everytime. All you do is announce that groups 1 and 2 will play groups 3 and 4. You instantly have two teams. It's quick with no time spent picking teams. More time to play the game. No hurt feelings. It's fair and the kids see that it is fair. There are no complaints. See p. 65 for 'Band leader' information on team coloured bands for easy identification of groups during a game.

Another time, you may choose to play groups 1 and 3 against 2 and 4, or, of course, any other combination. Mix and match for fairness. Other alternatives can be to play, for example, 1 and 2 girls against 3 and 4 girls and 1 and 2 boys against 3 and 4 boys, etc.

## 2. In-class intergroup competition

Children will also happily get involved in fun intergroup competition in class. Groups and individual numbering of children enable learning opportunities and easier classroom management. For example:

- Question and Answer (Q and A) process

With identification numbers, you are able to readily organize children to create and ask questions of each other. For example, a child numbered one in group one can pose a question to a child numbered two in group two. Number two tries to answer and number one says whether the second child was correct. Points are awarded for correct answers, and points are awarded to the first child if he/she knew the correct answer themselves. This, of course, helps to prevent questions being asked that are beyond the grade level, and keeps the questioner double-checking their own knowledge. Questions should be on curriculum currently being covered or that has previously been covered.

Child number two in group two now has a question for number one child in group three. Of course, any combination of 'questioners and answerers' identification numbers can be used. Conveniently the numbering process makes it easier for you to keep track of which children have participated, and those who are yet to ask questions or answer them. This record can be kept over several days until everyone has had a turn, i.e perhaps have a few questions asked each day. Since you are choosing the numbers, children never know who they will be questioning, or if they will be the one to answer the question for their group - it is an impartial process.

Alternately, have numbered slips of paper in a container and ask a child to take a piece of paper from the container and read out the number. A second child takes a second number from the container. That process selects which numbered child will ask which numbered child. Children like the chance aspect of this selection process. They are interested to see who is going to be involved and whether it will be themselves.

In order to be fair, use the identification number system so that everyone, over time, has the opportunity to pick a piece of paper out of the container. Thus you may say, "Today all people numbered three will be picking numbers from the container."

- Q and A application

Spelling - Children ask each other the spelling of words from their grade spelling list.

Times-tables - Children ask each other to answer a times-table question.

I believe that there is room for children to both learn their times tables academically and by rote. It is important that children understand what is being done with numbers in the times tables, but also learning the times-tables by rote makes children quicker with mathematical computation generally. Thus, in my teaching, I included learning by rote. I expected children to master the recitation of times-tables. This process of learning, I found, enabled children to more readily answer any times-table question. We chanted a different times-table each day, sometimes as a class, sometimes as a group, sometimes just the boys class-wide or of a group or just the girls. As you can see below, growing ability with times-tables worked well with the Q and A in group competition.

- Q and A, times-tables and the selection process

Place slips of paper, in a container, numbered 2 to 12 (representing times-tables 2 to 12). Children numbered in each group will, when asked and without looking in the container, pull out a times-tables number. This number will dictate to a predetermined group which times-table they have to recite. You can ask a child to do the 'blind' selection for another group. Some groups rejoice in getting an easy table to recite, others moan if theirs is a difficult table, but again the fairness of the process is noted by all - sometimes you are fortunate, at other times you have to deal with a difficult times-table. But the rest of the class hear, again, the table, and again have the opportunity to reinforce their knowledge or correct their knowledge. It's fun, point-earning, and effective in learning the tables - and it does not take long.

You, of course, can select different topics/curriculum for children to consider, using the Q and A process. It is a reinforcement process for learning curriculum that you are able to employ whenever you see fit.

- Jot note games

Part of the learning of jot-note taking (starting on p. 140) involves intergroup competition- specifically lessons 5 and 6.

### 3. Group projects

I recommend developing jot note capabilities first, see p. 140. This will help children feel more comfortable in doing the research needed for project work.

A class-wide topic can be divided between the four groups. Thus, for example, a study of ocean life may engage group one in researching deep sea fish, group two close-to-the-surface fish, group three arctic waters, and group four researching coral reefs. Each group's work is further subdivided amongst individual children. Pictures, diagrams, maps and written work can be displayed on each group's wall space for other groups to see. Presentations of the material that children have researched can then be made by groups to the other groups. This approach to research can, of course, be applied to other subject matter.

# THE FOUR COMMUNITIES CLASSROOM TEACHER'S MINDSET AND PRESENTATION

Successful Four Communities Classroom teachers present, consistently, a professional and authentic face to children; a face that clearly conveys personality. This is important for children in their establishment of a constructive relationship with you. It also, of course, distinguishes you as an individual in your own right, and demonstrates to children the validity and importance of assertion of self.

But while each teacher demonstrates difference, there is a commonality that runs through Four Communities Classroom life processes. Some of these shared understandings and approaches gleaned from throughout the book are listed below.

- The teacher should always look for opportunities to encourage children's own innate sense of responsibility.

- The teacher believes that children, rather than being disciplined, prefer being given an opportunity to practice responsibility and self-correction.

- One statement or a (speculative) question posed by the teacher can trigger a class discussion, focus attention, open minds, and create some productive teaching moments. Depending on the opportunity this presents, you can expand discussion for thirty to forty minutes or more, introducing further related thoughts and questions. This approach works effectively for many learning opportunities, including curriculum, and can be used effectively as a stimulus for research.

- When possible, teachers should refer back to children's contributions. Engagement of the children's ideas and thoughts reinforces the importance of participation in the learning atmosphere of the room. While referencing children, the following questions reside in the back of the teachers mind:

1. Will what I am saying enable this child to start/continue feeling valued as an individual?

2. What sense of faith in self and confidence am I helping to build in this young person?

3. What effect am I having on the child's perception of his/her relationship with me?

4. What message am I sending to other would-be contributors in the classroom?

5. How will my responses to children impact upon the good teaching and good learning environment?

- Referencing children's thoughts and ideas can be a good avenue to two-way communication, especially when the teacher finds his/herself talking a lot. When moving from a teacher-dominated information-giving and child-learning process to a shared process of engagement with children, be sensitive to changes in children and the class as a whole. Guide changes towards validation of children, their thinking processes and towards constructive behaviours by all. Become the guide and model for the development of mutual regard.

- When the classroom is home to a shared life-process, benefits accrue for teacher and children in the form of an enhanced learning atmosphere.

- The emphasis is on discussion. Teachers may give instructions on class procedures and teach curriculum subject matter, but it is important that children feel they are contributing and/or can contribute. Children should not sense that you see them as empty vessels to be filled - recipients of the implication that you know best. You may know best, but that's beside the point. Engage and interact with children so that they and you feel like partners in their classroom endeavours - the creation of positive learning relationships - a shared sense of 'we' in the classroom that respects individuality. Every interaction with children should reinforce this positive learning relationship foundation.

- In the Four Communities Classroom the meaning of 'teacher knows best', is redefined. It transcends "I'll tell you all you need to know", to a more subtle expression of understanding learning process in children and how mental growth is facilitated. Children start to see you as their wise guide in the classroom.

- It is important that the children become part of the foundation of what it means to be in this class - an awareness that should never be absent from the collective consciousness of the classroom. Learning experiences, significant on the day, should not be allowed to fade to a memory through lack of use, but be allowed to be part of the accumulating learning experience of life and learning - a gathering wisdom. In other words, 'problems or opportunities', moments, and days should not be wasted.

- Consider trying out constructive ideas that may arise in class. Use, and make reality, those ideas that contribute to good teaching and learning. Lack of use can leave them as intellectual exercises, with constructive and lasting change lost.

- During discussion, take children from what they know and feel comfortable commenting upon to the next step of consideration. How far you explore any topic with your class will depend, of course, upon their age and your sense of their readiness for more sophisticated understandings. Start with more readily-dealt-with thoughts and questions and consider following with an occasional use of more challenging propositions that will demonstrate to children that perhaps there is more to think about here. Such processes can act as door-opening exercises for the mind. Children can sometimes surprise you with sophisticated thoughts.

In the Four Communities Classroom children are given tools for constructive learning, constructive relationship, and constructive development in their processes of becoming - their life's journey enhanced.

The common framework of the Four Communities Classroom, will, with the teacher's individuality and the individuality of each child, produce different expressions of learning and mutual regard. This is why every year will be different and stimulating.

# CHAPTER THREE

## TEACHING CHILDREN HOW TO DO JOT NOTES:

## FURTHERING CHILDREN'S CAPACITY AND OWNERSHIP FOR LEARNING

**Introduction**

This chapter outlines how children can learn to effectively take 'jot notes' - recording in point form information they hear or read. This skill builds the ability in children to discern what is most relevant and to rapidly capture pertinent facts, so that they can reproduce the information in sentence form or make a well-informed verbal presentation.

The series of eight jot note lessons (starting on page 143) enables children to effectively learn jot-note skills while building ownership for learning and faith in themselves through an awakening of six self-sufficiencies.

**Self-sufficiencies**

1. Faith and self-sufficiency in acquiring knowledge and information from the written and spoken word.
2. Faith in self to use discernment effectively when acquiring knowledge and information.
3. Faith in self to be able to impart information learned.
4. Faith in self in offering opinions arising from discernment.
5. Faith in being able to share and be open in dialogue with others.
6. Faith in self to venture with confidence into arenas of information, learning, and dialogue.

Capacities for self-sufficiencies in learning are enhanced through the following three inherent aspects of jot-note taking:

1. **Exercise of discernment**
   "What, of this information that I am hearing/reading, should I include in my jot notes?" When children are asked to make jot notes from information received, verbally (listening) or through reading, they engage in making decisions regarding the main points of information.
   Danny grade 7.
   *"Jot notes are good because you are not trying to write everything - you write down what you think is important.."*

2. **Organizing information**
   This includes organizing jot-noted information into coherent written and/or oral presentation. Children will assess the adequacy of their jot notes and the adequacy of their communication ability i.e. "How well am I making myself understood?"

3. **Reproducing information in their own words**
   Through jot-noting processes and reporting, children experience and practice reproducing information in their own words.

These three skills are valuable to learning processes since, through their practice, children also build capacity in:

(A) listening to the teacher, taking notes, and offering their own understanding of the lesson, either verbally or in written form. (emphasized in lessons 1, 2, 3, 4, 5, and 8)

---

Children should not be expected to jot-note everything. In developing jot note capacity, the teacher has, for occasional use, an additional teaching methodology to draw upon, as well as an additional learning experience for children.

**(B)** researching topics in the library, and on the internet, and offering their understanding of the research in their own words, either verbally or in written form. (temptations to plagiarize defeated) (emphasized in lessons 6 and 7)

To achieve the three learning capacities for jot-noting, there are four listening-to-the-teacher skills to be attempted and eventually (to varying degrees) mastered by children.

**Four listening-to-the-teacher skills**

1. Learning to take responsibility for handling verbally presented information on a single hearing; learning not to rely on repeated information from the teacher. Everything repeated means that there is time for only half as much teaching/learning in a day.

2. Learning to decide what information, in a verbal presentation, needs recording in jot note form for immediate future reference (reporting back orally or in writing).

3. Learning to use abbreviation as a tool for more rapid collection of the information and facts raised in the presentation.

4. Learning to use the abbreviated jot notes taken during a lesson and convert them into sentences that will make sense to another listener/reader.

Children, of course, will, as in all learning situations, have varying success in acquiring jot-noting skills. Some children are more quickly able to 'catch on' to what is being required of them, others will make slower progress.

My experience has been that the slower child can make gains, since the jot note process engages the mind's inner dialogue in selecting relevant facts - information channelled through the process of jot-note taking. Thus, the information being received and the jot-note process become one - a very significant tool for learning.

Initially, information the child is asked to listen to is contained in a simple sentence (see lesson one). A simple sentence makes it easier for children to cope with, what is for them, a new way of thinking and makes it easier for them to consider the main questions attached to jot noting skills -

1. What is this about?
2. What is the information?
3. Can I tell someone what I have just heard?
4. Can I write this information down?

However, for the child who has heard the information, but not been able to write down any of the information, you verbalize the first question -

1. What is this about?

The slower child may have no answer. In this situation I continue in conversation with the child and ask, "Well is it about flowers?" "No". "O.K. Was it about horses?" "No". O.K. So what was it about?" That is when I usually start to get some rudimentary response - perhaps not complete, but correct as far as it goes. Now you can steer the child to the second and third question.

2. What is the information? and,
3. Can you tell me what you have just heard?

"Was there anything else that you can remember?" Gradually most children are able to report on at least some of what the sentence is about. Contained in the child's side of your conversation with them, inevitably and importantly, is their report in their own words of information they heard. "O.K". Now take the child to the fourth question and ask, -

4. "Can you write that down?"

The child writes the information. Their writing may have spelling mistakes, and be offered in a poorly constructed sentence(s), but they have breached a barrier. The child has internalized the information given to him/her and reproduced it in their own words. Practice is now needed. Gains will be made.

Beyond such a one-on-one conversation with an individual child, there are also, as for all children, two other main incentives that the teacher provides - 'an incentive-to-try communication' and 'an atmosphere of inclusion'.

### Incentive-to-try communication

I often use the 'give-it-a-try' encouragement in my communication with children. "Don't worry if you miss some of the information, just put down/capture whatever facts you can. Give it a try - see what you can do." This approach can take pressure off the child. It's important that children do not feel overwhelmed.

### Atmosphere of inclusion

The atmosphere of inclusion is an important aspect of the Four Communities Classroom. Discussion and contribution to discussion are key elements, in the atmosphere of inclusion. (For full details on classroom discussion and contribution see chapter two, 'Creating the Four Communities Classroom: The teacher's role, the children's role, and sharing development'.)

Thus in an atmosphere of inclusion, ask children to volunteer and read out what they have written. By asking children to volunteer what they have learned from their jot notes, or to volunteer to read their sentence, other children in the class can add to their understanding of what is being required of them. Volunteering information becomes a form of class discussion, where difference in presentation of the same information is considered a matter of distinction in children; we are all different, therefore, our work will be presented differently. (See p. 110, on 'Learning the importance of difference')

As in any class-wide discussion, no individual child is picked out and asked to contribute. Instead, contribution remains an open invitation to be taken up by children as they feel comfortable. However, children do, of course, observe others taking up the invitation. The decision becomes an ongoing thought process; involvement at some level is, therefore, a part of every child's experience. The same dynamics apply during discussion in community groups. Usually, in group discussion, you'll find a greater percentage of children feel comfortable contributing. Often group discussion is, for some children, a more comfortable process for them, where building confidence in themselves can more readily bring them to the point of wanting to contribute to the larger arena of class discussion.

So with emphasis on 'giving-it-a-try' and feelings of inclusion, the following eight lessons can be used to enable children to begin the process of mastering jot-noting skills.

## Summary

### Jot-noting skills include:

- **Building self-sufficiency**
- **The four listening-to-the-teacher skills**
- **Exercise of discernment**
- **Organizing information**
- **Children reproducing information in their own words**

*Please note that differences in who we are as individuals will always impact upon all elements of jot-note taking skills and is an awareness that must be understood by children in order for them to be successful throughout the following eight lessons.*

*Thus, the discussion activity 'Learning the importance of difference', (p. 110) , is an important prelude to teaching jot-note taking.*

### Children listening to children skills

For more information see p. 132, 'A listening-to-others [and the teacher] awareness activity.'

**Lesson One**

## Practice listening to the teacher and then writing a simple sentence:

(opening up the way to effective self-assessment in children and prelude to learning how to take jot notes)

---

Remind children that everyone agreed that good teaching and good learning is an important part of the Four Communities Classroom, and that you want them to practice listening to information. "For this," tell the children, "you will need a pencil and paper ready on your desk. In a minute I'm going to give you a sentence that I want you to write down. I will say the sentence at a normal speaking pace, just like I'm speaking to you now."

Make it <u>very, very</u> clear that you are going to say the sentence just once. You are not going to repeat the sentence.

I usually make up a short sentence that is immediately pertinent to the children, day, and place. Thus I may say, "Today is (day of the week and date) and it's a beautiful/sunny/cloudy/windy/rainy/foggy/snowy day at _____ school, and we are in Mrs./Mr. _____ grade _____ classroom.

I've yet to have a class where at least one child isn't ready, or hasn't paid proper attention and cannot write the sentence, or simply doesn't know what is being asked of them. "What was that?", they ask, "can you repeat the sentence?" (often this problem extends to several children)

"No," you say matter-of-factly, "I said I was going to say the sentence once."

"Can this be true," they think, "I've always asked for information to be repeated." Since it now becomes clear that you don't intend to bail them out, they find themselves just having to sit there while everyone else is getting on with the work they are also supposed to be engaged in. But, don't be concerned, they are learning an important lesson.

Give the class the time they need to write what you have said. "Pencils down when you have finished." Five minutes later most of the attentive children are finished their work! The inattentive ones are still feeling left out and wishing they had listened better.

(It's a slow start to a process that eventually becomes so much easier for the children that they will be able to write jot notes on a 15 minute lesson and reproduce the information in their own words in a page or so of writing. Be patient.)

"Who would like to read to me what they have written?"

Hands go up, readings come in. Thank children. Quickly it becomes apparent that children's sentences vary.

> TEACHING NOTES

(I've had children quickly 'correct' their sentence to conform to a child's to whom I've said - "that's right." The immediate thought being - "There is only one correct answer and I have little or no faith in my work, so I am probably wrong because the other child was told his work was good.")

Uncertainty regarding the ability to self-assess represents for children a major barrier to effective learning. It is a barrier that resides, to some degree, in many children, and it is one that can be overcome. This is a point where you can start to help children to develop effective self-assessment skills. (However, the one or two non-listeners are already in an active state of self-assessment on their need to listen in class.)

Don't say anything directly to any children who may have changed their work and thus 'corrected' their work. They may feel silly enough at getting their work 'wrong'. They will understand fast enough, as you remind the class of the significance of difference in all of us. (See 'Learning the importance of difference', p.110) "Differences in us mean that differences between us appear in our work. It's O.K when one person's work reads differently from another person's work." When you point this out to children they have a window of wonder opened up in their minds.

You may want to ask the children in a wondering tone, "Why is it, when we have all heard the same information, that all our sentences are different?" You may hear from the children, or you can supply the answer - "Because we are all different, we will write the information down in different ways. Isn't that amazing? The information has to be correct, but it's O.K if it's given back to us in different ways. In fact, it would be unlikely that we would all write precisely the same way. In fact, what you have all been doing is putting the information down in your own words. Well done!"

"O.K I'll give you another sentence and let's see how many different ways we get back this information."

Now this is fun. Participation is becoming attractive.

It is also becoming attractive for the children who weren't ready the first time. In my experience it's rare, although not impossible, that children will put themselves through another round of asking for the information twice.

"O.K. everyone get their pencils poised over the paper." "Are you ready this time?" (looking at those who weren't). They nod yes. "Good."

Launch your next sentence. So that children start to feel comfortable with the process, it should contain approximately the same amount of information/facts as the first sentence.

> **TEACHING NOTES**

I once used the sentence - "Mr. Sterling has two dogs - a black and tan German Shepherd and a white fluffy Samoid, that love to play in the yard."

Tell the children, "Don't worry about spelling, just try and write down as much of the information as you can."

Emphasize the word 'information' rather then using the word 'sentence'. The children are not taking down dictation, but are trying to capture the information that your sentence contains.

Again ask for volunteers to read out what they have written. Comment on the variety.

Broach some additional thoughts to emphasize the 'O.K ness' of children's work.

- **Order of information.** "Jim wrote about the Samoid dog first. Was he right?" Yes. "Why?" Because his information about the Samoid was correct. <u>The order in which Jim wrote the information is up to Jim</u>.

- **Additions and interpretations.** "Sarah wrote that the German Shepherd's coat was black and tan. Did I mention the coat in my sentence?" No. "So was Sarah wrong in mentioning the coat?" No. "It was fine for Sarah to talk about the coat because the black and tan colouring referred to the coat. Sarah added information that fitted the information in my sentence, and that is fine. Well done Sarah." (Now Sarah really likes this type of work!) Sarah added information that, in effect, is an interpretation. <u>Additions and interpretations that fit the information and follow the sense of the information, are good.</u>

Now everyone hears Sarah getting praised and children start to realize that it's O.K to be different in their work as long as the information is correct. (This is a demonstration and encouragement of the self-assessment process, although, of course, children don't think of it in these terms.) It is unlikely, however, that children in your class will be 'correcting' their work again without carefully assessing the validity of what they have done.

- **The use of alternative words.** Children may call the yard the garden, or write that the dogs liked to play outside. These are all acceptable. <u>Alteration of wording within the meaning of the information is O.K</u>.

- **Missing information, but always trying for more.** Do not make children feel inadequate if they change the information somewhat, or miss information. Remember you asked the children to give it a try, and giving it a try is what they are doing. <u>Missing information is O.K. but we always try to get as much as possible</u>. For children, this thought is important to help them experience some success. Feeling that one's efforts are meeting with some success means children will be more willing to keep trying and to keep improving.

**TEACHING NOTES**

Individuality in children's jot-noting will mean that you will see variables in their notes from one child to the next.
- Order of information - O.K
- Additions and interpretations - O.K
- The use of alternative words - O.K
- Missing information but keep trying for more - O.K

Depending on time and your sense of the classes readiness to continue, you may decide to give the class a third sentence. However, do not tire the children. Remember it is best to finish the lesson on a note of high willingness to participate, maintaining the perception of 'this-is-fun'.

Ask the children if they know what jot note taking is. You will be able to channel answers into a statement that says that taking jot notes is what they have been doing - listening to information and putting it down in their own words.

Now that the children know the process of listening and writing, you could, perhaps, build their familiarity with the process by giving them one sentence each morning for the next two or three days. This need only take about 10 to 15 minutes each day for the children to listen to the sentence, write, report on what they have written, and be celebrated for their variety of reporting on the information contained in the sentence you have given them.

## Lesson Two — Learning what abbreviations are and how to use them

Understanding abbreviation and its usefulness, lays further groundwork for jot note taking.

Start the lesson by asking children if they know what this word means as you write it on the board - ABBREVIATION. Usually there are some children who do.

Chalk in hand and ready to make a list, say, "Can anyone tell me of an example of an abbreviation?"

Days of the week, someone may say. Mon. means Monday, Tues. means Tuesday.

Months of the year. Sept. means September, Oct. means October etc..

"Yes. Notice how abbreviations always have a period after them to show that they are an abbreviation."

You may get many more examples of abbreviations from the class.

Ask the children, "When writing down a jot-note sentence in your own words, would it be less work to write abbreviations where possible?"

My Daughter *Can't Wait* for Monday Morning!

> **TEACHING NOTES**

Yes, they say, that would make things a lot easier.

"O.K. let's try it." And you give the children a sentence where abbreviations can be used. You may be able to create a sentence from some of the abbreviations the class have given and that you recorded on the board.

Ask, "Who managed to write some of their sentence using abbreviations?"

Hands go up. "Good."

Now you take the children to the thought that when they are trying to capture information and facts in a spoken sentence they not only can use abbreviations that everyone would recognize, but they can use abbreviations of their own.

"Using abbreviations are a good way to speed up the capturing of information and facts - it is a good idea to use any abbreviation that helps."

Use your sentence from the previous lesson to demonstrate. Write it on the board.

For example:
Mr. Sterling has two dogs - a black and tan German Shepherd and a white fluffy Samoid, that love to play in the yard.

Ask, "Are there any words in this sentence that you could abbreviate?" Suggestions may include Bk/tan. G.S.

It's important that children create abbreviations where meaning is not forgotten later. Thus say to the class, "Bk/tan may be O.K., but could the meaning of G.S be forgotten? Could we use an abbreviation for German Shepherd that we would be more likely to remember?"

G. Shep. may be offered, or perhaps Ger. Shep.

"Yes, either of those abbreviations would work better. Which one you use is your choice. No one is going to check what abbreviations you use. But it will be important that your information and facts are correct. You decide what abbreviations you use so that you get the information right in your sentence."

Ask children for more abbreviations that they could use for information about the dogs.

Here the children have a chance to practice the creation of useful abbreviations that they, according to their own decision, may use.

Validity of anyone's idea comes from the consideration of its usefulness rather than the teacher passing judgment. This is a learning opportunity for children where self-assessment of the usefulness of an idea becomes the deciding factor.

*My Daughter Can't Wait for Monday Morning!*

> **TEACHING NOTES**

Give the children another sentence, again with approximately the same amount of information as the previous sentences. Tell the class to try and capture as many facts as they can, but to continue to save time and too much writing, by using as many abbreviations as they can.

"How many used some abbreviations?" Hands go up. "Good." Ask for volunteers to read their sentence. When you have heard some sentences, again remark on the differences such as:

    Order of information

    Additions and interpretations

    The use of alternative words

    Don't make children feel inadequate by drawing attention to information that they might have missed.

Again, give the class a third sentence if you feel the class is able and won't be tired by the additional work.

## Lesson Three

### Determining the most important information/facts and using further time-saving abbreviation

Ask children to use the clock on the wall, or their watch, to time you while you read aloud four sentences. Ask them to count the seconds. Perhaps wait until the clock's second hand reaches twelve before reading. I used the following.

(1st sentence) *Beavers are among the most skilful builders in the animal world.* (2nd) *These busy animals are famous for constructing dams across rivers and streams.* (3rd) *A dam holds the water back so that it spreads out into a deep pool.* (4th) *Here the beavers build their homes, called lodges.*

From 'Nature Cross-Sections' by Richard Orr, Pub. Scholastic Canada, 1995

The children reported that I took 18 seconds. Try it, you'll find that speaking at a fairly slow pace, these four sentences will take about 18 seconds to read. One could say, therefore, that each sentence took approximately 4 to 5 seconds to read.

Point out to the children that to speak a sentence takes about five seconds. They will agree that you didn't read very fast and it still took only five seconds.

Now count the seconds the children take while they write their first and last name. Children will often take between 3 to 12 seconds to write their own name.

> TEACHING NOTES

"If it takes five seconds to speak a sentence of perhaps 12 words, and if you take five seconds to write the 2 words of your name, then you can see that very quickly you are going to get behind in writing the information contained in a spoken sentence. Thus, no one can write information as quickly as it takes to speak information"

Say to the children, "We can do two things to help us with this problem."

"Don't write all the words that are in the sentence, just the words that have the most important information. The words that you do decide to write you write as abbreviations."

To move the class forward from this point <u>choose one of two options</u>

1. Put up an overhead of the four sentences that you just read to the class.

And say, "If we are not going to write all the words, what words would we miss?"

"Let's take the first sentence."

## *Beavers are among the most skilful builders in the animal world.*

"What words would we miss?"

Children will tell you that words like, 'are', 'the' and 'in' don't need to be written.

### OR

2. Write the first sentence on the board and ask, "What words would we miss?

"O.K., so what do you think are the most important words that tell us information and facts? What would you want to remember to put into a sentence?"

Various ideas may be presented by different children. If you wish, underline the words they choose. They may offer as the most important facts the words skilful, builders, beavers, among, world. Don't pass judgement. Let the children judge. Remind them that when they are writing jot notes they have five seconds to write down the words they feel are most important. Writing out two whole words takes them five seconds. Even if they abbreviate the words it may take them more than five seconds if they write lots of words.

This forces the children to reconsider, and they will then whittle the words further to perhaps beavers, skilful, builders. "O.K.," you say, "now if we could abbreviate just those words then you have a good chance at capturing the most important facts in five seconds."

"Does anyone have any ideas about how to abbreviate these words?"

> TEACHING NOTES

Hands go up.

I was offered the abbreviation skilf. for skilful. I wrote it on the board. Someone said that the abbreviation's meaning wouldn't be easy to remember. This short exchange gave me an opening to start introducing what I had already intended to explain to the class.

"There is no time to look at what someone else is doing - each person has to make quick judgements themselves, first about what words are the most important and secondly how to abbreviate them."

"In the heat of the moment of listening to the information and capturing facts there is no-one judging you on what words you capture and how you abbreviate them."

I want children to put thought into how they see themselves when they capture facts - a change in perception as their role as learners where they start building faith in their individuality of effort. I want children to become comfortable with both the process of capturing facts and in their own efforts, through knowing that:

1. there is no 'right' abbreviation.

2. anyone can use whichever abbreviation they wish, as long as they are able to understand the abbreviation themselves.

3. they are in charge of their abbreviations and no one else need to be able to understand the abbreviations that they use.

4. sometime we may use an abbreviation and then don't remember its meaning, but that's part of learning how to get better at using our own abbreviations.

5. they are in charge of deciding what words they are going to capture and how to abbreviate.

6. it's unlikely that everyone will choose exactly the same words to capture.

The aim of capturing important words and abbreviating is so that each child can, as the next step, write sentences that, as correctly as possible, clearly explain the facts of the information. (information written/spoken in their own words - this is where difference is celebrated.)

Interactions with the class are used as opportunities to reinforce the above six elements of jot-note taking that also, simultaneously, emphasize the individuality of everyone. Thus, the child who offered the abbreviation skilf. is left alone to consider for herself the abbreviation's usefulness while, at the same time, she and others are happy to stay open to further suggestions. Everyone's comfort and dignity are cared for. Hands continue to go up and further abbreviation ideas are offered for the word skilful.

*My Daughter Can't Wait for Monday Morning!*

> TEACHING NOTES

- Skful.
- Skfl.
- Sful.

Is there a right one? No. You make an abbreviation choice that suits you and one that you think you will most likely be able to remember.

This exercise in abbreviation ideas is, of course, repeated for the other most important words in the sentence. Thus, three learning reinforcements occur:

- building understanding of the process of jot-noting,
- building faith in own judgement, and
- learning to be an effective assessor of one's own work.

The process, faith in judgement and learning to be an effective assessor of own work, are elements that are reinforced with consideration of the 2nd sentence.

## *These busy animals are famous for constructing dams across rivers and streams.*

"What words in this second sentence are the most important?"

Children start to realise that the information about 'the animal' has been covered in the first sentence, as has the word 'construction' with the building reference, therefore, this information doesn't need capturing again. The new information in the second sentence is contained in the words 'dams', 'rivers', 'streams'. Thus, through careful consideration and class discussion, children start to arrive at these words as being the most important to capture in their jot notes.

"O.K., does anyone have any ideas about how we could abbreviate those words."

Very short words like 'dams', someone may say, don't need abbreviating. "Yes, you may decide that some words are just as easy to leave as whole words".

The remaining two sentences, of course, are considered in the same way, reinforcing process and, very importantly, reinforcing validity of self in decision-making, while at the same time learning the need to assess the effectiveness of ones decisions.

# Lesson Four

**Part One**  **Further practice in using time-saving abbreviation and determining the most important information/facts**

**Part Two**  **Children sharing jot note information with others in their Four Communities Classroom group**

### Part One - Further practice in using time-saving abbreviation and determining the most important information/facts

I do not insist on children listing their jot notes down the page, but I do tell them to do so. In other words I teach a process for children to adopt that helps many in the process of jot-note taking. I instruct children to prepare for taking their jot notes by numbering down the page.

1.
2.
3.
4.

I find that this helps children focus on something specific, rather than leaving everything open-ended. "Try to capture four facts," I tell them. "If you can get more that's better, but see if you can capture at least four facts."

Most children do better than four, but, at this stage, it is less intimidating for children to aim at a quota of four. Children are not helped if they feel pressured.

Remind children of what they need to think about when doing jot notes. They should not write too much by writing whole sentences. It's important that they try and keep up with the information. To do this they have to make rapid decisions about:

- which words are the most important to write down.
- how they are going to abbreviate the important words.

"In yesterday's lesson we worked as a class doing jot notes. Today we are going to practice jot-noting by working on our own. So, in a minute, I'm going to read a paragraph. It has a similar amount of information as yesterday's paragraph."

Remind the children that this paragraph is only going to take about 18 to 20 seconds to read, and at the end of those few seconds they will need to have captured four or more facts. So everyone must listen carefully and make their own jot notes.

> TEACHING NOTES

For this lesson, from an adaptation from 'Nature Cross-Sections' by Richard Orr, Pub. Scholastic Canada, 1995, I read the following:

*Inside the lodge, beavers are safe from enemies because all the lodge entrances are underwater – and even though it is built with branches and mud, the roof of a lodge is so strong that even a grizzly bear would find it hard to break in.*
*Beavers are most common in Canada and the U.S.*

When the children have finished their jot notes ask, with a matter-of-interest tone (not a tone of judgment), how many children captured facts:

- by writing jot notes - (as distinct from attempting to write whole sentences)?

- by making some of their jot notes whole words?

- but can see now that some of their whole words could have been abbreviated?

Ask children to volunteer words they wrote that they now think they could have abbreviated, and ideas for abbreviating.

These general questions help to reassure children whose efforts may not have been perfect. Your response to their answers should be designed to build comfort both with you and the process that they are engaged in. Remember, taking jot notes from information read in a matter of seconds is a challenge. The children are remarkable at making strides in this process, but they must feel comfortable as you and they proceed.

### Part Two - Children sharing jot note information with others in their Four Communities Classroom group

Announce that you are going to want everyone to turn their captured jot-note information into sentences. But before they do this you are going to ask them to sit on the floor in their groups to discuss what they know about the information that was read to them. This will give everyone a chance to look at their jot notes as they listen to each other and, as they listen, to see how they can make changes to improve their jot notes.

Tell children that we don't want them to read out their list of abbreviated jot notes to their group. We want everyone to look at their jot notes while they tell others what the information is about. There is no value in just reading out their list of abbreviated words. Everyone needs to interpret for their group what their jot notes mean. This is a useful exercise for children as they have to be able to look at their jot notes and place the knowledge/information into spoken sentences. Plus, children are engaged in listening to others to see

> **TEACHING NOTES**

if they can glean further information to enhance their own jot notes. You may want to point out that if anyone cannot interpret their jot notes for others, i.e. they don't understand their own notes, then obviously, the next time, they will have to think more carefully about how they write their jot notes.

On occasion I find that, given too much time to consult with each other, some children start to write sentences being dictated by another. Telling the children that you are only going to give them a couple of minutes or so to share information with each other in the groups avoids this possibility. This will seem quite alright to children, since getting and capturing information in a short time is how they have been working all along.

You may want to ask how many children have added to their jot notes after listening to others in their group.

When two or three minutes or so have passed, tell children that they are to go back to their desks ready to write their sentences. However, it is important, at this stage, to prepare the children. Tell the children that they can now draw upon the information in four ways.

"You have information -
1. in your jot notes,
2. in the extra jot notes you made listening to others in your group,
3. also your memory from listening while the paragraph was being read,
4. and the memory of listening to others in your group."

Thus tell children:
- to use all they know from their jot notes, and all that they have in their memory to put the information together to write their own sentences.
- that the information is theirs now. The information belongs to them to write in their own words.
- that they can write as many sentences as they want.

Remind children that talking was for when they were in their discussion groups, and that the desks are for writing quietly. Now it's time for writing quietly.

Also remind the children that because we are all different:
- everyone will be writing their own sentences, and everyone will be writing the information differently.
- that it is going to be very interesting to see how many different ways there will be of writing the information.
- that it would be very strange if anyone's writing was exactly the same as someone elses.

My Daughter *Can't Wait* for Monday Morning!

> **TEACHING NOTES**

The expectation of difference in everyone's writing relaxes children as they launch into their sentence making. It helps children to know that they do not need to look across to others' writing, and it also raises awareness in children that looking at what someone else is writing is counter-productive. It would take away the excitement of difference.

Sometimes it helps children to focus if they think of someone that they are telling the information to. "Pretend that you are at home telling your mom or dad what you learned about beavers today."

When children have finished writing, invite them to volunteer their sentences. Everyone can now hear many different ways the information was written. Differences are, of course, remarked upon and celebrated. After a while, say, "Isn't amazing, that when everyone heard exactly the same information that there are so many different ways of writing it." This statement encourages many others to offer their effort. They want to tell what they have written. This process celebrates not only children's work, but also their uniqueness. Therefore, children's contribution should NEVER be criticized.

Do not worry about, or draw attention to, those children whose contribution sometimes has information missing. Children are aware of how their effort compares, they tell themselves what they have missed and that they will have to keep concentrating if they want to get good at this jot-note taking. The children will be self-assessing (a skill they are developing) and in your class they will want to improve. Always thank children for their contribution.

## Lesson Five — The first jot note information game (where children use information)

Depending on time and your sense of children's readiness you may wish to make lesson five continuous with lesson four.

There are a number of stages to this lesson, all of which need to be explained to the children at the start.

### The rules of the game
1. Announce to the class that you are going to read a paragraph to group one. And group one are going to take jot notes on the information. Then you are going to read a different paragraph to group two and group two are going to take jot notes on the information in that paragraph. Group three will have a paragraph of their own to jot-note, and, of course, group four will have their paragraph too to write their jot notes from.

> **TEACHING NOTES**

2. After all the paragraphs have been read, the children in each group will go into their discussion circles to share with each other what they think their paragraph is about. Everyone will be able to add to their jot notes.

3. After 2 or 3 minutes everyone will return to their desks to write in their own words the information in sentences.

4. Then a volunteer from group one will read the sentences he/she has created. If anyone else in the group has information that was missed by the volunteer, they can either say what it is or read out their sentences. When group one has told all that they know about their paragraph, then, if they haven't missed any information, the group will earn 10 points. If they have missed out information they will get fewer points. Half the information, for example, will earn 5 points.

5. Anyone from group two, three or four can now earn three bonus points for their group if they can say anything that group one forgot.

6. Each group, in turn, will go through the process, and each group will be given the chance to pick up bonus points if they think information has been missed by a group.

So you tell the class:

- "Every group will need to listen very carefully to their paragraph so that they don't miss out any information when making jot notes, otherwise they will give other groups a chance to pick up bonus points."

- "You may want to listen closely to other groups paragraphs, and take jot note on those too, if you wish, so that if they make a mistake you will be able to get some bonus points for your group.

The kids love this, especially should another group not be paying adequate attention, enabling them to earn bonus points at the other group's expense. No group wants to lose points and then see another group make bonus points from their mistake. The stakes are high!

You will have a very focused class, just waiting to capture as many facts as possible. Many children write jot notes on other group's paragraphs in the hope of being able to earn bonus points. But writing extra jot notes or not, everyone is listening and committing to memory as much as they can. It is excellent training for focusing children's minds. Children experience constructive competition and develop for themselves the incentive to do well. The children make huge strides in the jot-note taking process, internalizing information, organizing information and creating sentence construction that conveys understanding.

*My Daughter Can't Wait for Monday Morning!*

TEACHING NOTES

**Playing the game**

Once all four groups have heard their paragraph and written their jot notes (stage 1), steer the class through stages 2 to 6, reminding, as you go, what is expected for each stage. Thus, for example, when stage four is reached, make sure that everyone from, say, group one, has said all they know about their paragraph (or story, as I refer to it at times) before you open it up to the other groups to try to earn the bonus points of stage 5.

Disagreements may arise at stage 5, - a group insisting that they were right and the bonus-seeking group are wrong. Don't settle these disputes with an answer, but tell the class that we will find out who is right when the disputed paragraph is read a second time. But, before you do the second reading, continue to invite the other groups to offer more information that they think group one may have missed, or got wrong.

At this stage you have not yet awarded points to either group one or the groups working for bonus points. On second reading of the paragraph, the children will then hear your point awarding decisions. (At times, you may wish to consider children's assessments as to how well group one did, and the validity of other groups efforts to earn bonus points). On hearing their paragraph a second time, children are extremely focused to see how well they did their jot notes, sentence writing, and explanations of their story, especially if other groups took issue with their work. Outside the 'guaranteeing-of-motivation-and-fun' process of point awarding, there is no need for any teacher-assessment of the children's work - children will have given themselves as close a scrutiny as anyone. Children's scrutiny of their own work, especially within the community context of striving, creates an inner dialogue of assessment and resolve. In children's subsequent work, the teacher gets to observe the benefits.

When information from the second reading is compared to group one's efforts, and the other three groups responses, you will often find further opportunity to highlight differences in children's thoughts and work. In other words, you may become engaged in assessing whether disputes between groups are based upon:

- actual facts contained in the sentence.

- interpretation of meaning by children.

OR

- alternative word usage that actually conveys the same meaning as the original paragraph.

These questions need to be explored with the class, within the context of their contributions.

**TEACHING NOTES**

The following serves as an example:

With information from a paragraph stating that *'a bee will return to the hive and dance a special dance telling the other bees the direction and distance of pollen,'* a child wrote about the 'journey and distance'. The boy had substituted the word 'direction' with the word 'journey'. Remember he had captured facts in seconds in his jot notes and then wrote the information he had learned in his own words - interpretation and alternative word usage is, therefore, virtually guaranteed. This process, underlines difference in us all. Thus the boy's work is valid. And, by inference, all children's work is validated as long as the deciding question is met (tell the children) - "Do your sentences give the right understanding?"

After this game, children may ask "Can we do that again?" You may wish to let them play the game again with another set of paragraphs, today or tomorrow. It will be good practice.

## Notes for Lessons Six and Seven

### Reading, researching and jot-noting

Lesson six and seven (pp. 159 and 161) are designed to enable children to begin the process of mastering research skills, and reproducing printed information in their own words - more jot note skills.

To achieve the learning capacities attached to reading, researching and jot-noting there are a number of skills to be attempted and eventually (to varying degrees) mastered by children. These skills are:

- learning to decide what facts, in a book/article, need recording in jot note form for immediate future reference (either to report back orally or in writing).

- learning to use abbreviation as a tool for more rapid collection of the information and facts raised in the book/article (without further reference to the book/article)

- learning to take the abbreviated jot notes and convert them (to be written in their own words) into sentences that will make sense to another listener/reader.

**Lesson Six**

# The second jot note information game (where children use their eyes for getting information)

The same six stages from the first jot note game (lesson five, see pages 155 and 156 ) are used. Remind the class of these stages. "Except, this time," tell the class, "each group will get its information by using their eyes, by looking at an overhead transparency projected on a screen."

I prepare four paragraphs on an overhead transparency(ies) that contain approximately the same amount of information as used for lesson 5 - written at appropriate grade level. (I find that using linking themes such as animals, or oceans, or a particular specie work well - for example, you can prepare the children by saying that all these paragraphs are about bees, or about rainforest creatures, etc.) Overheads are displayed, one paragraph of information at a time. Thus, the first paragraph of information is for group one, the second for group two, etc. "Again, anyone can try to earn bonus points and can choose to write jot notes on another group's paragraph."

I find that after experiencing the game from lesson 5, children are usually particularly focused on this second game, and try to be prepared enough so as not to create opportunities for others to earn bonus points.

Tell the class that to read these paragraphs would take about 20 seconds, and, therefore, that is approximately the amount of time they would have to write their jot notes. But, since they will be using their eyes to read the information for themselves and then write jot notes, that you will give them twice as long. In other words, each group will have their paragraph displayed for about 40 seconds, maybe even 45 seconds.

"O.K., are you ready group one?" "Here is your paragraph."

And so you proceed, group by group, putting each group's paragraph on display one at a time. That completes stage 1.

- Options for stage 2 *(from lesson 5)*

*After all the paragraphs have been read, all the groups will go into their discussion circles to share with each other what they think their paragraph is about. Everyone will be able to add to their jot notes. As an extra challenge you may choose to skip this stage, and tell children that they can write their sentences from their own jot notes, without discussion with others. This should be announced before the display of the overheads. This can provide incentive for any child who thinks that they needn't work too hard since they will be able to get the information from others in their group during the group discussion stage, i.e. 'I'll just tag on to other peoples effort.'*

*TEACHING NOTES*

1. The approach of sharing information with others before writing, and,
2. the approach of writing from their own jot notes, independently and without reference to others, both serve to expand children's learning capacity. Therefore, give children opportunity for both approaches.

The validity of approach No. 1 is that it provides children with a number of learning experiences:

- Being part of the dialogue in hearing others' understanding of the information.
- Being involved in the exercise of making yourself understood.
- Being involved in an internal assessment of one's own knowledge in comparison with others'.

Also important:

- Knowing that there are many valid sources of information.
- You can be a valid source for others, especially if you have done your 'homework' and are able to convince with sound argument.
- Being able to assess for oneself the validity of what another is saying.

The above are all discernment-building capacities; important for the Four Communities Classroom learning environment and, for effective life-long learning.

See p. 156, Lesson Five (the first jot-note game) and repeat stages 3, 4, 5 and 6.

At stage five, again there may be disagreement, and again let everyone have their say – first, the group whose paragraph it is can speak, and then the other groups who think that they have information that will earn them bonus points can put up their hands to speak.

The second viewing of the information can then take place where everyone assesses their work against the original information source. Points are awarded - ten points for groups that have a full description of the information, less for those with information missing. Three bonus points for groups who were able to identify missing or incorrect information.

Children will sometimes add information that was not included in the original paragraph. Since this work is a prelude to more self-directed learning, interpretive learning and a dialogue of learning I don't discourage children from adding information. I tell children that if they are involved in researching a topic in the library and/or on the internet and they know something that is relevant, then it is O.K to include the information they already know.

> NOTE: For this game, adding information to a paragraph is O.K. However, once children are involved in a research project they will, of course, need to check the validity of their knowledge against information gleaned from the library or the internet.

**Lesson Seven**     **More practice at getting information through the eyes - seeing information**

This lesson brings children closer to goal (B) first outlined on page 141.

Goal (B) is … 'children building capacity in researching topics in the library, and on the internet, and offering their understanding of the research in their own words, either verbally or in written form. (temptations to plagiarize defeated)'

You want the children to become comfortable with taking information from books - reading and putting information into their own words (not plagiarizing). This lesson is essentially the same as lesson six, except that instead of reading from overhead transparencies the children read from a book.

The ideal is to use a projector that will project anything that is placed on it. Images of three dimensional objects as well as pages of a book can be immediately screened. Alternatively, a page could be computer scanned and projected from a computer. If either of these technologies is not available, provide each group with a different book with a page and paragraph indicated that you want the children to read.

In lesson seven I increase the amount of information for children to jot-note; perhaps double the information handled in lesson six. Doubling the information represents a further challenge, so you may decide to perhaps triple the time that you give children to make their jot notes - say perhaps 2 minutes.

If you are projecting the information, you will, of course, have precise control over viewing time.

However, if groups are handling books, you may wish to time pairs of children for 2 minutes before they hand their groups book to the next two children in their group. Although perhaps harder to administer, the advantage of this approach is that this can be going on simultaneously in all four groups.

If children say that they wished they had more time then, if you like, grant their wish. Give everyone a second chance to see the information. (This is exactly what they would be doing if they were doing research in the library). But, in this exercise, give children the time you think they need. Perhaps another minute would do. The important thing is not to give children so much time that some are tempted to start writing the information verbatim. It is important that this must still be a jot-note taking exercise.

With jot-note time over, and before asking children to write information in their own words, you have a choice.

**TEACHING NOTES**

1. Have children proceed directly to writing with no discussion.
   Or
2. Have children discuss in their groups what they think the information is about.

Mix and match these processes on different occasions.

When children have been looking at books in their groups, and, therefore, have not been able to see the information other groups were working with then, of course, there can be no competition over the information and no possibility to earn bonus points.

In this non-competitve circumstance, and after children finish their writing, read aloud the original information and ask children to assess their own work, giving themselves a mark out of ten before handing it in for your assessment. You may want to tell children that if you agree with the mark that they have given themselves that they will earn a bonus of two points for their group.

However, with groups of children who, viewed the on-the-screen display of each group's information, you can go through the discussion/point earning/bonus point earning process as outlined in lesson five, page 155. You also have the option, of course, to re-display the on-the-screen paragraphs seen by each group.

## Lesson eight

### Getting information through the ears - hearing information

Lesson eight brings goal **(A)**, first outlined on page 140, to a useful place for teaching and learning in the classroom:

Goal (A) is ... *'children building capacity in listening to the teacher, taking notes, and offering their own understanding of the lesson either verbally or in written form'*.

By the time lesson eight is completed, children should feel comfortable taking information from the teacher's spoken word (including curriculum information) and putting information into their own words (verbalized and/or written) This level of attainment in children will bring to conclusion this series of lessons on jot-note taking skills.

Lesson eight moves the children considerably forward in the amount of information to be listened to, and therefore, the amount of time they are listening to information and the amount of jot notes they will end up taking. Lesson eight represents a big jump for children.

> **TEACHING NOTES**

To help them cope with the increased demand of more information and, therefore, more jot notes, I give the increased amount of information to the children through a story. (I do not use curriculum information at this point.)

A story is more likely to carry itself in the child's memory. Children very often place themselves in a story - "what would I do in this situation?" Later, when the children are asked to write the story in their own words, from their jot notes and memory, they are far more likely to be successful. Meeting with success in telling the story in their own words helps children become more assured of their ability to take jot notes and to report back what they have learned.

Success will mean different levels of competence for different children, but even the slowest child is able to make some headway. The saying, 'practice makes perfect' is especially applicable, and because your children are engaged in continuing to practice something that they have developed an understanding for, they are not likely to feel lost and frustrated. Everyone can achieve.

### **The Story**

I told a personal story, (not private or confidential). The one I usually chose to tell was the adventure I had traveling by ship across the Atlantic. Depending upon the capacity of your children, tailor your story to last 5 to 15 minutes.

Personal stories work well because you can just stand and talk connectively to children. Children show interest, and are readily engaged. I talk at a normal speaking pace. They know jot-note taking, and in this setting, and at this stage of their skill acquisition, children seem quite willing to engage in what is, for them, a mammoth jot-note taking session.

You may wish to introduce the use of headings. Then you can, during your story, tell the children, O.K. here is another heading. 'Leaving Port'. Write your jot notes under this heading. 'The Emergency Drill on Board Ship'. Write jot notes under this heading. 'The Day of the Storm at Sea'. 'Arrival in Canada'.

The use of headings helps children to keep their notes and their memory organized. The use of headings is an approach that children also find helpful with learning curriculum. Headings can be used as a step towards children taking full responsibility for their own jot note organization. In other words do not feel that in all lessons where children are jot-noting that you should always provide children with heading announcements.

You may wish to mix and match curriculum lessons with both heading announcements and no heading announcements.

TEACHING NOTES

**The completion of children's written account of your story**

Upon completion of the written accounts, take in children's work and assign a mark out of ten that reflects the amount of information they have managed to include. These marks should focus on the jot-noting and reporting-in-own-words skills only. (Do not detract from the jot-noting by marking for sentence structure, spelling or tense. These abilities can be the focus of lessons specifically aimed at these skills.)

Also collect children's jot notes. You will likely find that children who have written the fullest account have been the most successful in capturing facts and points in their jot notes. They had lots to refer to.

When returning children's work you may like to praise the class generally for becoming good jot note takers. Point out that the mark they have earned for their work is a result of how many facts that they were able to include. "I am pleased to see that everyone can do jot notes, but if you can try to capture more information in your jot-notes then you will find it easier to write your information."

Where information is short in the written work, and short in the jot notes, you may like to write a comment on children's work. For example, 'Good work Jane, as far as it goes, but you have no information on the arrival (etc.)'

As in all classes, the work handed in will vary between that of an excellent standard to writing that is missing detail. However, very importantly, you will likely have all children's work reflect a vast improvement over their efforts from lesson one and two. In other words, all children will have likely demonstrated knowledge in jot-noting, and writing from jot notes. This can be built upon. No child should now be unaware of what is required, and everyone should have some sense of how to proceed.

# Building On Jot Noting Skills

Once you have taken children through the eight jot-note lessons they are ready to use their new-found skills. Look for something to teach from the curriculum that will enable children to use these skills successfully. Importantly, everyone has now reached the stage where jot-note development can occur in tandem with curriculum acquisition. Start with something small, slowly building the challenges over subsequent lessons. Use some of the techniques and games outlined in the eight jot-note lessons that are familiar and fun, such as the group competitions around knowledge.

The group competitions, and group discussion/sharing of information will help slower children to feel comfortable and help them not to be left behind. To help children build and develop their jot noting skills make these processes ongoing; jot-noting and learning curriculum enhanced by each, simultaneously.

However, requiring children to take jot notes for every curriculum-based lesson is, I feel, unreasonable and too great a burden, and may have the effect of making jot-noting a chore rather than being a fun challenge. Consider asking children to do jot-notes occasionally - perhaps once or twice a week.

You may find some children voluntarily using jot notes on all sorts of occasions. That, of course, is great. Others may ask your permission, which, of course, is also great. Both are instances of children taking responsibility for their learning processes. There are, of course, no guarantees that any child will volunteer to take jot notes. Do not worry. Children knowing how to do jot notes when asked is a huge step forward. It is, of course, wonderful when children want to take jot-notes. However, do not require all children to take jot notes, because some are voluntarily taking jot-notes. This could put a uncomfortable spotlight on ardent children, a position they may choose to shy away from in the future. This is, of course, not what you want. Say, "Well yes, certainly, you can take jot-notes anytime you like! If you feel that it would help you, then it's a good idea. Take jot notes whenever you want to - that's great! There will be times when I'll ask everyone to take jot notes, and other times when you decide. Whenever you think that it would help your learning, you can choose to take jot notes without asking permission."

What would be the effect of this statement upon individual children and the class as a whole? There are a number of potential benefits that are opened up. The children who are engaged in voluntarily writing jot notes, or who asked permisssion, are affirmed and feel very good about themselves. These children are also, automatically, leading by example. Quiet but spontaneous positive leadership occuring in your class is part of the Four Communities Classroom, and is an example of the experience you want children to have.

**TEACHING NOTES**

Other children will now engage in an inner dialogue, wondering what decision they will make regarding jot-notes. Thoughts may include:-

- Oh! A part of my learning is up to me?
- And part of other children's learning is up to them.
- That feels different from what I'm used to.
- Other children are making decisions for themselves - shouldn't I?
- What am I going to do?

Thoughts of this nature can represent for many children an additional incentive towards accepting responsibility for self.

And, furthermore, jot-note taking has now become an ongoing positive influence that is being used spontaneously in your classroom. Thus, with children voluntarily jot-noting, with others following suit, this will be part of the influence, in your classroom, of assuming responsibility for self. For some, it may take the next grade for the spontaneous jot-noting choice to be made. But, in the meantime, all children are living in an environment that makes taking responsibility for self a well-accepted option. This can have day-to-day benefits where responsibility for self may show up and be exercised in other ways by children.

- **The reluctant or slower child and jot-noting**

For those jot-note hold-outs, there is always the planned jot note session. You say "For this lesson, I want everyone to take jot notes. I will be collecting your work and giving marks for your jot notes AND your finished writing. Yes, this is for everyone!"

Thus from time to time, make jot-noting part of children's curriculum learning experience. You'll find that jot-note taking enables the most reluctant child's learning to progress - even the ones who produce little on the page. Since they are involved in their group discussions, and the group competitions, I find that even these children gradually hone their skills. Engage children - ask them what they know. Slower children can feel success in being able to tell you what they know - a step in confidence building and perhaps a step towards feeling more comfortable with writing what they know. A child imparting even a little knowledge is the beginning of being able to impart more, as comfort and confidence grows. That is something that you and the child can celebrate.

Have fun!

# CHAPTER FOUR
## GROUP DYNAMICS WITHIN THE FOUR COMMUNITIES CLASSROOM, AND BEYOND

Children within their community of the Four Communities Classroom become engaged in group dynamics. Learning benefits accrue, through the discussion process, development in children's verbal communication skills, and, through relationship, the enabling of greater confidence in self.

*Vanessa, grade nine, recalling grade five.*

**"Grade five is where I really changed. I was that little person who sat in a corner and read. I never wanted to go and speak in front of the class. In the Four Communities Classroom groups you had to speak your opinion or just sit there and nothing would happen for you, and you think, well this isn't working for me.** *(the power of inner dialogue)* **With the groups you have to put in what you want to get out or it's just not going to come. That's when I changed. It was in grade five that I became energetic and learnt to speak for myself. I remember Erica and Kristine telling me that I had changed a lot."**

Although individuals may have similar experiences, inner dialogue will, of course, vary, with varying outcomes. See 'Children's life experience', and 'Tentativeness precedes steps forward,' p. 193. Positive experience will usually begat positive outcomes - variously expressed amongsgt the children in your class.

This chapter explores group dynamics with the purpose of enabling teachers to build constructively on relationship changes that can occur between children when grouped. This knowledge can be used to more creatively and constructively move from problem to solution in sharing with and guiding children in dealing with learning and behavioural issues in the classroom.

The intent is to consider grouping dynamics to better understand what is happening in the groups. This can lead to more appropriate responses to children, their concerns and behaviour.

The chapter is in two parts:
1. General grouping concepts Four Communities Classroom grouping
2. The dynamics of group integration

Provided are general comments on group dynamics (applicable to many human grouping situations), as a foundation for the focus on classroom particulars. Two classroom case studies are used as illustration.

### 1. General grouping concepts and Four Communities Classroom grouping

All groupings, whether of adults or children, will be engaged in autonomy (of individuals) and integration (of the group) dynamics, that are processes of interplay between members and the group. The interplay is essentially an integrative engagement for individuals from which, through acceptance by the group, an individual's autonomous sense of well-being can develop. Human need for acceptance and belonging is met through integration, and achieved through grouping. This autonomy and integration relationship is consistent with our internal ecological and biological processes.

> **Ecological pattern - autonomy and integration**
> The individual's autonomy (either of the individual cell or organism) cannot be absolute; its autonomy is dependant upon integrating with surroundings/habitat/environment; its externalities. [Ed. from 'Mutuality in healthy process.' p. 250-251]

In fact, constructive integration with an externality (e.g. a group, another person, an environment) is an essential element for the development of constructive autonomy in the individual.

Group dynamics of autonomy and integration are foundational to cultures, with an interplay that impacts both the individual and the group as a whole. In groupings, these interactive dynamics of autonomy and integration are not always in balance, i.e. individual autonomies can be subsumed by integrative group pressures, or visa versa, to the detriment of both the individual and the group. Balance between autonomous and integrative elements exists when compromise is shared and benefits accrue to the individuals and the group as a whole; a process, in fact, of mutual regard between individuals and group.

> **Ecological pattern - healthy life process within healthy surroundings**
> In the science of living systems this process of health is described as autonomy (of the individual) and integration (with surroundings) being in a state of mutuality. It is a foundational and intimate connection, where the health of each is dependant upon the other.
> This concept of health for both autonomy and integration has implications in understanding:
> - all relationships within the environment.
> - human relationships.
> - relationships involved in the learning processes of school. [Adapted from appendix (ii), p. 251]

While other species fit into a contained ecological niche, it is our frontal-cortex, cross-ecological niche endowment that gives us the capacity to depart, in our person-to-person relationships, from an autonomy and integration balance. But, it is also through the intelligent application of frontal-cortex thought process that we can choose to work towards constructive balance. This is achieved through communication.

Group dynamics can have constructive and destructive outcomes. Group dynamics are at the heart of all cultures be they national, ethnic or tribal; in structures, such as families, churches, businesses, corporations, governments, educational institutions and classrooms; also in clubs, pubs, youth groups, groups of friends, and so-called counter cultures, and even in temporary short-term groupings. These are all groupings where entrenchment of perspective can exist and an institutionalizing process can reign. Entrenched or not, all groups will exhibit some type of commonly-agreed-upon group consensus with which to make sense of the world. Significantly, and especially where integrative pressures prevail, this can, at times, oblige some individuals to compromise aspects of their autonomy.

Sometimes such compromise is only too clearly recognised by the individual. Given, perhaps, the integrative force of economic and/or social pressure there is an acceptance of compromise.

- **When autonomy is being besieged by integrative demands**

In school, becoming (individual autonomy) and belonging (group integration) can be compromised when children feel uncomfortable with their peer group culture, the school's cultural expectations or a combination of these. Outcomes from dynamics of compromise may diminish constructive development of the child and create difficulties for the school. Both the individual's autonomy and the group integration (the school) can be adversely affected. When 'becoming and belonging' are adversely affected, children feel unhappy and disengaged. [Incidentally, it is elements of these dynamics that are at play when feelings of homesickness are experienced - the individual's autonomy is not feeling 'at home' in the new integrative surroundings. As we know, time to adjust (one's sense of autonomy) can be the cure and, perhaps, having one's contribution to the new community valued, speeds the process of becoming and belonging.]

In school, the ideal environment for children is that in which a culture works towards meeting good teaching and good learning goals, and which is celebrated by both children and their school equally; autonomy of the individual and integration with the school dynamics in balance. Although unstated in these terms in the classroom, it is this balance, effecting becoming and belonging, that is the goal in each community in the Four Communities Classroom. It is this goal that Four Communities Classroom system is designed to address.

I would like to consider three distinct, but interactive, aspects of autonomy and integration group dynamics, and comment on their effect upon becoming and belonging in the Four Communities Classroom.

### 1. Autonomy and integration dynamics between the individual and the Four Communities Classroom group

Children in the Four Communities Classroom are well positioned to engage constructively in autonomy and integration dynamics since, within their groups, they are required to interact with only six or seven people, rather than having to contend with one large whole-class group. Significantly, this is empowering for children as, in a smaller group, they can have a greater and more easily-exercised influence, and, therefore, are more readily able to engage in the shaping of the smaller group's code, or culture. Acceptance and exercise of identity are easier to achieve. This also presents an opportunity for exercising self-correction, in working towards a balance of autonomy and integration within the group.

Teachers are able to facilitate this process by monitoring interactions and selecting the most constructive group make-up for children.

### 2. Autonomy and integration dynamics between the groups of the Four Communities Classroom

Security, acceptance and belonging fill the human need for integration. The marvel is that this need finds such different expression from group to group and culture to culture. Within the global community the tragedy is that these differences of expression, arising from a common need, have often fuelled suspicion, defensiveness and conflict rather than understanding. Each group has tended to autonomously pursue its perspective, with little regard for integrative accommodation with the perspectives of other groups. Thus, while the integration dynamics of becoming and belonging are seen as the stuff of life within groups, they're generally given short shrift in the relationships between groups. When there is little balance between autonomy and integration, either within groups or between groups, there is little room for mutual regard.

However, with mutual regard as foundational to the Four Communities Classroom, children are in an environment where constructive relationships between groups can be learned and practiced.

### 3. Autonomy and integration dynamics between groups as well as with individuals in other groups.

The Four Communities Classroom is structured to encourage groupness, with an emphasis on becoming and belonging within groups. Children create their sense of groupness through group names, earning points, group discussion, group bulletin board displays, etc.. While a sense of distinction between groups develops, there simultaneously develops a feeling of mutual regard for all, through each child also being an integral part of the larger community of the classroom. As the confidence of each child grows, within his/her group, the child's enhanced sense of self equips him/her to better function as an individual within the larger community of the classroom; feelings of inadequacy or defensiveness are reduced. These are the conditions that favour mutual regard process. Mutual regard is difficult to accommodate when self-esteem is low, or feels threatened. Knowing how to be part of and a contributor to one's own community, while recognizing one's belonging and value to a larger reality, is an important concept to be exposed to and to learn - especially important socially, economically and environmentally in the wider world.

*Vanessa and Kristine, grade eight, recalling grade five.*

**"We'd laugh and say to each other, 'I am me and you are you and together we are us.' It's like making a statement that on our own we are ourselves and together we are us, but we are always our own person. We learnt that in the Four Communities Classroom. It brought it out in us."**

Some elements of grouping

- Cultural influences upon an individual are integrative influences.

- All human groupings maintain implicit and explicit expectations that are part of the group's distinguishing features and a display of cultural identity.

- The previous 2 elements are implicit to group identity.

- Group dynamics provide a sense of security, partly obtained through a building of an individual's identity that arises out of group association.

- Grouping is a way of looking after of our innate human need for security, acceptance and belonging, universal and common to all people.

Being in groups within the Four Communities Classrom strengthens the individual. The individual develops a greater sense of self-knowledge and discernment, within the context of the group.

---

### Acceptance, becoming and belonging, and the exercise of identity in the group setting

I came into the classroom one day and saw one of my Four Communities Classroom groups with stickers they had made and placed on their foreheads. My first thought was to order the stickers removed, but quickly realized that these children were exhibiting perfectly healthy group dynamics and, with very clear and simple actions, were speaking volumes on acceptance, belonging and security. They were also having fun, but looked at me enquiringly. Their action was, of course, an expression of belonging in their group. My smile reassured them that nothing was amiss. However, had this group-action been disruptive, I would have used the classroom rights to seek remedy. Then such an exercise would represent a learning opportunity in the examination of their group dynamics in terms of integration with other groups and impact upon constructive learning. In other words, in the Four Communities Classroom, display of groupness is O.K when it is in harmony with good teaching and good learning for all groups, and is in accord with mutual regard.

Since children are not generally expected to be able to articulate rationale for their expressions of becoming and belonging, but instead rely on their feelings to judge its rightness, I believe it would have been confusing, if not damaging, for me to have mistaken this group's actions for disruptive behaviour and, in turn, overridden and negated them.

Thus, if behaviours in the classroom meet the mutual regard and good teaching and good learning imperative, be ready to let it happen. But when behaviours are not constructive, draw on classroom rights to guide the children. Good teaching and good learning should not be compromised.

The forehead stickers ran their course, and, within a week, they disappeared. It was the children's process, and, within the bounds of good teaching and learning, time taken was theirs to decide. Becoming is a self-discovery journey of many steps, with nuances of difference for each child.

<u>Footnote.</u> From p. 243, teacher thought box **"… awareness as to what constitutes productive tolerance limits (is) important to teaching and learning in the classroom."** Appendix (i) 'The foundations of living systems: processes of change, difference, potentiality and learning in the classroom'.

## 2. The dynamics of group integration

This section is a brief consideration of some of the integrative group elements (that may have constructive or negative affect) and some associated challenges that groups may encounter. It is presented with a view to providing further insight into events and dynamics that could occur in classroom groups, and to enable constructive monitoring and intervention by teachers. Some integrative elements and challenges for groups are:

1. Provision of group-selected secondary experience and information. (constructive or negative)
2. (Peer) group pressure to conform. (constructive or negative)
3. Outlining of expectations and procedures. (constructive or negative)
4. Affirmation processes of group belonging and identity (constructive or negative)

   perhaps leading to -
5. Denying acceptance of others (sometimes leading to a group security paradox)

Groups may mix and match these integrative elements, ranging from functional to more dysfunctional application and result.

There will be varying displays of these elements, according to the degree of group cohesion and the personalities involved. It is unlikely that negative rallying-round techniques will be used by the group to exclude others. Under the teachers' watchful eye, it is the functional, rather than dysfunctional expression of the integration elements that should prevail. Generally, for a newcomer to the class, introduction to the group culture is a welcoming experience.

The Four Communities Classroom provides a context for group autonomy and integration dynamics and, through discussion, in an atmosphere of mutual regard, an opportunity for children to seek, exercise and positively express autonomy and integration dynamics. Such opportunity brings about constructive learning in children about self and others. The following case study serves as one illustration of group dynamics in the classroom.

### The story of Ryan - a case study from grade five

I was forewarned about Ryan. He was to arrive for a fresh start, mid-year, from another school. In order to facilitate this 'fresh start', I decided to put him with a group that had established good cohesion and group norms. This group's self-regulation was enabling it to function constructively and contribute to good teaching and good learning generally. Its internal self-organization extended to setting up its own group library system, whereby its members could display books on a nearby shelf and borrow from each other. The children welcomed Ryan, but naturally did not want their group function to be disrupted. They set about introducing Ryan to their group culture and engaged constructively in the four elements of integrative activities, i.e -

1. *Provision of group-selected secondary experience and information.*
2. *(Peer) group pressure to conform.*
3. *Outlining of expectations and procedures.*
4. *Affirmation processes of group belonging and identity.*

The group informed Ryan of their ways, means and conduct. Ryan wasn't interested.

The group selected information for Ryan, to tell him about themselves as a group. Ryan wasn't interested. The group outlined the norms they chose with which to guide their behaviour. Ryan wasn't interested.

It turned out that Ryan wasn't really interested in making a fresh start, but wanted to carry on the disruptive ways that propelled him out of his previous school.

For whatever reasons, and despite the problems he encountered with this attitude, it likely made more sense to Ryan to stick with what he knew and had honed, producing feelings of being in control to whatever degree he could manage, rather than trying to accommodate the more foreign (to him) system of the group. Attempts to satisfy an emotional need drove Ryan, as it does us all. But Ryan chose ways that were damaging to himself and others. He was not, however, a bully. Ryan did not use intimidation.

In fact, Ryan's coping strategy involved bringing other children onside to lend support. Ryan's solicitation campaign appeared to be based on the assumption that surely, given a choice, anyone would be more interested in subversive behaviour than getting on with 'boring old school work'. He was their man to lead the way. Thus he set about challenging the group's function. His intention appeared to be to power his way into the group and establish new and disruptive group norms; his group members were to become colleagues in subversion - supporters of Ryan's perceptions.

There is power to be had by children who are able to challenge established norms and replace them with their own version.

In a regular classroom, the Ryan's of this world can usually find some who will join their power base. It takes a particularly strong class ethic to enable an entire class to isolate and overcome negative influence. Children such as Ryan are often able to exert a diminishing influence upon good teaching and good learning.

But in the Four Communities Classroom group that Ryan found himself in, there was a group cohesion that was more than his match. He was unable to turn anyone's head and, instead, found that, after some renewed efforts to give him a second chance, he, in fact, was marginalized and then rejected by the group. He tried, a number of times, to exert influence, and appeared perplexed and puzzled at each failed attempt. He was, however, unable to learn from these experiences and continued to fail within the group.

The children came to me and asked that Ryan be moved to another group. I knew that this could represent an opportunity for Ryan to take power, as other groups were not as strong in resolve. I declined, saying that giving Ryan more time would probably be helpful. The children agreed to persevere, although they were very concerned about the affect Ryan was having on their point earning capacity. To help the group in its efforts to help itself, to help Ryan; in fact to help the entire class, myself included, I tried not deducting points from the group for Ryan's point losing behaviours. That didn't help. The group came to me, unbeknownst to Ryan, with a signed petition, outlining, in writing, their concerns. Points lost or not, his presence caused more disruption than their group wanted to handle. I had to act.

I decided to confide in Ryan that his group no longer wanted him. He was concerned. I asked if he wanted to be in the group. Yes, he said, that was important to him. (With no audience, his system cannot work, i.e. the group was merely to be turned into a tool to meet Ryan's needs.) He didn't like the rejection contained in the petition. We discussed what behaviours he thought would endear him. Interestingly, he had no difficulty in outlining them.

"O.K.", I said to the group, with Ryan by my side, "Ryan is very concerned and wants to work hard at being accepted by the group." The group rather sceptically agreed to another 'fresh start'.

Well, of course, this chat with Ryan was insufficient to resolve anything, and I was left wondering how to turn this problem into a learning opportunity for all.

Perhaps it comes from the mindset that the Four Communities Classroom teacher develops, but a concept of **'visiting rights'** came to mind. Ryan could earn his way into the group by showing he could get along with them.

In re-introducing point loss for Ryan the next morning, the inevitable happened. I said to Ryan, "You have lost your group ten points, so now you will bring your desk over to mine and there you will sit until you have managed to earn back the ten points. Earned points will allow you to rejoin and repay points to your group." (With Ryan's desk next to mine and no audience, there would be no point loss, but I would be obliged to use the slightest reason to award Ryan points, in order to make the visiting rights concept work). I continued, "You will be allowed, as the day's lessons and work proceed, to visit your group for fifteen minutes and then you will return, with your desk, next to me. On subsequent days, anytime you earn five points you will be able to visit your group again. Each successful visit and interaction will mean that the time allowed with your group will extend by fifteen minute increments. Thus, the first successful visit of 15 minutes will lead to the next visit being 30 minutes, as long as it remains successful, which, in turn, will open the way to a 45 minute visit, etc.."

This worked. Ryan's capacity to modify his behaviour was not stretched to breaking point, as even he could make an effort for short periods. Away from the group he had no audience for his power moves. And like us all, Ryan preferred acceptance over rejection. He learned to work on behaviours acceptable to his group and the return to isolation gave him the opportunity to consider events and recover, before his next try at integration. The group learned to deal with a sizeable difficulty and find accommodation for Ryan. While Ryan never totally emulated the other members of the group, he did abandon his disruptive behaviours and did, in fact, find his fresh start. It was an important turning point for Ryan. He grew happier in school, as he discovered easier and more satisfying ways to meet emotional need.

**A summary of group dynamics and challenges that the group and Ryan found themselves involved in**

- Through consensus (and living out the Four Communities Classroom mutual regard ethic), strong protocols had been established by the grade five group to meet their needs; emotional contentment through acceptance, constructive relationship and learning.

- The newcomer appeared to want to meet his emotional needs, as he saw them, through taking power and control, on his terms.

- The group used integrative elements to welcome a new member.

- The strong sense of group integration, established by its members, in turn, gave back strength to individual members (autonomy enhanced through constructive integration), making it easier to resist takeover.

- The group attempted rejection (No. 5. Denial of acceptance, p. 172) of the non-conformist new member, to maintain group identity and integrity.

- Rejection compelled the new member to revisit his attitude and consider different ways to achieve his needs. But help was needed in this. Although the new and rejected member could express what he needed to do, he possessed insufficient capacity (perhaps now lost from his lexicon) to regard externalities with a sensitivity that would enable constructive learning to come out of the experience.

- The group decision to try again made it easier for each child to play their part in trying to integrate the new member.

- The children worked as a group to decide, organize, and act, to bring the teacher into finding a solution that would be an act of shared responsibility.

- Shared responsibility made it easier for individuals, and the group as a whole, to cooperate and apply a possible solution to the problem.

- The group, as a whole and as individuals, including Ryan, was involved in feedback, self-monitoring and self-correction, in response to the externalities that they themselves had created. Reinstatement of emotional equilibrium was the yardstick for the process, and the discovery of a new basis of emotional security was the hope for Ryan.

Ryan and the group were able to engage life-learning in bite-sized chunks - application, internal reflection, regroup and application.

**The dynamics of:**
- **autonomy (primary experience) and**
- **integration (secondary experience)**

**at work for Ryan, his group and the teacher**

Children will always have their own thoughts [**primary** autonomous experience] and Ryan's story offers an example of the teacher providing the structure [**secondary** integrative experience] for children to engage in constructive, self-directed learning [primary experience engaging both autonomous (themselves) and integrative (others) elements]. This type of pattern between primary and secondary experience and autonomy and integration, is an important and essential element of the Four Communities Classroom.

However, mutual regard, for example, cannot be taught effectively only through teacher-supplied secondary experience lessons on values. In such situations, the expectation is that the child's autonomous thoughts will be carried along by the integrative secondary statements of the lesson. The child is told this is best because of the reasons supplied. There is little or no room to feel or experience the context of what is being transmitted. It is an attempt to establish autonomous thoughts without primary experience.

In the Four Communities Classroom, the exchange between primary and secondary experience, and autonomous and integrative elements, enabled the nature of regard to change for both Ryan and the group. The group learned that mutual regard between like minds is one thing, but that, sometimes, it can take increased thought and effort to relate to others effectively and that, therefore, mutual regard has different qualities and manifestations, according to the personalities involved. The group learned that, especially when confronted with difficulties, effort directed towards establishing mutual regard offers a way to a more manageable and productive relationship. The opportunity that Ryan's presence provided, (a contextual learning opportunity), also showed children that there are times when the mutual regard process results in the positive outcome of a constructive association, but not necessarily friendship. Although friendship may, of course, develop from constructive association.

Ryan was introduced to a regard process that offered him a more satisfactory and constructive way of interacting with externalities; the development of mutual regard: his autonomy more in balance with integrative processes. His happier disposition suggested that he found that he enjoyed coming to school more. Certainly he seemed able to make a more constructive contribution to both his and others' lives.

- **The power seeking child in class-size setting and smaller groups**

Placed in a regular classroom, a power–seeking child may take an approach similar to Ryan's, or use bullying devices to create an 'insider group' that will exert its will upon other children. (See 'Moving forward with bullies - the story of Jason, p. 195, where a different approach, alongside group process, was used.) Containing bullying problems in a class-size setting can be unwieldy, perhaps obliging the teacher, in assuming responsibility, to consider more imposed regulation and consequence; 'You will do this. You won't do that'. The application of increasing levels of imposed regulation can sometimes require a forcefulness that overrides sensitivity to the group as a whole, or to individuals. 'These are the rules, with consequences - follow them!' In a classroom where the teacher assumes full responsibility and, when deemed necessary, forcefully applies it, children may find themselves adopting a getting-by approach to their learning process, to cope with the disruptive child[ren] and the teacher's response. This is self-regulation taking place within both imposed circumstance and imposed regulation. This can alter the atmosphere of the classroom, be counter to achieving successful outcomes, and be hard on both teachers and children. Within a Four Communities Classroom group, a power-seeking child is confined to his/her group in attempting exertion of will, with or without others on side. When the problem is confined and contained to a small group, constructive learning opportunities can more easily be explored, when attempting to effect change, than in the more unwieldy arena of the entire class.

Groups that develop a strong sense of identity will likely be able to integrate a power-seeking child, or isolate the child if he/she refuses to contribute constructively. When this happens, the child is forced into some internal reflection. Also, groups sometimes find such a situation spurs incentive to establish greater resolve and identity. The teacher's job is to monitor situations such as these (an easier job than when a 'problem' child has an entire class available to influence) and provide assistance to the group and the child. Again, as in other situations, remedy should be sought that offers learning opportunities for both the group in dealing with difficulties, and the child whose relationship skills appear limited.

As members of society most people are in groups of some sort. It is through shared responsibility and intelligent engagement that society and the individual grow. Responsibility for the social relationship is not entirely assumed either by the individual or society. Therefore, in school, it is a mistake, I believe, for teachers to ignore the opportunity for growth, inherent in bringing children together while simultaneously assuming all responsibility for behaviours and outcomes. While not intended, children can be left feeling that their sense of responsibility is incidental. This does neither the children, teachers, the school, or society a favour.

In Ryan's case, group process combined with visiting rights proved effective.

## Additional thoughts on grouping children

1. <u>Group rights:</u>
   <u>Guiding groups to more effective functioning</u>

Occasionally, groups may need extra discussion on what type of individual contributions help make a good group, enabling children to effectively examine what makes a group work well together. However, in my experience, the need is rare and, therefore, should not be used unless you have a class that, after some practice, seem unable to function constructively in groups. Usually, as children start to become more familiar with the Four Communities Classroom process, good group practice evolves. This needs time. The teacher needs to monitor the ups and downs of progress, and only involve children in discussion of what constitutes satisfactory group process if development stalls.

Most groups of children will likely not only manage well enough, but continually hone their group skills, through practice.

But if your class is not making progress in group process, sit the children in their **group discussion circles**, likely insisting on talking stick leader process (see p. 53 for details), and pose the question, written on the chalk board:

*'What rights do you need in your group to help your group work well together?'*

As you did in your original classroom rights discussions, ask the recorder to list their group's thoughts and ideas. Perhaps allow five or ten minutes, and, because your class has demonstrated poor group skills, move around the groups constantly, offering comments to maintain focus and awarding points for effective discussion process.

Also, using the same format as for classroom rights: (chap. 2, pp. 92 - 104)

- have groups highlight their five most important group rights.
- through a plenary session, produce a list of the children's group rights on the chalk board.

- add to the list if children think something important should be included.
- refine the list by having class discussion on each right.
- ask children to review their refined list to see if they, personally, like the rights. If there are no objections, then ask, "Who created these rights?" This establishes, clearly, the children's ownership.
- have children create a wall display of the rights they have chosen and discussed.

The display of group rights is important, it becomes a reminder for all children of the behaviours necessary for effective group function. In groups that don't function well, there are often children who blame others. A child demonstrating behaviours consistent with group rights can legitimately avoid blame, with an expectation of a better effort from others.

2. <u>Opportunities for children to visit other groups</u>

As much as you may try, it is impossible to arrange group membership to suit everyone all the time. In a class of thirty children, divided into four groups, there are in excess of a billion possible group combinations. Most children, therefore, find themselves in groups that include friends, people who aren't particularly friends, and, maybe people they don't get along with - a bit like the adult world of work. Many children accept their group situation, but if the phrase, "I want to be in the same group as my friend", becomes tedious for you, and your explanation that groups will be changed at Christmas and Easter seems insufficient to some, 'opportunities for children to visit other groups' can act to dispel objections.

Place children's names in a tin, labelling one tin for each group. Every morning and afternoon, have a child - without looking - take a name out of another groups tin. Use tins in numerical order. The child whose name is picked is given the option to sit with a group of his or her choice for the entire morning (or afternoon). Put a check mark on the slip of paper bearing this child's name to show that he or she had an opportunity to visit, and place the name slip back into the group tin. This child will not be able to have the opportunity again, until every name slip in their group has been picked and check-marked.

Points earned by the visiting child go to their home group. Children who disrupt the group they are visiting have their visit cut short. Children love the visiting idea, although not all children want to visit another group and will pass when their name is called. This is perfectly O.K. When this happens, pull out another name slip to give the visiting opportunity that morning or afternoon to another child.

3. <u>Your role as a member of each group</u>

Groups are encouraged to create their own identity, one which reflects its membership. The teacher's connection with each of the groups is a point of reference for them on 'How are we doing?' Important feedback comes from the moment to moment interactions of each day. The awarding of points is also a form of feedback. Connection through feedback makes the teacher a focal point for all four groups. Thus, the teacher is, in a sense, a de facto member of each group, although the relationship with the group is, of course, different from that of the child group member. The child's membership, unlike the teacher's, involves development of sense of self and the feeling of belonging inherent in group identity.

The teacher's membership need not necessarily be a stated one or even one children are aware of. If you choose, you can make it more an invisible guiding hand that communes with groups as needed.

Sterling, S., 2001, p. 83.
*"(teacher's should) embrace leadership that designs for and nurtures participation, co-creation, healthy emergence, and self-organization."*

For groups, the teacher is the foundation from which explorations are made into group process development and curriculum acquisition. I found that, on occasion, groups enjoyed the novelty of my drawing up a chair to sit with them for a moment; short enough and infrequent enough for novelty, but not long enough to impinge upon their group dynamics. Sensitivity to children's response is key. (See 'The teacher as a group member', p. 40.

*Vanessa, grade eight, recalling grade five.*

**"You were like a mayor who came round to each neighbourhood and said, What can we do to make it better? You helped us help ourselves."**

4. <u>The pre-arranged single group meetings with the teacher</u>

You may wish to consider pre-arranged meetings with, perhaps, one group per week, after school or during lunch for 15 to 20 minutes, for an informal chat on whatever topic arises. In this way, you would meet once with each group, over a four week period.

Meetings can be a light hearted exchange of views and thoughts; a point of connection between you and the children. The opportunity to relate to you in their group setting, where children are most practiced in relationship with others, can be very affirming for children. This presents an opportunity for children to connect with you more closely than they could in the wider class environment. Children's fellow group members are able to observe your affirmation. The teacher becomes, in effect, a role model for children in how to relate to and perceive other children.

5. <u>The impromptu single group meeting with the teacher</u>

You can also meet on an impromptu basis, whenever needed. (See p. 218 for a case study - 'The recess impromptu single group meeting with the teacher' - (this time with group 4)'. Impromptu meetings can be a forum for airing problems, irritants or concerns and offering guided discussion to help the group and its individuals to resolution.

Sterling, S., 2001, p. 88.
*"... develop an inclusive (teaching/learning) model where everybody feels valued and able to make a difference, the educational benefits ... will be enormous."*

# CHAPTER FIVE

## THE FOUR COMMUNITIES CLASSROOM: ACCOMMODATING DIFFERENT AGE GROUPS

*The basic premise of the Four Communities Classroom remains the same, regardless of the age of children. Community, communication and relationship are fundamentals of life. But, as in all communities, interaction is shaped by its participants. Thus, classes made up entirely of grade 2's, or grade 3's, will create and live their classroom community life differently from children in grade 5, which will differ from grade 6, and so on. The personalities in a classroom, also, of course, have a bearing, making one grade three class, for example, different from another. It is these different personalities, brought together for a year to create a community unique to them, that makes each year different and interesting.*

*However, differences in age and maturity of children do affect the way in which the Four Communities Classroom is introduced and how it evolves.*

*To help teachers get started, I offer some suggestions for shaping the introduction of the Four Communities Classroom at different grade levels. Thus, the following information is an adjunct to the main text in chapter two, and should be used in combination.*

## Grades Two and Three

In grade two (of course, only just out of grade one), many children may be unsure of what is expected of them, including how to relate to others in the group setting. An understanding of the concept of community is unlikely in very early childhood, and, therefore, children may need a lot of guidance and practice in becoming confident with the culture of the classroom. You may wish, over the first month, to get to know the children before assigning them groups and introducing the Four Communities Classroom. Or you may prefer to put the children only into groups initially and introduce later the various elements slowly, over time, giving due regard to practice and growing familiarity.

Grade three children are usually mature enough to start the Four Communities Classroom process immediately.

### Section 1 - Elements from 'Developing the Four Communities Classroom' modified for Grade 2 and 3 (see p. 33)

Elements numbered 2 and 3 can be merged concurrently:

**2. Asking THE foundational question.**

Very young children respond well to the foundational question. They know why they are in school. Establishing the importance of good teaching and good learning as a mainstay of your classroom is readily achieved.

**3. Towards good teaching and learning**

Couching questions in open-ended terms (as on p. 35) may not be specific enough for very young children. They are, however, able to put thought into what would be the best environment in which to learn, such as being quiet when the teacher is talking and even being quiet when someone is speaking in class, so that we can all hear. Also, "does arguing help you to learn?" This may be all you would do, especially with grade two children.

**4. Groups**.

Tell the children that we have groups because you think it would help with learning. Explain how everyone can have a job to help their group work really well, just like people have jobs to help their community. (Children like jobs. It makes them feel they can make an important contribution. A sense of purpose is good for children's self esteem, as it is, of course, for all people. Start discussion by asking questions such as, "Can anyone tell me what a community is?" (People grouped together.) And, "What jobs do people have in the community to make the community work?" Jobs discussed, (and you may find yourself contributing to these), may include mailman, policeman, teacher, shopkeeper, street cleaner, reporter, doctor, caretaker, etc..

And you say, "Our groups are like communities, because we are people grouped together, and we could have jobs that need to be done to help our group."

When giving jobs to children, you can discuss the group community needs, and relate them to the outside community. For example, mailman may equate with the book collector's job of passing sheets of paper; reporter equals the recorder; policeman equals the talking stick leader, because he/she keeps order during discussion; street cleaning is everyone's job, and translates to keeping the floor clean, and we can all be caretakers by keeping our desks tidy. You may not find parallels for all jobs, but the idea is that all communities need people to do jobs, and our classroom community groups are the same. "Jobs are needed to make our classroom work well." All jobs are shared in rotation; everyone is included in having responsibility for jobs. Children do not mind doing jobs that don't appeal to them when they know that jobs are rotated.

By asking questions about community, groups and jobs, you have invited children to engage in an inclusive-of-everyone process, that makes them want to participate. Ideas will likely come quickly from the children. Thus, without articulating a purpose for the Four Communities Classroom that small children may have difficulty understanding, you are, instead, engaging children in the formulating and sharing of ideas, and practicing listening to each other; some essential elements of the Four Communities Classroom discussion process already underway. The greater logic for young children is that the groups enable fairness in job sharing. You should also mention the fact that if it appears that some children are not getting along very well you may have to move people to different groups.

**5. How we have classroom areas for each group to care for, use, organize, and decorate for classroom life and learning.**

Young children will need guidance. Have specific structures and expectations of how you see children functioning in their group corners. Don't leave it open-ended for children to deal with. You may want to create specific tasks that signpost children, and/or arrange for adult help for each group. This would be a good time to invite parents into your classroom. Or you may want to recruit the help of teacher aides or, perhaps, older students, to guide children in decorating their corner. Let children list their needs and what they want their corner to look like. You may decide to let children choose two or three group colours, perhaps with a mini-lesson on complementary colours and hues. By combining help with children's input, children are better able to get in tune with what it takes to effectively discuss, agree, plan, and execute the decoration of their corners. This example in the guidance and practice needed for young children to become confident with the culture of their community classroom can be extended to include other group activities. Such interactions will become important to children in their learning in the Four Communities Classroom.

**6. Points**.

Young children like big numbers. Earning 2 or 3 points at a time won't seem impressive. You may wish to give points in multiples of three, or five, perhaps saying, "You can have two lots of 3 points, or three lots of 5 points, if your group can tell me what that adds up to." Or at other times, just give points out. Points are seen by children as awards, validating constructive behaviour. Scores, totalled at the end of the day, enable groups to monitor how they are doing. Interest will be high. Keep an eye on point totals, so that no group falls so far behind that they lose interest. Every group must feel that it has a chance at being as good as the next. This, of course, underlines the importance of choosing group membership carefully, to ensure point-earning potential is reasonably even, as it can sometimes be difficult to award children who find themselves in a fractious group. Also, very importantly, the awarding of points must take into account individual limitations, so that a less able child can still earn points and feel good about doing so. Feelings of acceptance can come through a child's point contribution to the group. Scores that reach a certain agreed upon number trigger prizes for a group. Prizes can be very inexpensive; age-appropriate and popular are novelty store items such as stickers, little cars, bracelets, book marks, decorated pencils, erasers.

**7. Discussion.**

Children will already be aware of the fact that you have involved them in discussion. You can highlight how discussion has been helpful by asking, "What things have we decided by discussing our ideas together?" And you can say, "You have been so good at thinking carefully and talking about your ideas, that I think that there may be other times where we'll decide what we will do by discussing." "We could have group discussions to decide, for example, what name you would like to pick for your group" This, of course, creates the need for talking stick leaders, and recorders. Your adult helper can assist children in learning how those jobs are done, and how the others in each group are expected to interact with the children who have these jobs. A teacher of a grade 2/3 split, found that very young children benefited from routine. For group discussion, children were required to sit on the floor within their circle of desks, as the older children do, but with their knees touching, and in the same order as they sat in their desks. The routine prevented time wasted with children jumping up to sit elsewhere in the circle and even outside the circle. Young children seem to really like routine and also the sense of order provided by the talking stick leader in keeping discussion organized, and giving everyone a fair chance to contribute. A foundation of this sort, so embraced by young children, is, of course, significant in establishing a strong sense of self in relationship with others.

You could have practice discussions, encouraging the sharing of thoughts and reasons, in groups and with the class as a whole, on various topics; perhaps, favourite food, favourite television show, what they liked about grade one (the previous grade), favourite time of the year, etc..

**8. Group names**.

Again, provide parameters for young children. Pick one theme or category, of equal appeal to boys and girls, e.g. birds, jungle animals, prairie or savanna animals, oceanic creatures, etc.. Have children decide on group names, within your chosen theme, perhaps with the use of adjectives, such as the Flying Cardinals, the Proud Lions, etc..

**9. Group jobs.** See the previous page - **4. Groups.**

**10. The purpose of numbering students, work in/out trays, work record keeping**.

All of these elements work well with young children. The numbering of students makes classroom organization easier, as you not only have the structure of the groupings, but a system of organizing across groups. For example, instructions like, "All children who are number one do this, all with number two do that, all with number three get their coats on, all with number four go to the chalk board, all with number five do art, etc. Also being fair, so important to children, is easier when assigning those jobs that crop up only occasionally. Instead of trying to remember who hasn't had a turn yet, just keep track of the fact that it's the turn, now, of all the number fours, and you can rotate these jobs group by group. You seldom get challenged with 'it's not fair he/she did it last time', or 'how come it's always group three who get all the extra jobs?' The system is not only seen as fair, it's defensible, contributing to children's contentment with the classroom culture.

The work in/out trays are part of the book collector job. With the carrying of paper back and forth, this job, of course, can be readily understood and carried out by all age groups.

Work record keeping is the teacher's, job and, of course, is not affected by the age of your class.

## Section 2 - Elements from, 'Developing the Four Communities Classroom - Discussion Forums' modified for grade 2 and 3 (see p. 71)

### 11. Classroom Rights

The concept of classroom rights is introduced through three activities - (A) The Balloon Rights Activity, (B) Human Rights/Needs Activity, and (C) Classroom Rights Activity. These activities will be a challenge for very small children, requiring them to mentally juggle, and discuss complex concepts. To enable youngsters to feel comfortable and make progress, the activities have to be modified.

### (A) The balloon rights activity

(From a modification by grade two and three teacher Marie Gaudet, Saskatoon, Saskatchewan, Canada.)

Give children seven of the ten rights. It is less to concentrate on.

I suggest the following:

The right to my own bedroom
The right to clean air
The right to an allowance
The right to love and affection
The right not to be bossed around
The right to food and water
The right to time for play

Make photocopies of '**The balloon ride for grade 2 and 3 children**', p. 190, for each child, with the seven balloons carrying the 'rights' messages. Tell the story of each child riding in a hot air balloon kept aloft by throwing out weights which are also rights. See p. 125 for more information. Hand out the photocopied sheets and ask children to cut out the balloons, read each balloon right, and put their name on the back.

- Individual Ranking (the first balloon ride)

Say to children, "Look at all the balloons, decide which balloon right you would throw out first, because it is least important, and put it at the top of your desk. Then choose which balloon right you would throw out second and place that underneath the first balloon." Continue directions, until children understand the ranking process, and are able, according to their own thoughts on priorities, to have their seven balloons arranged in a ranked column. If children change their minds during this selection process, they can readily move their balloons into a different order. When children are sure that they are satisfied with their choices, they can number the balloons from one to seven. Number one will be placed on the least important balloon right, thrown out first, and seven on the last, which they consider to be the most important balloon right. The balloon has 'landed' when the rights have been ranked.

- Ranking in Pairs (the second balloon ride)

Have each child partner with another, and lay out their balloons in their ranked order, for each other to see. Children explain to each other why they made their choices. They then imagine they are on a balloon ride together. Since children are sharing this ride, they will now have to agree on which right they will throw out first, second, etc. Once a balloon right is discussed and ranked, one child's balloon is discarded, while the shared balloon, equally owned by both children, is put into its place in a new ranked column. Again, while the two children are making their selections, the order of the shared balloons can be readily changed. When both children are in agreement, they re-number the balloons from one (least important) to seven (most important).

- Ranking in Two Pairs (the third balloon ride)

Children now group together in two pairs of two, and lay their balloons out for the other pair to see, giving reasons for their ordering of the balloon rights. In this, their third and final balloon ride, children will now decide, as a group of four, the order in which to place their shared balloons. Again, one set of balloons will be discarded, and the shared balloons, equally owned by all four children, will be arranged, through group consensus, in order of importance in a ranked column. Although the process achieves the object of ranking rights according to children's sense of their importance, the children's focus is on the balloon ride and having to keep the balloon aloft by, one by one, throwing out rights that they feel they can most do without. The story line (on page 125) is important, as it maintains interest and fun. The story, therefore, should remain the basis of your communication to children on this activity. When groups "have landed their balloon" with all rights ranked, leaving their most important right not thrown away, groups number again each balloon right - with a one that the group first discarded and a seven for the right the group decided to land with.

With four children sharing their thoughts there will likely be much discussion. As balloons land, you may wish to keep the class appraised, "We now have three groups that have safely landed their balloon." This announcement will often hurry along slower or more argumentative balloon riders.

- Plenary discussion

Please read page 76 to guide the plenary discussion. However, with young children, focus on simplicity and brevity - achieve the desired outcome while interest and attention levels remain high.

Perhaps briefly hear from children in each balloon group their impressions of the ride, and, combining this with your observations of each balloon group's process, impart to children some important awarenesses about getting along with others. Or, simply wrap up the activity with your observations. Be non-judgmental so that children don't feel criticized. You may decide that the most appropriate tone is a lighthearted one. You may wish to use some of the following points to focus children's attention.

1. If you don't speak up, decisions may be made that you don't like or agree with.

2. If you don't speak up, you only have yourself to blame if you don't like what's happening.

3. If you don't listen to other children's ideas, they may not want to listen to your ideas.

4. If you don't listen to everyone, you may miss out on some good ideas and thoughts of others.

5. The groups who vote fairly make the best progress.

6. In your community groups, you will be making decisions perhaps daily or weekly. What you have learned today about talking and listening to each other can help you to make your group the best that it can be. That will help your group to earn the most points.

The purpose here is to highlight some effective group process foundations; awarenesses that children can take to their community groups.

(B) Human rights/needs activity

- Reading the true story of hardship

The story I read is from Helene Tremblay's book, 'Families of the World' (see page 82 for more details) It is written at a grade eight level, and, therefore, language and extent of detail will need to be modified for grade 2 and 3. You may choose to use other true stories that will enable children to consider what is missing in some people's lives, and the rights they need, to live properly.

- Group discussion on human rights

After hearing the story, it should not be difficult for young children to make a list of what people should have to live properly. But they may have difficulty understanding the difference between 'needs' and 'wants'. This will not necessarily present problems, since you will be asking the children to underline four or five of the most important rights that they listed. This may eliminate 'wants' without having to explain the difference. However, it is not necessary to ensure accuracy in this endeavour. The point is children will have a chance to reflect on families more needy than themselves, and be made aware of the needs of others. Also, they will be introduced to the process of group/class discussion needed for the classroom rights activity and important to building the Four Communities Classroom.

- Class discussion to refine and rationalize the listed outcomes from group discussion

The process outlined in the main text should be modified to reduce the amount of time required in order to maintain young children's attention span and interest. You can still go around the groups, asking each for an item from their list of rights that everyone should have. However, after each item, ask if other groups have thought of the same thing, even if they may have said it differently, and invite further thoughts. Young children can get sidetracked, but this consultation process with each group will offer an opportunity for children to practice staying on the topic and maintaining focus. Summarizing relevant contributions, at various junctures, helps in this process. However, in the interests of expedition, every item does not need to be explored, especially those that seem straightforward. Thus you produce, with children's input, a list of rights on the chalk board. Be sure to thank children for their contributions and congratulate them on thinking of so many rights that people should have.

- U.N. Declaration on the Rights of the Child

As the wording and concepts are complex, you may choose not to bring the U.N. Declaration on the Rights of the Child to the attention of grade two and three children. Any reference should be kept brief, with perhaps the indication that adults have created a list of rights for children and they would be very impressed with the list you have made.

(C) Classroom rights activity

- Group discussion on classroom rights

Children need to be given a focus for classroom rights. The need for rights has to be linked to why children come to school. When you asked THE foundational question, children agreed on what school is for - for good teaching and learning. They also now know about the importance of rights for people to live well. It is now a small step to what is needed to learn well. To link these understandings, take your class through a thought process, by asking a series of questions; questions that may, at first, produce more thinking than answers. But that's O.K.

Remind children of what they have agreed upon in discussion - we come to school to learn, and rights are important in making people's lives better.

"So", you wonder, "could rights also help make our life in the classroom better and help us get better teaching and learning?"

Hmm. You'll get children thinking. But to take them where you want them to go, children will likely need more focus, some direction as to what you might be getting at.

"Could we think of any rights, that we could give each other, that would give us better teaching and learning?"

(You may get answers; some that are on course, and perhaps some that are off base. Field them as you go.)

"So, for example, if someone is trying to talk in discussion, but children aren't listening properly, what right could we give the person who is talking?"

"Does that person have a right to be listened to, or is it O.K to just ignore him or her?" "If it was you trying to say something, would you want to be listened to?" Well, yes.

"So. Would it be a good idea, in our classroom, to have the right to be listened to?" Yes.

Give an example.

"Is being listened to a right that, you Barry, could give Mary. Could you listen to Mary?" Yes.

"Is being listened to a right that, you Mary, could give to Barry. Could you listen to Barry?" Yes.

"So you both could give each other the right to be listened to?" Yes.

"Barry gives Mary the right to be listened to, and Mary gives Barry the right to be listened to."

This is a demonstration to the class of how rights are desirable and something that children might want, and that the rights children give each other are reciprocal.

To be sure that the overall concept is understood by all children in the room, you may decide to give more examples of children giving each other the right to be listened to.

You have arrived at this juncture by asking a series of questions that lead and enable children to apply their own thinking to the concept of rights. You are involving them in a process which is predominantly a primary experience.

Thus, you have reinforced the primary experience, with its encouragement and validation of children's thinking, as part of learning in your classroom. Also you have introduced the idea that they are part of each other's learning environment. This leads to an awareness that, instead of, perhaps, unwittingly interfering with other children's life in the classroom, a child can make conscious decisions to make positive contributions, and that other children are empowered with the same choices regarding children around them.

"Now, I'm wondering, are there any other rights that we could give each other that would make life in the classroom better for us?" "I'm thinking that if each group sat on the floor in their discussion circle, we could see if groups could come up with more ideas for classroom rights." "So, we need the recorder to take their pencil and paper to write down people's ideas, and the talking stick leader to make sure everyone has a chance to speak. Now everyone can go and get ready for a group discussion." Adult helpers would be helpful, in this early part of the year, to facilitate group discussion and/or recording.

Emphasize, "Choose classroom rights that we can give someone and they can give us."

As described in the main text, have groups highlight (in preparation for class discussion) their five most important rights.

- Class discussion to refine and rationalize the listed outcomes from group discussion

Again the process outlined in the main text should be modified to reduce the amount of time required and not strain young children's attention span and interest. It should be in line with children's previous class-discussion experience. Thus class discussion should follow the pattern adopted in the human rights activity.

Go around the groups, asking for one item from their list of rights, and ask if other groups have thought of the same thing, even if they may have said it differently, and invite further thoughts. Start creating a list on the chalk board, as ideas for rights are raised and discussed, and summarize relevant contributions as you proceed. In the interests of expedience, every right may not need exploring, especially ones that seem straightforward. You will need, though, to be diligent, to ensure that the list of rights and their implications are fully understood and children can feel ownership. As this may be time consuming, you may have to re-visit this process over a number of days, until it is completed to everyone's satisfaction.

You will be involved in an orchestration of maintaining interest, motivating, building understanding and ownership, keeping children on topic, focusing discussion, making summaries of contributions, and producing a list of rights on the chalk board.

Thank children for their contributions and congratulate them on thinking of important rights for the classroom.

In the main text, it is suggested that children's rights should be declared in art form, creating a collage for display and reference. You may, with grade two and three, prefer a more personal approach for each child. Hand out larger photocopied balloons **(see p. 191, 'Classroom rights for grade 2 and 3 children')**. Draw enough lines on the balloon for each child to personally write each of the rights the class has chosen. Also have a space where each child can sign their balloon, indicating that they are in agreement with the rights. Also, in the 'basket' of the balloon, place a photograph of the child having a nice ride in their balloon. A small school photograph is ideal. Completed balloons are fixed to the wall close to each group. Wherever children look they will be able to see balloons carrying their classroom rights message, for easy reference.

For information on 'Using Classroom Rights', and 'The Importance of Difference', I believe the main text will act as sufficient guide.

'Self-correction' may be a concept that is beyond the understanding of very young children and, in most cases, is not needed, as classroom rights enable most children to constructively advance their concept of self in relationship with others.

*I would like to thank and acknowledge Marie Gaudet for advice on the application of the Four Communities Classroom to the grade two and three classroom.*

## Grades four and five

I think it is fair to say that, in most situations, resistance to change is still, generally, very low in grade four and five children, and most will respond well to the constructive development of relationship and responsibility in the Four Communities Classroom. Also, I believe, most grade four and five classes can be approached from the standpoint outlined in the main text, without modification beyond that required by variations in class character and teacher personality.

However, the U.N Declaration of The Rights of the Child, if not presented with a modification of language, will require a mini-lesson, explaining some of the more complex concepts contained within the list of rights. Differences between grades four and five will likely be most noticeable in the sophistication of discussion. Interestingly, though, much of this difference becomes less obvious in a split 4/5 grade class, when the grades are distributed evenly throughout the groups. Therefore, go straight to the main text, and enjoy your year with your grade four and five children.

## Grades six, seven and eight

The higher the grade, the more likely it is that resistance to change will occur. With each successive grade, children become more acculturated to the familiar, which may include a system of relationship and learning which emphasizes individual over community function. Acculturated in this way, the disruptive child may see no needs beyond his own, perhaps making school days time for on-again, off-again disruptive episodes, and perhaps obliging other students and the teacher to develop systems of coping, rather than connecting.

Some children, especially the disrupters, may not be impressed that you are changing the rules of functioning, just when they may have responses to school 'off to a fine art'. With resistance to change, introducing and establishing the Four Communities Classroom can present more of a challenge for grade six and seven teachers and likely even more for the grade eight teacher. Although it should be said that, in the higher elementary grades, getting 'response to school off to a fine art' doesn't necessarily translate to happy, contented and confident children. Thus, in introducing the Four Communities Classroom, there will be both resistance to change, but also a welcoming of change, especially if it enables the child to more readily make sense of the world. The latter, though, is an awareness that usually comes over time. Conscientiously approached, the Four Communities

Classroom system is likely to afford the teacher an increasingly easier and enjoyable year. Bear in mind that fluctuation is also an ecological dynamic.

Capra, '96, p. 186.
*"...all living systems exist in continually fluctuating environments,..."*

What should be the approach to children in these grades?

Grade six and seven, and especially grade eight children often think that they are close to being grown up. Treat them as grown-ups in your interactions, while at the same time thinking of them as children. This has a positive affect upon children's sense of emotional wellbeing, as they are, in their view, being accorded the level of respect that an adult receives. Meanwhile, you are not setting them adrift to find their own way. When trying to make sense of a world that, as one gets older and more aware, becomes more complex, guidance is vital. Be generous of heart.

You are introducing a new way of perceiving the classroom's learning environment; changes that include encouraging debate, discussion and dialogue between children, with the teacher as facilitator and guide. This is at a time when children are starting to question more and when making sense of the world is becoming more challenging, as a broader range of awarenesses begin to develop. You will, therefore, be challenged. You will be expected to provide defensible perspectives that enable children to develop clarity on issues of self within a broader context; self in relationship with externalities. As an externality of some significance, the teacher becomes an important yardstick in a challenging life journey. You could say that you have come along at the right moment.

The Four Communities Classroom dialogue is more readily orchestrated if your higher grades have already experienced the Four Communities Classroom in previous grades, since the introduction to change will not, of course, be a factor.

If you are as new to the Four Communities Classroom as your class is, then I think it is important to declare to grade six, seven or eight students, right off the bat that, this year, you want to try something new. "It is a system in which student's ideas become an important part of teaching and learning. I thought we could experiment with this to find out if it helps us in the classroom. So I thought it would be a good idea for us to explore this together. And it starts by first moving all the desks. Let me explain." You can then proceed with developing the Four Communities Classroom as outlined in the main text.

This approach is inclusive, and invitational. It is not an imposed directorate and, very importantly, does not put you in the position of having to make things work. It is, instead, a shared responsibility. And, just in case this is somehow interpreted as being able to proceed with a less responsible attitude to work, add, "However, this does not mean that we will do less school work. Curriculum still has to be covered. It is how we proceed that will be different."

There will, then, especially with grade seven and eight students, be a much greater sense of carving out the shape of your Four Communities Classroom as distinct from the younger grades who are generally more pliable and willing to follow the teacher's lead with the thought - If the teacher says this is good, then it must be.

# High School

A few thoughts.

Progress can be made in the high school classroom to constructively engage ecological process. However, high school structures, based upon the North American system, are not conducive to creating the Four Communities Classroom model. As in all of life, ecological dynamics exist in high school, but organizing learning to embrace an ecological sense of community is made difficult by five structural factors, and complicated by student emotionally-based factors.

## Structural factors

1. **Organization of the school day**
   Individual students find themselves in different groupings of students with every class they attend, making the creation of community more difficult.

2. **Organization of the school year**
   With the academic year divided into semesters, there are three end-points and, therefore, three times in the year when any building of classroom community comes to a close.

3. **Organization of curriculum transmission**
   The organization of curriculum transmission affects the school day and, in high school, requires students to pursue, independently, the attainment of each grade. Thus, there is little structural rationale for learning connections to be established between students during the school day.

4. **The huge buildings that house many high schools**
   Travelling independently between classes requires little communication or need for association between students, other than between friends. The small fish in a large pond syndrome tends to be prevalent. One's presence can appear to be immaterial to the school.

5. **High school and the big wide world**
   The next step for high school students is the larger outside-world. This is where one may experience a dwindling sense of local community amid growing globalization pressures, although perhaps offset by social media. Should high schools examine ways to take on a greater leadership role with more emphasis on communication, empowerment and consideration of and practice in what constitutes community and the buiding of confidence?

## Students factors

1. **The long-term acculturation process of schooling.**
   The long-term process of schooling tends to produce in student minds:
   - perceptions of the meaning of education.
     (Perhaps seen in terms of passing/failing and the validation of self within the context of curriculum knowledge acquisition)
   - strategies for staying emotionally safe.
     (For some this may involve emotional detachment from the school's curriculum-centred process. For some, introducing discussion into the classroom [foundational to the Four Communities Classroom] may generate feelings of being exposed to other's criticism and, therefore, may not garner enthusiastic participation.)

2. **The period of adolescence.**
   Adolescence is a period when students:
   - are still developing their frontal cortex (p.265).
     (If this development is taking place in an environment that views curriculum and its transmission as being of primary importance, and emotional development as secondary or even incidental, could this environment affect emotional development, and, in turn, affect frontal cortex development and curriculum learning potential?)
   - may be uncertain about the validity of their inner thoughts.
     (Are students provided forums for the exercise of thinking skills with others and the development and sharing of ideas?)
   - are searching for peer acceptance.
     (Acceptance in any form is a preferred state for most students. Achieved within a community ethos, this could be a powerful and constructive influence for students and school.)

For further thoughts on the teenage years see appendix (v) p. 297, 'The teenage years - pulling away from parental attractors'.

| The right to my own bedroom. | The right to clean air. | The right to an allowance. |

| The right to love and affection. | The right not to be bossed around. | The right to food and water. |

| The right to play. |

**The grade 2 and 3 balloon ride**

See p. 183

---

This page can be photocopied

My Daughter *Can't Wait* for Monday Morning!

# In our classroom we all have the right to:

**The grade 2 and 3 classroom rights balloon**
See p. 186

This page can be photocopied

My Daughter *Can't Wait* for Monday Morning!

# CHAPTER SIX

## CHILDREN IN ACTION - CLASSROOM CASE STUDIES

While the teacher is in charge of the class journey, each child is in charge of his or her own thoughts, arising from what they see, hear and feel. For each child, it is very much a personal journey. Therefore, the teacher must consider throughout each day what the children are going to see and hear to ponder upon, and how they may feel.

As we can see in the mission statement (p. ii), all children in the Four Communities Classroom are engaged in the development of:

- considered thinking processes in relationship with others.
- awareness, at an emotional level, of the importance of reciprocation.
- understanding that difference in thinking is an expression of the individuality of us all.
- understanding that learning is often enhanced through interpersonal communication.
- understanding that our own and others' feelings are part of our communication process, as we grow and learn.

## The child's perspective

What do children know and how, perhaps, will they feel while being introduced to and engaged in these processes?

What children do know is that teachers like them to face the front of the room and pay attention. Children (new to the Four Communities Classroom) are, however, not usually accustomed to listening to each other in the learning process. As a Four Communities Classroom teacher, you are taking children into unfamiliar territory. Much will happen. Development will include the building of processes of relationship, reciprocation and mutual regard, and the accompanying development of neuronal connections in the brain [appendix (iii) pp. 276 - 286].

This will be challenging for the children, as new patterns of organisation and ways of making sense of the world are presented for consideration. Children's presence means awareness and awareness means involvement. The events of your Four Communities Classroom are now happening in their world.

- **Positive curiosity**

As we are all ecologically disposed to relate and react to our externalities, many children's involvement will be positive and approached with a sense of anticipation and curiosity.

- **Positiveness on hold**

Sometimes, however, involvement can be negative. This may be displayed in grudging, and/or passive behaviours likely a child's established self-defence strategy against already formed attitudes to 'school stuff'. The child has prejudged and has 'decided' not to like anything on offer. In such cases, you are seeing a state of mind that has started to lose capacity to mutually regard externalities, and, therefore, is losing capacity to maximise learning potential. Do not let children who appear to be in this state of mind deter you. It is for such children that the Four Communities Classroom is particularly important. Patience, understanding and a new environment that is ecologically balanced can usually, in time, enable all children to do better. Take encouragement from children who appear more ready to be constructive, and move the class forward through their involvement, and be patient with children who are finding their way.

- **Children's life experience**

Children's life experience, in and out of the classroom, will influence their response to their world. This life experience will influence relationship processes, involving perceptions, feelings and self-esteem, and their sense of place within their world, including the Four Communities Classroom.

For many children it will be an experimental journey of hesitancy and tentativeness prompted by not wishing to feel exposed in new and unknown territory. Alongside, there will be weighing up, and trial and error participation as private thoughts abound, some of which may be shared in class discussion.

- **Tentativeness precedes steps forward**

Tentativeness precedes steps forward, especially in the cautious and/or considered thinker. This is why the teacher does not insist that any individual child make a verbal contribution at any time. It is sufficient to know that thoughts are always occurring, so learning is occurring. A child will verbalise thoughts and ideas when he/she feels comfortable. The teacher will gain some insight on development processes occurring as children reach a comfort level for them where they choose and share their thoughts and ideas. However, some children learn much from just listening - secure and happy in their particular comfort zone. Interestingly, one of my more silent class members said, in later years, of his Four Communities Classroom experience, 'I liked the discussions we had best'. His subsequent successes over his school career indicate that, likely, much constructive thinking was occurring in his unspoken thoughts.

Throughout this process, children will be engaged in tentative monitoring mode (how do I feel?) and monitoring others; deciding, moment to moment, at what level to participate.

- Is this a safe thing to do?
- Will I be O.K?
- How did the other kid fare when he/she ventured to say something?
- What was the teacher's response?
- What did I think of the teacher's response?
- Was it safe for that kid?
- Maybe I'll dip my little toe into the water and see what I feel like.

Feelings are an important part of these responses and are, for many children, important 'look after myself' questions that need primary consideration. Most of us tend to monitor our feelings, in relationship to what is happening around us.

## Four Communities Classroom case studies

These following case studies, originating from different schools, classrooms and grades that I was invited in to, I believe, will serve to illustrate how mind processes are engaged, and the way in which children tend to use Four Communities Classroom tools in the shaping and development of both classroom life and their personal potential.

### Introducing the Four Communities Classroom to a grade 6 class. The story of Matt - the boy who couldn't be bothered to try

Matt appears to have lost interest. He couldn't care less. He can't be bothered to offer an opinion or to vote and, although he appears unhappy, he seems, more than anything, to have given up. Perhaps classroom experiences, generally, have left him cold and feeling 'why bother?' His face is hangdog; probably an outward expression of his state of mind. With his thinking curtailed, by, it seems, conclusions and closures, he isn't expecting much; anticipation abandoned, a narrowly-conceived attractor [appendix (i)] firmly in place.

But Matt can't stop hearing and he can't stop his thought processes and, although his mind is using a negative filter, is it possible that what he is hearing about the Four Communities Classroom and the thoughts being generated could overwhelm his apparent resignation? No one knows. But there is a chance that positive primary environments will penetrate his apparent negative outlook. All a teacher can do is start the Four Communities Classroom process, hope and watch. Any reassessment of Matt's view of the classroom will be his process. The teacher is the provider of the ecological classroom environment, while Matt, alone, is privy to his own thoughts and evolving possibilities (the inner dialogue).

One day, Matt puts his hand up! Will he make a comment, or ask a question; will this be a positive contribution? His hand is up, you can't let this opportunity slip. With no special fanfare, you just say, "Yes Matt?" And out it comes; an intelligent well thought-out contribution. Can you believe your ears? Yes!

Is this the turn around? It is not always that fast, but it is the sort of start that bodes well for a turn around. It represents hope. Any turn around could well be a transitional affair, with backward and forward moves, and it will be with Matt holding the cards. The teacher's job is to to continue to offer Matt a primary experience environment that hopefully continues to resonate and provide the beginnings of hope so that Matt will extend his stay at the table of participation. Without it appearing evident, the teacher stays alert and sensitive to Matt. It's an arms-length caring that does not put any spotlight on Matt that may cause him to retreat from this try. It is a first step, and Matt might venture now to explore further.

Matt's contribution was on classroom rights and the question of the right to be different. The class had already been discussing for some time the efficacy of the various rights that the groups had proposed and which I had recorded on the chalkboard. Rights were discussed in random order, according to which child's waving hand I pointed to, and not many rights were left to consider. We had just agreed on one right and were ready to discuss another. It was at this point that Matt decided to put up his hand for the first time. He proposed that the right to be different is important, as it encourages recognition of people as individuals. Having just turned eleven years old, he didn't put it quite like that, but he did support his statement by saying that if everyone were the same it wouldn't work, and gave an example. He was clear and to the point. Immediately, hands went up, and child after child argued for Matt's view, with just a few children offering alternative thoughts. The topic quickly came to a vote, and the children established Matt's thought 'the right to be different' as a classroom right.

What could be better?

Up to this point, Matt had been silent, deciding not even to vote on anything. When questioned on not voting, he had said he didn't care about having these rights for himself. With seeming intransigence he was not prepared to shift from his position, even in a participatory atmosphere of sharing. But he was, however, listening and thinking and, as something was apparently (finally) making sense in his mind, he slowly opened it. Maybe, he thought, this could be O.K. Perhaps we can suppose that his mind had started to see validity in what was going on around him.

At this point, I would speculate, Matt had decided to give the rights some consideration and that the right to be different was actually important to him. Further, he decided to announce his thoughts in class; likely a big step for him. He formulated his argument and presented his case with clarity. These are all higher-order thoughts that he engaged in, of his own free will. And this is very important, because if I had pushed for this to occur, I probably would have, at best, achieved nothing, and at worst generated resolve to resist, and deepened negativity. By engaging in his own private thoughts (in response to his changing environment), and then deeming it safe to voice those thoughts, Matt had, in fact, of his own volition, moved to a different state that offered more promise for learning. Private thought in response to externalities, leading to behavioural change is an important part of children's personal journeys.

Thus, perhaps, we can say that new patterns of organisation and ways of making sense of the world began occurring to Matt, and that his experience felt good. Feeling good goes a long way towards bringing about positive change. It is a process, and process requires time. The amount of time will vary from child to child. Many factors will decide the course of Matt's journey, not the least of which will be the results he experiences from further efforts and teacher/class reactions. This is a crucial point for both Matt and his teacher. But, what next? Maintaining the Four Communities Classroom structure with its enabling interactive classroom atmosphere, is a vital role for the teacher, and especially important for children like Matt.

---

## Introducing the Four Communities Classroom to another grade 6 class. The story of Joe who prefers diversions over learning

Joe appears resentful, angry, intelligent, aimless and bored; a child who sees see little purpose in being in the classroom. He engages in half-hearted efforts that he usually scuppers so that they do not develop constructively. He quite likes the idea of amusement at others' expense, but with no great commitment to this endeavour. Commitment to anything, positive or negative, isn't high on his agenda, and he generally seems unhappy.

First event. Day one. Joe volunteers for a job; but, through careless application, fails to perform it adequately. Perhaps the job offered some diversionary appeal, the novelty of which soon wore off. It would have been all right if half an effort could have been sufficient. 'Who cares?' shows on his face.

Second event. Day two. Joe makes two or three contributions to class discussion that are purposely trite and dismissive. He appears to want to indicate to the class his assessment that this whole enterprise is of little value, and why would they want to be part of it anyway? This backfires, because the rest of the class feels good about what is happening, and any power Joe has is not enough to negate that; the class disregards him. Perhaps he hoped there would be some amusement value in causing this initiative to fail. Who knows what power and control outcomes might arise from that? That's one attempt where he would have relished success. Now what? Time will tell. But at the end of class Joe wants me to notice his cash contribution in the collection box for the Terry Fox Charity Run. Interesting hmm?

Perhaps new patterns of organisation and ways of making sense of the world are already occurring to Joe, and he is realizing that they feel good. Feeling good goes a long way towards bringing about positive change. It is a process, and process requires time. The amount of time will vary from child to child. It is a personal journey.

---

## Moving forward with bullies - the story of Jason

### A mid-year case study;
### Meeting a teacher's request to change a traditional grade 5 classroom to a Four Communites Classroom

Jason sits at his desk with an appearance reminiscent of a mafia don, looking as though he is deciding, minute by minute, how and when to use his unchallengeable control. He is 10 years old and big for his age. Having disrupted the class, he will listen to the teacher's reprimand, but teacher-correction has short-term effect, creating a short period of hibernation before he stirs again. The rest of the class knows this, of course, and, given this uncertain respite from Jason's intrusions, serious curriculum learning effort is difficult to maintain. Thus, the children, even the better behaved, are not working well, and the teacher is feeling worn down; enthusiasm increasingly difficult to muster. And, of course, Jason has his coterie of followers, who are given his permission not to apply themselves to work in any serious manner. Some are a bit scared of Jason and find joining is the easier option, while others appear to think Jason's regime is quite amusing. The latter constitute a form of inner circle.

What does the teacher have to offer that is better and more interesting to Jason than this nice little situation that he's managed to carve out for himself? Appeals to fairness, consideration for others, that doing well in school is best for him in the long run, or threats of various types (e.g. loss of privilege, can't go on the field trip, detention, bring in your parents, etc.) may cause concern for many children, but Jason is one of those exceptions. In Jason's mind, the immediacy of daily control appears to outweigh other considerations, even if, for awhile, he seems convinced to behave more appropriately. So ensues a cycle of hope raised and then eroded, which is wearing for all. Meanwhile, in a classroom where children are generally more dispirited by than approving of Jason's antics, Jason's control provides him a questionable high. But having established a reputation, he feels compelled to maintain it. He has created a behaviour trap for himself that is hard to break. With his sense of well-being options limited, and increasingly less satisfying, Jason moves on to more continuous and heightened control devices. The primary one he holds over class members is the threat of bullying; verbal, physical and implied.

This year survived (not enjoyed), does not necessarily mean the end of problems. Long-term prospects for Jason's education, and intelligent development of his mental capacities, are left in a questionable light. Likely, future behaviours will be founded on the ones Jason has established in early years, with self-identity further coalescing into a negative form. This, of course, would translate into an uneasy school career, and possible problems in adulthood. Children sharing future classes with Jason may find themselves, as this years class did, trying to develop their learning capacities, while coping with additional burdens; not a good learning environment.

It is this type of situation that can cause teachers to ask, 'Why do I have to spend 90% of my time with 10% of the kids?' This is not a good thought for parents, if their child is part of the remaining 90% of children receiving 10% of the teacher's time and energy. And with the administration's curriculum imperative thus compromised, the teacher's stress levels rise.

There are not many happy people here. The joy of learning, and teaching, has fallen away.

Is there a way forward for Jason or for the other children who may find themselves in the same class, the same school, the same education system. Is there a way forward for the principal, and the teacher? The short answer is yes, and it lies within Jason. But the teacher is key. The conditions have to be right for the effective function of self and others.

Creating the right conditions, therefore, is key, and it is the teacher's job to provide those conditions. For Jason, new patterns of organisation and ways of making sense of the world not only need to occur to him, but also need to encourage him with feelings that are more satisfying and rewarding than those created through his current actions. The classroom environment has to be such that this new awareness is self-generated by Jason; with change feeling good.

Since change is a process, it requires time. The process will be Jason's personal journey; prediction of outcome impossible, but hope high, with ecologically sound principles in play; providing room and scope for living system dynamics such as emotion, self correction, mutual regard processes; all constructively re-engaging with Jason's already-existing ecological foundation. (See appendices.)

The teacher provides this supportive classroom environment; the framework for learning to build constructive relationships. It is this learning that will bring Jason to many points of decision. Now, as he decides how to act or respond he will have an opportunity to make sense of his decisions through the filter of mutual regard process. This may take some time. It will demand patience on the part of every stakeholder. Jason will certainly need help and classroom support to undertake change.

NOTE. The following should be used in the Four Communities Classroom context only. In isolation, it will not work properly.

**Two keys**

The first key to releasing Jason and the rest of the class from a cycle of bullying is a classroom discussion, which will focus on the importance of being different. There is no reason why the children should not be involved in seeking resolution to this major problem of Jason's bullying, as they would with any other problem the class may have.

**Problem or Opportunity?**

Thus:
- The first key, in the Four Communities Classroom, is class discussion - (a *primary experience*) see p. 51- class and group discussion. Also see appendix (iii) p. 278 - primary experience.
- The specific key is the discussion of 'The Importance of Difference', *(the particular primary experience)* See p. 110.

Enabling children to understand the importance of difference is an essential part of building the Four Communities Classroom, mutual-regard-relationship environment. When mutual-regard relationships begin to develop, it becomes increasingly difficult for bullies to function.

**Three links**

Thus the teacher is engaged in forming links between:
1. Importance of difference
2. Building of mutual regard relationship
3. Creation of an environment difficult for the bully to function in

These links provide the teacher with a powerful tool to confront the problem of bullying, and a tool that also becomes the children's. This is vital if the children are to perform their pivotal role in working towards solution.

In being fully engaged as members of the class discussion they are part of what is going on. This is not a session where children are sitting and listening to the teacher.

Before proceeding, let's look at the methodology of the 'teacher talk/children listen' approach.

- **The secondary experience classroom response to bullying**

The teacher's 'speech' response, although obviously indicating great concern is, for the children, a secondary experience.

Regardless of how much sense and wisdom the teacher speaks, and regardless of how well argued and presented, convincing a bully to take responsibility and ownership for the problem and then decide to change, will likely be uphill work. The teacher's speeches may leave the children with some hope, but not empowerment to effect change. The children who watch bullying taking place in their classroom, among their peers, are the ones, potentially, with the most influence with bullies.

Bullying impacts children's everyday lives.

Thus, for them, bullying is a primary experience. The secondary-experience talk provided by the teacher enables little development of control of the situation by the children.

Each child's process of interpretation of the teacher-supplied, secondary-experience talk is isolated from others; each child is left with his or her own thoughts and decisions on the subject, knowing that, above all, they don't want to invite the bullying from which no-one is immune. The private thoughts engendered by the children receiving information carry little or no weight in the realization of a solution, unless they can engage in a primary experience discussion forum where consensus can lead to shared thoughts and group empowerment. Without this, although the bullying is of great concern to all, substantial change is unlikely.

- **The primary experience classroom response to bullying**

So let's take a look at what constitutes effective/positive change process. To be constructive, change and learning has to take place through consideration of relationships with externalities; a process, in its most sustainable form, distilled in the words 'mutual regard'. And the avenue to mutual regard is participation which is a primary experience.

Discussion is a participatory primary experience. It is not an orchestration of a situation but a spontaneous evocation of children's thoughts, ideas and emotional response to a situation. Of course, this does not mean that the teacher does not have a hand in initiating and facilitating discussion, with some agenda attached. But the children quite readily recognize the teacher's role in the discussion process and still appreciate the spontaneity and opportunity the discussion affords. They are, after all, putting up their hands of their own volition and making contributions of their own volition; they are listening to each other, thinking and responding; they and you are building understanding and consensus; they are taking ownership. And, very importantly, children know that they are part of a shared process, since when they share their thoughts, they also share their feelings.

Thus, each child is involved in a primary experience that will help to minimise thoughts and feelings of isolation from other children's thoughts and feelings. Open and available to each child are comfortable feelings of being part of group understanding, resolve and intent. This is very empowering for the class as a whole and the individuals within it, but disconcerting for the bully, as he starts to see his power dissolving. It is hard to hold a selfish view which is counter to an understanding with firm foundations and that is seen to be shared. Making it harder for the child to function as a bully is, of course, exactly what you and the class want.

- **Back to Jason and our case study**

Back to the situation of bullying and control, in which Jason has invested so much, and the predicament in which this class and teacher find themselves. In order for Jason to take responsibility for his actions, first the teacher has to take responsibility — not for Jason's actions, but for the environment that enables his actions. The teacher's focus, right now, is not on disciplining but on the job of building (both apart from curriculum, and alongside curriculum) constructive identities within children and appreciation of mutual regard; building in children an ability to know and develop self, and participate in relationships with constructive externalities.

This is fundamental to the Four Communities Classroom, of course, but with a child like Jason as a starting point, where do we begin?

Start with some directed, purposeful nuance.

**Firstly:**

Do not provide Jason with any recognition, beyond that of being a class member. Even the slightest disapproving recognition of Jason's disruptive behaviour will serve as fuel to his fire. If, however, it appears to the class that Jason's assumption that he can dominate carries no weight in your eyes, the children will be signalled that Jason's currency of control can be depreciated.

**Secondly:**

Adopt a mindset, whether you are convinced or not, that <u>everyone</u>, without exception, wants the best for themselves and others. This is a foundational thought for the teacher and, usually sooner than later, also that of the children's. This forces Jason, at some point, if not to adopt a positive attitude, to argue for his negativity. A position supported through negative reasoning is very hard to maintain and Jason will find himself confronted with the daunting task of having to justify his position, if not always to you, certainly to himself. Thus a choice is laid out that becomes the basis for his subsequent journey; an isolated endeavour versus community acceptance. It is hard for Jason to avoid pondering which alternative is the most satisfying. It will almost certainly be a two steps forward, one step back process. Don't give up on him. Fruits of success in teaching can sometimes be someone else's to enjoy. However, there is a good chance that it will be you and Jason who get the opportunity to explore a successful relationship.

Thus, with two nuanced starting points tempering everything you do and say, the new reality for you, Jason and the class is about to begin.

Implying, through word and deed, that everyone wants the best for themselves and others, has a powerful effect. If you find yourself in receipt of negative assumptions from a child or children, your perplexed expression, either verbal or facial, will imply the need for explanation. You may even ask for one. Such explanations, if attempted, usually tail off. You continue as if, perhaps, it was just a case of your misunderstanding and the child did not intend to be negative. It leaves the child with the job of making sense of his or her thoughts and motives, while you continue with your two-pronged nuance of positive assumption.

In an atmosphere of positive goodwill, launch the Four Communities Classroom environment as described in chapter two. Through discussion, establish the foundational statement that school is about good teaching and learning. Even Jason is attentive for a while. The set up, classroom layout and discussion is new. Jason likely feels a need to understand it. The rest of the class may be surprised and encouraged by Jason's apparent acceptance of a new regime. The teacher makes no comment, and hopes that this will last. It doesn't. Jason doesn't want to relinquish control. Wanting to signal to all and his coterie in particular, that it will be business as usual, Jason turns to a variety of his disruptive devices to again swing attention and control his way.

The first crucial event is thus precipitated. The class needs you to deal effectively with the challenge. You examine his chosen behaviours, perplexedly, in the light of the Four Communities Classroom foundational statement that school is about good teaching and learning. How is this helping when we are looking to you Jason and others to help us achieve a good teaching and learning environment? There is an implication here that we are looking for leaders who can help. The implication is that you think he fits the bill. Your emphasis is on positive reinforcement suggesting strengths that obviously a fellow like him must have, rather than censorship for what he has done.

The approach chosen for this interaction with Jason can be private (as in taking him to one side and having a quiet conversation) or public, or some combination of both. The need for little reminders and reinforcements should be expected; combinations of whispered or more public communication. Occasionally, perhaps, a knowing glance between you and him can be effected.

Jason may find it too difficult to respond favourably for any reasonable length of time, i.e. time to allow you to make reasonable progress in introducing the Four Communities Classroom to the class, and you may find yourself having to ask him to leave the room. In response to his objections you reply that you would much rather him stay in the room, but he is preventing good teaching and learning from proceeding. Put the onus on him. Whether he can stay is up to him. He'll likely stay, with good behaviour restored – for a while. Then, eventually, you may have to say, "I'm sorry Jason, you are going to have to leave the room".

Your options – (a) leave him outside the room to wonder, for some minutes, what is in store for him. (b) go with him and ask him why he thinks he is out of the room. Or some combination of these options as you see fit. Tell him that he is more than welcome back into the room when he figures he's ready to help good teaching and learning. Ask him what he thinks that means and how he feels he can help. Leave the decision to Jason. He might opt to return to the classroom right away. Verify that he is in fact ready. "Yes", he says. "Good", you say, "I am very happy to hear that." Now the onus is on Jason to prove that he was right when he said he was ready. (Do not say something like, "We'll see", or "I'll be keeping an eye on you." This sends a message that you don't have a lot of faith in him, and that you will, no doubt, be forced to accept some responsibility for any subsequent bad behaviour. Such messages will create resentment and undermine both him and you). Partners in resolution, you and he return to the room on a positive note. If he fails, it's his failure not yours, and he, again, puts himself through another dose of facing responsibility for his own decisions.

- **Requiring Jason to deal with his behaviour and his decisions**

Throughout this process, Jason has not been disciplined as such, but rather has been required to deal with his behaviour and the consequences of his decisions. He has not had the pleasure of observing your annoyance or any other emotion you might feel. Jason must not know how you are feeling and it is not his concern. Don't hand him a control lever to work you with. The consequences of his actions are the way they make him feel, and if he has created feelings he doesn't like, he is the one who has to do something about it. You are not assuming responsibility for his behaviour or his self-created feelings. You are providing an environment where he has little choice but to assume responsibility. Up until now Jason has conducted his school career in a way that has enabled him to dodge responsibility for his choices. It has been quite a ride, letting the teacher deal with the problems he's left in his wake. Enabling Jason to re-engage with responsibility is infinitely more important than any curriculum learning you might achieve with him, and is, in fact, a prerequisite. Thus, engaging with responsibility is vital to Jason, if he is to benefit from engaging in the curriculum effectively and engaging in mutual regard with his externalities - others around him.

- **Problems or opportunities**

Through his disruptive behaviour, Jason has, in fact, given you an opportunity to help him re-engage with responsibility for self. It is helpful and positive to see the problems in your classroom not as difficulties but as fertile ground for learning opportunities. Likely, Jason will be providing you with quite a few opportunities. You have to be ready for them. Keeping nuance in mind, you will, in the environment you provide for Jason to operate in, impart the message, "Responsibility over to you Jason".

And thus you proceed, moving forward in establishing for the class an understanding of how the Four Communities Classroom runs.

Are your bullying problems now a thing of the past? Not likely, but you are on the right track, because the majority of the children in your classroom like what they see and hear, and start to recognise that they are forming a collective will that's likely capable of standing up to Jason. Reluctant followers take their leave of Jason's influence, and even his 'inner circle' starts to waver. The 'inner circle' children often have problems of their own. Jason gave them a place to hide, where they could avoid confronting their problems. Now, with Jason otherwise engaged in a new dynamic, he has little to offer them. They are looking for security and your new classroom atmosphere of mutual regard looks appealing. It could actually be easier and nicer to join this mood of newfound confidence building in the classroom than cling to the vestiges of Jason's waning influence. The individual problems experienced by the 'inner circle' children will likely at this point, become more evident. This will enable the teacher to offer better-targeted attention, empathy and help. Teacher Mrs. Peters, *"Things became more clear and defined as to what various children required."*

As his power and his support slip away, Jason's isolation deepens. He is not happy. Expect resistance from Jason. It is not an easy time for him. You've usurped his reign.

It is important to keep a close eye on Jason, right now, in less supervised situations; in hallways, and at recess. Let other teachers on recess and lunchtime supervision know of the situation you have with Jason, and alert them to the fact that he may use child-play as a cover for bullying, and that some intervention may be required. Perhaps you can avoid such possibilities by finding responsibilities for Jason during some of these times – helping you in preparations for projects, finding books in the library perhaps (alert the librarian), colouring wall displays, etc. Make him feel important and helpful. Intersperse these events for Jason with the inclusion of one or two good kids in an enterprise. These events then become integrative in tone, rather than becoming perceived as spotlighting a problem kid. Be sure to maintain communication with these helping groups as they proceed. To totally remove the spotlight perception, engage other individuals or groups of children that don't include Jason. "We all can help with our classroom".

This process is evolutionary in nature; everything geared towards celebrating children for their contribution. Children start to recognise each other for their contribution – a mutual regard process. Jason gets included, perhaps in cautious ways by the others, but children are generally quick to say, "Hey that's good Jason".

When children are empowered to offer their hearts and minds, with confidence, to a mutual regard community, they are also going to offer Jason some constructive feedback. These are the beginnings of good feelings for Jason about himself in school; feelings that are important for every child, Jason being no exception.

Jason's teacher reported to me that, as the overlay of bullying behaviour faded, it became apparent that Jason was depressed. Whether this depression resulted from his lost status, or from some other, more deep-seated, cause that, in Jason's case, led him to bully, or from some combination of these is hard, if not impossible, for the teacher to determine.

That is a degree of insight that a psychologist may be more qualified to comment upon, and indeed the school system's psychologist may be invited to participate in helping Jason and his teacher to move forward. A teacher with increased awareness and sensitivity to Jason is likely to be more able to determine his needs. But much of how Jason perceives himself will be affected by his externalities and the other children's interactions with him. The Four Communities Classroom, with its mutual regard ethic, will have a lot to offer Jason, and will always be open to positive contributions from him. Like all of us, Jason will be encouraged by constructive feedback from his environment.

Unlike the effects of bullying, Jason's opportunities for positive empowerment will not detract from the other children's progress as they explore their own self-image and identity, and those of others, through group community processes. Much is to be learned in communion with others, and the more confidence each child has in self and relationship, the better situated he or she is to learn.

At the end of the school year, Jim, a former 'inner circle' child, wrote a poem to his teacher, celebrating her. Jason wrote a card to Mrs. Peters saying that she was the best teacher he ever had. These unsolicited expressions of positive emotion indicate that these children experienced positive bifurcation processes. The odds for a good year, next autumn, for these children, are greatly improved, and especially so if they experience, once more, another Four Communities Classroom with their next teacher.

Adopting the tenets of the Four Communities Classroom appears a favourable way forward for children, the school, the principal and the education system; especially so if the progress realized in 'the Jason situation' is multiplied by other children with similar problems in the school system.

## Quietening the bullies turmoil - a grade 6 boy's story

*It should be noted that teachers are seldom in receipt of all the circumstances that make up a child's life and, in fact, not only cannot but, usually need not be. Teachers do, however, need to move forward as constructively as possible on what confronts them at the time. Keeping the following in mind may, at times, prove helpful.*

It's the start of the school year, but, the 'fresh start' anticipation, held by most, of a new beginning in the next grade is being clouded by the boy with poor relationship skills.

Why do we think this? There is a complaint about bullying. He's carrying on his reputation for bullying from last year. Already, at this very moment, he's in trouble with the teacher and principal; he's not happy. But a teacher who knows him from the previous year says, "I've never seen him show remorse before."

A bullying mind that appears to be in remorse is wonderful, because it could demonstrate that a mind is admitting that it is unhappy with its situation, and, therefore, is a mind that might be willing to consider alternatives, should they be offered. However, apparently remorseful or not, the bullying mind is one that is essentially not happy.

First let's look at the situation in front of us. The boy appears bright. Brightness does not, however, necessarily enable children to cope better. Children can find themselves challenged in trying to make sense of the world; sense-making that, perhaps, has been further complicated by inconsistent personal life experiences. The mind cannot find satisfactory, constructive reasons for things, so why try to join in, to contribute? Resulting emotions may include feeling down, unhappy and unfulfilled. We are all emotionally driven and the boy will, therefore, try to make sense of these feelings. This may result in trying to decide whether something is wrong with self or others. This is a time when self-esteem is vulnerable to erosion and may be already depleted.

Emotional dictates within all of us mean that we need interaction with others - all needing some sense of control over our situation. It is no different for the bullying boy. If these emotional needs are not met through constructive relationships, then they must be met in other ways. Often other ways elicit behaviours that others don't like. Bullying can result.

Being a bully enables the child to seize control. With control seized, he ensures interaction and relationship on his terms, and his identity is established. He decides the parameters of interactions. Life's confusion is put on hold, he feels some purpose for a while. It is a poor substitute, but better than nothing. He has had a self-recognition fix. It will hold him for the day - hopefully. If he can find others who are bullies, it's helpful, as he then has a source of affirmation for both himself and his actions.

Perhaps there doesn't seem to be a way out of this bullying behaviour, and really, perhaps he doesn't have to think about that if he has 'moral' support from others; self-justification facilitated; self-image and feelings about self, while not perhaps the best, good enough. With seemingly no viable alternative, he thinks, he may as well accept that 'this is the sort of person I am.' More bullying behaviour helps to confirm to self that he is right in his assessment of self; further bullying turns into a process of self-justification.

But, of course, below the outward show, there is a person of low self-esteem, and a diminished sense of self. The bully will feel that he/she is highly vulnerable to being exposed. Therefore, maintaining a front becomes essential and, because we are emotionally driven, we must, above all, look after our self; temporary fixes are aways better than no fixes.

Fixes for the bullying mind, beyond the temporary, may seem unavailable, and/or too difficult to tackle, especially for the mind with low self-esteem. The bully's mind is not, I would think, well positioned to apply remedy to itself and create more balanced relationships with others. Such thoughts would, I believe, present, to the bully, a difficult thing to contemplate and to interpret as success; bullying is the easier option; success seen in different terms.

'Successful' (for the moment) bullies are, perhaps, those with a momentum that creates acceptance from the majority; this is the way things are around here. The bullying culture is too large, too established for any individual to change it. The recipients of the bullying increasingly become the focus for its continuance; the victims of a desperate exploitation to feed a need. Nobody dares challenge it, nobody wants a spotlight on them. Negative lessons abound for all, even for bystanders.

(I believe where reporting to adults has resulted in censor of the bully, that the bully feels his/her identity is so under attack, he/she turns to the only self support they know - further and, perhaps, heightened bullying behaviours. This, of course, can result in a worsened situation for the bullied child. It's no wonder that children so often choose to endure in silence.)

Bullying can be more established in high school, as it may well be that the perpetrators have lived much of their lives within these damaging parameters. Help in constructive self-esteem building, and in the building of a constructive view of the world is required.

In elementary school there is less history to overcome, and perhaps, as in our bully's case, he is the only child in the class struggling with the problem. The best time to start helping the child, before there is a chance for a bullying culture to become re-established, is at the beginning of the school year.

- **Can solution be found in behaviour contracts?**

Do behaviour contracts in class result in clearing confusion in the bully's mind? Behaviour contracts can have the effect of causing some self-consideration of what's wrong with self. But, it seems to me, well structured processes with considerable assistance and support, are essential.

However, the behaviour contract, while hopefully illuminating for the child, could, I believe, prove to be a difficult spotlight for the bully to handle. He may feel resentful. He may be inclined to emotionally support himself through further bullying; assuaging, for the time being, the feeling of resentment, and the threat to his identity and sense of control. I feel that behavioural contracts will not necessarily help in moving the bully constructively forward, especially when applied solo with no follow-up.

- **Solution through self-directed discoveries**

I feel that the more effective avenue for bullies to deal with their problems is that of the self directed discoveries. Self-directed discoveries are a way of looking after self that does not leave bullies with the feeling that, in the process, they have submitted to another's idea. Individuals need to feel in control; a need that we all seek to fulfil. It is the teacher's job to provide a classroom environment where children's need for individual control over self is constructively enabled.

The environment and interactions within the Four Communities Classroom provide a way for the boy/girl to work through their own confusion to a more comfortable sense of self. The Four Communities Classroom enables children, whether they be bullies, victims or bystanders, to build and contribute toward positive classroom environments. (See 'The Story of Jason', page 195.)

- **The use of praise for a healing bully**

Be careful, be judicious. Yes he/she needs feedback, but most will come from the social environment - gradually, developmentally. It gets better, faster according to his/her behaviour and relationship efforts. Too much praise may be interpreted as a process of push towards improvement by authority, rather than a process of self decision and self control. Praise from the teacher, being a secondary experience, can generate resistance, whereas the process of self decision and self control enables important primary learning to occur; the usually less contrived, and therefore, greater assistance coming from feedback from peers for constructive relationship behaviour.

---

Generally, in bullying situations, The Four Communities Classroom provides a sense of self, established through constructive relationship processes.

In the brief time I spent in his classroom, the bullying boy showed remorse indicating that there is hope for change.

---

### The story of a grade five/six class - reluctant participants in their own affairs
### Or
### Children not recognising what is in their best interest

I was taking a class of grade 5 and 6's through the refining process of the rights that they had thought up; 27 of their own ideas on what they considered would be useful in enabling them to enjoy their classroom for the year. No small enterprise but, unlike all the other classes I had worked with, the import of this exercise had not appeared to have struck home. Yes, they had all participated in the creation of their list of rights, but having completed this, the general consensus was, 'We don't really want to think about them anymore. Thank you anyway'. (This had been, after all a huge learning curve, and apparently with no marks attached.)

They were nice kids; polite and agreeable and, overall, working well and quietly at their desks. The task of getting through the curriculum, apart from the usual range of ability difficulties, was proceeding smoothly. Teachers would call it a good class. It is a rare class, however, that does not present some extra challenges and this class had a couple of needy children, with some difficult social/learning problems. Nevertheless, the teacher could survey this group, breath a sigh of relief and think, 'I wish the class coming up next year was as good. Oh well, we'll deal with that then; meanwhile I've got a good year. Thank goodness. It makes up for some of those tougher classes I've had. And I've had some, I'll tell you'.

Will this class ever become tough to teach, perhaps when they are in grade eight? Ask this of a grade 5/6 teacher and the response may be, "They might. Could be. That's why I am not a grade eight teacher. I don't know how grade eight teachers do it."

As you have probably gathered, I am laying the groundwork for a number of points and questions:

1. Why should it be almost expected that classes of children should present increasing challenges, as they get older?

2. Is it possible to build on children's positive attitude to school, so often displayed in the younger grades, so that children are able to retain a positive mindset as time goes by?

3. What has caused, in this instance, a good class to become fairly reluctant participants in their own affairs and to not recognise what is in their best interest?

I would like to look at the last question first.

- **Some speculation**

My answer is, I don't know. But don't these circumstance give one cause for concern? What could have possibly happened to this class? What series of experiences could have occurred for the children to judge that, since this was not work required of them in a written form to be evaluated by the teacher, this exercise was optional, superfluous, something that others in the class might want to bother with, but 'count me out. I'll just sit and watch, I won't be a nuisance, let me know when you are done, and I'll probably make an effort again, when you've got some real work for me. And, oh yes, I'll go along with whatever you decide'.

I wonder if this speculation is correct? Assuming that it is, can I figure out why this might be so? Well I have more thoughts, more speculation, but of a more general nature that takes me beyond my interactions with these particular children.

If the conjecture has relevancy, schooling, perhaps, has had the effect of distilling some children's thought patterns to the point where they assume that 'their own affairs' are catered to best through thinking within parameters required to do school work and being good, and that thoughts outside of these parameters are personal and not actually relevant within the school environment. It is, of course, a very general statement, and if proof were possible within educational process, grounds for and against the speculation could probably be established, from class to class.

However, beyond the speculation, when we combine evidence of children demonstrating disinterest in matters important to them, and with our knowing that they will eventually develop to the point where questioning begins, should this not be a matter of concern for educators and prompt the key 'teacher thought' question:

> **When and under what circumstance is it best for children to start to develop, as part of constructive relationship with others, brain capacity that enables intelligent questioning, and carefully crafted independent thinking?**

However, let me return to the children on hand and the situation I find myself in.

(This is a situation, incidentally, that is typical for teachers, i.e. unexpected happenings that cannot be anticipated in planning. For best results, the 'best' prepared lesson has to be presented by teachers with the capacity to accommodate the unexpected).

How right are my assumptions regarding the children's thoughts? I don't know. But the weak responses of some, the silence of many, certainly conveyed partial interest at best. My speculation may fit. Matters of the mind, especially in wanting to understand others, are so imprecise.

But, outside of ordering compliance, or exhorting children to contribute (such concreteness, deceptively, has its appeal), teacher sensitivity, in the light of our speculation, can be a useful, though tentative, response. The value of speculation, I believe, should not be underrated. Speculation is a process and product of the mind, and should, therefore, be given some weight; we have the mind for speculation – we can use it; the mind's speculation can help in guiding our sensitivity and sense of others. The teacher demonstrating mind process, in interaction with children, is a wonderful way for children to learn about and trust their own humanity; seeing the teacher's mind in action.

Determining accuracy of the speculation may come from responses you generate. However, if you tell the class what you think they are thinking, it probably won't help. Whether in agreement or not, you may still not elicit a response that prompts constructive discussion (the purpose of this particular interaction).

But getting to the bottom of the class's motivating thoughts is seldom essential to moving forward. The relevant question for you is, have you gleaned enough of a sense of the children to know how to prompt them to reappraise their thinking sufficiently to begin constructive discussion?

Since this class was not responding very well to the opportunity to discuss, it didn't seem as though discussion was going to get this class discussing. Slow starts do happen sometimes. Sometimes the older and more set in their ways children are, the more likely they are to be resistant - fear of feeling vulnerable making them reticent to express themselves. Once taken hold, such reluctance can be a powerful inhibiter in class interactions with peers.

Thoughts around inhibiting influences upon children provide an answer, in part, to question number one.

1. Why should it be almost expected that classes of children should present increasing challenges, as they get older?

Resistance to discussion can begin to show as early as grade six, but can be much more established by grade seven and eight.

Of course, there are always exceptions. In all grades, there can be bright and outspoken people, who are only too keen to let you know their opinions. If you give them an opportunity it is as though the floodgates have been opened. Even when it seems that you've given carte blanche for a takeover, you can regard this as an opportunity. It is, in fact, great as you've got some speakers. You, however, insist upon process. Process allows for opinions and counter opinions. This is not anarchy, it is discussion. You are on your way.

But back to the reticent five/six split grade where there was this prejudicial weak response. What did I do? I decided to act on the assumption, that, of course they wanted to share their views, and I ask how can anyone know what those thoughts are if they don't speak. Everyone has thoughts. "Maybe," I said, "everyone thinks that everyone in the class can read their minds and therefore, they have no need to voice them."

I asked a student if he could read the mind of the person sitting next to him. "No," he replied. Then I asked the second student the same question regarding the first student. The answer was, "No." "Well," I said, "apparently you aren't mind readers." Is anyone in this room a mind reader? No. "O.K," I continued, "so how are we going to tell what someone is thinking? I would like you to open your mouth (demonstrating in an exaggerated way and causing some amusement) and try letting some words come out, so others aren't forced to mind read. Do you agree mind reading is impossible? Do you know what he is thinking? Would it help if he spoke?" All this is offered in an incredulous and amused tone. It works. The kids start putting their hands up and thoughts are expressed. The class keeps the ball rolling, as they hear views about their classroom rights that they perhaps don't agree with, think are incomplete, or need modifying. "Now we know what each other are thinking." I said, "That's great – well done everyone. Now we are discussing. Now we will be able to come up with some rights that we want for ourselves in this classroom.

(Thus, 'On my feet', I had speculated, tentatively thought and responded. I had made suggestions that I felt would move the class forward. But at no time had I resorted to disrespectful tactics. Only the most positive assumptions regarding children's state of mind will produce positive outcomes. At all times the children, and you, must be able to maintain dignity).

Question number two.

2. Is it possible to build on children's positive attitudes to school, so often displayed in the younger grades, so that children are able to retain a positive mindset as time goes by?

I say, yes, but it is easier to maintain if it becomes the modus operandi experience for children before their emotional shields are erected too high.

How clever you all are is always a good assumption to work with and, with this grade five/six class, as their discussion process starts to gel, it is the stance I take. And they are clever. Class discussion offers the opportunity to show it.

The right to education, and the right to learn come under discussion. Is there a difference? The children say that education is an organised activity, and that learning happens all the time. Of course, they don't say this immediately, but this is what starts to emerge as they listen to each other's ideas, and they nod, murmur, and say 'yes' in agreement, as I offer a summary of their discussion.

This class of children, expressing higher order thoughts with their peers as audience, presents an excellent challenge to developing mental capacities. The precision of expression of evolving thoughts is variable. Sometimes it's just amazing, at other times children try hard and are not always satisfied with their effort. But what we do know is that self-correction processes are at work at all levels of thought. The teacher thanks every child equally for their contribution.

## The story of a grade four class where silliness reigns. A mid-year case study. Help had been requested

Creating an atmosphere of silliness in the classroom were three Silly Billy's (boys and girls) with some Silly Billy hang-on's. Fun came from silliness. Laughter and added commentary, which often occurred, was assured, if someone was silly. Fun and silliness were synonymous. Work was so frequently punctuated with silly commentary and laughter that the teacher's focus tended to one of fun spoiler in order to reduce disruption. It didn't take the children long to discard the salutary effects of disciplinary talks and restore the atmosphere to one of fun and silliness. Relaxing with this class almost became an expression of abrogation of responsibility to teaching and learning.

The class had a boy who appeared tuned-out, and lackadaisical. Another boy, who was athletic, apparently viewed his athletic achievements as merit enough, frequently resorting to disruption and sullenness when required to sit in class. This added to the class's air of immaturity. Yet there was also considerable brightness in the class.

Containing the silliness, connecting with the non-connected and channelling the brightness became the challenge in communicating with this class. Increasingly, as the term progressed, this challenge seemed the dominant reality, and, for the teacher, it became wearing. Hope for signs of some development of maturity were fading. Individually, these were nice kids, but it became difficult to look forward to school in the morning. This is not a welcome feeling for a dedicated teacher. And so ensued daily emotions of guilt and frustration. Increasingly, the year seemed one to be endured rather than enjoyed. I was asked to help.

- **The communication challenge**

The introduction of the Four Communities Classroom did not change the communication challenge inherent in this class, but what it did do was offer a way forward to engage, constructively, with the communication challenge. The journey to this goal began.

The key question: Apart from the way the children operate, collectively as a class, what else fuels the communication challenge? The answer lies in another question; who is accepting responsibility for this class and its immaturity? The teacher. As long as the teacher accepts this responsibility, the children will let her. Without acceptance of responsibility on the children's part, there will be no appreciable development of maturity.

The use of the Four Communities Classroom is the route to evoking, in children, responsibility and ownership for development of their own maturity. It is also the route to addressing the communication challenge, and the route to developing an atmosphere of good teaching and learning.

It should be said that we do not expect grade four children to be mature beyond their years. But we do expect a level of maturity in grade four children that complements, rather than impedes, their learning and intelligent development.

And so the story of this class unfolds, a story of both individual and shared experience in the Four Communities Classroom.

This is a mid-year introduction to the Four Communities Classroom. I start by arranging the class into four groups, laying out some parameters as to how we will operate; explaining that we will build understanding over the days and weeks ahead, and that we will continue developing our community classroom, as the year progresses. The 'we' suggests that this will be a shared endeavour of children and teacher – an important part of the Four Communities Classroom experience. To achieve this, I explain, we have to learn how to have class discussions, where we talk and listen to each other. They listen attentively, as is usual for any group of children, or adults, when introduced to something new. I tell them that we will be learning many new ways of doing things in our everyday classroom life. This is all presented, of course, in language appropriate to grade four comprehension.

Learning to listen carefully to the ideas of others, respond to those ideas and offer ideas of one's own is often a new experience for children. Learning to take part in this type of effective group discussion, is an essential avenue of primary experience, and its process needs to be taught to all groups and all grades especially those that have not been accustomed to voicing and sharing ideas. In this case, we learn by doing, 'right off the bat', when I ask, What are we in school for? Why do your parents send you to school? Hands go up, answers come in, and we quickly establish our foundation – we are here to engage in good teaching and learning. This is reinforced by saying that everything we do and talk about in our classroom will be to help good teaching and learning. Would your parents think it a good idea if we sent home a letter saying that each morning we would do things where we learnt nothing? 'No' is chorused. The foundation is laid, understood and agreed upon. But this will be a foundation that children will need reminding of from time to time.

So now we have accomplished two protocols simultaneously – established that the good teaching and learning foundation will be our reference point for all subsequent life in the classroom, and begun the development and understanding of discussion and its role in the classroom. Of course, this first exposure to class discussion is only the beginning. Much more has to be learned and realised, for children to be able to use this primary experience effectively. (For further information on building discussion skills in children, see chap. 2.)

Agreement on good teaching and learning and the introduction to discussion are foundational to all classes although, of course, sophistication of language and rate of presentation are modified for different age groups (chap. 5). Using these elements as incontrovertible protocols in focusing this particular class is essential.

The children have demonstrated that they need something strong and engaging for them to focus collectively upon. Without that common, agreed-to and understood framework, they are not going to, in the near future, it seems, break clear of the distractions of silliness. Consistency, then, of formula, and insistence on maintenance of class protocols, is key. Thus, with this class, I enable children's expression and growth, through constant reference to our established protocols of functioning, and reference to our growing understanding of the development of these protocols. It is essential that one thing builds upon the next, with few and only minor deviations allowed. Children are strongly encouraged to make their contributions and build their sense of responsibility to self and others, within fairly inflexible guidelines. Again, focus and consistency is key. Moving forward from this point is a goal, waiting for the development of sufficient maturity that won't happen overnight, but will evolve through sensitive interaction between the teacher, individuals and the class as a whole.

The children respond. So far so good. There is no problem in getting contributions; there are more than enough children willing to speak (although, as usual, there are a number who are yet to feel comfortable speaking out). There are contributions that come from earnest faces, sometimes offering carefully considered thoughts, with words that appear to be subject to careful choosing, sometimes anxious to make their point understood. There are contributions that are trite and off the point that sometimes lead to laughter and loss of focus, leading some to forget to listen to the next contribution. Side conversations spontaneously occur and keeping the whole class focused, as a unit, on the discussion at hand demands energy.

But for these children the communication challenge is on and they are, for the most part, engaged.

For example. 'The right to share' is discussed. Such a right is likely to lead to the perception of the right to help ourselves to other people's supplies without asking permission, which in turn, of course, is likely going to involve argument and hurt feelings.

A cautionary note is not offered. The teacher's job is to bring the class to this realisation, through discussion, and/or demonstration, as I do in this instance, by taking a child's possessions while stating my 'right' to be able to share. I ask the shocked children, "Is this what you want with this right? Is this the effect you want?" "No", they say. "So what are you trying to achieve? What do you want for yourselves?" I ask. "Do we need to reword this right, and how? Or do we need to drop this right?" Discussion, ideas, thoughts come forth, until we are able to word a statement for voting on; a statement for the children to consider and, thereby, hopefully reach consensus.

With this kind of focus, there's not much room for silliness.

Any point that is brought forward by children is dealt with, through discussion. One cannot be tempted to avoid the discussion process on items that you know are problematic. We are establishing important perceptions of self and thinking, which must not be short-changed. The children are allowed to work through their thoughts. They will come to the right conclusion. If they don't, it usually means that the parameters of the discussion are not properly understood by them. The teacher has to work with children's contributions with the addition of some gentle, guiding wise words to build understanding. The process of discussion is also a process of airing and listening to various points of view. The children are reminded that they need to listen carefully so they can decide for themselves how they will vote. If a child does not like what they are hearing then they can put up their hand and speak. And perhaps they can persuade others to their point of view. That is their opportunity and their challenge. It becomes apparent that to do this, and make it fair for all, they must give others the courtesy of being listened to.

> **Ecological pattern**
> Processes of mutual regard, responsibility and reciprocation are foundational for the ecological classroom. (pp. 253 and 256)

Again, reminders are part of this process. Without needing to use the word reciprocation, the children are engaged in learning its import and meaning. Mutual regard is experienced, not intellectualised, and an environment that encourages responsibility for self and others is building.

The message is, the responsibility for you and your thoughts is yours.

If, at times, things are going nowhere, or advances look as though that they might slip away, I turn to those children who have previously provided useful thoughts, and summarize theirs and other contributions to move the discussion forward, thus establishing beachheads that we will not fall behind. As we are building our classroom rights, the use of summaries also enables us to put people's ideas to a vote.

You may have dissenters opposing a winning vote. That's fine. Go with the decision of the vote; it is what the majority of the class wants. And this is another point of relationship learning – all will not be persuaded; alternative views are part of difference; and this difference can be recognised and accepted calmly. There is no cause for fights or name-calling.

This process needs more orchestrating with our 'Silly Billy' class than most classes I have worked with. No-one is left out of the discussion and this important medium serves to give all children assurance and encouragement. Reminders are given that those given the courtesy of being listened to, should extend the same courtesy to other speakers. Meanwhile, silliness is discouraged on the grounds that it is not helping us with good teaching and learning, while fun and laughter, an important part of classroom life, is allowed, and commentary is made through the formal hands up process only.

This whole rights discussion serves the silly billies well for it is not just to establish rights, but also to simultaneously immerse the children in an extensive process of mutual regard, responsibility and reciprocation. In fact, the simultaneous processes complement and enable each other. This proves very engaging for the children, as they find themselves giving careful consideration to questions affecting how their classroom will function.

> **Ecological pattern**
> The purpose of the rights discussion is not just to establish rights, but to immerse children in an extensive process of mutual regard, responsibility and reciprocation.

This whole process takes time, and I am cognisant of the children's attention span for engaging in this mentally demanding higher-order thinking and development of discussion skills. I have been taking the class through a huge learning curve. They get tired, so I stop at the first signs of fatigue. The next day, after they have had a chance to, literally, sleep on their experience, I resume the discussion. Over the next few days, I allow whatever time the class needs to complete their rights discussion. This is the most efficient use one will ever make of time in the classroom. It has proven, in many classes, to pay back huge dividends, in the form of a more smooth-running class, with enhanced ability to engage with each other and more effectively with the curriculum.

Towards the end of my stay with this class, the silent children are speaking out, with verbal language skills that have been advanced through practice. We discover that the lackadaisical boy has some great thoughts, which he offers eagerly, and defends in discussion. Our athlete is presenting his views, although he still works on maintaining his 'cool' image. We do not try to change children's self image from without. Children are engaged in their own growth. They are provided a nurturing environment in which they will develop, constructively, at a rate they feel comfortable with.

We are all beneficiaries of hearing contributions and thoughts that otherwise would not have been spoken. And the children, who have contributed from the beginning, now speak with greater confidence; many signs of nervousness and anxiousness calmed. It is a gradual and visual transformation, occurring before my eyes.

If silliness breaks out, it is now easily contained, as we all now know how to handle ourselves more effectively.

# Feelings and learning in action - a personal account of a young boy

I think I was eight years old when the day came to learn fractions. Hmm, I wonder what that is about? I know numbers, I know how to count and do all sorts of things with numbers, you know, add, subtract, multiply, divide. What else could there be to do with numbers? I was curious. Not a bad state of mind for learning – curiosity. It is certainly aligned to interest. I was ready. Or so I thought.

The lesson was presented academically. There were no visual aids to look at or handle; no effort made to weave in a practical understanding. The teaching was limited in its approach and, therefore, addressed itself to only part of my brain's learning capacity. At eight years old, what did I know about my brain's development processes? What did I know about teaching? But I did know how I felt, and my feelings gradually changed to worry. I didn't understand what my teacher was talking about. She asked questions that I didn't understand. My ideas about how they should be answered didn't match up with some answers which received a 'yes'. Perhaps it will become clear as the lesson proceeds, I thought, but it was becoming worse. My feelings were worsening too.

But I kept my mind on the task, and it was a task too. I had to do something to make sense of this. Nothing I had heard was helping me in my sense-making process, so I started to devise something that would carry me through, so that I could restore some respectable feelings about myself. After all, this wasn't going to go away. I knew that fractions, from now on, were going to be part of my life, whether I liked it or not, and I didn't want to have my life complicated by feelings of inadequacy. So I devised a system by which I got the right answers, most of the time – that's O.K., not everyone, always, gets everything right. I could live with that.

Goodness knows what system I devised all those years ago, but I do remember thinking, that if what I am doing isn't right, it's not really very good. So, as one in charge of myself, I decided, correctly, that I had better check with the teacher. I waited in line. It seemed there were a number of others struggling too, needing lots of help. I just needed some verification, some small adjustment probably, and I'd be on my way.

What! You're doing it like that? No, No! Forget that! You've got it completely WRONG!

Well can you guess what this response did to my feelings? I was devastated. The rug had been pulled completely out from under my feet. Now, if I ever got the answer right, even if I figured out how to do it properly, the teacher would think I had gone about it the wrong way and give me an 'x'. Where was I to turn? The teacher. But she didn't have much time for me, certainly not enough for my learning needs. She spent some time repeating the explanations that I had already, apparently, clearly shown were beyond me. I left the front of the room none the wiser in terms of fractions. But some learning of another type became firmly fixed.

- I learned that my relationship with my teacher was not as good as I had thought it was, otherwise she wouldn't have made me feel so bad. People who like you don't do that.

- I learned that if you devise a way to get through, don't reveal it. It's better to fake it as long as possible and face the downfall later. Either way, it's going to hurt, so put off the problem. Besides, you may stumble on the correct solution eventually.

- I learned that I had probably come to the end of the time that numbers and math were accessible to me, because surely it wasn't ever going to get easier. I concluded that I can do many things, but I can't do math; likely because I am not very clever. Other kids are lucky because they are clever. Some of my friends can't do it either, so that helps a bit, but it's horrible when they get it and I still don't. I don't want to be on the wrong end of the class's clever/stupid spectrum.

I didn't like these thoughts. I didn't like that I would have to be more measured in future with my learning processes. Learning became less of a shared process, more of an emotional protection process.

I wasn't old enough to know that my thoughts had validity, that I had demonstrated creativity and that I wasn't stupid.

Did my teacher intend any of the lessons I had learned? Of course not. She would probably have been horrified to know what I was thinking. She was there to teach curriculum, and that is what she did. She probably thought that, given the varying intelligences of the children in her class, not everyone would be able to get it, but what can one do? Martin is apparently one of those children who won't be able to get it. Too bad.

The emphasis was on the importance of getting through the curriculum!

Many years later, when I was the teacher teaching fractions in elementary school, I recalled the feelings of my eight year old self. In my class everyone got it.

## Grade six class introduction/discussion on the point system

I am explaining how points can be won, but also occasionally lost. For example, since being late for class holds up proceedings and inconveniences everyone, a loss of points can occur if a group member is late after recess. Three minutes multiplied by thirty waiting people, equals ninety minutes lost.

But, a boy wonders, is it really fair that the whole group should lose points if one of their group is late? A better response, he thinks, would be to keep that person in after school, and not punish the whole group by taking away points.

This draws appreciative agreement from class members. Thus, while contradicting me, he seems to have spoken for others.

### Problem or Opportunity?

This boy is doing exactly what we want children to do - he is thinking (as apparently were others) and demonstrating that he feels he has something worth saying.

However, is this particular thought of the boy's going to enable us to set up a useful workable agreement for the class? Perhaps. One could pursue this. However, I think my idea is better.

**Two options**

1. The Four Communities Classroom Response

Since it appears that the concept of losing points for lateness needs to be supported with further reasoning, we could discuss and seek consensus through process.

Or

2. The Teacher Assumption of Responsibility and Control Response

In order to get on with my instructions on point-earning I could, instead of reasoning, shut the boy's idea down by saying, "I find it works best my way, we've got a lot to do this morning and we can't lose time on this. We must get on with our work."

- **Possible unintended fallout**

As good as I may feel my idea is, and, therefore, not requiring further discussion, shutting down the boy's contribution conveys an unfortunate message to all students - if you do have any thoughts, keep them to yourself, because they are not wanted, and likely not valid.

Result - ideas, creativity and, positive expression are devalued, and also seeded are relationship frustrations with the teacher. Although school-work may get done, the unintended and more powerful lesson to these children is:

- Thinking is only valid, when it falls into line with the teacher's instructions.

- The teacher's instructions and the teacher-approved thinking is the basis of this relationship.

- The teacher has to take responsibility for some things, for reasons the child cannot be expected to understand.

While a child may accept adult power, the child, is, as we all are, in a constant quest to make sense of the world. As the child gets older, increased questioning can eclipse acceptance.

As one considers what to do next in this situation, there are some important thoughts to keep in mind.

Providing children with the opportunity to question, in their attempts to make sense of the world, is important to their development.

One never actually has control over what another thinks. Thinking is innate to human beings. Thus, the question of what thought processes are being generated in the children in your class and what messages they are receiving, always exists. Once matters/issues are broached, we do not want to leave children with the impression that we feel that they are unable to think effectively. However, children need to also know that, though their thinking is a valid process, thinking never reaches an absolute state. Thinking is always subject to reflection and review, and reaction by others and rethinking.

- **Opportunity**

Now, if I do not shut this boy down, I either have to go along with what he suggests and, with the class, discuss details of how this is going to work, or I have to provide more basis for my 'better idea'.

Either way it will be a process where all ideas and contributions have to be supported with thinking and reasoning. This is the approach that, in the Four Communities Classroom, is in continual process. Since much of our intellectual growth can arise from organising thoughts and presenting them to others, so that they are able to consider them, we use this opportunity for growth and fair consensus.

Is there a risk here of surrendering authority to the class? No, there is not. There should never be any diminishment of self. Any diminishment of a teacher will likely mark the beginning of the end of children receiving a good education from that teacher. Providing the best education to children is not achieved through losing control. In this case, far from losing control, I am demonstrating the value and importance of thinking and democratic process. However, if the children had interpreted that as licence to 'take over' then I would have explained again the important principles of good teaching and learning, retaining fully the reins of responsibility for the class that is ultimately yours.

If that meant laying down the law then so be it. (See page 215, The Story of Brent.) My job is to figure out how (and in what measure) to provide opportunities for these children to exercise responsibility and engage in constructive questioning.

I say to the boy, and, of course, also to the class for their consideration, "Yes, we could punish late-comers after school, but it seems to me that a group should be able to rely on its members to arrive on time and not waste the time of the group or the rest of the class. If the group is able to rely on you as an individual then, perhaps, you in turn will be able to rely on them. The group should be able to rely on you to not lose points."

Although not part of a planned lesson, through the circumstantial life of the classroom, the idea of reciprocation, without using the word, has been introduced to the children. Sooner than later classroom life will present such opportunties. They should be taken advantage of. Learning in context is always powerful.

In this instance, the powerful idea of reciprocation is immediately demonstrated to the children. Reciprocity is important in the relationship building process, and helps with the process of acceptance and belonging in group dynamics. Children usually find this concept significant.

The boy, with his idea, is not put down. He will continue to feel comfortable in presenting his thinking, and others will be making mental notes that it is safe, even good, to speak in this class. Foundations are being laid. My 'better idea' is agreed upon by this class and would, I believe, satisfy most.

But should further arguments have been presented in favour of individual punishment in the lateness circumstance, then I would have continued discussion without any arbitrary closure, continuing to build confidence in the safety of speaking. In continuing to facilitate class discussion, I would have offered:

- Further reasoned reaction to children's newly offered arguments.
- Invitation to others to express their ideas on the subject, both in response to my arguments and to the boy's.

At some point I would bring the issue to a vote.

(I have found that usually the class will vote in favour of the best solution.)

However, if the vote had gone in favour of the individual punishment, then I would have gone on to discuss what the punishment will be. Let's look at that possible scenerio. Up for discussion is also the question of how effective individual punishment will be in arriving at a point where the class's time is not wasted by late-comers; reminding the class that our ultimate measurement of all that we do and decide is maximising good teaching and learning.

If the class still votes in favour of late-comers being kept in after school you have a less than best outcome. You know that the benefits of group connectedness and reciprocation have lost a valuable building influence, and you are stuck with some, perhaps daily, after-school duties.

What to do?

You remind the class that we have all agreed that school is about good teaching and learning and, therefore, the success of their solution will be measured by the good teaching and learning yardstick. Any solution must deliver what we want - good teaching and learning that cannot be subject to the dalliance of late-comers. If their solution delivers - no more late-comers - then that is wonderful. Their solution has worked, and well done everyone. "However," you say, "if it doesn't work after, say, a week, we will use my solution."

You've have now established some win-win situations.

The class may want to 'prove' their solution is best, and make their expectations clear to all concerned. The result - good teaching and learning is not interrupted by late-comers, and a sense of cohesion is built.

The class will have proven that they can effect change - this is good for the self-esteem of individuals and the class as a whole. The image of self and of the class as a unit is a good one.

This may not be the most likely outcome and children may still come in late after recess. Now the children are experiencing concrete results of their thinking and the need to reassess; a fundamental thinking/consequence process of life. You haven't told them that they were wrong, they have experienced thinking, decision-making and its results. Experiential learning is powerful. Their frontal cortex has grown. Not a bad bit of teaching.

Now you are ready, and so are they, to try your idea, and thus to experience further beneficial influences on group connectedness and reciprocation, as well as a good teaching and learning atmosphere no longer interrupted by late-comers.

An important process that is also occurring here is that the life of the classroom is being used to learn a wide range of life lessons.

- Community works best in a democracy, when self is seen in the context of others and their needs.

- That success and one's own interests are often best served by considering others.

- That this process becomes a validation of children's sense of self, as it becomes apparent that their views are needed in the construction of their world.

These points are not learned in one exposure, but through the life of the classroom, on an ongoing basis. One assesses classroom activity and interaction for opportunities to build and enhance children's learning experience. Many occasions for this arise daily; not necessarily planned. Within a short time, it becomes second nature for the teacher to use opportunities in both small incidental ways and in the way outlined in the late-comers example. However, there are times when you may decide to by-pass some opportunities and instead use perhaps a quick look that says, it's now time to do that page of math. This makes clear that, with your relationships-for-learning atmosphere in place, the establishment of curriculum priorities are an important part of learning and school. In other words, children are not allowed to 'learn' that discussion process can be spun into a time-wasting device. That is not good teaching and good learning.

Sometimes, teachers express concern about the amount of time that is spent on such processes. It has been my experience, and that of teachers that I have worked with, that some careful investment in dealing with circumstantial issues pays curriculum dividends, in a greatly enhanced learning atmosphere.

---

## Disruption of group discussion. A mid-year case study in a grade six classroom

The boy gets up from his seating position on the floor, moves away from his group discussion, and sits on the edge of his desk, and, with legs dangling over the front, rocks the desk with sufficient energy to cause the desk to teeter back and forth on its front legs. This, of course, creates a noise. The boy is supposed to be sitting with his group, in the discussion space, in the centre of the horseshoe arrangement of their desks. Group discussions are underway on rights that all people should be able to enjoy, regardless of where they live in the world.

*Problem or Opportunity?*

**Two options**.

Option 1. Teacher assumption of responsibility

The teacher adopts a quick and immediate assumption of responsibility for the boy's behaviour leading to:

(a) a sharp demand for him to get back into the circle.

(b) walking up to the boy and asking him to get back into the circle, perhaps in whispered tones.

Teacher response (a) can create a sullen response in the boy; a negative emotional reaction which, of course, is never good for building good relationships for learning. One incident like this sends out a poor relationship signal to the boy and to the other class members who have witnessed your response. It is likely going to take a lot of time and effort on your part for the boy to feel comfortable with you again. There is one caveat to this. If the boy happens to be well recognised by all students to be a trouble maker and you are aware of his self appointed role/reputation, then different responses may be in order. See the next case study, the 'Story of Brent'.

Teacher response (b) will create much less negative feeling, especially if whispered, because at least you kept it a private communication with the boy.

Option 2. The shared responsibility response

The teacher sees this situation as an opportunity to exercise the boy's own innate sense of responsibility. Responsibility practiced by students is always a good thing.

If the boy catches your eye, beckon him to come over to you. Or perhaps ask another student, nearby, to ask him to come over to you. The walk over to you will usually have some sobering effect, but you going to him is O.K too.

Draw the boy's attention to the fact that there are 25 students in this room. Ask him, if all of them decided to rock their desks, how much learning/discussion would be going on. He will probably say zero or not much. You agree with his assessment and point out that he, therefore, is unlikely to be learning much either. Ask if he knows what he has to do to put things right. He'll likely say he knows. So you ask him if he could go and put it right. He says he could. So you invite him to do just that. He goes back to his group and re-enters the discussion. You have not actually said, "Get off the desk, stop rocking the desk, or stop making that noise." You haven't told him to get back into the group to discuss. There has been no reprimand.

What is the state of his feelings right now? What would you feel if you were him?

You have drawn on the best, most responsible part of the boy. He may feel slightly silly for needing your input to correct his behaviour, but those are feelings he is most likely to direct at himself. He, after all, caused the interaction. You haven't made him feel silly in front of the class, because it was a private conversation. He also has had the opportunity to present some rationale to support his behaviour, but didn't, because he decided he couldn't really justify what he was doing.

What do you think will most likely occur in this boy's thinking process, when making future behaviour choices in his group/class?

Is this foolproof; will this boy's decisions always be the best? Not necessarily. But it may not take too many similar incidences for the boy to improve his self-correction processes. You offered him this opportunity and he took it. His emotional disposition is now such that he is certainly on the path to learn effectively, and contribute to other children's learning environment; at the least, not to be disruptive.

---

The next story looks at the need for balance between self-assertiveness and mutual regard, and the link to dignity.

### Dignity and the story of Brent and the story of Bill (the need for the teacher to recognise children's intent and respond appropriately)

<u>Brent</u> - in a grade 7/8 class. A story that includes **the rebuilding of dignity**.

Outside on a sunny day, the *'Listening-to-others [and the teacher] awareness activity'* (for information on this activity see page 132) has gone well, and we all troop back into the classroom and return to our groups. There is the general noise that can be expected when thirty people settle into their desks. But, as the room becomes quiet, the noise of children from another classroom passing our open door becomes noticeable. No one has thought to close the door. Brent sees his opportunity for display and, while we are all well aware that Brent would more likely welcome distractions than find them an annoyance, he speaks in an almost pious voice, explaining that the noise outside is bothering him and could he, therefore, please have the door shut. Coming from Brent this 'reasonable' request is a problem. From someone else it probably wouldn't be.

If I close the door, which needs to be done, anyway, then Brent has just demonstrated to the class that I, the teacher, can be fooled. Mr. Sterling thinks I am so good. Brent has turned responsible behaviour into a charade. The message to his classmates is, 'You too can fool the teacher'. When fooled, the teacher's authority is undermined. But how can I censor him for making such a reasonable request? Brent, no doubt, thinks he has me over a barrel, especially as the Four Communities Classroom is where children are given the opportunity to engage and demonstrate their own sense of responsibility. If my authority is undermined, then the ethos of the room and what it stands for is eroded. Children will feel less secure and confident in explorations of self and constructive relationship. Children may retreat inside themselves since no one wants to risk looking foolish.

So without comment I go over to the door, observed by all in silence. All know that this is a test. I close the door and turn directly upon Brent, just when he thinks his comment has worked, and I say, with a strength of meaning that is to be completely understood, "Don't you ever do anything like that again. You know, the class knows, and I know that your request was not meant to be constructive. Obviously, the door needed closing. Please, in future, confine your contributions for us all, to responsible constructive thoughts."

This, of course, makes it quite clear to the whole class that I have not been taken in, and what's more, the consequences for attempting to do so can be embarrassing. Brent's cockiness is replaced with a look of foolishness. Brent's attempt to impress the class has failed, and now his best bet is to keep a low profile, in the hopes that this will be forgotten. Which is what he does, and he also works at building a relationship with me that is more constructive for him and me. I, of course, respond positively to enable him to rebuild his dignity. Brent is never a problem again and he does, in fact, begin to make positive contributions to his group.

This story illustrates that there are times when the 'law' has to be laid down. I find that, in the Four Communities Classroom, the situation that Brent precipitated is fairly rare. But, although the atmosphere of the classroom is one that builds towards mutual regard and assumption of responsibility, there are times when it has to be made clear, in no uncertain terms, that there are lines that self-assertiveness cannot be allowed to cross (see p. 257). It is important to note, therefore, that ultimate responsibility for the successful running of the Four Communities Classroom lies with the teacher (something that each child requires) and that no child's assertiveness can be allowed to disrupt that process.

*Be firm when you have to be!*

**Bill** - grade 5. A story where **dignity is maintained**.

In response to my introducing discussion, democracy and ideas, as a function of the Four Communities Classroom, Bill, a boy full of enthusiasm, pricks up everyone's ears when he suggests that it would be a good idea to vote on agreeing not to do any work in the afternoons. I say, "Sure. If you can all get notes from your parents, endorsing the idea, and you can also get the principal to agree, then we can perhaps do that. Bill doesn't think this is likely to happen, and, of course, the proposal is dropped. I have proceeded on the assumption that this is a humorous suggestion and so the interchange is kept light. (Also, this exchange indicates that the influence of autonomy and integration dynamics is not necessarily an arrangement contained within the classroom, but can include other factors; the school, the parents, and the communities that the school is part of.)

Incidentally, in the story of Brent, if it had been Bill who had asked for the door to be closed, I would have probably said with dry humour, "Oh, I'm very sorry Bill, perhaps you would like to close the door. I am so pleased that you have plans to work hard." He would have smiled. The class would have said, "Yeh Bill, get to work." No harm done. Connection through humour for everyone.

*Sometimes humour can be the most constructive mutual regard response.*

I was well aware that Brent's motivation wasn't humour, but self-assertiveness without mutual regard. Responding to it as humour would likely have caused Brent to generate a number of ambiguously humorous events, with which to push his luck, and slowed his progress towards mutual regard considerably. Also, this behaviour would have impaired the class's sense of comfort as we worked towards Four Communities Classroom process. Connection is not always possible through humour.

Conversely, lecturing Bill would have introduced a sour note, noted by all, and perhaps have created a small hurdle in the intelligent building of constructive relationships.

In essence, the child's intent is everything. Seeing and getting to know each child as an individual will help you recognize intent and enable you to respond appropriately. This is important for the building and maintenance of dignity.

---

## Dignity over discipline and the avoidance of a battle of wills in relating to the class

As we have said, relationship process is of primary concern in the Four Communities Classroom. This includes demeanour and perception, which impact relationship dynamics, both on the teacher's part and the children's. I believe that the more successful teacher will be neither too tentative nor too authoritative in relating to a class, preferring instead to convey dignity.

- **The teacher**

In a teacher's general approach to the class, being overly tentative, or overly assertive, can have a deleterious effect on how children perceive the teacher. Any resulting adverse responses by children can, in turn, affect the teacher's assessment of children's behaviour. This can lead to situations where the teacher feels it is necessary to introduce or heighten disciplinary measures to maintain control and constructive learning environments. A sense of dignity, for teacher and children, becomes harder to achieve.

The overly authoritative teacher can undermine the dignity of children, by making them feel inconsequential, and elicit dismissive or resigned attitudes.

The overly tentative teacher may convey to children, accurately or not, insufficient dignity and classroom authority.

Either of these perceptions make it difficult for children, under the scrutiny of their peers, to align themselves with the teacher and, therefore, to relate constructively to the teacher.

If there is little constructive relationship occurring between the teacher and the class, it will be difficult to engage children in a successful Four Communities Classroom experience. Also see the Four Communities Classroom Teacher's Mindset And Presentation, p. 137.

- **The children**

With a class of 25 or 30 children, each forming their own perceptions from day one, any teacher can be misread by a child. Brent, in that grade 7/8 class, (p. 215), where I went in to help, was that someone for me. As I had not adopted the more **secondary-experience traditional** techniques he had become accustomed to, his perception appeared to be that I was an easy-going soft touch, and he was going to show the class just how soft. Thus, in his assessment I, likely, was seen as overly tentative. It was important, therefore, for me to quickly and decidedly correct his perception with some unquestionably assertive response. Self-assertion (see pp. 256 and 287) is an ecological imperative and, when required, you provide. With my dignity intact, the rest of the class could feel comfortable, leaving Brent the job of reassessing his perception and behaviours.

*When the opportunity arrives, role-model self-assertion and dignity, thus enabling it in others.*

As you set out to build relationships in the Four Communities Classroom, you will find that the more years that children have experienced row-teaching culture, the more adaptation you will require of them. Younger children, therefore, are more likely, under new conditions, to accept and build a relationship with their teacher. Also significant to the building of relationships is the encouragement of independent thought. This translates, especially in grades 6, 7 and 8, to greater levels of questioning. Teachers of these grades have to be prepared to enable children to verbally exercise their need to make sense of things. This means creating a safe environment in which children can voice their ideas, knowing it is your job to maintain dignity for all in the new context of learning that you are placing them in.

It is always possible for the teacher to misread situations.

When it becomes apparent that you may have misconstrued what happened, DON'T stick to your guns. You will only create that raised-eyes-to-the-ceiling expression and all the disparaging thoughts that go with it. But when you know that you made a mistake, apologize, "I thought it was this because of that, but if everything is fine, then it's fine."

*When the opportunity arrives, role-model self-correction.*

Children will fall over themselves to forgive when you say sorry.

Sometimes children will try to convince you that you have misread a situation when you haven't.

Children may say, "No I wasn't talking and I was paying attention." You reply, "Well that's good then, I don't have to worry about you." Or, "Great, I thought you were talking, but if you weren't - no problem." Or, "I'm sorry, I thought you were talking, I must have been mistaken, I was just concerned that the people around you were being disrupted by you." Responses of this type are non-confrontational, they don't force children to defend an indefensible position, perpetuate a deceit, or engage in a battle of wills. The child knows he/she was talking and knows that children around know. Whether he/she thinks you are fooled or not (although he/she will harbour serious doubts), the child will engage in inner dialogue, debating the comfort of the exchange and how many more times they want to invite such attention.

Most children realize that too many such incidences could well invite a greater degree of teacher-correction. Since resolve to self-correct can be strengthened in such situations, children who do not usually create problems are also reinforced in their behavioural choices. Dignity remains intact for all.

*Allow self-correction to occur in children when you are able to.*

All children are given an opportunity for success when self-assertiveness, mutual regard and dignity are balanced and integral to classroom function.

---

## The recess impromptu single group meeting with the teacher - (this time with group 4)

It was early in the development of the Four Communities Classroom in Mr. M's grade 5/6 class, when group four reported that they couldn't reach consensus on a group name. In fact, it quickly became apparent that there was quite a bit of dissension and polarization between the four girls and two boys that made up the group (boys were in the minority in this class making the provision of equal numbers of boys and girls in all groups difficult). With children in group four divided down gender lines, and not being able to find a way to agree, their future as a well functioning group was in question. "The boys are being unreasonable," I was told. "It's not fair," said the boys, "We are outnumbered, and the girls vote down our suggestions every time."

Routine monthly discussions, where the teacher sits with a group to listen to concerns and/or successes the group is experiencing can be a valuable assessment process for the teacher, the group, and the individuals within the group. But group fours situation couldn't wait a month. So I immediately arranged a meeting. "Let's talk about this over recess and see if we can find a way to sort this out."

In the Four Communities Classroom it is always important to see problems as opportunities. Therefore, I wondered how this could become an avenue of learning for these children.

Guiding thoughts for the Four Communities Classroom teacher in this situation are:

1. This is a group problem - not a teacher problem.
2. By joining the group over recess, I will, for the meeting, become part of the group.
3. How are **we** as a group going to tackle this problem? (The teacher does not assume sole responsibility for resolving the situation.)

Opportunity

At recess we all sit in group discussion mode - cross-legged in a circle within the circular space created by the group's desks. I tell the group that we are going to listen to each other and all have an equal vote in working towards a solution.

I ask for the children's take on the problem. Different and divergent points of view are offered. The girls say that the boys think their idea for a name 'The Hippopotamuses' is silly. The boys, however, say that their "compromise" of adding 'Call of Duty' to the name was outvoted, "just because the girls always vote us down."

The girls explain to me that 'Call of duty' is about armies and war and that they want nothing to do with war in their group name. The boys scoff and say, "So what, it doesn't mean that we like war. The girls just vote against everything we say - it's not fair."

So I say, everyone is not going to do well as a group if they always argue along boy/girl lines. Effective groups listen to what everyone says, and each person is responsible to vote according to whether they can agree or not with what is being said. It is nothing to do with voting according to whether the idea comes from a boy or a girl. We are people here. That is what is important. It is by listening, and in return offering your reasoned ideas, that good decision-making comes about. That is what each group needs to strive for in order to be an effective group, especially when in competition with the other groups.

I ask each group member, in turn, if they have anything that they would like to say regarding what I have said. One girl says that she agrees with me. She thinks that would make things fair. Others make similar statements - both boys and girls. So I put it to a vote. They all put up their hands in agreement.

"So, how do we use this new-found agreement to solve our name problem?" I ask. One girl repeats, "I think that war is wrong and that, therefore, I want nothing to do with a war-type name."

"Is that a reasonable request, not to have a war type name?" I ask of the others. The boys say, "Well yes, we suppose so." Then suddenly one of the boys says, "What about calling ourselves 'The O-So-Cool Hippopotamuses'. Turning to the girl who voiced concern about war, the others ask if that is O.K by her. Yes, she nods. We vote on it. The suggestion is carried.

I ask, if we can all agree, in future, to listen better to each other, regardless of whether the thought is coming from a boy or a girl. Yes, they all agree. "O.K", I say, "It's up to you to make it work."

## What Four Communities Classroom dynamics were in practice and what was experienced by group four?

Emotion is an **ecological imperative** and a dynamic process that includes other ecological imperatives. [See appendices (ii), (iii), (iv)]
- **communication**
- **mutual regard**
- **self-correction**
- **primary learning experience**

In this case, unhelpful emotions arose from polarization that encouraged less than helpful stances in viewing each other. The boys scoffed at the girls, convincing the girls that boys wanted only to obfuscate and obstruct. They weren't, therefore, happy with each other.

At the end of the **communication** process a new understanding of each other was arrived at and a new understanding of how to work together agreed upon. This represented a **mutual regard** process that held a good chance for reciprocation to be part of group interactions. Children were given the opportunity, working with the teacher, to create a non-polarized environment, where they could listen and engage in an inner dialogue of **self-correction**; constructive thoughts building, from within from which to make a contribution. How would that feel? What emotion would be experienced? These are the questions that the child uses to evaluate the experience. This is a **primary learning experience** that has the power to create constructive change and the power to last - especially if put into practice over the time group four is together.

A follow-up meeting with group four would probably be a good idea. I mention this to the teacher. The teacher, by keeping an eye open, can determine when would be an appropriate moment. If, at some future date, further dissension is observed and possible resolution seems to be escaping them, it may be a good idea to help the group revisit the outcomes of the first meeting. However, if everything appears to be going fine, the teacher may want to wait until the next monthly meeting to confirm that things are indeed going well. He/she can decide at the time whether it will be helpful to just observe mutual regard in action or to invite anyone to vocalize the sentiment. Mutual regard does not necessarily mean consensus. It means a willingness to listen and consider others' points of view.

When group four had a problem they told me about it. Make sure that all your groups know that they can bring seemingly unresolvable problems to a recess discussion. Soon, groups will understand the role of this impromptu recess discussion opportunity and build understanding of how to use it wisely.

(For more information please see p. 178 on pre-arranged and impromptu single group meetings with the teacher)

---

**The message from the case-studies**

The classroom environment has to be such that new patterns of organisation and ways of making sense of the world start occurring. These patterns are self-generated by children as change begins to feel good. Feeling good goes a long way towards bringing about positive change.

Creating the right conditions, therefore, is key, and it is the teacher's job to provide those conditions.

### The classroom community moves on

The many connections and friendships built and strengthened during the year are often obliged to undergo a rather artificial end in June or July. For the entire school year, the teacher had been at the centre of the community he/she and the children created together. So it is very likely, upon return to school in the fall, that children will feel a sense of loss that they are no longer in their community with their teacher. These are valid feelings that deserve recognition. Much will have been achieved in developing understanding of self in relationship with the teacher and others. It is a year-long experience to be valued and cherished. So it would be counterproductive, if not damaging, if this were to be overlooked. This is an important piece of life process. Yes, the teacher has a new class, and so do the children, but brusque references to 'moving on' can undermine the meaning of community and connection, and the sense of self that children developed through community.

Community and connection, to mean anything, especially for children, must feel valid - always. The arbitrariness of changing grades and teachers should not be accompanied by an arbitrariness applied to emotional connection. Take care to maintain connections with the children. At recess, invite them in to reminisce when they appear at their old classroom door. Children will move on when they feel ready, secure in the knowledge that who they are and what they achieved together in the Four Communities Classroom had meaning.

New beginnings do not have to mean the end of connection. Moving on to new explorations are facilitated if the old foundations still appear strong and valid.

You have, for a season, enabled growth in a group of children, and positioned them to continue to build upon this secure foundation of ecological process.

## These tables record grades achieved in the Canadian Test Of Basic Skills (CTBS) by a Four Communities Classroom grade five class in the 1990's.

- The Canadian Test Of Basic Skills has been replaced with the Canadian Achievement Tests.
- The children's names have been omitted and the alphabetical order of the class has been altered.

The CTBS tests where administered in October of the grade 5 year and again in October of the grade 6 year. As of October, on average, children are expected to be able to score a 5.2 norm in grade 5 and a 6.2 norm in grade 6. There were 30 children in this class, but since five of the children were either absent for all or part of the test administered in grade 5 or grade 6 these children's results were incomplete and their scores have not been included in this table.

Table One

| STUDENT | Vocabulary As of October in grade five | Vocabulary As of October in grade six | Reading As of October in grade five | Reading As of October in grade six | Math Concepts As of October in grade five | Math Concepts As of October in grade six | Math Problem Solving As of October in grade five | Math Problem Solving As of October in grade six |
|---|---|---|---|---|---|---|---|---|
| 1 | 4.5 | 7.9 | 5.9 | 7.9 | 5.1 | 7.2 | 4.9 | 8.8 |
| 2 | 6.1 | 8.7 | 6.3 | 8.3 | 4.3 | 7.5 | 6.0 | 7.7 |
| 3 | 6.9 | 9.7 | 6.3 | 9.5 | 6.1 | 8.0 | 7.0 | 9.0 |
| 4 | 4.5 | 6.0 | 5.5 | 5.7 | 4.5 | 4.8 | 4.9 | 5.1 |
| 5 | 2.3 | 3.2 | 3.0 | 5.1 | 4.5 | 4.2 | 3.8 | 4.3 |
| 6 | 6.0 | 6.5 | 6.7 | 6.6 | 3.9 | 5.8 | 3.8 | 5.1 |
| 7 | 5.6 | 6.4 | 5.5 | 5.6 | 4.5 | 5.6 | 4.4 | 6.3 |
| 8 | 4.5 | 6.6 | 4.2 | 6.2 | 5.4 | 6.3 | 5.5 | 5.6 |
| 9 | 5.4 | 6.7 | 4.5 | 5.5 | 5.1 | 7.1 | 4.9 | 6.2 |
| 10 | 5.0 | 6.9 | 5.2 | 4.8 | 4.9 | 6.4 | 5.2 | 6.2 |
| 11 | 4.3 | 6.3 | 3.9 | 6.2 | 6.0 | 6.6 | 5.9 | 7.1 |
| 12 | 6.1 | 6.6 | 6.1 | 7.2 | 6.0 | 5.8 | 5.5 | 5.8 |
| 13 | 6.9 | 9.1 | 7.0 | 8.8 | 5.6 | 7.7 | 6.2 | 8.6 |
| 14 | 3.5 | 5.8 | 4.6 | 4.8 | 3.5 | 3.6 | 4.9 | 5.4 |
| 15 | 6.6 | 8.1 | 7.8 | 8.7 | 6.7 | 7.2 | 6.2 | 7.1 |
| 16 | 5.3 | 6.3 | 4.3 | 6.5 | 5.7 | 5.9 | 4.4 | 6.8 |
| 17 | 6.1 | 6.7 | 5.6 | 6.8 | 5.4 | 7.1 | 6.6 | 7.7 |
| 18 | 6.0 | 7.2 | 5.5 | 6.9 | 5.1 | 5.8 | 5.4 | 7.1 |
| 19 | 2.8 | 5.2 | 3.0 | 5.1 | 3.1 | 5.8 | 4.4 | 6.3 |
| 20 | 6.7 | 7.2 | 6.8 | 7.7 | 5.2 | 6.4 | 5.7 | 6.8 |
| 21 | 6.3 | 6.7 | 7.0 | 8.0 | 5.8 | 6.9 | 6.0 | 8.1 |
| 22 | 4.0 | 4.0 | 3.7 | 4.7 | 5.1 | 6.1 | 4.1 | 5.8 |
| 23 | 7.4 | 9.7 | 6.0 | 8.7 | 6.8 | 9.5 | 7.3 | 9.8 |
| 24 | 5.2 | 6.3 | 5.5 | 5.4 | 4.7 | 5.2 | 4.7 | 6.5 |
| 25 | 6.6 | 8.9 | 7.1 | 8.7 | 6.5 | 9.2 | 6.4 | 8.5 |
| Average grade for the classroom | 5.4 | 6.9 | 5.5 | 6.8 | 5.2 | 6.5 | 5.4 | 6.9 |
| Increase - grade 5 to 6 for the class as a whole | +1.5 yrs. | | +1.3 yrs. | | +1.3 yrs. | | +1.5 yr.s | |

Table Two

| Child's overall score Oct. grade 5 | Child's overall score Oct. grade 6 |
|---|---|
| 5.1 | 8.0 |
| 5.6 | 8.0 |
| 6.6 | 9.0 |
| 4.9 | 5.4 |
| 3.4 | 4.2 |
| 5.1 | 6.0 |
| 5.0 | 6.0 |
| 4.9 | 6.2 |
| 5.0 | 6.4 |
| 5.0 | 6.1 |
| 5.0 | 6.6 |
| 5.9 | 6.4 |
| 6.4 | 8.6 |
| 4.1 | 4.9 |
| 6.8 | 7.8 |
| 4.9 | 6.4 |
| 5.9 | 7.1 |
| 5.5 | 6.8 |
| 3.3 | 5.6 |
| 6.1 | 7.0 |
| 6.3 | 7.4 |
| 4.2 | 5.2 |
| 6.9 | 9.4 |
| 5.0 | 5.9 |
| 6.7 | 8.8 |

My Daughter *Can't Wait* for Monday Morning!

Caveats to keep in mind when reading the table

Children's scores can, of course, be affected by their emotional state of mind on the day of the test, their competence at test-taking, and whether they feel rested, etc. A low score does not necessarily indicate that the child is having difficulty in that area of school work. The table offers only a general understanding of children's level of competence in the four areas tested (vocabulary, reading, math concepts and math problem solving). For example, it is likely that child #1 did not have a good day in grade 5 in the test measuring math problem solving. It seems too remarkable that she would come up virtually 3 1/2 grades by the time she was tested again in grade 6.

Teachers have the advantage of being able to compare scores with the general level of work the child does in the classroom. We are, of course, only privy to the test scores.

Within the parameters of this caveat it is, however, fair to say, I think, that one can take away a general sense of where children stand at each grade level. Certainly, I think that a high score, unlike a low score, does more closely reflect a child's ability. In other words I am not sure that one can score significantly beyond one's ability.

Although these tables are only one snapshot of children's performance in a Four Communities Classroom, I feel they do offer an encouraging glimpse into those aspects of education that lend themselves to measuring.

Table One Observations

- Average grade increase for the whole class, noted at the bottom of the table, is between 1.3 and 1.5 years - an overall average increase of 1.4 grades in one year for the children in this class.

- It took this class their first 4 years to move approximately .17 above grade norms (scoring, as a class, by grade five, 5.37 rather than the 5.2 norm). But after experiencing the Four Communities Classroom in grade five this class jumped an additional 1/2 a grade above grade norms. Thus, by October of grade 6 the class average stood at 6.8 (over 1/2 a grade above the norm). Many children achieved beyond this class average.

- Over half of the class recorded at least a two grade level increase in at least one area - they are the children numbered one, two, three, five, eight, eleven, thirteen, fourteen, sixteen, nineteen, twenty one, twenty three, and twenty five.

- Children who had gradually fallen behind in the years prior to their grade five Four-Communities-Classroom experience (averaging less than full grades, i.e. 0.7 to 0.8 of a grade per year) all achieved at least a full grade increase in at least on area in grade five, (and in some cases up to two full grades). See the children numbered five, fourteen, and nineteen.

- The number of children with scores above the 6.2 norm after their grade five year:
    In vocabulary            20 children (80% of the class), averaging 7.4
    In reading               14 children (56% of the class), averaging 7.9
    In math concepts         14 children (56% of the class), averaging 7.4
    In math problem solving  16 children (64% of the class), averaging 7.6

Therefore, over half the class, by grade six in October, averaged scores of 7.6, or, in other words, had achieved grade levels over half way into the grade seven year.

Table Two Observations

- The number of children scoring below the 5.2 norm after their grade four year - 14
- The number of children scoring below the 6.2 norm after their grade five year - 9 (now 1/3rd fewer scoring below grade norms)

- The number of children with an overall score of 5.2 or more after their grade four year - 11
- The number of children with an overall score of 6.2 or more after their grade five year - 16 (Number of children scoring at or above grade norms increased by 1/3rd)

Dear Parents or Guardians,

This year, exciting things are happening in our classroom. The children have created four communities- one in each corner of the room - where each child can develop a sense of belonging.

We are still following the curriculum and covering all the subjects, but with an added sense of anticipation and interest. The children in each group are in charge of their own corner where being in-charge carries responsibilities; each child taking responsibility both for themselves and for the group as a whole. Exploring this relationship is an ongoing part of children's daily experience, and part of the development of a positive learning atmosphere.

Class and group discussions are also a way of life and learning for us; learning to listen to others and receiving consideration in return. Through discussion, each child is learning to recognize the value of his/her thought processes and developing confidence in expressing thoughts, ideas and opinions. Children are learning that to have a voice means allowing others to speak.

We are creating this classroom environment based on Martin Sterling's book, 'My Daughter Can't Wait for Monday Morning'; Child-driven Responsibility For Sustainable Education In Happy And Productive Classrooms - Bullying Sidelined'.

It has been shown that children participating in this teaching model, enjoy the opportunity to build constructive relationships in classroom groups. Many of the children report that they have made more friends during the year, than in previous years. Importantly, bullying is reduced, and largely eliminated. Children say that coming to school is something they look forward to. Peace of mind in a happy learning environment has proven to maximise interest in learning and improve grades, as children develop greater capacity and ownership for learning, consideration of others, and confidence in self and their own abilities.

'My Daughter Can't Wait for Monday Morning' outlines a model for building a good teaching and learning atmosphere, and, with this solid and proven system, the journey is ours to own, shape and explore.

We look forward to reporting our progress as the year goes by.

Kind regards



Grade    teacher

# Appendices:

Thoughts and explorations that inform my approach to how children think and learn in happy and productive classrooms; the ecological link to the 'How To's

## Appendix (i) Processes of change, difference and potentiality - foundations of existence and of living systems

The foundation of existence is viewed through the interconnected and dynamic processes of communication, feedback, bifurcation, far from equilibrium states, order and chaos. The dynamics of interaction mean that nothing is in a set state and, therefore, everything is always in process. Process contains the seeds of potentiality and change, along with the creation of difference. The application to living systems is explored and, by extension, the dynamism occuring in children's lives in the classroom.

## Appendix (ii) Ecological foundations

A discussion on the importance of self, including the importance of identity and self-organization, recognizing that effective cognitive process is fundamental to constructive integration of self with surrounding environments.

## Appendix (iii) Difference, commonality and the importance of emotion

Consideration of the concept that self is emotionally driven and that quality of interactions with environment affect both emotions and cognition and, therefore, learning - factors that affect quality of memory, state of mind and brain development.

## Appendix (iv) Living systems and self-descriptors

Considers constructive enabling of children's inner thoughts to effectively contribute to interactions and communication within the classroom - autonomy and integration dynamics of living systems in action. Highlights the joy and success of classroom life when founded on an effective development of self and environment.

## Appendix (v) Communication and behaviour in the classroom

A discussion on consideration of nuance (as a factor arising from self), and the containment influence of externalities (attractors), that can influence the quality of communication process and, therefore, emotions, memory and learning process.

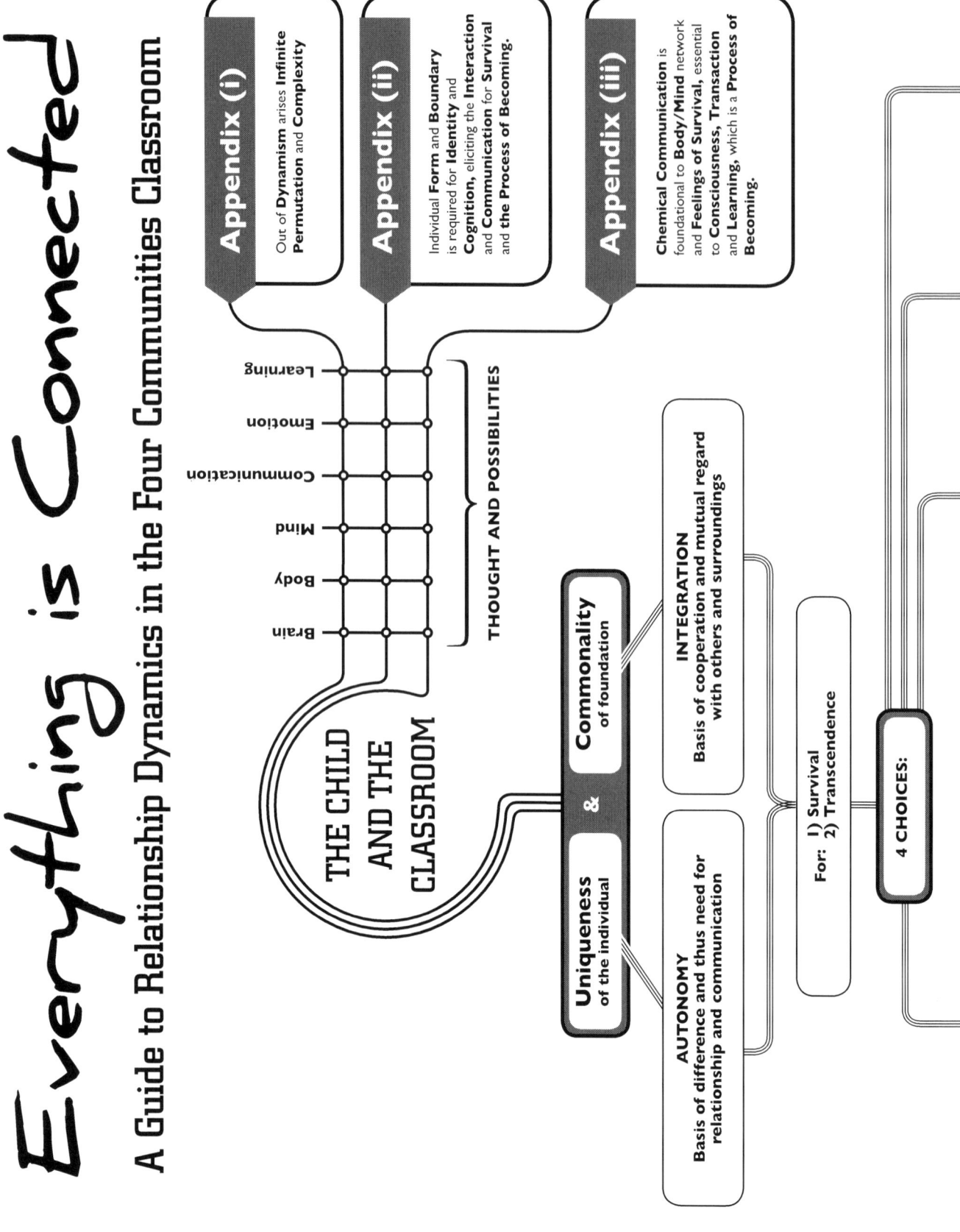

# Everything is Connected

## A Guide to Relationship Dynamics in the Four Communities Classroom

**Appendix (i)**
Out of **Dynamism** arises **Infinite Permutation** and **Complexity**.

**Appendix (ii)**
Individual **Form** and **Boundary** is required for **Identity** and **Cognition**, eliciting the **Interaction** and **Communication** for **Survival** and **the Process of Becoming**.

**Appendix (iii)**
**Chemical Communication** is foundational to **Body/Mind** network and **Feelings of Survival**, essential to **Consciousness**, **Transaction** and **Learning**, which is a **Process of Becoming**.

Brain — Body — Mind — Communication — Emotion — Learning

**THOUGHT AND POSSIBILITIES**

THE CHILD AND THE CLASSROOM

**Uniqueness** of the individual & **Commonality** of foundation

**AUTONOMY**
Basis of difference and thus need for relationship and communication

**INTEGRATION**
Basis of cooperation and mutual regard with others and surroundings

For:
1) Survival
2) Transcendence

**4 CHOICES:**

My Daughter *Can't Wait* for Monday Morning!

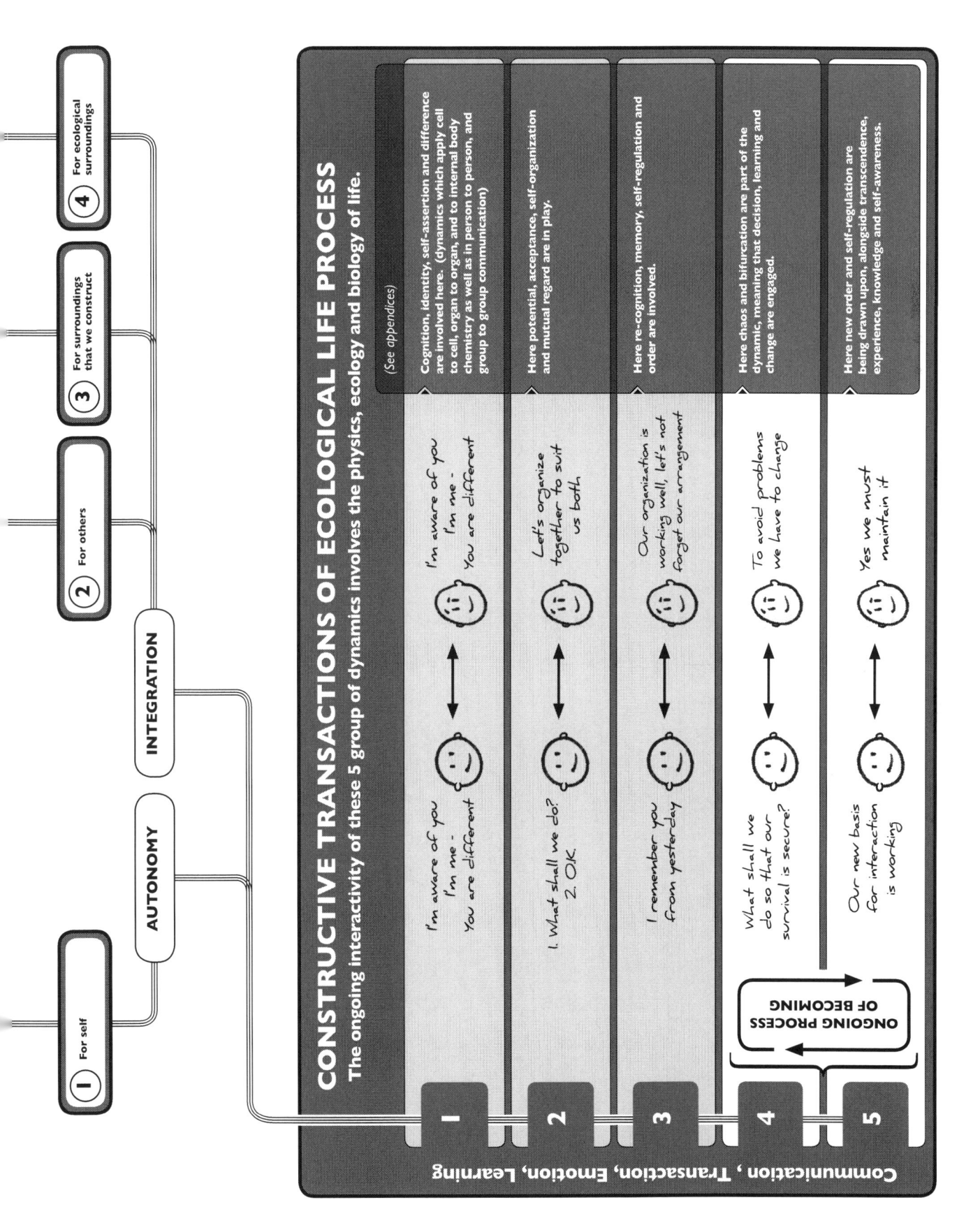

# CONSTRUCTIVE TRANSACTIONS OF ECOLOGICAL LIFE PROCESS

**The ongoing interactivity of these 5 group of dynamics involves the physics, ecology and biology of life.**

*(See appendices)*

1. Cognition, identity, self-assertion and difference are involved here. (dynamics which apply cell to cell, organ to organ, and to internal body chemistry as well as in person to person, and group to group communication)

2. Here potential, acceptance, self-organization and mutual regard are in play.

3. Here re-cognition, memory, self-regulation and order are involved.

4. Here chaos and bifurcation are part of the dynamic, meaning that decision, learning and change are engaged.

5. Here new order and self-regulation are being drawn upon, alongside transcendence, experience, knowledge and self-awareness.

| # | Left | Right |
|---|------|-------|
| 1 | I'm aware of you / I'm me - You are different | I'm aware of you / I'm me - You are different |
| 2 | 1. What shall we do? / 2. OK | Let's organize together to suit us both |
| 3 | I remember you from yesterday | Our organization is working well, let's not forget our arrangement |
| 4 | What shall we do so that our survival is secure? | To avoid problems we have to change |
| 5 | Our new basis for interaction is working | Yes we must maintain it |

**ONGOING PROCESS OF BECOMING** (between 4 and 5)

*Communication, Transaction, Emotion, Learning*

Hierarchy:
- AUTONOMY
  - 1. For self
- INTEGRATION
  - 2. For others
  - 3. For surroundings that we construct
  - 4. For ecological surroundings

The Sterling System for Ecologically-based Sustainable Classrooms

227 My Daughter *Can't Wait* for Monday Morning!

# Appendix Contents

| | | |
|---|---|---:|
| (i) | **Processes of change, difference and potentiality -** <br> **foundations of existence and of living systems** | 232 |
| • | **The dynamic world of living systems** | 233 |
| 1. | The quantum realm - a foundational theory for existence | 234 |
| 2. | Chaos and order, far-from-equilibrium states, and bifurcation - dynamics of change and learning | 237 |
| 3. | Chaos theory, tendencies and attractors of containment | 239 |
| 4. | Communicative feedback - at the heart of living systems and life in the Four Communities Classroom | 241 |
| 5. | Review of the dynamic foundations of living systems | 245 |
| (ii) | **Ecological foundations for productive, happy learning** | 248 |
| 1. | Ecological foundations of identity and relationship | 249 |
| 2. | Identifying boundaries | 249 |
| 3. | Externality | 250 |
| • | Mutuality in healthy process | 251 |
| 4. | Towards a balance of autonomy and integration dynamics | 252 |
| 5. | Ecological dynamics and us | 253 |
| 6. | The process of becoming - in nature and within ourselves | 254 |
| 7. | Cognition and mind - a process of knowing and perception (not necessarily conscious, or remembered, by all species) | 254 |
| 8. | Cognition, autonomy, integration, self descriptors, and having the ability to assert self | 256 |
| 9. | The ecological heritage for all | 257 |
| • | Fundamentals of the ecology of life: a summary | 258 |

**(iii) Difference, commonality and the importance of emotion:
 connections to productive, happy classrooms** — 260

- **DNA - foundation for difference and commonality** — 260

- **Molecular communication, feelings and emotions** — 262
    1. Integrated body systems - a blueprint for cooperation — 262
    2. The role of emotions - the great motivators — 263
    3. Staying on the ball. Self organization in reference to externalities equals learning flexibility — 264

- **Growth, development, communication, and learning in the brain
 and nervous system** — 265
    1. Neuronal development — 266
    2. Neuronal development in reference to externalities — 266
    3. Communicative intelligence, neuronal development, emotions and peptides — 267
    4. The brain and emotions — 270
    5. The mind's inner dialogue and external surroundings — 271
    6. Social influence and brain capacity — 272
    7. Brain capacity - relationship patterns of emotion, memory and learning — 273

- **The brain, consciousness and mind** — 275
    1. A physical structure for the brain but not the mind — 275
    2. The mind, and the quantum realm — 276
    3. Infinity of the mind — 277
    4. Mindful of intelligence or mindful of wisdom? The measure of intelligence — 277
    5. Minds in the classroom - a re-definition of what classroom
       responsibility means for teachers — 278
        - Primary experiences — 278
        - Secondary experiences — 278

**(iv) Living systems and self-descriptors: constructive inner dialogue and the joy and succcess of life in the classroom** ........ 282

1. The self-descriptors .......... 283
2. Self-descriptors in the classroom - emphasising an innate capacity .......... 284
3. One self-descriptor in action prompts another - autonomy and integration dynamics of living systems in action .......... 286
4. Self-descriptors and group function .......... 288
5. The essential nature of difference and the ecological communication imperative .......... 289
6. Ecological diversity and self-descriptor referencing to the surrounding environment .......... 289
7. Ecologically sound communication, tendency and the process of becoming .......... 289

**(v) Communication and behaviour in the classroom: the containment influence of attractors alongside nuance, discernment, and learning** .......... 292

1. The relevance of nuance, and tendency to the development of discernment in the classroom .......... 293
2. The mind, nuance and containment influence of curriculum learning .......... 295
3. Containment influence, categorization, customary thinking, and organizational closure .......... 296
4. Cultural containment influence and customary thinking .......... 296
    - Detaching from parental containment influence - teenage exploration of self .......... 297
5. Classroom culture and its containment-influence attractors .......... 298
    - Detaching from school containment influence - when classroom protocols may contain seeds of frustration for children .......... 298
    - Can frustrations (and bullying behaviours) be abated within peer-group containment influences? .......... 299
    - Teacher and children working together - learning beyond curriculum .......... 299
6. Containment influence of the 'neon light' face of the corporate world .......... 299
7. Nuance and discernment, and the containment influence of texting with phones .......... 301
8. Nuance and discernment viewed alongside the containment influence of attractors .......... 301
9. Seeking balance between nuance and containment-influence attractors .......... 302
10. Maximizing learning in the classroom - engaging discernment, while seeking the balance of nuance with the containment influence of attractors .......... 303
    - Discernment, primary experience, feedback, mutuality and the process of becoming .......... 304

## (i) PROCESSES OF CHANGE, DIFFERENCE, POTENTIALITY - foundations of existence and of living systems

### Introduction

As a non-scientist, I do not presume to offer a comprehensive scientific discussion. I am indebted to the scientists and other thinkers on whose work I have drawn for an understanding of the theory of living systems. I explore what I see as connections between physics, living systems and life in the classroom, in a discussion that I hope will make sense to educators in considering processes of change, difference, potentiality and learning in the classroom

I have found it useful to consider these links in creating a teaching model which has proven to enhance children's learning experience in school.

The theory of living systems and systems theory, are terms that refer to an overarching concept of far-reaching proportions, describing levels of existence and relationships, from non-living to living; in short the ecology. These theories, sometimes collectively referred to as new science, consider life in an holistic sense, where everything in the living and non-living world is seen in the context of its connection to and interactions with everything else.

As we, and our children, are part of this ecological interactive world, I have found it useful to consider links between new science and our understanding of children's learning needs and processes.

In the search for understanding of existence, the approach of classical science, originating with Rene Descartes (1596 - 1650) and Sir Isaac Newton (1642 - 1727), has been to determine the basic building blocks of existence, to shed light on deterministic patterns, and to build understanding upon principles that can be contained within a mechanistic cause-and-effect coherence. Thus, compartmentalization became the route to the analysis and mastery of knowledge and the understanding of existence.

This contained a search for universal laws; for precision in scientific research and understanding; a quest for the absolute.

This quest for identification of the absolute and the compartmentalization of knowledge as a way to understand the world became, it seems, the driver in determining how we should educate children; a process arising out of concern for 'getting things right'(see pp. 8-9).

It was in the continuing search for the absolute that the atom was discovered; and later quantum physics, with 'particles' smaller than the atom. The discovery of quantum physics, however, presented the possibility of not only a far less predictable world, but a dynamic world of unimaginable complexity, rendering definition of the absolute an ever more elusive, if not an impossible quest.

Hence arises the question, if we are part of a world of unimaginable complexity, and beyond that which classical science has been offering as a rationale for quantifying the nature of existence, what implications, if any, does that have for our quest for 'getting things right' in education?

Sagan and Druyan, '92, Introduction.
*"...bear in mind the imperfection of our current knowledge. Science is never finished. It proceeds by successive approximations, edging closer and closer to a complete and accurate understanding of nature, but it is never fully there."*

Stemming from the unfolding revelations, the theory of living systems is a work in progress; an evolving science that is the focus of work in many fields of endeavour. It is an unfolding of complexity of systems that are sustaining for life.

Sterling, S., 2001, p. 54.
*"... sustainable systems are those which are self-organizing, self-healing, and self-renewing, and that are able to learn in order to maintain and adapt themselves."*

We, and all life, are derivative expressions of this self-referential process. The ecological system evolves and changes in response to an environment that is a reflection of its constituents.

However, unlike non-human species, which remain unquestioningly within an ecological niche, we, as humans, are shapers of our social environment. We have the capacity to choose to be self-sustaining in the organization of our own communities, including the contexts we surround ourselves with, the classrooms we create, and processes of interaction and learning we engage children with.

Although we are heavily influenced by our self-imposed acculturated processes, children are closest to the derivative view of the ecology; the freshest outcomes of its process - not yet fully acculturated.

Thus children are the ones who, as they set about their lives and learning, must contend most with any dichotomy between ecologically-based processes of being and societal/cultural mores. In other words, the ecologically endowed foundations (our ecological core) that guide development processes in children may not be well accommodated within cultural contexts, including the culture of education and learning. Often tensions resulting from the mismatch have to be absorbed by the learner. This can be an inhibiting influence upon development. To unwrap this concern, I look at the description of existence provided by new science.

With educational concerns as the focus, I offer a general explanation of the holistic nature of new science, living systems and the ecology.

I should also point out that I see three levels of discussion that can be pursued in studying new science:

1. The general overview offered in this book and its implications for education.
2. The discussions offered in my source books which go into much greater detail, including detail of individual scientists' work, while at the same time offering a synthesized argument for an overarching concept of new science.
3. The science from the primary sources of research.

The thesis offered in appendix (i) is that there is a continuum between the complex activity of the invisible sub-atomic 'particles' of quantum physics that is being discovered and the 'concreteness' of the world we can touch, see, and hear - i.e life and nature.

Chopra, 2000, p.12.
*"Physics informs us that the basic fabric of nature lies at the quantum level, far beyond atoms and molecules.*

It appears that quantum physics is foundational to ecological process, and since relationship is a foundational concept of quantum physics (p. 234) there also exists a parallel in the importance of relationship to ecological processes.

Capra, '83, p. 77.
*"... the world view emerging from modern physics can be characterized by words like organic, holistic and ecological."*

There are parallels to be noted between the concepts of quantum physics, the ecology, life and nature, and, as we are part of nature, parallels with our particular interest in learning as an indivisible element of life.

## The dynamic world of living systems

I draw on Capra, Chopra, Briggs and Peat.

Physics tells us that there are dynamic and interacting elements that shape the physical world. There are elements of consistency and change that are always at work in both living and non-living systems. Since these dynamics apply to all events, they contribute to the connectedness of all things, and to the perception that nature is an holistic endeavour.

These concepts are considered from the perspective of understanding their dynamic effect and application to children and the classroom as living systems. Since new science is holistic, this discussion can be attempted from many starting points. I will begin with quantum physics, as *"...many believe (it) to be the most fundamental level of reality"*. (Briggs and Peat '90, p.181.)

# 1. The quantum realm - a foundational theory for existence

Chopra, 2001, p.10.
*"The quantum realm is the fountain head of pure potentiality, giving rise to the raw material of your body, your mind, and the physical universe."*

> If the quantum realm reveals the potentiality for the mind and body, will this contribute understanding to the educational endeavour of developing human potential?

Chopra's reference to 'fountain head of pure potentiality' underlines the limitless potential for difference. (See 'Learning the importance of difference', p.110)

Chopra, 2000, p.12.
*A quantum, defined as the basic unit of matter or energy, is from 10,000,000 to 100,000,000 times smaller than the smallest atom. At this level, matter and energy become interchangeable. All quanta are made of invisible vibrations ... ("called quantum fluctuations") waiting to take physical form"*

The constant interactive movement of sub-atomic 'particles'*, ever changing in complex patterns, forms the foundation of possibility and relationship in living systems of life, and in nonliving systems (like the weather).

(* Quantum physics can be difficult to conceptualize, since it deals with sub-atomic 'particles'; with 'particles', inside atoms, that are up to "100,000,000 times smaller than the smallest atom" and cannot be seen. Particles can also fluctuate to being wave-like. The use of the term 'quantum particle' is, therefore, not a precise description, but used as a utility in my discussion of the quantum realm.)

Quantum physics reveals a realm of limitless potential. Limitless potential is the basis for difference - differences between specie and individuals, including differences in children.

Quantum 'particles' in moment-to-moment ceaseless unpredictable movement seem chaotic. But 'particles' always affect each other through relationship; *"patterns of probability" (and) "interconnectivity."* (Capra, '83, p. 80.) In that there is order and consistency.

This dynamic nature of limitless potential and ceaseless, unpredictable movement, suggests a fruitless search for the absolute. To cease the search for the absolute in the classroom is to accept that life in the classroom can be a wonderful full-of-probability adventure, with limitless potential.

Physicists say that the 'particle-like' particles:

- are in constant movement.
- move in complex patterns.
- are constantly affected in their movement by the movement of other particles.
- are involved in constant relationship with other particles.
- are sensitive to each other.
- are the environment for other particles.
- exhibit patterns of probability and interconnectivity

If these elemental aspects of quantum physics are the foundation of nature and we are constituents of natural existence, perhaps we can draw a parallel here with children and life in the classroom and begin to see that no particle or child is an 'island'. David Bohm in 1951 speculated *"on the analogies between quantum process and thought process."* (Capra, '83, p. 86.) Thoughts are in constant movement and move in complex patterns. In children, thoughts are constantly affected by the thoughts of other children; are involved in constant relationship with other children; are sensitive to each other; and are the environment for other children's thoughts and actions - patterns of probability and interconnectivity underway.

Sensitivity of particles to each other suggests that a kind of mutuality occurs between particles. Movement is ceaseless and the sensitivity of relationship makes every particle's move unpredictable. From this unpredictability arises infinite possibilities that make it difficult to predict outcomes.

In recognising this dynamic and sensitive interaction in the classroom, we enable a naturally occurring mutuality to take place between children and facilitate infinite possibility.

> **If the quantum realm is the fount of unpredictability and infinite possibility, could education, when focused on measuring children's level of attainment of pre-planned goals, be diversionary to the more fundamental need of enabling exploratory and learning processes to occur in elementary school children?**

Chopra continues, 2000, p.169.
*"Quantum physics prove(s) that the infinite variety of objects we see around us - stars, galaxies, mountains, trees, butterflies and amoebas - is connected by infinite, eternal, unbounded quantum fields, a kind of invisible quilt that has all of creation stitched into it. Objects that look separate and distinct to us are in fact all sewn into the design of this vast quilt."*

This 'quilt of connection' concept is in keeping with the understanding of new science; that reality is full of interconnectivity through relationship, with inherent possibilities and probabilities. This brings with it a reduced reliance upon classical determinism as being descriptive of reality.

> **If individuality and limitless potential for difference lie in the quantum realm, it seems that this must have implications for teachers when assisting children in their development.**

In quantum physics, individual particles are extremely sensitive, in the course of their movement, to the movement of other particles, and, of course, other particles to them - all having been influenced by others already. It is a series of moments that are ceaseless. Therefore, movement is a constantly evolving and changing process of moments.

> **Perhaps the classroom is a quantum physics-based reflection of a constantly evolving series of non-linear moments.**

Capra, '96, p. 30.
*"The subatomic particles have no meaning as isolated entities but can be understood only as interconnections, or correlations between various processes of observation ..."*

The evolving and changing process of moments is non-linear, and is entirely unpredictable as to the course of any movement; the permutation possibilities are unimaginable. Bohm calls this process, involving *"infinitely sensitive feedback with the whole"*, quantum potential. (Briggs and Peat, '90 p. 183.)

With such unpredictability, there is chaos, but also order, in that interactions contain a process of mutuality. There seems also to be linear deterministic qualities. These qualities have been experimentally demonstrated; whatever is done to one particle is *"instantaneously registered by a change in the whole system, thus affecting the other particle."* (Briggs and Peat, '90 p. 184.)

It appears that quantum physics means dynamics of:
- movement and relationship
- mutuality
- infinite possibility and potentiality
- chaos and order

Since relationship affects change outcomes, relationship is critical. The understanding of quantum particles and understanding the relationship between quantum particles seems as one.

Capra, '83, p. 80, quoting Niels Bohr.
*"Isolated material particles are abstractions, their properties being definable and observable only through their interaction with other systems."*

Thus, how particles 'look' and behave, can only be understood in the light of how they are affected by other particles. So we can say that particle behaviour and 'look' is affected by the environment created by other particles. Only through interaction can properties be defined and observable. Properties that emerge from these interactions are called emergent properties.

If we parallel this again with life in the classroom we see that, in life, definition emerges from environmental interaction.

> **There are key words that arise in quantum physics description that have application to the consideration of children and learning, and as such, may serve as a useful foundation in the consideration of education. Of particular note are the words, 'potentiality', 'relationship' and 'emerging properties'.**

> **In children there are emergent properties that arise through relationships between individuals, groups, and surrounding environment.**

Thus, the concept of relationship in quantum physics seems important and foundational in providing some illumination upon more readily observable existence, giving substance to the concept that existence occurs through relationship.

Certainly it seems in physics that non-relationship means there is nothing to be observed. Therefore, isolation can only be referred to as an abstraction while emergent properties (the outcome of interaction) arise from relationships with others in the environment.

The classroom environment exists through relationship; each child's behaviour affected by the environment created by the other children and the teacher. No child is an 'island'. When we create a classroom environment conducive to the free flow of thoughts and interactions, in an atmosphere of mutual regard, constructive behaviour will likely be an emergent outcome.

> **Does the idea of observable actuality arising in the presence of relationship have application for emerging properties in the classroom?**

Capra tells us that the complexity of quantum physics appears in nature as a complicated web of relationships and makes nature unified. Humans are, of course, not outside of these connections. Thus, there appears to be an overall quantum-based pattern to both existence and to the ecology.

Says Capra, '83, p. 80, 81.
"...*modern physics reveals the basic oneness of the universe. ...As we penetrate into matter, nature does not show any isolated building blocks, but rather appears as a complicated web of relations between various parts of a unified whole.*"

Capra, '83, p. 88.
"*All the material objects in our environment are made of atoms that link up with each other in various ways to form an enormous variety of molecular structures ...*"

Capra brings us insights into the significance of relationship, ceaseless movement, and change and the uncertainty of obtaining a precise measurable outcome - all factors involved in the consideration of nature and the ecology. Thus, it can be said, with humans being part of the ecology that:

1. we are part of, and contribute to, environment and emerging properties.

2. relationship is foundationally important to us.

   Children are also, of course, part of the ecology.

> **Environment and relationship play crucial roles in the properties or qualities that emerge in children. Thus, it appears fair to say, the ecology's living system process offers insight into the weight and importance of classroom environmental influence upon children's development.**

But alongside this oneness are the dynamics of chaos and order, far from equilibrium, and bifurcation; dynamics integral to change and learning.

## 2. Chaos and order, far-from-equilibrium states, and bifurcation - dynamics of change and learning

Briggs and Peat, '90, p. 150.
*"... in the laws of unpredictability, chaos, and time - (lie) the secret of natures creativity."*

Again language can be confusing, as the word chaos is usually associated with something to be avoided; an undesirable state of disorder and erratic randomness, whilst order, once achieved should be maintained. But chaos theory describes, instead, complex motion and change process.

Without motion the dynamics of change would cease and a state of equilibrium (entropy) would ensue. A state of equilibrium means nothing can happen - no movement, no energy, no transaction, no dynamism.

James Lovelock, p. 35.
*"The state of disequilibrium is one from which, in principle at least, it should be possible to extract some more energy, as when a grain of sand falls from a high spot to a low one. At equilibrium, all is level and no more energy is available."*

Therefore, movement, energy, transaction, and dynamism require disequilibrium - a state of being that is far from equilibrium.

Capra, '96, p. 176.
*"... an organism in equilibrium is a dead organism. Living organisms continually maintain themselves in a state far from equilibrium, which is a state of life ... (and) nevertheless (is) stable over long periods of time..."*

Thus, being in a state far from equilibrium is a dynamic existence interactively involving movement, energy, and transaction. Such dynamism can remain stable (see 'Attractors of containment', p. 239), but can also undergo stress, bringing a system close to chaos and a need to adapt. Adaptation occurs through bifurcation - a fork in the road, a point of 'decision'. It is through bifurcation that a system moves to a new order; a process of change and of learning. Instability can characterize the chaos/bifurcation process in its passage to order.

Taking on board new information can be a transition from what was perceived as a stable state to a need to adapt and to consider alternatives: a self-organizing striving for stability with the engaging of bifurcation choices.

As systems are dynamic, it means chaos/order transitions via bifurcation are ever present and are inherent in life, nature and ecological process.

Briggs and Peat, '90, p. 137.
*" ... a property of far-from-equilibrium chaos is that it contains the possibility of self-organization."*

Capra, '96, p. 25.
*"...understanding the pattern of self-organization is the key to understanding the essential nature of life."*

Thus, systems operating far from equilibrium are subject to instability and bifurcation leading to development of a new direction. Outcomes can affect the quality and pattern of self-organization. This can represent a developmental and evolutionary process; an increase in complexity - a process of learning.

Similarly, it seems, the far-from-equilibrium state would be an important part of children's learning process. Within children's minds, bifurcation would create a fork in the road and a point of decision, requiring choices that can lead to change, development, learning and increased levels of awareness.

Capra, '96, p. 186.
*"Since all living systems (including us) exist in continually fluctuating environments, and since we can never know which fluctuations will occur at the bifurcation point just at the 'right' moment, we can never predict the future path of the system."*
My bracketed words.

> **It is important to recognise that fluctuating influences make the teaching and learning process imprecise.**
> **However, the classroom learning environment is influential and vitally important to the bifurcation processes of each child.**

By allowing constructive thoughts, actions and relationships to flourish in the classroom, rather than striving for a predetermined set state, children are enabled to arrive at individual and collective bifurcation points from which growth and change can emerge.

Capra, '96, p. 177. Bifurcation can be evolutionary and developmental.

Thus:

> Learning, can be described as,
> - being brought to a point of bifurcation, (fork in the road) a chaotic region, with a moment, or moments of instability (in what is known, thought or believed), thus moving into a different state where, perhaps beliefs and behaviours are altered.

Thus, through change, a learning process occurs. Since learning cannot be unlearned, the process is irreversible. It is chaos and order in mutual interaction. The occurrence of thousands of such bifurcation processes increases the number of learning 'events' and, therefore, results in complexity, and complexity of evolving systems - children's minds moving forward to a higher order.

Briggs and Peat, '90, p. 144.
*"...thousands upon thousands of bifurcation points (constitute) a living chronology of the choices by which we evolved as a system ... to our present form."*

The current state of a system is a reflection or record of previous bifurcations: *"a crystallization of the system's history."* (Briggs and Peat, '90, p. 144.) All species are reflections of their bifurcation history; an evolutionary history. Bifurcation is an evolutionary process.

Capra, '96, p. 177.
*"The existence of bifurcation at which the system may take several different paths implies ... indeterminancy."*

In a positive sharing environment, accepting of children's thoughts and ideas, children can build a strong bifurcation history of learning, growth and creativity; a pattern that can be lifelong.

> What implications are there for classroom life generally when, at the foundational level of existence, fluctuating life processes mean that probability and a striving for stability occurs alongside creativity?

> **Learning and bifurcation in the classroom**
> **Bifurcation processes:**
> - influence relationship connection to surroundings and others.
> - mean adaption and consideration of alternatives and an engagement with choices.
> - are part of the creation of, and learning from, complexity.
> - mean a self-organizing striving for stability. (See 'attractors of containment' on opposite page.)
> - are part of mutual interaction.
>
> However, fluctuations in the environment make it difficult to predict the form bifurcation will take, and what will be absolutely learned.

- **Classical order or the far from equilibrium state?**

While bifurcation is uncertain in outcome and difficult to measure, by contrast, classical science is based in concepts of set states, in pursuit of certainty, order and containment, and prefers to study order, precision and absoluteness. Classical science, therefore, is useful and effective when considering systems that are less prone to bifurcation, where states are more set and measurable. For life on earth the solar system is an example of a system closer to being in a set state.

But set order can exist alongside bifurcation-prone order. For example, the solar system affects weather that is always subject to bifurcation changes.

Thus, it is not a matter of classical science being trumped by new science, but rather that classical science is insufficient to describe dynamic systems that evolve and change. Children are an example of a dynamic system.

Briggs and Peat, '89, p. 24.
*"... in the nonlinear world - which includes most of our real world - exact prediction is both practically and theoretically impossible."*

Thus, those that are striving for certainty can find that they are constantly at odds with the evolving ecology of life; unable to accurately predict future outcomes, unable to understand the significance of bifurcation points, often taken unaware by unforeseen emerging properties, often trying to determine remedial action, often clinging to an illusion of certainty, often falling short of hoped for goals.

By embracing uncertainty and the positive outcome of chaos/order bifurcation in the classroom alongside the relative certainty of curriculum acquisition, one can, in fact, enhance the learning process, as it settles more comfortably into the ebb and flow of the evolving ecology of life.

> **Since school is filled with life and teaching, and learning is a dynamic process, it seems that a perspective based upon predetermined expectations alone will not sufficiently reflect school processes and, therefore, will also be inadequate in guiding educational initiative.**

As each individual child in the classroom evolves and changes from minute to minute, there is dynamic group influence. Environment affects life and life affects environment. Awareness is key. In a safe, affirming environment, children can be open to qualitative growth and change.

It is interesting to look at a list of words that appear in discussion of the dynamics of the quantum realm, chaos and order, far-from-equilibrium states, bifurcation and change and consider their relevance to the classroom environment:

- relationship
- probability
- possibility
- interconnectivity
- linear and non-linear
- individuality and group influence,
- unpredictability and uncertainty
- indeterminancy
- infinite permutations - potentiality
- sensitivity
- mutual evolution and change
- emerging properties
- complexity.

## 3. Chaos theory, tendencies and attractors of containment

I continue to draw on Capra, and Briggs and Peat.

Chaos theory also introduces the term **'attractor'** to describe containment influences and tendencies within systems.

Says Capra, '96, p. 177.
*"Whatever the system's initial conditions, it will be 'attracted' towards a stationary state of minimum entropy (change), as close to equilibrium as possible and its behaviour will be completely predictable."*

Systems that are close to equilibrium are limited in their function and tend towards predictability. This limiting effect within the system is known as the 'attractor'. The result is that a system's cycle of function is limited in its range (the limit cycle of the attractor) and creates repetitive action (as in a pendulum - Briggs and Peat). Though continuing to repeat the action, left to its own devices, a system will change with the slightest change in its conditions. Thus, when the pendulum's swing is slowed by friction and air resistance the pendulum is not able to continously follow its path and will eventually come to rest.

However, when you look at a pendulum powered by a motor to keep it swinging, you have a controlled mechanically-boosted attractor - unaffected by friction and air resistance - an attractor where the pendulum movement is sustained.

Unlike man-made systems, nature combines influences of change with a variety of containment-influence attractors in order to maintain conditions that favour sustainability and balance in the ecology.

Say Briggs and Peat, '89, p. 37,
*"The ability of limit cycles to resist change through feedback is one of the paradoxes discovered by the science of change. More and more, researchers are appreciating the way nature has of coupling continuously changing things together in order to end up with systems that effectively resist change."*

As illustration, Briggs and Peat, '89, p. 38, talk of the balance between change and the order of containment-influence attractors to maintain sustainability in predator/prey relationships. *"Here is a collection of many individuals, each one behaving randomly, yet all somehow creating a highly stable and organized system."*

Thus the ecology demonstrates its capacity for self-organizing stability.

Lovelock speaks to this capacity, '89, p. 52.
*"The earth spins before an uncontrolled radiant heater, the sun, whose output is by no means constant. Yet right from the beginning of life, around three and a half eons ago, the Earth's mean surface temperature has never varied by more than a few degrees from its current levels. It has never been too hot or too cold for life to survive on our planet, in spite of drastic changes in the composition of the early atmosphere and variations in the sun's output of energy."*

In terms of attractors Capra says, '96, p. 197.
*"Extensive research has shown that a wide variety of living systems - including genetic networks, immune systems, neuronal networks, organ systems, and ecosystems - ... exhibit(ing) several alternative attractors."*

Consideration of containment-influence attractors and their influence on the dynamic nature of the evolving process of life can, perhaps, provide insight into the role and affects of containment and tendency in children's learning. [Appendix (v), p. 292]

Capra, '96, p. 206.
*"While behaviour in the physical domain is governed by cause and effect, the so called laws of nature; behaviour in the social domain is governed by rules generated by the social system and often codified into law. The crucial difference is that social laws can be broken, but natural laws cannot. Human beings can choose whether and how to obey a social rule; molecules cannot choose whether or not they should interact."*

In guiding children, therefore, it would seem, the closer we get to the ways of the natural world, allowing for the natural flow of the positive containment influences of attractors alongside bifurcation and change in the classroom, the more readily children will *"... move from the universal to the unique, towards richness, and variety. This, of course, is a well known characteristic of life."* Capra, '96, p. 177.

In viewing children in terms of derivatives of ecological process - their behaviours, relationship, individual tendencies and learning - we can see examples of attractors (containment influences) in action. Appendix (v) offers thoughts on how containment-influence attractors affect behaviour in the classroom (and beyond).

In recognizing these behaviours, it is important to note that, as Capra says, despite the attractors' constraining influence on relationships in dynamic systems, everything is in a constant state of relationship change, making it difficult to make precise measurements of what is happening or what is about to happen. As such, a dynamic system is hard to measure and predict because it is constantly changing. With the influence of attractors, as Capra points out, we can only make predictions about the quality of how things will behave in the ecology.

Capra, '96, p. 134.
*" ... this does not mean that chaos theory is not capable of any prediction. We can still make very accurate predictions, but they concern the qualitative features of the system's behaviour rather than the precise values of its variables at a particular time. The new mathematics thus represents a shift from quantity to quality that is characteristic of systems theory in general. Whereas conventional mathematics deals with quantities and formulas, dynamical systems theory deals with quality and pattern".*

> **An individual child is formed from cells that, affected by attractors and change influences, work together in a dynamic system. Should we be giving greater consideration to *"the qualitative features of the system's behaviour rather than to the precise values of its variables at a particular time"*. (Capra, '96, p. 134.) What effect does this have on educators' systems of evaluation?**

The classroom, a dynamic system subject to both social expectations (attractor) and the constant state of change arising from its membership, can be an environment conducive to positive change; a place where good outcomes and relationships can flourish in a state of mutuality.

My Daughter *Can't Wait* for Monday Morning!

## 4. Communicative feedback - at the heart of living systems and life in the Four Communities Classroom

Feedback is something that we all like to get. We like to know that we are understood by others. Sometimes we might ask questions (ask for feedback) to help us understand what another person thinks of our actions or thoughts. Sometimes we may look for feedback clues, such as facial expressions, and other indications of mood such as approval, interest, annoyance, amusement. This is part of relating to others. Feedback, of all types, is part of communication.

Since feedback, along with constantly evolving processes of movement, relationship, and mutuality are part and parcel of ecological process, our desire for feedback would appear to arise from our ecological core.

As Briggs and Peat, '90, p. 183, explain, "... *the quantum potential - which every quantum particle possesses - is an infinitely sensitive feedback with the whole.*"; a feedback process that perhaps can be thought of as foundational to mutuality. Living systems respond with mutuality to their surroundings through communication [sometimes chemical, see appendix (iii)] and the receipt of feedback. Mutuality, communication and feedback in humans is, of course, expressed verbally through an attitude of mutual regard.

It follows that children, as living systems, adequately respond to their surroundings through communication and feedback, especially in an environment of mutuality or mutual regard.

With discussion process being an expression of communicative feedback, it seems important that it is part of the classroom experience. Mutual regard can especially be part of discussion if there is some "…infinitely sensitive feedback with the whole" that results in constructive networks.

This has guided my thinking on how children develop and learn and, together with the teacher, create happy productive classrooms in an atmosphere of mutual regard, with discussion at the heart of all teaching and learning; constructive networks forming.

> To what extent would concepts of network and discussion processes be relevant to children's learning experiences in the classroom?

- **Negative and positive feedback**

There are two types of feedback - positive feedback and negative - which are two continuously interacting dynamics that form networks and function within the mutuality imperative.

The terms negative and positive feedback are not value judgments.

**Negative feedback balances and regulates**, providing foundation within the confines of attractors (containment).

Richard Monastersky (Barlow '98, p. 28).
*"Negative feedback reduces any changes in the system and therefore helps to stabilize it."*

**Positive feedback magnifies change** and contains the potential to modify attractors. However, without the balance from negative feedback, the change can be so great that the system can be made vulnerable to damage.

Richard Monastersky (Barlow '98, p. 28).
*"Positive feedback … (can) destabilize a system."*

Living and non-living systems usually need a balance of negative and positive feedback. It is the interactive nature of positive and negative feedback that enables each individual system to maintain mutuality in the interest of a healthy environment. This mutuality of need creates stability in the ecological system.

Capra, '96, p. 63.
*"... purely self-reinforcing feedback phenomena are rare in nature, as they are usually balanced by negative feedback loops constraining their runaway tendencies."*

Briggs and Peat, '90, p. 25-26, illustrate by considering feedback processes engaged by a thermostat and also by a microphone. They say that negative feedback can be seen in thermostatically controlled devices. So, for example, a thermostat will trigger a furnace to operate. The heat produced by the furnace will cause the thermostat to shut off the furnace. When the temperature drops, the thermostat will again trigger the furnace to operate. This system of negative feedback is self-regulatory; attractors (containment influences) in action.

Positive feedback iterates; it repeats the same feedback continually - self-reinforcing. The feedback is not a self-regulatory influence, as is negative feedback, but an amplifying influence. It builds on itself. The screech of a microphone is the result of this process; amplified sounds are picked up by the microphone and fed back into the amplifier to be amplified further.

Systems, in both of these examples, consist of parts that are relating to each other through feedback processes.

As Capra says, it is rare in nature that positive feedback processes will exist in isolation as, without some self-regulatory negative feedback influence, positive feedback would have a spiralling runaway effect; attractors overcome. Positive feedback in isolation would mean no regard for the environment and associated systems - no mutality or mutual regard relationship. Thus, 'self' would be adversely affected.

A system's dynamism depends on a system providing input to itself with a balance of both negative and positive feedback, as in self-balancing, self-regulation and self-reinforcing. [See self-descriptors appendix (iv) p.282 ]

> **Could the dynamics of the spiraling runaway effect of no mutuality (with no self-regulatory negative feedback) be behind loss of order and control in the classroom? In other words, the loss of constructive network pattern in the classroom is caused by positive feedback (feedback without self-regulatory influence) in action; the attractor of school's purpose overcome.**

Moreover, 'self' does not operate in isolation. Each entity of living system 'self' operates in relationship with other entities of self, be it a cell (a chemical information system), an individual (a system consisting of cells), an organization (a system consisting of individuals - consisting of cells), an ecosystem (a system consisting of a group of individuals in a sustaining environment), or a combination of all of the above.

Capra, '83, p. 81.
*"nature ...appears as a complicated web of relations between various parts of a unified whole."*

- **Complexity and communication feedback**

Complex ecological relationships operate far from equilibrium, and thus go through states of chaos and order. Relationships are not simple cause and effect arrangements (as with the furnace example).

Negative feedback is self-regulating and resists change; attractors maintained. But positive feedback can trigger bifurcation, modify attractors and cause change to occur. While change is occurring through bifurcation, negative and positive feedback communication continues. Thus, as the change to a new order starts to form, feedback communication will continue to influence the shaping of the change. Simultaneously, the feedback communication contributes to a new level of self-regulatory negative feedback, needed to keep the new order in balance. Thus, in the interest of ecological integrity, mutuality is maintained in the new order.

In the creation of a new level of order, there is, as there was in the old, fluctuating influence between negative and positive feedback.

This fluctuation between feedback processes, during bifurcation, enables the ecosystem to adapt, develop, change and learn. This causes the ecology and life transactions to become more complex. The increased complexity makes communication more complex. Thus, to ensure the viability of self, there is the need for mutality of communication, feedback (negative and positive) with other entities of self; a mutually sustaining network.

This complex process is especially focussed in human lives. Thus, communication, learning and complexity are linked.

Since we humans make the world increasingly complex for ourselves, this link between learning and complexity is an important ecological perspective for teachers. It underlines the need for increased sophistication in human communicative ability.

The structure and process of the Four Communities Classroom, grounded in communication through discussion, enables an environment where children and teacher, together, can create a mutually-sustaining network, engaging negative and positive feedback to create a happy, productive learning experience, true to the ecological imperative of each living system.

> **To maximize learning potential in the classroom, and to maintain constructive network patterns, what forms of interconnectedness and communication feedback would children require?**

While the balance between positive and negative feedback helps to guard against the damaging domination of one type of feedback over the other, it is not, however, a cut-and-dried process, but a fluctuating and dynamic one.

Capra, '96, p. 294.
"All ecological fluctuations take place between tolerance limits."

This would seem to suggest that life-sustaining balance between positive and negative feedback arises from relationships of cooperation in ecological systems.

> **Sensitivity to life fluctuations, cooperative relationships, and awareness as to what constitutes productive tolerance limits are important to teaching and learning in the classroom.**

The Four Communities Classroom teacher can gently monitor this fluctuating environment. She has the tools to facilitate children's choice of responses and behaviours that help create dynamic sustaining conditions for life, in the classroom and beyond.

> **What interactions of positive and negative feedback in the classroom will create complex thinking in children's minds, and cause the breaching of bifurcation points to enhanced learning and new levels of mental organization?**

Through discussion, the dynamism inherent in combinations of positive and negative feedback engenders awareness of others and mutual regard; a healthy balance of autonomy of the individual and integration. with others This can build diversity as well as complexity, enabling the child, (an ecological system) to create in itself an increasingly, ever-ready state of adaptation to meet changing conditions. Complexity and diversity equals flexibility and minimises vulnerability.

> **If self-sustaining attributes of flexibility and the capacity for diversity are the processes of a healthy ecology, what would children need to experience in the classroom to put these attributes into practice themselves?**

Briggs and Peat, '90, p. 165.
"It appears that the greater an organism's autonomy, the more feedback loops required both within the system and in its relationship to the environment".

The healthy, autonomous system, it appears is engaged in a continuous learning curve; more feedback loops meaning increasing system complexity with increasingly complex exchange and transaction.

When we create a learning environment in which children can explore ideas together, we encourage feedback loops that create continuous and constructive learning.

> **Increasingly complex feedback goes hand-in-hand with increasing development of individual autonomy, and forms the basis of continuous and constructive learning. To what extent are we enabling children's written and verbal communicative skills to be commensurate with the increasing complexity we are creating in their surroundings?**

> **To what extent is the life-sustaining living system dynamic between a child and its surroundings utilized as children move through the grades? This question is particularly relevant, as teachers aspire to help children develop the human facility for responsibility to self and environment.**

> **How and what are we doing, in schools, to prepare children for a world that we are making increasingly complex?**

> **In education, an increasing sophistication of endeavour and communication would reflect the ecology's learning curve process as we increase the complexity of our human impacted environments. This is an important ecological concept for educators.**

Having considered the patterns of life systems, we see how feedback affects how a system develops its organization through connections between behaviour, relationship and communicative feedback.

Humans, including children, also look to communicative feedback for guidance to make sense of their world, through the examination of the relationship, behavioural pattern and organization of others in their surroundings.

Capra, '96, p. 187.
*"This self organizing, the spontaneous emergence of order, results from the combined effects of non-equilibrium, irreversibility, feedback loops, and instability (chaos/order)."* [Bracketed words are mine].

There is, through self-organizing feedback, harmony in ecological relationships that ensures continuity of right-conditions-environment for life, and for us, in the living of life, an opportunity to contribute to and participate in the right-conditions-environment. In essence, the dynamics of ecological sustenance and sustainability provides a foundation for symbiotic cooperation.

The Four Community Classroom is founded on the concept of symbiotic cooperation. A classroom environment that affords its constituents the opportunity to self-organize in response to feedback as it creates for itself a right-conditions-environment for cooperation as a way of life in the classroom.

> **If symbiotic cooperation is fundamental to ecological process, and we are derivatives of ecological process, to what extent should we enable in children's minds ideas of cooperation as a way of living and learning?**

> **Should the life-sustaining feedback of environmental process provide us with a guide for shaping feedback offered in the classroom? Should feedback in the classroom be about maintaining the right-conditions–environment for constructive life and learning? What form would that take?**

When we enable an environment where mutual regard and cooperation can flourish, the seeds we plant fall on fertile ground. Children respond to an innate sense of what feels right.

# Review of the dynamic foundations of living systems

In review, let us consider our link to the theory of new science; our conscious and unconscious human connection to the ecology. It seems that the quantum realm, chaos theory, and theory of living systems exhibit a commonality of concept which is underlined through terms such as bifurcation, far-from-equilibrium, feedback and attractors. Also the concepts and terms share many words.

## INTER-RELATED CONCEPTS AND WORDS

- unpredictability and uncertainty
- infinite permutation potential
- indeterminancy
- sensitivity
- mutuality
- cooperative interaction
- chaos
- order
- evolution and change

- relationship
- probability
- possibility
- interconnectivity
- linear, non-linear
- individuality and group influence
- complexity
- emerging properties
- development

- learning
- tendency
- fluctuation
- no absoluteness
- quality
- pattern
- self-organization
- communication
- network

From these theories, which are a convergence of many scientists' work over a considerable period of time, a cohesion appears to emerge; a common thread linking elements of existence in which relationship between living and non-living entities is seen to be a series of ceaseless and dynamic moments.

We learn that relationship processes involve feedback, bifurcation (point of decision and learning), order and chaos that make outcomes unpredictable and contain change, development and evolution. Tendencies, qualities, pattern, and network form and develop in mutuality to ensure maintenance of the context for life. Self-descriptors (appendix iv) guide self-regulatory function, while bifurcation allows tensions to find new expression. Fundamentally, it seems, there is a cooperative learning that leads to self-organizing ability; an ability that enables a symbiotic context for life and the environment. Life-forms, whether microbial, cellular, animal, human, plant organisms or the entire planetary function, exhibit the same dynamics.

**Can understanding the ever-changing, evolving nature of the ecological dynamics of life enable a deeper understanding of ourselves, and our learning capacity, and deepen understanding of the dynamics engaged when teaching?**

These thoughts have led to the creation of the Four Communites Classroom; the combined parts of the whole working together to create an ecologically sound environment that is self-sustaining in its mutual regard processes of evolution and change.

We humans are ecological beings, we are part of ecological expression, and we are part and parcel of the unified whole.

Moreover, with our mental capacity, we perform a conscious role in the ecological process. We have powers that enable an ecological engagement that goes beyond that of other species and their contained function. We are able to facilitate our learning through our consciousness of wide-ranging possibilities, and our desire for personal development.

We have a conscious choice in decision-making, especially at bifurcation points in our lives. We can also choose and precipitate bifurcation.

> **To what extent do we recognize children's conscious thought processes as expressions of ecological process, and to what extent do we constructively enable such processes?**

However, within our bodily structure, beyond the purview of conscious control, much activity continues with the same level of symbiotic and cooperative unconscious self-organization that exists throughout nature (e.g. pumping of the heart, experiencing goose bumps, healing of cuts, eyes adjusting to light or dark). We exhibit, therefore, both conscious and unconscious self-organization.

Reciprocity and sensitivity to feedback maintain the sustainability of an infinitely complex ecological system. As history has shown, humans sustainably excel, for the good of all, not through imposed dominance, but through reciprocity and sensitivity to feedback. We are part and parcel of an infinitely complex ecological system.

> **To what extent do we enable children to appreciate the effect of reciprocity in interaction with others and develop sensitivity to feedback in the classroom?**

Each of us, including our children, has a highly sophisticated ecological core. Surely, this is a gift of nature to be recognized, in all its power and wonder, and nurtured in the children in our care.

> **To what extent do we recognize the fact that each child has an ecological core and is ecologically driven?**

The Four Community Classroom nurtures this gift of nature. The Four Communities Classroom model provides teachers with the tools to engender responses and behaviours that help create dynamic sustaining conditions for life in the classroom and beyond.

### Discussion is an enabling tool

Through discussion, the teacher can engage the child's mind and emotion, bringing to life and consciousness the dynamics of living systems through relationship processes.

- **Communication and feedback**
  Affected are the quality of decisions made in those relationships, which help shape the **pattern of organization** between individuals.

- **Relationship processes**
  We learn that relationship processes that take place in discussion involve feedback and bifurcation (fork-in-the-road point of decision, change and learning). We recognize that bifurcation - the point of change in the dynamic between order and chaos - is an important part of children's learning process, enabling development and increased levels of awareness.

- **Order and chaos**
  We can see that the dynamics of order and chaos (that can make outcomes unpredictable) are a natural part of this process that contain change, development and evolution - all part of learning.

- **Bifurcation processes**
  The bifurcation processes, triggered by discussion, increase the number of learning events.

- **Increased learning events** create complexity which, in turn, can make communication more complex - sophistication increased. Thus, one can say discussion, learning and complexity are linked.

- **Increasing complexity**
  Since we humans have tended to make the world increasingly complex for ourselves, this link between learning and complexity is an important ecological perspective for teachers to consider. It underlines the need for increased sophistication

in our ability to communicate in a meaningful way. Facilitation of written and, especially, verbal communication should, therefore, be the foundational mainstay of education from which other learning stems.

Capra, '96, p. 282
*"To be human is to exist in language. In language we cordinate our behaviour, and together in language we bring forth our world."*

By making discussion a foundational element in your classroom you automatically bring to life the physical dynamics of the ecology, enabling every child, as an ecological being, to find expression.

(See p. 57, 'How to create and build constructive discussion and communication process between children'.)

## (ii) ECOLOGICAL FOUNDATIONS FOR PRODUCTIVE, HAPPY LEARNING

**Introduction**

In building a Four Communities Classroom, the teacher creates an environment that reflects the tenets of ecological literacy and guides children towards learning to live in accord with those around them.

Within each child are the elements that are foundational to ecological expression and include every aspect of our being, from internal functioning that is largely unconscious to our conscious awareness of self and surroundings.

While other species exist within an ecological niche, which keep them in symbiotic accord with their environment, humans do not. We have powers of reasoning and the ability to make the choices that are ecologically sound. We could but, too often, we do not. Cultural constructs take the place of what Capra calls 'ecological literacy'.

Capra, '96, p. 295.
*"The survival of humanity will depend on our ecological literacy, on our ability to understand these principles of ecology and live accordingly."*

To explore ways to create a classroom environment in tune with this ecological imperative, I found the following ecological elements not only provide a useful reference, but also a valuable guide in providing insight into understanding children, and their processes.

- boundary, individuality and difference (identity)
- trading of needs (transactions)
- relationship
- mutuality and mutual regard
- self-organization
- communication.

As we consider how the dynamics of quantum physics and associated theories (the basis of living systems theory) appear foundational to life and the ecology, we see how the dynamism of life is expressed in the ecology through individuality and difference; each living entity being distinct from other living entities. Since identity, individuality and difference are essential to dynamism within the ecology, the survival of individuality and identity require transactions that maintain dynamism; a trading of needs, a relationship of mutuality. These connections of relationship cannot occur without constructive communication systems. However, without individual identity, nothing can be identified or communicated with. So it becomes apparent that identity, communication and relationship are fundamental to ecological process and life expression. This is true of relationship connections between individual cells within organisms, and relationships between complete organisms, from the most simple to the most sophisticated. Humankind, every adult and child, is a highly individual, sophisticated, complex organism.

Seeing children as dynamic life expressions of the ecology, with identity, communication and relationship imperatives, can broaden awareness of their learning processes.

I consider the ecology and the link to children in the classroom under the following:

1. Ecological foundations of identity and relationship
2. Identifying boundaries
3. Externality
4. Towards a balance of autonomy and integration dynamics
5. Ecological dynamics and us

> "The survival of humanity will depend on our ecological literacy, on our ability to understand these principles of ecology and live accordingly."
>
> Capra, '96, p.295,

6. The process of becoming - in nature and within ourselves
7. Cognition - a process of knowing and perception (not necessarily conscious, or remembered, by all species)
8. Cognition, autonomy, integration, self descriptors, and having the ability to assert self
9. The ecological heritage for all

## 1. Ecological foundations of identity and relationship

Having looked at the patterns of relationship in new science we see patterns of self organization through relationship with externalities, via feedback. In quantum physics, although infinitely minute 'particles' are difficult to define, we have seen that relationship appears foundational to the movement of the particles. This relationship process is also evident in the ecological process and more readily observed since the 'particles' of life (cells, organisms, individuals), have, by comparison, the property of substance and boundary that brings concreteness to relationship. In this examination of the ecological system, we see that identifying boundaries is both essential for entities to exist and to the occurrence of relationship processes between them. So for children, who are ecological beings, we can see that the concept of boundary as foundational is important. Boundaries are essential to a child's individuality and difference. Making 'the essential need for boundary' a conscious thought can constructively alter relationship perceptions of self and others. Recognizing that self-organization through relationship with externalities, via feedback, is an ecological imperative, points the way to creating a classroom environment where children are given the opportunity to self-organize through relationship, via feedback through discussion.

> What effect would the thought of the 'essential need for boundary' to life process have upon classroom life?

## 2. Identifying boundaries

The earliest boundaries for life are those of membranes. A cell, for example, is surrounded by a membrane. The membrane defines the cell as a distinct system from other cells.

Capra, '96, p. 163.
"...the cell membrane ... a boundary of the cell, ... encloses the network of metabolic processes (within the cell) and ... limits their extension." (bracketed words are mine)

Each cell, contained within its membrane, has an internal purpose and process. The membrane defines the limit of the cell's metabolic process and contains its identity and pattern of organization. Thus the membrane enables identity, purpose, and a pattern of organization to emerge.

Ludwig von Bertalanffy, (Barlow, '98. p. 106.)
"An astounding multiplicity of processes goes on in even the simplest cell, so arranged that its identity is maintained in this ceaseless and tremendously complicated play. Equally, every living being displays in its organs and functions a purposeful construction, adapted to the environment in which it normally exists."

A cell's purpose, contained within its membrane, includes relationship with its surrounding environment, and includes communication and feedback processes. The cell has to be able to relate to its surroundings in order to live. To do this, the cell has to be, and is, an active member of a network, (the larger organism). The cell's existence contributes to the existence of the larger organism, which in itself has its own identity.

The cell is a constituent of the larger organism's pattern of organization. Thus while the membrane serves as a mark of identity and purpose, it is not a mark of separation.

> A child's identity is not a mark of separation from others. Identity and definition are essential to the establishment of relationships and patterns of organization. A child's sense of identity (autonomy) does not exist in isolation. Relationships (integration) are important in developing identity.

Using a system of chemical communication [see appendix (iii)] the cell plays its part in the network of the larger organism. In turn, the larger organism has its own definition and identity with which to relate to its environment in life; its externality.

It is important for each child to have the opportunity to develop and strengthen their awareness of boundary, their individual identity and their value, as an individual, to the well-being for the classroom as a whole.

> The classroom is an integrative element. The child is essentially an autonomous element (although no individual is ever totally autonomous). The classroom forms an externality for the child.

## 3. Externality

Externality is a term I use to refer to the habitat/environment that surrounds an individual. For a cell, the externality is the inside of an organism of which it is part. For plants and animals the externality is the environment and habitat which they collectively create and in which they live (in conjunction with weather/climate). A healthy externality, where sound ecological relationships exist, enables life to flourish.

For children in school, the externality is the classroom environment, which they collectively create and in which they live.

> **Ecological pattern - healthy habitats**
> The classroom, must be, as is the larger organism for the cell, a healthy habitat, in order for individuals and groups to do well and make constructive contributions to the class.

So how do we create a classroom where sound ecological relationships exist.

> Classically-based classrooms tend to be heavily integrative externalities for children, at some expense to the child's autonomy.

In the theory of living systems, the definition and identity of a cell or larger organism (such as a child) is recognised as a pattern of organization. Therefore, a child is a living-system pattern of organization.

Each child has a pattern of purposeful organization which forms its identity.

Two important ecological concepts arise from the relationship between identity and surroundings:

1. The individual (with its identity) cannot exist in isolation.
2. Healthy autonomous existence is dependent upon integrative and symbiotic relationship.

Thus reciprocation is important to the health of habitat. The cell needs a healthy larger organism to exist within, and healthy cells are important to the larger organism.

Says Sterling, S., 'Linking Thinking', p. 25.
*"The health of the bigger system and the health of its subsystems are intimately connected."*

- **Mutuality in healthy process**

The larger organism forms the habitat or environment for the cell. It must be healthy for the cell to be healthy. Plus the habitat or environment surrounding the larger organism must be healthy for the health of the larger organism and thus for the cell. Healthy habitats begat healthy individuals and cells. Conversely, diminished habitats can result in diminished individuals, which in turn may exert impacts that have diminishing effects upon the habitat.

What we see emerging is that a balance of individual autonomy and its integration with surroundings is essential to a healthy ecology.

This concept of autonomy and integration, in a state of mutuality, is vital in considering healthy life process, within healthy surroundings. It is a foundational and intimate connection, where the health of each is dependant upon the other. This concept has enormous implications in developing understanding of all relationships within the environment, including human relationships and those we have with children in the classroom. In our relationships, the mutuality imperative is expressed as mutual regard. The use of mutual regard in working towards an environment of balanced autonomy and integration has direct application to successful learning process.

Since the living systems of life are always in process there is significance to the phrase *'working towards balanced autonomy and integration'*. Ecological balance arising from 'working towards' is part of ecological process and, therefore, our conscious focus and contribution should also be upon striving for ecologically sound autonomy and integration balance. The following questions are relevant to the striving for autonomy and integration balance in the classroom.

> **To what extent does the connection between individual wellbeing and the classroom habitat speak to the state of children and their impact upon self and others?**

> **In what ways could enhancing classroom habitats enable children who are struggling with their sense of identity and with curriculum demands?**

> **Do children feel they have a sense of purpose in the classroom? How do children see themselves in the classroom - what is their sense of identity?**

The individual's autonomy (identity, purpose, and a pattern of organization) (either of the cell or larger organism, including the child) cannot be absolute; its autonomy is dependent upon integrating with surroundings/habitat/environment; its externalities.

> **How will children's sense of purpose and identity affect their interactions and patterns of organization in their classroom surroundings?**

This interaction between organisms (patterns of organization) and the environment is known, in the theory of living systems, as structural coupling. This means that the living system is coupled with the environment and interacts with it. This interaction affects organism behaviour. Behaviour is the response to perceptions or cognition of the surrounding environment. Cognition and behaviour are linked.

> **It is important to consider the quality of structural coupling the child will experience within the classroom.**

These processes of patterns of organisation, structural couplings, cognition and behaviour, are ones of relationship and are all processes involving autonomy (self) and integration with surroundings. These relationship processes work within the dynamics, described in appendix (i), of feedback, attractors, pattern, far from equilibrium states, chaos/order, bifurcation, self-organizing, development and learning. All these processes are interdependent.

Since interdependencies are dynamic, they are ceaseless in their interactions, and they are in constant states of change and development. This dynamic state of interdependence creates a context for life, as all elements participate in the stability of life through ceaseless relationship processes. However, because states of chaos and order arise out of dynamic process, there is fluctuation between stability and instability. This is where processes of bifurcation and positive and negative feedback come in to have a mediating effect on fluctuations and instability, especially in terms of reining in the destabilizing effect of self-reinforcing, runaway iterating positive feedback (pp. 241-242). The relationship dynamics of the ecology display a balancing act capacity between autonomy and integration, but one humans have to consciously engage.

It is important, therefore, to recognize the relationship dynamics of the ecology constantly in play within the classroom and, rather than controlling or striving to orchestrate, gently guide children with a positive, affirming hand.

> **Since children are living systems and part of living system process, how are the relationship dynamics of the ecology reflected in the life of the classroom?**

**Ecologically, a constructive sense of autonomy means:**

- the existence of a biological boundary that marks and defines self.
- being distinct from others.
- having a sense of purpose.
- being engaged in self-organization.
- being responsible for self.

**Environment and our integration with it means:**

- **Self is surround by, or immersed in, an environment/habitat.**
- **Other children, such as a class, form a surrounding environment/habitat for each child.**
- **Each child in class is a contributor to other children's environment/habitat.**
- **There exists a relationship between self and environment, ecologically known as structural coupling.**
- **Self is integrated by the environment/habitat.**

**Relationship between self (autonomous element) and environment (integrative element) means:**

- **Individual self (autonomy) with a good sense of well-being will be a constructive influence on environment/habitat (integration). Good autonomy creates good integration.**
- **A constructive environment/habitat (integration) will have a constructive influence on individuals (autonomy). Good integration creates good autonomy.** (See p. 14, Ms. Eva's observations.)

Since autonomy and integration are dynamic and, therefore, fluctuating, constructive outcomes arise from a 'working-towards-balance' mindset. In a close-to-balance state, these foundational dynamics enable a sustainable in the ecology; one dynamic not dominating the other.

> **Ecological Pattern**
> **A balance of autonomy and integration for the child in the classroom is a foundational dynamic for sustainable life in the classroom.**

## 4. Towards a balance of autonomy and integration dynamics

Unfortunately, a working towards an autonomy and integration balance does not always exist in the classroom. Often integration in a classically-based classroom means an emphasis on control with imposed rules and regulations, where the child's autonomy has little room for development. The child is required to fit the classroom; integration imposed over the development of autonomy.

Inadequately developed autonomy equates with uncertainty as to how to constructively contribute to the habitat. This can lead to behavioural problems on the part of the child and the perceived 'need' for increased levels of imposed rules and regulations to maintain control on the part of the teacher; integration dynamic increased, autonomy dynamic decreased, resulting in out of balance dynamics. The outcome can be children unsure of themselves, perhaps rebellious, encouraged to seek acceptance elsewhere, diverted from constructively developing themselves and their surroundings. Alternatively, if schools/teachers 'give up' on integration efforts, children are left to decide their own form of autonomy; autonomy not necessarily balanced with constructive integration. Dominance of either dynamic is damaging to the building of constructive environments and constructive selves.

To be constructive, the dynamics of autonomy and integration need to be in a state of working towards balance.

So to summarize:
- the well-being of a child is dependent upon the well-being of the integrative nature of the class.
- the well-being of the class is dependent upon the well-being of its members.

Thus we have a mutuality dynamic of:-
enhanced habitat = enhanced children = enhanced habitat = enhanced children = enhanced habitat.

Individuals and their environment flourish when one enhances the other, linking responsibility and reciprocation.

**Self is responsible for self, but, in exercising that responsibility, self is also responsible for its surrounding environment.**

This means that:
- Enhanced classroom habitats create happier children more willing to make constructive contributions to self (autonomy) and environment/habitat (integration).
- Valued children have an enhanced sense of self, work better, and are better able to contribute to the class habitat.
- Constructive self is engaged in forming constructive patterns of interactions with habitat.

## 5. Ecological dynamics and us

Ecological dynamics in nature ensure ecological stability. However, the human mind, with a choice of action, can be a destabilizing influence. This destabilization may arise from undervaluing the importance of mutuality or mutual regard, with its accompanying self-reinforcing iterating positive feedback. Unless iterating positive feedback is modified by the regulation provided through negative feedback, living system dynamics will not necessarily produce constructive results.

> **Do circumstances exist in children's classroom lives that may cause destabilization to occur?**

In situations of human social domination, for example, positive iteration feedback may arise from a structure of perceptions and/or rules that are not sufficiently responsive to change pressures. Destabilization occurs. Although the iteration of expectations and demands contained within the rules may appear to be the best route to status quo maintenance, further dynamics come into play.

Instead of solely maintaining the status quo, effects may also include the marginalization of mutuality processes, curtailing the natural evolution of balance and development.

When such human-specie iteration is introduced into expressions of ecological process, social or environmental, the resulting imbalances can bite back. The bid for status quo can, instead, create imbalance.

Thus seeking permanence through iteration, can, over time, be an illusionary and fruitless endeavour with consequences that can engage negative expressions of life dynamics. Whether constructive or negative in effect, dynamics are always in play, nothing is fixed; all is in a state of becoming. However, when focused on the ecology and patterns of nature, of which we are a part, we can live, respond and react more closely aligned with the principles of the ecology.

By creating a classroom environment focused on the ecology, children are given the opportunity to flourish and enjoy productive happy learning.

> **Classrooms are arenas where there is a constant display of living system dynamics, both in positive and negative behaviours. The dynamics of life are always functioning. How can the recognition and use of life dynamics be used constructively in the classroom? What level of responsiveness to children's concerns would enable an enhanced learning environment to develop in the classroom?**

## 6. The process of becoming - in nature and within ourselves

Ilya Prigogine, (referenced by Capra), has, in a sense, summarized his work in the title of his book, 'From Being To Becoming'. It is conceptually important, say Prigogine and Capra, to move from the idea of set states of being, to ones that are in a constant process of becoming. It can be said that life is a process of becoming.

The process of becoming is accomplished through a series of accumulating moments, capable (but not necessarily) of producing sustainability in both nature and humans. In humans, our conscious thinking capacity, in concert with the process of becoming, suggests a foundation for learning and development. Thus, it seems, we are endowed with the capacity to make a constructive contribution to the ecology's sustainable balance process, and also to avoid the 'bite back'.

> **In a series of moments, life is a process of becoming - it does not stop. Thus, when classroom work-goals are achieved, moments still continue. Since classrooms are life-filled, they are non-stop centres for the process of becoming. How effective are classroom environments in enabling constructive processes of becoming? How many moments are enabling? What signifies a constructive moment in the process of becoming?**

The process of becoming, involves structural coupling (interaction between organisms and the environment) within processes of cognition, mutuality and autonomy and integration relationship. All of this occurs through the dynamics of feedback, attractors, pattern, far from equilibrium states, chaos/order, bifurcation, self-organizing patterns, development and learning, and complexity.

To summarize, the 'Process of Becoming' rests upon the ecological dynamics of life and is always in action in nature, within ourselves and within the life of the classroom. To facilitate constructive processes of becoming in children, it needs to be recognized that:

- **agreed upon protocols** for life in the classroom empower each child. (See classroom rights. pp. 92-109)
- **moment-to-moment events** in a child's life should arise within a classroom atmosphere of mutual regard.
- **disagreement and problems can be used as teaching/learning opportunities** to create constructive moments; disequilibrium events that can lead to learning about difference, the consideration of alternatives, and the learning of mutual regard. (see chap. 2, especially 'Problem or Opportunity' banners.)

A healthy environment requires autonomy and integration dynamics always working towards balance.

I would like now to focus on the role of cognition in nature.

## 7. Cognition and mind - a process of knowing and perception (not necessarily conscious, or remembered, by all species)

Capra, '96, p. 171.
*"Mind is not a thing but a process - the process of cognition, which is identified with the process of life".*

Drawing on Maturana and Varela's Santiago Theory of Cognition, Capra sees the process of life, through cognition, as a process of knowing, (within ecological niches) saying that the simplest of organisms are capable of perception.

Capra, '96, p. 170.
*"A bacterium, or a plant, has no brain, but has a mind".*

Capra, '82, p. 296.
*"Mind is a pattern of organization."*

Cognition and mind is essential to the structural coupling that links individuals to surroundings. It is a process that first involves individuals' cognitive ability and, secondly, determines their resulting behaviour; a pattern of organization engaged. In order for individuals to determine behaviour that is appropriate to their surroundings, they have to be cognizant of their surroundings. In order to be ecologically sustaining, behaviour has to be in symbiotic mutuality with the environment. This applies to both the natural environment and to himan constructed environments.

However, human constructs may not necessarily be ecologically viable.

When the human construct overlays the naturally occurring environment, responsibility falls to humans to maintain an environment in symbiotic mutuality with the ecology and our ecological core. Classrooms are, of course, human constructs.

> **What effects upon children's cognition and resulting behavioural choices will a classroom environment likely trigger?**

In interactions in nature, cognition has to be ecologically appropriate and viable. Ecological viability means that the integrative web of ecological existence is not compromised. Thus ecologically sound structural coupling contributes to an ecological pattern that maintains the health of all organisms and species, and their supporting environments; organisms coupled with environment.

Not all organisms and species have a nervous system or a brain to apply to cognition processes, but nevertheless cognition remains an ecological imperative.

Capra, '96, p. 97, quoting Maturana, 1970.
*"Living systems are cognitive systems, and living as a process is a process of cognition. This statement is valid for all organisms, with or without a nervous system".*

William D. Hamilton, writing with Robert Axelrod (Barlow, '98, p. 138).
*"... bacteria are highly responsive to selected aspects of their environment, especially their chemical environment; ... they can respond differentially to what other organisms around them are doing; ..."*

So, it would seem, from the smallest to the most sophisticated entity of life, cognitive ability is present and necessary.

Cognition, in the case of bacteria, is a sensing ability; in this instance, a chemical sensing ability that enables cognition and response to environment; a predetermined survival living system of the ecology, operating through automatic cognition devices.

Humans, of course, use consciousness in the engagement of cognition - essentially a primary experience - and, in addition, have memory capacity that enables a process of re-cognition to occur. These capacities of cognition and memory are important contributors to learning capacities. Bacteria, and some organisms that do have nervous systems and brains do not have the capacity to re-cognise. Some creatures, for example, rely upon processes of territorial possession; contained in life and behaviour by cognitive mechanism rather than re-cognition and discrimination abilities. (Hamilton and Axelrod, p. 142.) However, despite our cognitive and re-cognitive abilities, our additional powers of reasoning and the ability to choose, we do not always make good behavioural choices.

While the behaviour of other entities, existing within cognition constraints, keeps them in symbiotic mutuality with the environment and gives each its ecological niche, it is not so easy for humans.

Sagan and Druyan, '92, p. 230, point out,
*"The dominance of relationships in the same bit of forest within the communities of, say, owls, bears, racoons, and humans are generally beneath the notice of sparrows."*

It is much easier to be an 'ecologically-correct' sparrow than a complicated human with power of choice. But, for both, a sustaining environment is key to survival.

> **To what extent do we enable children to exercise discrimination, reason and discernment, and to consider the validity of their choices?**

> **How can the classroom environment enable children to practice making constructive and discriminating choices in their lives?**

Cognition and perception (of an environment) in children is a primary process that can trigger behavioural choices within the environment. (It is an engagement of the child's autonomy integrated within the environment.)

Thus:

- primary (experiential) learning opportunities where children learn to discriminate, reason and discern, mean that children are engaged at a constructive emotional level - children well positioned to apply discernment to their behavioural choices; children at one with a good autonomy and integration fit.

- children's cognition (or perception) of their classroom environment will affect their behavioural choices.

- a hostile or isolating classroom will make children feel uncomfortable and isolated. This may cause withdrawal, and may spur the creation of a counter-culture that seeks acceptance and comfort elsewhere. In effect, the counter-culture may be viewed by the child as a better autonomy and integration fit.

- an accepting and considerate classroom environment will more likely engender constructive primary and emotional reactions; a good autonomy and integration fit.

Since the focus of secondary experience education is upon secondary experience learning processes, the primary experience aspects of children's cognition is not always given much accommodation. However, primary cognition processes are always occurring within each child. The Four Communities Classroom teacher balances primary cognition experience with secondary experience learning (imparted knowledge). See pp. 92, 93, 175, 278, and other index references for secondary experience. Combining primary and secondary experience opens the door to more balanced and enhanced learning.

## 8. Cognition, autonomy, integration, self descriptors, and having the ability to assert self

In determining survival within environment, cognition and behaviour processes enable the entity to both establish and assert self (self which includes the elements of autonomy, identity, and difference), and integrate self with its environment. From this, we can say that life process is a process of self determination contained within an environment.

Ecologically, to assert self is a responsibility to self and, when responsibility to surroundings is made in equal measure, self-assertion is beneficial. Constructive feedback from surroundings is more likely to occur. This is responsibility to self, and the importance, ecologically, of self-assertion.

> **How can children be encouraged to assert themselves in harmony with their externality of the classroom environment?**

Self-assertion is foundational to the existence of all life and foundational to the theory of living systems.

The assertion of self [involving self-descriptors such as self-regulation, self-balancing, self-maintenance, and self-organization - see appendix (iv)], is an engagement of autonomy of self in an integrative process with externalities. Integral to these processes of self within the environment are feedback loops engaged with cognition and action/behaviour.

These are life processes of mutuality that apply as much to the cell that is surviving and contributing to its organism, as to larger organisms (e.g. plants, animals, and humans), surviving and contributing in their wider environment.

And again, in humans, we find, self-assertion takes on an enhanced significance. With the added endowment of consciousness, memory and choice, we can choose, in our use of self-descriptors, an approach to self that makes us the best we can be. Humans have, perhaps, unlimited potential, with a capacity for learning beyond that of other species where functioning is contained within their ecological niche.

When we consider the child in the classroom in self-descriptor terms, we see that the child's sense of autonomy is engaged in an inner dialogue of supporting self in the classroom environment; assertion of self. The child uses cognition, and re-cognition in shaping his/her perceptions, and uses self-descriptors such as self-regulation, self-balancing, self-maintenance, and self-organization, along with feedback in his/her interactions. In this ecologically sound process the child will learn, develop his/her knowledge, and shape actions and behaviours. The teacher has no control over these processes, but does have influence (negative or positive) through the surroundings she/he creates for children to engage their processes of becoming.

So what does this mean for the children in our care?

## 9. An ecological heritage for all

The earth presents, for all life-forms, a shared biological heritage of life dynamics and change. But as humans, with choice and powers of reasoning, we are outside the ecological-niche parameters that contain the lives of other species. We have the capacity to take responsibility for our behaviour and learning, and to decide what behaviours constitute a constructive accord with each environment we find ourselves a part of. As derivatives of ecological process, adults and children, from moment to moment, use and express all the dynamics of the ecology of life. Hence, with these dynamics within us all, children and adults flourish when constructively engaged with, and in tune with, elements of the ecology of life.

> **Having ecological dynamics within us all, children and adults flourish when constructively engaged with the ecology of life.**

It is the teacher's job, to assist children in their constructive development of these ecological capacities and to help them fully embrace the gift of their ecological heritage and infinite potential.

This is our responsibility, because the consequences of our actions, for good or ill, are not confined to us alone, but cut across all ecological niches. Animals are unable to 'sell their souls'. We are.

Our ecological heritage confers on us a brain, capable of thinking, potentially, on virtually all aspects of existence. This capacity enables consideration of consequences before action which, in turn, brings responsibility. Consequence and responsibility are as one.

Our ecological heritage, given to us all, individually and collectively, is not to be squandered.

> **To what extent are children enabled to express themselves in accord with their ecological foundation, so that they can develop, in the classroom, their capacities to choose, consider consequence, and assume responsibility for their thoughts and actions?**

Through the capacities of memory and the acquisition of knowledge, we have the power of decision but, in turn, the responsibility for self and responsibility for actions: abilities and responsibilities that form the dividing line between ourselves and other species.

Sterling, S., 'Linking Thinking' p. 26.

Children's decision making capacities should be nurtured through *"...active and participative learning experiences and teaching methods emphasised, with high degrees of interaction between learners, and learners and teachers."*

It is the way of the Four Communities Classroom.

**Ecological heritage confers on humans the capacity to:**
- take responsibility for behaviour and learning.
- decide what behaviours constitute a constructive accord with the prevailing environment.
- flourish when constructively engaged with elements of the ecology of life.
- consider consequences before action.

## The fundamentals of the ecology of life: a summary

Understanding ecological process brings understanding to the life of children in the classroom.

1. The concept of self in relationship to externalities is paramount in understanding one's place in the ecology of life.

2. For self to exist, boundaries must exist, from which arise identity and difference.

3. For relationship to exist, communication, in some form, must exist.

4. Communication and behaviour require cognition; an understanding of place.

5. Self must have purpose, which again marks identity and difference.

6. Existence of a healthy self is dependent upon symbiotic relationships.

7. Autonomy of a healthy self arises from a healthy integration with externalities (an environment of mutuality).

8. Self and environment are always in the process of becoming.

## (iii) DIFFERENCE, COMMONALITY AND THE IMPORTANCE OF EMOTION:
### Connections to Productive, Happy Classrooms

**Introduction**

A child's pursuit of education and the success that can be achieved rest upon his/her consciousness and mind, intimately connected to the foundations of language, memory, emotion, the frontal cortex, indeed the whole brain, nervous system, and person. And this is all contained within the surrounding environment, including that of relationship with others.

Candace Pert reveals in 'Molecules of Emotion' that chemical communication underlies the ecological imperative for learning - p.263. It is the chemical communication in the body that drives a child's emotional responses to learning process and survival instincts.

Pert, '99, p. 146.
"... our emotions decide what is worth paying attention to."

These chemical/biological processes also employ feedback loops and the other dynamics of living systems science. Together, biology and the dynamics of living systems enable our learning capacities and processes. The curriculum, as important as it is, is not in itself the learning process, but rather a compilation of knowledge which is conveyed through the learning process.

The curriculum, however, imparted through an understanding of our chemical/emotional/ecological process of learning, is set to flourish, as are the children who are in receipt of it.

Further underlining our connection to ecological imperatives, Pert takes us into a study of the biology of the ecology which shows, perhaps not unexpectedly, that communication, learning and response, both consciously and unconsciously, are hallmarks of life on earth.

Speaking on this commonality of life on earth, Sagan and Druyan, '92, p. 138, say,

"... the teaming lifeforms of Earth...are all made of almost exactly the same organic stuff, the same molecules almost always performing the same functions, with the same genetic codebook in use by almost everybody."

Out of this commonality comes huge variety and difference in species and the way species live their lives. Biology shows that the life of the ecology combines difference and commonality into a sustainable whole.

As derivatives of the ecology, we share this ecological commonality, while simultaneously expressing variety and difference.

With a view to enabling constructive learning in children, this chapter explores the role of emotion in learning, the significance of our shared genetic codebook and how all interaction in the classroom engages the mind and the body, working in concert through chemical communication.

### DNA - FOUNDATION FOR DIFFERENCE AND COMMONALITY

Difference is fundamental to life, and all people are, of course, living examples of difference, as is each child in the classroom. It is important for each child's sense of self and identity that they know that are part of this pattern of life. (See 'Learning the Importance of Difference' p. 110.)

I draw on Sagan and Druyan for the following, and make reference to living system dynamics.

DNA is a code of genetic information that forms foundations of difference and commonality. Chemical messengers within cells distribute information from the DNA's genetic code. Protein chemical messengers between cells distribute information from the DNA.

> "... the teaming life-forms of Earth ... are all made of almost exactly the same organic stuff, the same molecules almost always performing the same functions, with the same genetic codebook in use by almost everybody. ... sharing the same fragile surface layer."
>
> Sagan and Druyan, '92, p. 138.

---

> **Ecological pattern. Successful DNA sequences are ones that are in integrative balance with the environment.**

- DNA is self-replicating, self-regulating and self-correcting to ensure fidelity of information (a self-organizing process).

> **Ecological pattern. DNA sequences use the living system dynamics of self-regulation and self-correction.**

- DNA forms the genetic information that endows an organism with its appearance and behaviours.

Functional DNA ensures survival of the species in relationship to its environment.

Briggs and Peat, p. 160.
"*How the genetic code expresses itself is ... dependant on loops of feedback between the developing organsim and the environment.*"

Unconscious function of chemical processes occur in autonomous processes of self-regulation, self-correction, and self-replication, along with integrative processes of communication and response.

DNA information code is passed on through the genes. Fifty percent of the gene (DNA) information derived from each parent combines into a unique combination and, thereby, a unique individual is created; a new self ready to use its genetic inheritance to integrate and live in its environment.

> **DNA function not only makes each child a unique individual, but also provides a commonly-held endowment, enabling children to thrive within their environment.**

Genes are passed down through the generations; DNA codes are maintained. The magic is that though the same genetic codebook is in use by almost everybody each individual is unique; a common provenance from which difference arises.

> **Ecological pattern. Genetic difference is fundamental to the ecology and creates individuality. Every child in the classroom reflects that ecological endowment of individuality and difference.**

To summarize:
- DNA is the foundation for difference.
- DNA is part of the basis for individuality in children.
- A child's individuality confers sense of self.
- DNA is also the foundation for commonality.

DNA and children share, at different levels of function, ecological life processes of:
- autonomy and integration dynamics
- self–regulation and self–correction
- self-organization

In the Four Communities Classroom, the unique quality of every child is recognized and valued. Every child is encouraged in developing a constructive sense of self (autonomy) and is provided with an environment (integration) where self-esteem can flourish. Differences and commonalities are discovered in the process of class discussions; commonalities and differences recognised and celebrated. This environment is enhanced when each child is offered, as an ecological being, the opportunity to self-regulate, self-correct, and self-organize, as part of day-to-day life in the classroom. Extending beyond DNA, our feeling, thinking selves, live this self-regulating and self-correcting pattern of life [appendix (iv)].

# MOLECULAR COMMUNICATION, FEELINGS AND EMOTIONS

I draw on Pert, and Sagan and Druyan.

Emotion is a chemically mediated communication process within our bodies that is foundational to our feelings and our behaviours (including feelings and behaviours in the classroom).

Our life experiences, including survival processes, trigger emotions that we often refer to as feelings. And, as Candace Pert's research supports, there is a connection between how we feel and the chemical molecular communication in the body. The communicating chemicals are amino acids that string together to form messenger molecules. These messenger molecules are known as peptides.

Peptides, released by cells, float in the intracellular fluid, to carry information to other cells. Pert's work explores the deep biological influences involved in how we respond to every facet of our lives, including how we feel, the decisions we make, memory, and how we respond to learning; mind and body as one.

Pert, '99, p. 144.

"... neuropeptides can act as internal ligands to shape our memories as we are forming them, and put us back in the same frame of mind when we need to retrieve them. This is learning."

> If emotions and feelings are linked to learning what are the implications for the teaching-and-learning classroom environments that children find themselves placed in? How important are children's feelings in their learning process?

If the body and mind are one, with molecules working together in one finely orchestrated information exchange, how well must we care for the emotional well-being of the children in our care so that they can flourish in the classroom environment?

It certainly seems to follow that chemical molecular communication in the body (be it unconscious) has implications for how children think and learn - their beliefs, their expectations, their aspirations and how readily their minds open up to new ideas and information.

## 1. Integrated body systems - a blueprint for cooperation

With a symphony of connection in the body, Pert declares that the various systems of the body, the brain included, are not separate, but are locked together into a unifying whole.

Pert, '99, p. 172.

"... the brain, the glands, the immune system, indeed the entire organism, (are) joined together in a wonderful system coordinated by the actions of discrete and specific messenger molecules."

Sagan and Druyan, '92, pp. 129 - 130, on the internal functioning of organisms.

"Cells with quite diverse functions interact harmoniously. ... survival depends on the cooperation of very different constituent parts. (Our) brain, heart, liver, kidneys, pituitary, and sexual organs generally work well together. They are not in competition. They make a whole that is much more than the sum of the parts."

The body is a complex system of communicative self-organization; it is (especially in a healthy system) a complex system of individual organs (autonomously functioning) working in cooperation and balance with each other (integration with other organs); autonomy and integration in balance.

Thus, the endocrine system communicates with the immune system, the immune system communicates with the nervous system and the brain. In fact, the entire body is continuously engaged in communication. And all of this system is in receipt of brain-mediated information coming from an externality - monitoring senses of sight, hearing, touch, taste, and smell. And all of this communication occurs in a series of moments.

## 2. The role of emotions - the great motivators

As Pert describes in 'Molecules of Emotion', all peptides are emotion-mediated and they mediate emotion.

Peptides and their receptors are a chemically based system that is far older than the nervous system, and *"indisputably more ancient and far more basic to the organism. There were peptides such as endorphins ... being made inside cells long before there were ... neurons, before there were brains."* (Pert, p. 26.) Pert continues, peptides and their receptors have been *"the basic unit of language used by cells throughout the organism to communicate..."* With survival dependent upon a sense of fear and comfort, the emotional component can be seen as vital in the communication process. This emotional element of survival *"conserved for eons of evolutionary time, ... basic and fundamental to the survival of the species"*. (Pert, '99, p. 91.) - is essential to self.

Pert reiterates p. 131.
*"The simple physiology of emotions has been preserved and used again and again over evolutionary eons and across species."* (And) *"...crucial to the process of survival."*

Clearly, we have the physiology of emotions linked to the preservation of life, making emotions fundamental to life process, and survival of self. Again, self is essential for life.

> **Ecological pattern. Emotions are fundamental to life and survival of self. But, as Pert says, emotions are linked to learning process. Emotion, survival and learning are linked.**

The ecology in its survival process has been engaged in a learning process, often at unconscious levels. This makes learning both an ancient and fundamental attribute of ecological process, intimately connected to emotion.

Survival, therefore, has also been an evolving/learning process: a 'learning for survival' process made more complex and sophisticated with the emergence of neurons (nerve cells), with the accompanying integration of electrical and chemical communication. It seems that this was all part of a self-organizing process.

Sagan and Druyan, '92, p. 129.
*"Eventually there got to be many beings whose cells had specialized functions... Some cells ... were the conduits of electrical impulses, part of a slowly evolving neuronal apparatus in charge of locomotion, breathing, feelings, and - much later - thoughts. Cells with quite diverse functions interacted harmoniously."*

As humans, in charge of thoughts, we possess the electrical and chemical integration of peptide/receptor processes (be they unconscious) to conduct ourselves and our lives through a sophisticated process of conscious emotions and feelings that go beyond comfort and fear, hunger and thirst, to experience love, joy, loneliness, belonging, anger, sadness, pride, guilt, contentment, awe, worry, satisfaction, dismay, anticipation, hurt, excitement, courage, resentment, sullenness, jealousy, revenge, happiness, generosity, greed, empathy, sympathy, acceptance - the gamut of human emotion. All of these emotions are experienced, of course, with varying intensity, sometimes in combination, but always subject to change and nuance. Emotion is vital not only to survival but engagement in the pursuit of preferred environments, and more. We are complex beings and equipped for complex learning dynamics.

> **The many emotional nuances that humans experience and express create a complexity which includes the emotionally driven responses seeking survival, comfort, and learning. How are these emotion-led learning complexities accommodated in schools?**

These mood states of emotion (conscious and mindful to the brain), are mediated by peptides. But we are not conscious of peptide process itself and, therefore, our moods are integrated unconsciously into the body's communication processes, affecting our conscious behavioural decisions. Sometimes, though, we can be surprised by our emotional response to externalities and the feelings they evoke.

> **The experience of emotion, both in the states of consciousness and unconsciousness, is facilitated through peptide activity - one level of consciousness affecting the other. Could it be that some mood states in children (perhaps generated by an externality), but resulting from unconscious peptide process, create emotional confusion, making it difficult for children to make sense of self and externalities?**

Pert, '99, p. 145.
*"Emotional states or moods are produced by the various neuropeptide ligands, and what we experience as emotion or feeling is also a mechanism for activating a particular neuronal circuit - simultaneously throughout the brain and body - which generates a behaviour involving the whole creature with all the necessary physiological changes that behaviour requires.... and has a corresponding facial expression. It's part of the constellation of bodily changes that occurs with each shift of subjective feeling."*

(In her book, Pert outlines the health implications of emotional states).

As we explore this physiological concept described by Pert, it becomes evident that self is emotionally driven and that emotional response has implications for children's learning.

In the Four Communities Classroom how we feel is of paramount importance. We strive for an environment of mutual regard where self can find a comfort level, while integrating with others.

> **What conscious/unconscious processes are brought about in the classroom, and what is their emotional effect? How are children reacting/coping/benefiting, and at what level of emotional awareness?**

Younger children tend to learn with their emotions tightly connected to their actions. Older children may sometimes try out and experiment with 'self-protecting' emotional devices; emotions partly concealed. Adults may live with emotional devices that may include hiding of feelings from others.

Many recognise, intuitively, that emotional learning is an ongoing life process, and view it as learning about self and others (especially in relationships). As described by Pert, emotions are part of the physiological fundamentals of animal/human existence; an ecological foundation; an ongoing life process.

Emotion is central to the process of becoming, and an experience we all feel, moment to moment. Emotion, being part of the process of becoming, means that we never emotionally 'arrive', with emotions set. Emotions create an on-going chain of physiological/neurological reactions that are as constant as breathing.

> **Emotional worries can be an extra burden that, for the child, can over-shadow the learning of curriculum.**

> **To what extent do we pay heed to emotion in the learning environment and its effect upon behaviour in the classroom? Emotionally, much goes on within each of us as we live each moment.**
>
> **Can classroom environments be created where children's and teacher's moment-to-moment emotional journeys are founded upon reciprocal communication?**

### 3. Staying on the ball. Self organization in reference to externalities equals learning flexibility

The 'process of becoming', with its accompanying element of self-organization, is essentially a learning process with flexibility, (especially when constructive). Flexibility is exercised while referencing and responding to externalities to produce harmonious and, therefore, constructive relationships.

This flexible self-organization through reference-to-externalities process occurs in emotional response to relationships, in the relationship dynamics engaged between the brain and nervous system and the outside world (externalities), and in the self organization processes continuously engaged by the nervous system.

> **Ecological pattern.** The process of becoming, when referenced to externalities, leads to learning and self-organization flexibility. Are children's processes of becoming constructively enabled for learning and self-organization flexibility as they regard their externalities in the classroom?

A child's sense of self and behaviours arise from and are affected by:

- emotions and feelings via molecular communication, affecting the body, the brain and nervous system.
- the need for reciprocity of communication with others (a form of mutuality).
- self-organization.
- the emotional effect of the atmosphere in the classroom.

All of these aspects impact learning and benefit from a nurturing environment.

Teachers enable a nurturing environment by:

- demonstrating responsibility for the emotional environment of the classroom.
- being aware that children's emotional concerns can sometimes represent additional burdens that may dominate their learning endeavours.
- being aware that open, constructive communication can help to remedy or avoid emotionally induced learning problems.
- being aware that since learning sits on the biochemical processes of living systems, emotion is inextricably linked to all teaching and learning; neuronal (brain) development the outcome.
- creating emotionally secure environments to enable neuronal development which will enable development of self-esteem and the learning of subject matter.

> **Seeing children as dynamic life expressions of the ecology, with identity, communication and relationship imperatives, can broaden awareness of their learning processes.**

In the Four Community Classroom, children can feel emotionally safe in an environment of mutual regard, where each child's positive contribution is recognized and valued by both teacher and students. It is an environment where children can flourish and grow.

## GROWTH, DEVELOPMENT, COMMUNICATION, AND LEARNING IN THE BRAIN AND NERVOUS SYSTEM

I draw on Pert, Teske, Shatz, Diamond/Scheibel/Elson, Goldman-Rakic and LeDoux.

The frontal cortex of the human brain does not fully develop until the early twenties. (Pert, '99, p. 288.) Even beyond the twenties, the brain's inherent pliability gives it the capacity to continue evolving throughout life.

Teske, '96.
*"We (have) a brain that is constantly being shaped, in structure and function, by its history of developmental interactions with the outside environment."*

At any age, however, the brain's growth and development is closely aligned with emotional states and the accompanying chemical processes. Since teachers are shapers of and contributors to emotional states in children, they are, in all aspects of teaching and learning, both facilitators of brain growth in children and contributors to its pliability.

To better understand this process in the context of how children think and learn, I look at;

1. Neuronal development.
2. Neuronal development in reference to externalities.
3. Communicative intelligence, neuronal development, emotions and peptides.
4. The brain and emotions.
5. The mind's inner dialogue and its external surroundings
6. Social influence and brain capacity.
7. Brain capacity - relationship patterns of emotion, memory and learning.

## 1. Neuronal development

The brain is not a set structure. The brain's growth-to-meet-need capacity starts before birth and continues throughout life.

Towards understanding, within living system dynamics, these ongoing learning processes, this section examines the brain's inherent flexibility.

The process of brain development is a process of increasing the size of neurons (brain cells) and number of connections between neurons. When there is an increased demand from externalities, the brain has a built-in flexibility to grow more connections between neurons to increase learning capacity. Thus, learning and growth can occur in response to externalities; experiential learning.

Experiential learning is at the heart of the Four Communities Classroom. Together, teacher and children, through discussion, explore and share ideas that require the brain to expand and grow and be flexible enough to embrace new thoughts.

The development of the human brain is truly amazing. At the fetus stage of life, the individual's nervous system is under construction. Several hundred billion neurons are forming, which will be integrated into a functional mosaic by untold billions of interconnections (Diamond, Scheibel, and Elson p. 2-1). Humans are born with almost all the neurons they will ever have. However, brain size will increase as neurons grow in size and their axons and dendrites, the neuronal extensions that facilitate communication between neurons, increase in number. Axons and dendrites increase in number to facilitate increase in the web of connections between neurons (Carla J. Shatz p. 4). Greater complexity in the web of connections increases the communicative capacity of the brain and nervous system and is reflected in increased learning and intelligence capacity.

> **To teach children and stimulate learning is to stimulate an increase in axon and dendrite connections in the child's brain. In this regard teachers are stimulators of brain growth.**

Thus, brain flexibility and potential arise from the brain's ongoing capacity to increase axons and dendrites in its web of neuronal connections. This is a process that also starts to occur before birth. To enable axons to develop within the developing nervous system, action potential (nerve impulse) has to occur, says Carla J. Shatz in her chapter 'The Developing Brain'.

Before birth, before vision is possible, *"retinal (eye) cells ... spontaneously generate bursts of action potentials (nerve impulses) in the darkness of the developing eye." "... last(ing) several seconds ... followed by long pauses that persist from thirty seconds to two minutes." (Shatz, p.13.)* This nerve cell firing provides an interim nerve pulse in the fetus, to enable eye cell axons to grow to the correct place (at the back of the head) in the primary visual cortex of the brain. It is this spontaneous firing in the correct pattern which fashions the necessary neuronal connections. (Shatz, p.15.)

## 2. Neuronal development in reference to externalities

After birth, the rods and cones of the eyes will translate actual visual images into nerve impulses, (similar to the action potential nerve impulses) and the optic nerve system will 'find out and learn' how good its newly established optic nerve connections are at interpreting the visual world. In response to these now visually generated nerve impulses, the optic nerve system goes into a phase of building nerve axons that life experience reveals are needed, and eliminating those nerve axons that life experience reveal are not needed. This is a fine-tuning process that self-corrects initial errors in building the optic nerve. In terms of living system dynamics this is a process of self-organization through reference; the structure is to correlate to its function. (Shatz, p. 4.)

> **<u>Ecological pattern.</u> The nervous system engages living system processes of self-correction and self-organization in an act of learning-flexibility. Processes of being, fundamental in a child's life, are, here again, expressed within the child's body.**

My Daughter *Can't Wait* for Monday Morning!

Thus, the web of axons are not set at birth but, through self-correction and self-organizing processes, are enabled to develop and evolve. There is a structural coupling process occurring in the building of the functioning visual cortex; a process of flexibility that allows the nervous system to learn and render itself functional. We have all witnessed human babies learning to understand the three dimensional world, determining depth of field, and interpreting it into the ability to reach out and grasp something. This self-organization through referencing is both a conscious, and an unconscious process of learning. Thus, the brain self-organizes through the correlating of its structure to its function - axons and dendrites forming to create learning and understanding.

Similar to the visual system, signals throughout other areas of the nervous system refine the initially diffuse connections within targets. (Shatz, p. 15.)

Shatz, p. 4.
*"The neuronal connections elaborate themselves (self-organize) from an immature pattern of wiring that (before birth) only grossly approximates the adult pattern."*

Neurons, it seems, acquire greater specificity of function through increased complexity of axon and dendritic connections arising from stimulation and use. As the saying goes, practice makes perfect.

Shatz, p. 15.
*"The necessity for neuronal activity (after birth) to complete the development of the brain has distinct advantages. The first is that, within limits, the maturing nervous system can be modified and fine-tuned by experience itself…"*

Most importantly, it is activity and experience with externalities, our environment, that continues to shape the neuronal network of the brain and nervous system. It is an ongoing process that gives humans the capacity to acquire wide ranging skills and aptitudes. It is this capacity that enables lifelong learning to occur.

Within the Four Communities Classroom, children have the opportunity to reach out and explore together the efficacy of new ideas and information. It is this type of primary experience that can make a constructive contribution to the fine tuning of the nervous system.

Diamond, Scheibel, and Elson, p 1-1,
*"… significant …. is the ability. of the brain to change in response to cultural diversity - with measurable chemical and structural changes. Indeed, our brains literally add nerve cell branches (axons and dendrites) in response to training and learning, no matter what our age."* (bracketed words are mine)

> **The maturing nervous system is adding and deleting axons and dentrites in a fine-tuning process of learning through experience. To what extent does the classroom constructively facilitate children's axon and dentrite brain development process?**

## 3. Communicative intelligence, neuronal development, emotions and peptides

Structural changes within the brain involve both the growth and elimination of axons and dendrites, altering the web of neuronal connections and with it the brain's communicative intelligence. Since feelings are part and parcel of this process, emotional response will affect the chemical changes involved.

Pert, '99, p. 145.
*"…what we experience as emotion or feeling is also a mechanism for activating a particular neuronal circuit…"* The chemical changes are brought about through the action of the emotion-mediating neuropeptides.

Pert, '99, p. 294.
*"… emotions bring the whole body into a single purpose, integrating systems and coordinating mental processes and biology to create behaviour."*

Emotions are not set in relationship to the environment which is also in constant change. All is dynamic. In a series of moments therefore, emotion-mediating effects on body systems are dynamic.

In the Four Communities Classroom an environment of mutual regard creates a happy, emotionally secure atmosphere where minds more readily open to embrace knowledge.

> **Interactive responsiveness and the learning capacity of neurological structure is fundamental and foundationally important to the learning process of the child.**

The brain's communicative intelligence is, therefore, under constant review; part of learning, part of maturing. It involves both conscious and unconscious processes.

While these structural neurological changes occur at an unconscious level, we are, however, conscious of acquiring new mental or physical capacities, and also aware of varying emotions, though some emotions are unconscious and are engaged seamlessly with conscious emotion (Joseph E. LeDoux '94).

But, still, we are not conscious of the neuronal network doing this or that as we engage changes. Acquisition of mental capacity is, of course, a process of learning. Therefore, in imparting knowledge, teachers are facilitating neurological changes - the growth of axon and dendrite connections in the child's web of neuronal linkages. This is not occurring in isolation, but in concert with the dynamic relationships within the classroom and the atmosphere that is being created. This is part of the child's emotional dynamic that will have a direct effect on what and how learning takes place, i.e. the effect of neuronal changes occurring in the brain and nervous system. The neurons are self-organising, but will be in 'consultation' with the child's emotional state via neuropeptides (self-organization through reference).

> **Emotion, via neuropeptide processes, affect how and what is learnt. Is learning being facilitated by the emotional environment of the classroom?**

- **Children's surroundings, perception, and function**

    In biological terms, the child's being attempts to correlate to its function. But, since children are emotionally-mediated, perception of the situation is also significant. Thus the child is attempting to correlate to its *perception* of function. The word perception is important, since a child's sense of function is integral to the sense of self. A sense of self is perceived in relationship to surroundings and place. Therefore, perception of function and of self is closely aligned with the surrounding environment.

> **Ecological pattern. Structure (the child) correlates to function (as perceived by the child).**
> **A child's perception of self in the classroom will affect the growth and development of the child's brain.**

Since our perception of function and self, within our environment, is felt through a mood state, we affect ourselves. We affect what happens in our bodies and how we learn and behave. As Pert, '99, p. 294, says, emotions coordinate mental processes and biology to create behaviour. This is why self-esteem is so important. And this is why the relationship processes that a teacher establishes in the classroom are so important.

> **It is an ecologically sound desire for the child to feel a need for a teacher-provided, caring externality. The child's perception of the quality of his/her relationship with the teacher is the child's measure.**

However, children are not necessarily on roller-coaster rides of constantly altering emotions. An individual's core sense of self provides something of a constant in the relationship between emotion and externalities - be it a negative overlay in some, or a constructive stabiliser in others, depending on level of self-esteem. Core self-esteem processes are slow moving - the result of a series of emotionally-driven relationships in engagement with externalities, often over long periods of time - neuronal web evolution with some permanence. Such permanence implies the engagement of memory.

Thus, it seems we can say a child's state of self-esteem is representative of the accumulation of memory/learning processes. Pert, '99, p. 143, talks about a peptide link to memory, *"… biochemical changes that take place at receptors (on cells) is the molecular basis of memory."* Thus, memory is also part of peptide/neurological processes.

With peptide processes, including those of memory, occurring throughout the body, it is important to note that Pert p. 143, goes on to say, *,"… memories are stored not only in the brain, but in a psychosomatic network extending into the body."*

Memory is part of our psychosomatic network and affects all of our being.

In the Four Communities Classroom, each child is valued and nurtured in a safe and caring environment, created together by children and teacher.

> **Ecological pattern. Emotion is fundamental to the biological chemical processes of living systems.**

> **Since neuronal/peptide processes and learning processes are as one emotional process, to what extent are neuronal development, learning and emotion seen as linked imperatives in the schooling offered to children?**

In terms of neuronal adaptation, Diamond, Scheibel, and Elson (3-12) say, there is,

*"… a capacity of the nervous system for responsiveness to the environment throughout the lifetime of the individual. Considering the changes we go through in our life, learning and remembering, collecting experiences with each additional day of life, the neurons of our brain must undergo some very significant adaptations."*

Since birth, these peptide/neurological processes have enabled our learning and the formation of our perceptions, and it is through those perceptions that we view, relate and interact with externalities.

Every child begins their school experience with memory-involved perceptions as part of their self-esteem package. Our job is to create a positive learning experience and happy classroom memories where self-esteem can grow and flourish.

> **What classroom atmosphere will be provided by teachers and schools? What effect will these externalities start to have on learning/memory processes, not only in terms of neuronal changes while learning subject matter, but in terms of neuronal learning changes in relation to perceptions and self-esteem?**

Since neuronal change is a web of interactive communication indivisible from every thought and deed, it follows that, to realise best outcomes, curriculum acquisition must go hand-in-hand with equal attention to children's emotional needs. A happy, affirmed child will learn more.

Classroom atmosphere, self-esteem and learning (learning about relationship, knowledge and curriculum) are inseparable elements in a child's life and experience. All these elements are involved in the child's neuronal change processes. Neuronal learning developments are peptide mediated and are subject to emotion. Recognizing that people are emotionally driven, we can see that the atmosphere the teacher creates in the classroom is of paramount importance to the child. The foundation of constructive relationship process that the teacher establishes in the classroom can help engender feelings of connection, understanding and security and become the bedrock upon which learning and the acquisition of curriculum is built. Recognition that children's neuronal/peptide processes and learning processes are one, highlights the potential for the enhancement of children's learning processes and capacities.

## 4. The brain and emotions

Brain functions are emotion-mediated. As the mediators of emotion, a significant number of peptides are naturally-occurring endorphins. These endorphin peptides have their own receptors, known as opiate receptors.

Pert, '99, p. 134.
*"... opiate receptors are by far the densest in the frontal lobes of the cerebral cortex of the human brain ..."*

Opiate receptors are involved in degrees of inhibitory effect in the chemical pleasure/pain continuum that impacts alertness and readiness within the body and the brain. (Diamond, Scheibel, and Elson).

Pert goes on to say that the cerebral cortex shares many interconnections with the amygdala, one of the limbic structures, which plays a large part in our emotional life. So the frontal cortex is not only richly supplied with peptide receptors, but is in communication with the limbic system. The fact that emotion-mediation is part of the frontal cortex's functioning is, of course, in keeping with Pert's research that everything is connected and that communication occurs continuously throughout the body, brain and nervous system through peptides; Pert's 'molecules of emotion'.

Importantly then, thinking is (like other parts of our being), emotion-mediated.

> **If thinking is emotionally-mediated, what relevance is a child's state of mind to his/her learning ability in the classroom?**

Pert, '99, p. 288.
*"... the frontal cortex is ...dependent on the free flow of the peptides of emotion ..."*

Place this free flow of peptides of emotion alongside the higher-order processes of the frontal cortex and an important link can be seen between learning and emotion.

The frontal cortex is also known as the cerebral cortex or forebrain. The frontal cortex *"- the most newly evolved of the brain structures, and the ... most fully developed in human beings ..."* (Pert, '99, p. 134), is responsible for higher-order processes, such as reason, planning, forethought, prediction and decision making.

Pert, '99, p. 166.
*"... the frontal cortex (is) the part of the brain that gives us the ability to decide and plan for the future, make changes, to exert control over our lives ..."*

And, in consideration of frontal cortex functioning John A. Teske, '96, adds 'complex motor sequencing' and 'coordination' to the list. In other words the frontal cortex gives us the capacity to think.

Diamond, Scheibel, and Elson, 5-31.
*"The cerebral cortex ... provides the circuitry and connections that support our highest level of cognitive functions."*

When relating to children, it would appear important to factor in the effect of positive or negative emotions upon the frontal cortex and the impact on learning and behaviour. This connection between emotions and the functioning of the frontal cortex may also be of particular significance around questions of depression in children, quite possibly affecting classroom behaviours chosen by the child as well as the effect on their learning potential. Some teachers have voiced the opinion that bullying behaviour can stem from depression. Given Pert's findings, it would appear to follow.

Let's look again at some of the capacities of the emotion-mediated frontal cortex.

The frontal cortex:

- supports our highest level of cognitive functions (involving perception and learning) in combination with emotion.

- is responsible for higher order processes of:
  - reasoning - and emotion
  - planning - and emotion
  - forethought - and emotion
  - prediction - and emotion
  - decision making - and emotion
  - the ability to decide and plan for the future - and emotion
  - formulation of intention to change - and emotion
  - making changes - emotion
  - complex motor sequencing/coordination - and emotion
  - exertion of control over our lives - and emotion

When all of these 'highest levels of cognitive function' capacities are linked to positive and constructive emotions, it is probably reasonable to anticipate enhanced development and learning outcomes. But when these capacities are linked to a depressed and/or negative state of mind, then it seems not unreasonable to expect diminished outcomes.

Whatever the outcomes, the long term consequences are likely significant, as Pert states, '99, p. 288, *"In humans ... (the frontal cortex) does not fully develop until sometime in the early twenties ..."* Thus, perhaps, the obvious has been underlined for us all - happy children will be productive children and, therefore, will have enjoyed an enhanced brain development by the time they reach their twenties.

As Erica, a grade 7 student, reminisced on her productive year in our grade 5 Four Communities Classroom "It was a happy time." Happy productive learning. What more could a teacher ask for.

> **If the free-flow of peptides of emotions and their effect upon the brain's frontal cortex and its role in learning and behaviour is important in child development, it would seem important that the teacher be aware of these processes when creating emotionally secure environments for developing minds.**

When combined with the brain's possibly unlimited potential for increases in neuronal connections, the description of the frontal cortex's capacities seems to be a statement of a child's potential.

Diamond, Scheibel, and Elson, p 1-1
*"The human brain ... is still of virtually unknown potential"*.

Foundationally, children's potential and learning is dependent upon interactions with externalities, significantly including the classroom environment. This is learning that is often an interactive process with other people and integrated with relationship and emotion, engaging inner dialogue, and inner thoughts; all through a series of moments.

## 5. The mind's inner dialogue and its external surroundings

Children have inner thoughts, as we all do. As children perceive and learn about their externalities, they will try to make sense of them within the context of life experience. Questions may arise in the mind. Is there consistency in what I'm experiencing/being told? Do connections appear valid or do they jar with my inner feelings and thoughts? Are my own feelings and thoughts valid?

Patricia S. Goldman-Rakic, '92, p. 104.
*"... neuronal pathways in the prefrontal cortex update inner models of reality to reflect changing environmental demands and incoming information. Those pathways guide short-term memory and (affect) moment to moment behaviour. ...(and are mediated) by a balance of current, internal, and past information."*

When harmonious externalities occur in the classroom environment - whether reinforcing a child's perceptions or engaging alternative thoughts - an inner dialogue for substantial learning is created. This is learning that sticks, neuronal connections that stay around, neuronal connections that are not forgotten; memory in construction. Constructive inner dialogue enhances learning in the frontal cortex, so that the child is better positioned to constructively learn about the world, understand more about self (autonomy) and his/her place within it (integration).

> **Does the life of the classroom recognise, make room for and legitimise the child's inner dialogue?**
> **(box 1)**

> **Does the classroom provide a non-judgemental environment for the child's expression of thought processes?**
> **(box 2)**

---

Boxes 1, 2, 3, and 4 are referenced on p. 306 'Central thoughts for teachers'. Also referenced on p. 306 are boxes 5 and 6 from p. 301.

- **Exerting control over our lives**

Pert, '99, p. 166.
*"...the frontal cortex ... gives us the ability ... to exert control over our lives..."*

Care needs to be taken that children are not expected to assume responsibility, while being denied opportunities to assume control over their lives by exercising constructive inner-dialogue, where they are able to take responsibility for self. Children appreciate being able to use their emotions constructively for the learning process.

Awareness of the interactive nature of brain development, highlights for all those who interact with children the importance of creating an environment in which children can experience constructive positive growth.

While parents and teachers are at the forefront, the work and decisions of school administrators and educational authorities also have a major impact on teaching and learning environments.

Collectively we nurture the children in our care.

> **To what degree is the 'exerting control over our lives' an aspect of learning and facilitated by teachers? (box 3)**

A large part of this nurture is to be found in our willingness to respect children's feelings, not only teach but listen, make room for inner dialogue, affirm children's thoughts and ideas, lead with a spirit of mutual regard and share with the children the job of making the classroom a happy productive place to live and grow.

The Four Communities Classroom system is founded on this philosophy, guiding teachers and children towards the happy, productive environment they desire. The reward for teachers is in witnessing children's constructive communication with others and individual use of self-descriptors (e.g. self-correction, self-regulation, self-organization), which stimulates outcomes of:
- constructive growth of brain development.
- insight regarding self in relationship to others.
- an enhanced perception of self in relationship to others including the teacher.

## 6. Social influence and brain capacity

John Teske, ('96) offers a linkage between human socialization and brain development.

*"The human nervous system is likely to have evolved in ways which require social interdependency, not only for survival of groups but for the canalization of individual nervous systems ..."*

Teske tells us we have evolved through a two way street of interdependency; a process that renders us social creatures. This certainly seems to be reflective, if not derivative, of ecological communicative function between self-entities and externalities that lead to integrative fitness for group and individual survival. And, out of this social-interdependency has arisen the need for communicative capacity - language. Thus, social interdependency and language communication has become foundational for humans, both as individuals and within groups; everyone engaged in an evolving process of interaction with externalities.

This process of social and language evolution, occurring concurrently with the individual's neuronal growth capacity and developmental plasticity of the brain, is a self-organizing process referenced to externalities.

Teske, '96.
*"… the social nexus of our development is itself embedded within the biological unfolding of our species."*

We are social beings and when we place children and teachers, together for curriculum purposes, we are actually, firstly and primarily, engaging a social arrangement complete with ecologically-evolved-interdependency implications.

Thus, perhaps it should not be surprising that, in the classroom, the primary focus of children is the social/communicative reality they find themselves in with all the accompanying feelings and emotions, rather than the demands of the curriculum.

But also, within this social arrangement, each child's frontal cortex, complete with emotional linkage, is poised and hoping for (expecting) a nurturing and stimulating environment in which to learn.

Children are ecologically endowed for stimulation, nurturing and learning, and actually present perfect conditions in which to realise curriculum goals.

It is perhaps fair to say that a child's anticipation of nurturing stimulation is more likely to be carried into high school if it has been the child's experience throughout elementary school.

Children, poised for action and ecologically endowed to learn, present perfect conditions in which to realise, according to the expectations of many adults, the central goal of education; the learning and remembering of knowledge, curriculum and facts.

> **(box 4)** In the pursuit of curriculum goals, *will the ecological foundation of human emotional/neurological capacity be recognised, nurtured, cared for, and importantly, built-upon?* To build upon these capacities is to enhance not only the learning of curriculum, but brain development that will maintain openness of spirit for discernment and learning in the future; <u>opportunity maintained.</u>

> In not recognizing ecological endowment in the educational endeavour, while favouring only measurable curriculum attainment some children are 'turned off by school and learning'.
>
> Perhaps, for the 'turned off' child, there has been little legitimization of the social communication imperative and the inner dialogue that is part of each child's desire to make sense of their world; <u>constructive learning opportunity lost.</u>

How children feel about relationships with other children, teachers or curriculum and what is remembered, either from this morning or in times past, is intimately connected to memories of social communication and inner dialogue.

**Building upon the ecologically-endowed foundation of human emotional/neurological capacity:**
- **legitimizes and strengthens social communication with others in school, alongside the child's dialogue with self that is part of the desire to make sense of their world.**
- **enhances brain development, and openness of spirit to discernment and learning.**
- **enables and enhances learning of curriculum.**

Thus, it is important to recognize, nurture, care for and, importantly, build upon these foundations of human emotional/neurological capacity,

In contrast, a 'primarily-curriculum' emphasis can negate the child's self and impede social legitimatization of the child.

Within the Four Communities Classroom children have the opportunity to legitimize and strengthen social communication through discussion and, in an atmosphere of mutual regard, strengthen sense of self. These are children ready to learn.

## 7. Brain capacity - relationship patterns of emotion, memory and learning

Learning facts and interacting in relationships take a combination of emotion and memory. The interaction of social communication and inner dialogue is intimately and emotionally linked to memory - affecting what we remember, either from this morning or from times past. Emotional memory also affects feelings held about relationships with other children, teachers and curriculum.

Teske, '96.
*"Areas of the brain that are involved in emotion are also involved in memory; it is the emotional charge of an event that most directly determines how well it is remembered."*

Says Pert, '99, p.142.
*"All sensory information undergoes a filtering process as it travels across one or more synapses, eventually (but not always) reaching the areas of higher process like the*

*frontal lobes. There the sensory input - concerning the view, the odour, the caress - enters our conscious awareness. The efficiency of the filtering process, which chooses what stimuli we pay attention to at any given moment, is determined by the quantity and quality of these receptors at these nodal points. The relative quantities and qualities of those receptors are determined by many things, among them your experiences yesterday and as a child ..."*

The phrase, 'what stimuli we pay attention to at any given moment', and, moreover, remember, when linked to thoughts of quantity and quality of sensory input, are of significance to those engaged in teaching. Briggs and Peat remind us also that emotionally charged memory is affected by patterns of relationship, p.173, "A memory, like a sensation, is not an isolated bit; it is a pattern of relationships."

Pert, '99, p.143.
"... biochemical change wrought at the receptor level is the molecular basis of memory. ... a ligand ... changes the cell membrane in such a way that the probability of an electrical impulse travelling across the membrane where the receptor resides is facilitated or inhibited, thereafter affecting the choice of neuronal circuitry that will be used. ... (thus) memories are stored not only in the brain, but in a psychosomatic network extending into the body, ..."

Pert continues, p.143.
"The decision about what becomes a thought rising to consciousness and what remains an undigested thought pattern buried at a deeper level in the body is mediated by the receptors. ... the fact that memory is encoded or stored at the receptor level means that memory processes are emotion driven and unconscious, (but, like other receptor mediated processes, can sometimes be made conscious)."

Thus we have hugely interdependent interactions of being. It seems our bodies and brain are chemically linked through ligands that are emotionally responsive to our externalities and our relationship with externalities. This emotional, moment to moment interplay is the basis of cognition and memory. There is memory that enables recognition, and learning; a conscious process. But while there is this enabler of recognition and learning, there also is a process that causes memory to be discarded as being inconsequential. We can be either conscious or less conscious of these processes. At an unconscious level memory can be buried.

> **To maximise learning memory it is important to provide children with an emotionally secure classroom environment. There cannot, however, be control over the exact outcomes. As every child is different, 'what becomes a conscious thought and what remains an undigested thought pattern' is each child's personal process; they will make of it what they will. This is part of each child's inner dialogue, their humanity, and part of each child's personal journey. Thus from the outer experience comes the inner dialogue.**

> **What communication opportunities should be regarded and facilitated in school as important and integral to a child's education?**

Thus, we can say that, from outer experience, through communication and observation, comes the child's inner dialogue and learning memory. This process:

- **to be constructive, requires an emotionally secure classroom environment.**
- **cannot be predicted. Children are engaged in an inner journey; they will make of it what they will.**

**Our body and brain are chemically linked and are emotionally responsive to our externalities and our relationship with externalities.**

# THE BRAIN, CONSCIOUSNESS, AND MIND

I draw on Capra, Hagelin, Briggs and Peat.

Consciousness is a complex process associated with inner dialogue of the mind - self with self - that carries with it a high degree of unpredictability. Unpredictability of inner dialogue outcomes is an ongoing aspect of human interaction.

This inner dialogue consciousness in the child is very much a factor in teacher/child communications and relationships. Since these are very formative years for the child's brain and its exertion with mind, consciousness and thought, teachers do, during the child's time at school, engage the consciousness and mind of children in an important way - in the teaching and learning process, through curriculum, but probably more significantly for the child's thought processes, through relationship. The educational process, when viewed in these terms, seems to bring to the fore the need to consider mind and consciousness and what significance this holds for teachers in their interactions with and responsibilities to children.

The following offers an examination of these questions:

1. A physical structure for the brain but not for the mind.
2. The mind and the quantum realm.
3. Infinity of the mind.
4. Mindful of intelligence or mindful of wisdom? The measure of intelligence.
5. Minds in the classroom, and the re-definition of classroom responsibilities for teachers.

## 1. A physical structure for the brain but not for the mind

The brain has a physical structure, but investigation of consciousness and mind is complicated by its lack of a physical structure and place. The brain is an object; it can be identified. There is a deterministic form to the brain. But, although structured, the brain's complexity creates outcomes that are not necessarily physically contained, just as consciousness and mind, are not physically contained. The mind resides in no one specific place; you cannot, unlike the brain, point and say, 'this is the mind, this is where the 'thing' consciousness lies'.

Capra, '83, p. 376.
*"A true science of consciousness will deal with qualities rather than quantities, and will be based on shared experience rather than verifiable measurements."*

Lack of measurability certainly seems supported when we consider John Hagelin's statement, p. 61.
*"As the mind ... becomes less and less localized by the specific boundaries of a thought, awareness becomes correspondingly more expanded. When the faintest impulse of thought or feeling is 'transcended' in this manner, consciousness is left alone to experience itself."*

Hagelin makes a connection between mind, thought and consciousness that takes us into an area that we can probably identify with - the seed of an idea that is cogitated upon.

Consciousness is what Hagelin refers to as a unified intelligence, and the fountainhead of all known laws of nature. (DVD 2006)

While we are unable to see or touch the site of consciousness, it is vital to the quality of thought processes and the development of discernment regarding both inner dialogue and in interaction with the outside world.

> **To what extent should we engage children's minds and consciousness in classrooms with a qualitative emphasis rather than an emphasis that relies on verifiable measurements?**

Thus, although structured, the brain's complex relationship processes create outcomes that are not necessarily physically contained, just as consciousness and mind are not physically contained. But with mind and consciousness being fundamental life processes, what awarenesses need to be part of the teacher's mind and consciousness?

Teachers need to be aware that:
- consciousness and mind provide an avenue for intelligence along with development of discernment and wisdom.

And in the classroom teachers need to be aware that:
- quantifiable measurement appears to be inadequate in monitoring development of discernment.
- the engagement of children's minds in the life/learning process of the classroom is not measurable, but can be observed through increases in contribution in groups and the class.
- the persistently 'quiet' child is likely also benefiting from constructive classroom processes - again not immediately measurable (see p. 60).

## 2. The mind and the quantum realm

Briggs and Peat, '90 p. 189.

*"… human beings have evolved to exploit the quantum's individual unpredictability. Our eyes, nose, and taste buds are able to respond to just a few quanta of energy. The human nervous system (including the brain) is both classical and quantum in nature, exploiting processes at the quantum scale in order to achieve large-scale ends such as movement and speech. Thus the tension between individual quantum chaos and collective quantum order is able to create and drive increasingly complex scales of structure."* (my bracketed words)

This description of connectedness between the quantum realm and biology underlines this basis for life. Thus, perhaps, it should not be surprising that when the quantum realm, and chaos theory, along with associated words such as bifurcation and feedback, are examined in the light of our understanding of brain function, there appears to be a correlation. Consider whether the new science descriptive words, re-printed here from p. 245, have relevance for the physical brain, non-physical consciousness and the non-physical mind.

- infinite permutation potential
- indeterminancy
- sensitivity
- mutuality
- cooperative interaction
- chaos
- order
- evolution and change
- relationship
- probability
- possibility
- interconnectivity
- linear, non-linear
- individuality and group influence
- complexity
- emerging properties
- development

- learning
- tendency
- fluctuation
- no absoluteness
- quality
- pattern
- self-organization
- communication
- network

Their relevance would also appear to extend to children's relationship/development/learning processes; all ecological processes. The brain appears, in effect, to be H.Q. central for our conscious and unconscious engagement of these ecological processes, and probably this is why the scientific investigation of the brain's structure and interactive processes appear to offer an enticing route in attempts to fathom consciousness and mind.

Words of particular relevance, application, and persuasion seem to be 'infinite permutation potential', 'emerging properties', 'possibility', 'development', 'learning', and 'no absoluteness'. 'Chaos' and 'order' fit learning processes associated with bifurcation, although some may argue that 'evolution and change' cannot always be observed in all minds. This in itself, though, can be a descriptor of 'pattern' and 'tendency' (even if not always constructive). Other 'patterns' and evidence of 'tendency' may display 'sensitivity' and 'fluctuations', which may lead to 'evolution'.

Certainly all these 'relationship' processes would involve the communication process; processes with 'unpredictability' outcomes. Importantly too, each of these words do not describe separate and discrete phenomenon; all are related and interactive, i.e. one cannot talk about one without engaging all. If we apply these powerfully descriptive words to the human mind, and recognise the human brain as an ecological sophisticate, it is not hard to see how and why our minds are cross-ecological, and so powerful.

## 3. Infinity of the mind

The list of descriptive words on the previous page convey possibility. Words of containment or restriction do not appear, and neither does the word 'finite'. But the phrase, 'infinite permutation potential' is on the list. If the mind has infinite permutation potential, any discussion of mind is a partial consideration at best. It seems, therefore, that, in the search for mind and consciousness, one must rely to some extent on processes of speculation and conjecture which, interestingly, the mind seems to respond to quite well.

I have found the use of speculation and conjecture in the classroom works wonders for both inner dialogue, and the sharing and communication of learning.

When the teacher poses a question to his/her class, "What do you think ...?" or "What do you feel about ...?" this is an invitation for children to open their minds and respond, as their inner dialogue conjecture begins.

In contrast, with a non-inclusive not-to-be-questioned statement - "This is how things are."- children's inner dialogue and conjecture are more likely to remain contained - mind/consciousness potential contained.

And so emboldened, here are some thoughts, in my mind, on the mind.

Perhaps the mind is the essence of who one is, and the essence of aspiration, and the essence of downfall. Certainly, the activity of the mind would seem to be the precursor of both destruction and transcendence, and the avenue to status quo thinking, brilliance, mediocrity, empathy, imagination and creativity; the creator of perception and outcomes, and an avenue for difference. Also the mind, it would seem, is able to pursue multiple avenues, both at different times and simultaneously.

With children's minds in their keeping, it is a great responsibility for teachers and a sobering thought.

Ecologically, it can be suggested that the human mind, having transcended from the expression of simple ecological survival processes, has the ongoing power of transcendence. Evolutionary transcendence enables further transcendence, and becomes part of the process of becoming and possibility. Transcendence and possibility inherently enable choice. However, transcendence also enables the choice of non-transcendence. Thus, our minds are foundational and instrumental, in terms of transcendence, charged with choice in our process of becoming. It is through the power of choice, that the mind is empowered to be the creator of outcomes.

However, the conscious human mind is extraordinarily complex; it is not finite in what it can do, and therefore, not finite in itself; it cannot be captured or contained. With infinite potential for transcendence, perhaps we should be finding out what the mind can do within ecological context. As guides in the classroom, perhaps what is required is that we put our minds, our intelligence, into a search for the mind's wisdom potential, an infinite exploration with all minds on board.

## 4. Mindful of intelligence or mindful of wisdom? The measure of intelligence

Paradoxically, the human mind, having transcended beyond the instinct for survival, can become a force for destruction of both self and other species. Such is the power of our minds. This, it would seem, is intelligence without wisdom. Can there be intelligence without wisdom? Would choosing a wise mind be a transcendent choice?

If so, would we move towards wisdom by being mindful of our collective survival, mindful of our ecology, mindful of reference, mindful of mutuality, mindful of context? Would this be an intelligent thing to do? Do we have to link intelligence to wisdom to develop transcendent minds? Has intelligence, wisdom and transcendence been given into our care? In our hands, is the ecology's next move, in concert with humanity, to continue on its eons-age path of providing us with a sustainable way forward? Ecological dynamics will survive, with or without us. For ourselves and for future generations, we have a choice and a responsibility.

- **Can a link to wisdom be part of classroom life?**

Perhaps, intelligence alongside wisdom produces a truer intelligence, that exhibits ecological integrity, where mutuality is expressed through the use of mutual regard and discernment. If these elements are viable then the Four Communities Classroom's ecological base, where mutuality is expressed through the use of mutual regard and discernment, may be our route to linking wisdom to intelligence in classroom life. In the Four Communities Classroom, where discussion is foundational, there can be exchange of ideas that foster constructive mind process that focus not just on preferred outcomes, but on environments that are sensitive to positive mind interactions in children.

> To what extent should thoughts of discernment and wisdom be part of children's development of intelligence and learning process?

In guiding young minds in their formative years the wise teacher leads the way to intelligence with wisdom, as together they build the classroom environment.

## 5. Minds in the classroom - a re-definition of what classroom responsibility means for teachers

The mind is the shaper of things to come and intimately part of the ongoing process of becoming for each child. It follows that the mind should be at the centre of education and of learning. There are often 25/30 young minds in a classroom, in the process of becoming, presenting, for the teacher's mind, a significant responsibility - and opportunity.

- **Classroom responsibilities**

How does responsibility for mind development and processes of becoming compare to other assumptions of responsibility traditionally felt by teachers - the maintenance of discipline and the covering of curriculum? With these two elements under control, it is often felt that the achievement potential of each child will fall into place. But more could be gained.

The focus that assumes responsibility for discipline and curriculum vs. one that focuses on facilitating mind development can be the difference between the emphasis placed on secondary and primary learning experience. Within this difference lies an opportunity for realising further potential.

**Primary experiences** are ones that are felt; emotional responses to externalities and processes of discovery that give rise to internal dialogue in the mind. These are always with us, recognized educationally or not. These are processes that are often the most powerful in shaping perceptions of self and surroundings (constructive or negative), and decisions regarding what and how the individual learns and takes things 'on-board'.

**Secondary experiences** generally arise from teacher-imposed curriculum learning and discipline procedures that may leave little room for discovery or legitimizing internal dialogue. Secondary experiences provide information and rules that have been selected for learning and abiding by. Children can also have an emotional response to secondary learning experience, but more often in response to their sense of relationship with the secondary experience provider - the teacher. In other words, the child's sense of engagement will more likely come more from his/her understanding of the relationship with the teacher than relationship with the curriculum content.

The prevalence of teacher-held responsibility for assuring that children are mostly in receipt of secondary experience has arisen from the perception, held by many that teaching is an essentially secondary experience endeavour. The teacher dispenses knowledge, the children behave, listen and learn. This is a concept that has powerfully travelled from an individual's childhood learning experience into their adult learning experience, and on again to the next generation of children.

However, when we view the learning process in the light of our knowledge of the process of becoming it would seem that knowledge can be most effectively conveyed when the teacher uses these elements of primary and secondary learning experience in varying combinations to the best effect. Importantly, though, the primary experiences that should be offered in the classroom are the ones that not only respect children's processes of mind, but enable curriculum acquisition alongside a growing sense of self and discernment capacity. Possibilities enabled, rather than contained by the teacher's focus on discipline and curriculum.

Rather than assuming full responsibility for children's behaviour and learning, it can, therefore, be a shared experience of mutual regard and quest for knowledge. In the Four Communities Classroom children begin to readily take responsibility for best outcomes.

---

See pp. 19, 24, 25 and 175 for more on primary and secondary experience, and p. 197 for an anti-bullying approach using the primary and secondary experience perspective.

---

> **In offering constructive primary experience children are enabled to exercise their ecological heritage of self-regulation, along with the other self-descriptors.**

> **By enabling children's exercise of self-descriptors, teachers seldom have to consider resorting to secondary experience disciplinary measures in order to keep curriculum goals on track. In other words, teachers are able to relax on their traditionally perceived responsibilities, as children exercise and are enabled to develop their own sense of responsibility for self and others.**

It is important to remember that this building of responsibility in children can be set back, quite considerably, if inexplicably to the children, secondary discipline approaches are suddenly reintroduced to their classroom life. If, having established a classroom environment of shared responsibility for learning and behaviour, the teacher withdraws that ethos to more expeditiously deal with a problem, the response will be, "Are you trusting us with responsibility or not?" "What are we supposed to do now?"

Mrs. Dubray, Vice principal and grade five teacher.
*"The real strength of the Four Communities Classroom is that the kids take ownership for the Four Communities Classroom."*

Once children feel secure in the ownership role, teachers are able to concentrate on an enhanced program of curriculum acquisition and, more importantly, become true facilitators of children's processes of becoming.

Mrs. Dubray again.
*"The energy you are able to give to your children in terms of teaching curriculum is so much greater. There is significantly less stress, and it seems that children take on much more responsibility and carry on with their tasks. The Four Communities Classroom allows children to develop their abilities and blossom at their own level in a way that they feel safe."* (See the freedom/task concept for children - p. 75.)

Thus a re-definition of responsibility is described. Mrs. Dubray was able to shift the focus of her responsibility from maintenance of discipline and curriculum coverage, to facilitator of children's processes of mind and becoming, where behaviour and curriculum coverage became successful signposts in daily life rather than energy consuming, mind-marginalizing goals.

- **Opportunities of mind**

A teacher accustomed to assuming responsibility for each child's learning and behaviour may ask, does the infinite aspect of the mind mean unfettered, open vistas for everyone in the classroom? Does this mean that because we want to maximise learning potential, we have a classroom environment where anything goes? Well no. Successful ecological processes arise from mutuality. For a classroom environment to be sustainable, anything cannot 'go'. The best ecology for the mind is where minds regard minds. Thus, we may ask, with the enabling of the mind being the essence of learning, what, in the classroom, needs to be kept in mind?

The classroom is an arena for exchange of energy, where change and evolution will occur. This has to be a fluid process where mutual regard (a primary experience) and the potential for the development of mind flourishes. This is not to say that secondary experience is ruled out. Secondary-experience curriculum acts as a signpost, directing the discerning primary-experienced mind along its avenue of learning. It is the teacher who determines how she combines these elements to guide children in a sound learning experience

- **Emotion and inner dialogue in children, and the primary and secondary experience**

Relationship is foundational to human interaction. The child's mind forms perceptions in relationship to externalities, the classroom environment. This is an independent, responsive thought process of each individual child that the teacher has no control over and an important part of the relationship mix. Thus we ask ourselves, what is it that we want for our children? What externality would be most favourable in constructively developing our children's minds? How do we create such an environment? These are questions that lead to the teacher's provision of some secondary experience for children – what are we going to do and how are we going to get there? But then we pose a question that will open the door to children being able to constructively engage in primary experience. We ask ourselves, how will our children, with each of their individual minds, express themselves and participate in the life of the classroom environment? Then, in combination, secondary and primary experience produce this key question; what classroom structures will make primary experiences possible for children's minds?

This is important. Secure in an established classroom structure with a caring captain at the helm, children can launch happily into the learning adventure.

Secondary and primary experience are triggers for emotion. And since emotion is part of mind, mind is engaged through emotion. With the inclusion of the emotional component to consider in classroom structures, a further question arises; what types of emotions will produce the best learning outcomes and how will the secondary and primary experiences of the classroom impact the child's emotions?

For a practical guide and thoughts on enabling the exercise of responsibility in children, and the engagement of mind/thought learning processes in school, see chaps. 2, 4, 5, and 6.

- **Children's state of mind and the teacher**

In your interaction with children's minds, their perceived state of mind and emotion should be the most important factor guiding your relationship with them, both individually and collectively. I have found that primary experiences tend to create harmony and positive emotions in the child's mind and in the classroom as a whole. Happily, even most directives can be translated into primary experiences by presenting them in an inclusive way. Remember, "What do you think? What do you feel?" Never underestimate children's recognition of what is right.

Primary experience is an essential element of mind processes; primary experience and mind are as one. It is within this realm of primary experience that one can move forward more readily in the classroom, with children generally in a mindful, open state of mind.

Instead of relying only on secondary experience to shape minds, we become facilitators of children's inner dialogue and relationship, where they become architects and enablers of their preferred external environments for themselves and others.

This is living systems dynamics in action, where children understand the importance of individuality and difference (p. 110), alongside mutual regard; where change, learning and bifurcation are embraced; all important to inner dialogue of the mind.

> Ecological living system dynamics are inherent in each child, to be lived and expressed in the quest for sustainable relationship balance between the teacher and the child, and between the children. Minds are opened to discovery; potentials are explored. There are celebrations to enjoy.

The pursuit of this sustainable classroom life is a shared responsibility of teacher and children; the key to enabling transcendence in children.

Although the nature of the expression of living system dynamics is hard to predict, the quality of expression can be more closely anticipated. Welcoming living system dynamics into the classroom enables the infinite permutation potential in each child, complete with different properties emerging, pursued in concert with others. When discernment and sensitivity to cooperative interaction occur which, by definition, involves networks and mutual regard, it can be an especially constructive and qualitative process. Concepts of relationship, probability, possibility, interconnectivity, individuality and difference, group participation, and joy of being, are opened up for the mind. It is dynamic, evolving and ecologically sound. It is life.

Teachers do not have to take responsibility for shaping children's minds. Together, in the Four Communities Classroom, children participate in the creation of preferred external environments, enhancing both processes of becoming and curriculum processes.

## (IV) LIVING SYSTEMS AND SELF-DESCRIPTORS: Constructive Inner Dialogue And The Joy And Succcess Of Life In The Classroom

This journey into the natural world has left me with a sense of wonder; for our existence and how everything is as it is. The concept of being in a state of becoming seems enormously important to our understanding of the ecology as the ultimate reality.

That everything is in a state of becoming suggests a concept of existence that is endlessly evolving and finding expression. Our wonderful selves and the world we have been given to live in has been presented to us as a gift and a challenge; the baton of 'everything in a state of becoming' handed over to us.

Each one of us has a brain of incredible complexity. The brain provides us the capacity to engage in the earth's process-of-becoming in virtually countless ways and these ways are multiplied by the number of people on earth. We are born with the capacity to embark on our own personal journey in the earth's expression of becoming. It is our birthright.

Although we had no part in its creation, we now have everything to do with its future. Wisdom is ours if we exercise our response-ability within the mutuality foundations of the ecology that produced us.

The Four Communities Classroom philosophy is founded upon the theory of living systems where the quantum realm, the ecology and the biology of living systems have been translated into a language for education. Thus, we move forward with the thought that if we are derivatives of the ecology and biology and the physical dynamics of existence, it follows that our learning process and those of our children will follow the same path of expression.

All of these elements are building blocks, but probably the ones of most significance to children are of feelings, relationship and self. Thus, as we explore, in the How To section, how to develop and build a Four Communities Classroom for good teaching and learning, we focus on validation of the child.

Children in the Four Communities Classroom respond to ecologically-based avenues of learning, compatible with who they are as humans and who they are as children. In short, we give them the gift of a learning environment that resonates with their ecological core.

Children who have enjoyed a happy, positive life experience tend to readily excel in an ecologically-sensitive environment. However, too often a child's ecological core is overlain with defences, perhaps well-established in response to negative experiences, requiring time and patience on the teachers part. But I have found that, when children are provided with relationship dynamics, their ecological core, in time, responds with constructive outcomes. This usually becomes a process of self-validation. And when, through constructive relationship, children start to feel a sense of self-validation they find it easier to make sense of their world. The path to constructive progress can open up.

What you will find is that an environment that enables this validation of self for children also, automatically, engages the other ecological dynamics. For example, as a child starts to feel good about him/herself in relationship to others, a new order of perception of self and others begins. This is a process of development and learning. Positions previously held in the child's mind start to give way to alternative views.

Andrea, grade three.
*"I like the Four Communities Classroom because you can find out what people are like, instead of just saying, I don't like you and not even giving them a chance."*

In response to events occurring in the environment (bifurcation-engendered points of decision) the order of the child's perceptions start to move into the dynamic of 'chaos', the beginnings of change, [see appendix (i) ] as new perceptions start to evolve into a new order. These are internal and primary processes of the child's own inner journey (inner bifurcation process). So you have facilitated, in your living-systems-friendly classroom, a process that has engendered a combination of sometimes very thoughtful inner dialogue, alongside the externalities of self in relation to others. The child has been engaged and involved in bifurcation, leading to new perceptions; a natural process for nature's child.

When positive emotions are triggered, peptides flow with positive effect; another connection with the natural world. Peptides, as we know, link body systems, including the brain. [See appendix (iii) ] And when peptides [Pert's molecules of emotion - appendix (iii) ], flow in the brain, the brain's dendrite/axon development of neuronal communication process can become one of positive perception of self in relationship to others. Such brain development is an enabler of learning and, therefore, a fast-track to curriculum learning. The child's autonomy (sense of self) is engaged in an enhanced process of development, alongside and in relationship with his/her externalities - other children, the classroom, the teacher, the school and knowledge (integration). A positive balance between the dynamics of autonomy (of self) and integration begins to emerge; the ultimate state in development and learning potential for the mind. The environment for learning that you have created in your Four Communities Classroom has enabled a positive move in the process of becoming. Emotionally driven, as we all are, the child's ultimate reference point, that of feelings, has been nurtured. Positive outlook, perception and attitude are reinforced.

These processes have automatically engaged responsibility for self. There has been no coercion, no admonition from the teacher about the need to act responsibly. The environment is created; its denizens respond; it is the way of the ecology.

But simultaneously, the environment is affected; denizens/environment - each shaping each other. It is all a moment to moment orchestration, with good teaching and learning as guide. The teacher is the conductor, the facilitator, the conduit. Every element is engaged, from the dynamics of living systems to emotional response.

Let's take a closer look at some further dynamics - ones of exercising responsibility for self - that contribute to the joy and success of classroom life.

## 1. The self-descriptors

Exercising responsibility for self is an important aspect of life. Our minds handle the responsibility-to-self process through the dynamics of feedback-to-self. These dynamics are referred to as self-descriptors. And so self-descriptors, we can say, are the in-house moderators of our thoughts and feelings, providing continuous feedback for our consideration. Thus, self-descriptors also serve as a reflection of our sense of self and identity. Self-reinforcing feedback involves positive feedback to self, while other self-descriptors are processes of negative feedback to self. (For more on positive and negative feedback see p. 241.)

However, these built-in self-descriptors do not entirely centre on self. Our minds are equipped (and are able to choose) to think beyond ourselves. Children have this choice. And it is a good one, since in the striving for balance between autonomy of self and integration with others the use of self-descriptors become most beneficial when others are considered. Thus, in our relationship to externalities, through self-descriptors, we can effectively monitor our perception, behaviour and conduct in respect to others. In monitoring not only ourselves, but also our relationships, we are able to better understand what is going on around us and how events affect us.

Self-descriptors that operate constructively when referenced to externalities are:-

- self-correction
- self-regulation
- self-monitoring
- self-balancing
- self-limiting
- self-justification
- self-organising
- self-sustaining
- self-reinforcing
- self-assertion
- self-determination

So we may find ourselves asking, to what extent are my actions O.K, and to what extent do I have to keep track of and modify attitudes, behaviours, and actions? Thoughts such as these help to make constructive use of positive and negative feedback to self, and engender responsibility towards both self, and to externalities.

This constructive use of these processes, involving consideration of others as well as ourselves, can help smooth our way, and our children's way, in our interactions with others.

This is a natural ability children possess and we can encourage them to use to form strong positive self-images and sound relationships with others and the outside world. For some children the Four Communities Classroom becomes a place of reawakening for these natural abilities.

Thus, self-descriptors are self feedback thought processes of mind, often in the form of questions, engaged to help develop understanding of self in relationship to surroundings and shape our perceptions, attitudes and actions. These are important skills for children in school to develop and practice. Children practiced in such self referencing with externalities are children well positioned to intelligently engage with, and contribute to constructive learning in the classroom.

Self-descriptors are, therefore, the basis for responsible thought and action and form feedback to self. Each individual monitors his/her own actions and the response from surroundings. To what extent are my actions O.K, and to what extent do I keep track and modify attitudes, behaviours, and actions? Constructive feedback to self engenders responsibility towards self (autonomy), and to externalities (integration).

## 2. Self-descriptors in the classroom - emphasising an innate capacity

There is a lesson that I present to children on self-correction. It is described in chapter two, p. 113. With an introduction and class discussion it usually takes about 20 - 30 minutes. Discussion ends with a vote, where the decision is generally arrived at that the best teaching and learning comes from self-correction, rather than (constant) teacher correction. This agreement is posted on the classroom wall - a happy, decorative positive reminder of what we all agreed upon. We may need to refer to it as the days go by. You may find it helpful to look at p. 113 right now.

This lesson and discussion that you hold with the children creates an understanding of the concept of self-correction. Bringing this concept to children opens their minds to the idea that self can flourish in the classroom without the need for teacher intervention. This can be the beginning of a new feeling for children about self and the power of self in the classroom, and the beginning of the assumption of responsibility to self. It represents, in fact, the beginning of a balance of autonomy and integration in the classroom. The children, of course, do not understand, or need to understand the concept in these terms. It is, however, vital that self-correction becomes a primary experience for children (through discussion and exchange of ideas) and for legitimatizing innate feelings and intuition. It is after all, a process of self.

Vanessa, grade nine.
*"I like self-correction because it gives you some responsibility. Being allowed (by the teacher) to self-correct is the same as saying I trust you."*

Brittany, grade seven.
*"Self–correction is part of taking care of yourself."*

Should the teacher co-opt these self-descriptor processes, the effect will be counter-productive to constructive processes of self-awareness on the child's part. Telling a child what self-descriptor to use to modify behaviour is cooption that can only become an assumption of responsibility by the teacher and a supplying of secondary experience.

However, since self-descriptors function in reference to externalities, the teacher as an externality to the child is presented with a positive and concrete way to help and remind children of responsibility to self (and others). To help a child through the early stages of constructively exercising self-descriptors you may want to ask the child, "How will this action/decision or process, help or hinder good teaching and learning?" (See, 2. 'Asking THE foundational question', pp. 33-34.) For most children, if not eventually all, such questions supplied by the teacher become part of children's internal process of self-monitoring. In other words, they begin to automatically ask questions like these of themselves.

Becoming competent with the use of self-descriptors is a journey the child must take full responsibility for. He/she cannot be told how to feel. You provide the signpost. The child finds the way. Children's self-descriptors, by definition, can only be the child's own ordering of these dynamics and abilities; essentially an innate capacity.

Children are frequently able to answer their own self-descriptor questions satisfactorily, without the teacher being privy to their mental processes. Of course, you will know when a question has run its internal course unsatisfactorily, or hardly at all, when unsatisfactory class contributions are manifested.

When unsatisfactory class contributions arise, your response of "It looks like you need some teacher correction", alerts the child to the fact that careful consideration has not preceded action. The child will usually say that he/she does not need teacher correction. "Good," you say. And the child has an opportunity to re-evaluate, usually with satisfactory results. Disciplinary action is avoided, dignity remains intact. Emotions are kept in check. You are the externality with feedback. The child decides how to respond.

Essentially, throughout the self-correction lesson and on-going life in the classroom, a question begins to form in each child's mind. It is important that this question not be provided by you as a secondary experience, but that this question be allowed to be a primary thought, generated through classroom interactions and experiences. And this question is, 'Do I take control of the feedback I am getting with self-correction, or do I leave myself open for the teacher to supply feedback to me through teacher correction?' In other words, (and perhaps the form the question will take in a child's mind), 'What would I rather have for my life in the classroom, self-correction or teacher correction?'

However, should a child again invite teacher correction on a similar event or issue, accompanying your response with a look/tone of incredulity can prove effective. Each separate interaction should be treated, however, as a separate opportunity for the child to exercise self-correction. Life in the classroom will present many opportunities for self-correction practice; some children will need more than others.

If a child says that, yes, teacher correction is required, give the correction, and then ask why he/she was unable to self-correct. This approach makes it very clear that the child has a choice in the matter.

Will response always be satisfactory? No. But then you will get the opportunity to provide more feedback. Feedback may, occasionally, have to take the form of taking the child aside for a strong reprimand, likely to be noted in future considerations by the child. Yes, strong reprimands are still part of the teachers repertoire in the Four Communities Classroom (see 'The story of Brent the rebuilding of dignity', p. 215).

As we know, children learn at varying rates. Learning to use self-correction effectively can take time. But, always, interaction is engaged with the assumption of worthiness, and that a child is capable and wants to engage constructively with his/her own internal primary experience, and self-correct, with dignity intact. In this way, the tools of constructive relationship and communication remain strong and are, perhaps, even enhanced for use another day. At all times, your goal is to build a child's self-esteem and self-awareness so that, when emotionally ready, he/she is able to constructively take over the reins of self for self. Dignity-building leads to respect and responsibility for self.

**To summarize**

- **Self-descriptors are important enablers for children in building a positive sense of themselves.**
- **Teachers engage children with assumptions of worthiness. With dignity intact, a child can and will likely want to make constructive use of self-descriptors as part of his internal primary experience.**
- **Dignity-building is emotionally satisfying for the child and leads to respect and responsibility for self. (Dignity-building can be a great antidote for the child who seeks emotional sustenance from bullying others.)**
- **The goal is for a child, when emotionally ready, to take over the reins of responsibility of self for self.**

## 3. One self-descriptor prompts another - autonomy and integration dynamics of living systems in action

A glance at the self-descriptors on p. 284 indicates that a child who understands self-correction and begins to learn how to use it, also automatically engages with the other self-descriptors. So the teacher does not need to engage children in a process similar to that of understanding self-correction to create understanding of the other self descriptors. Children now have a frame of reference for developing responsibility for self and others. Through the concept of self-correction, a state of mind has been opened to the constructive exploration of self in relation to others and atmosphere of mutual regard within the classroom as a whole. The autonomy and integration dynamics of living systems are in action. Self-correction, with the other self-descriptors 'in tow', becomes a moment-to-moment enhancement of the decision-making process that is a part of every individual's life, generating such thoughts as:-

- How do I justify (in relationship to events and others) my thoughts and actions in the light of what I think and believe?
- How do I organize my thoughts and actions to create the best outcome?
- Is my thinking going to sustain me in this environment?

These questions constitute an ongoing, emotionally-mediated process that goes largely unremarked and seldom brought forth for detailed analysis. Events of heightened emotion that create casualties through lack of self-correction are often the ones that receive more notice; a problem for the child and for others. This is where, again, the teacher provides the question for the child to consider; the question that the child is apparently still learning to ask him/herself, "How will this action, decision, process, help or hinder good teaching and learning?" Emotionally laden situations can create fear and withdrawal in a child and act as barriers to the internal use of self-correction questions. It is important that children know they are in a safe place to explore their feelings. Guidance and patience are important in building, in a child, constructive emotional feelings.

In class discussion and in the everyday life of the classroom a child may consider questions around self-reinforcement, 'Am I right?' Do I reinforce myself by holding onto the idea that I have or do I look at it another way and perhaps change some of my thinking on this topic? In working towards resolution, the child will analyse and question sense of self, both from within and considering the possible opinions and perceptions that the external world may hold.

However, **self-assertion** is as important to sense of self as finding common ground with others.

Self-assertion is a process whereby we determine and project to others our individuality, our identity, our being, our self. Thus, self-assertion is a self-descriptor of identity and, therefore, important to the relationship process. Without that awareness of self, it is difficult to distinguish ourselves from others and then embark on a relationship. Thus while it is important to connect with others, we cannot lose our individual identity. However, self-assertion is not constructive when ratcheted to the point where relationships are negatively affected. Like every aspect of nature, it comes down to balance. When balanced with constructive relationship, self-assertion is the autonomy part of the autonomy/integration equation and, therefore, vital to life process. In equal measure to self-assertion, relationship is the integration part of the autonomy/integration equation and, therefore, also vital to life process. It is a process of self-balancing.

Every child is entitled to the vital process of self-assertion, and must be respected for their self-assertion contribution to life process. You can create a safe environment in which children can grow in their understanding of their mutual regard relationship and in which each child's life process can flourish.

The teacher's job is to be an enabler and source of assurance for each child's sense of self; a sense that enables constructive awareness through constructive relationship.

As this process and awareness grows within your classroom, the multi-faceted self-descriptor thoughts enable children to make constructive contribution to the autonomy and integration dynamics of life.

I remember a little boy in a grade four class where I was working with the teacher. This boy wanted to contribute to class discussion, but appeared very anxious about it. When he put up his hand, his legs would begin jigging up and down. While talking, he anxiously searched my face, presumably worried that he might not be saying the 'right thing'. It seemed very important to him to feel comfortably integrated into what was happening in class. I was his immediate environment and reference point to determine how he was doing.

I interacted non-judgmentally with him (and the class) and, over time, his concerns over 'right' contributions eased, opening up his mind to applying his own judgement of self and the efficacy of his responses. With only constructive feedback coming from the teacher he felt more assured of his own judgement when asking himself 'How am I doing?' Is my thinking sustaining me in this environment?

Non-judgemental acceptance of genuine attempt is crucial in developing comfort using self-descriptors. It was through this process that the boy was enabled and encouraged in his use of self-descriptors. He stopped looking anxious. When his hand went up, he started to look eager, happy, and confident, and his little legs were still. In a safe environment he had used self-descriptors to build a more confident awareness of identity and self - his sense of autonomy bolstered; confidence gained. He had made significant moves in opening his mind to his potential and building his autonomous capacity for self-assertion, in integrative balance with his surroundings.

**To summarize**
- **Self-correction opens the mind to the constructive exploration of self in relation to others.**
- **Thoughts of self-correction (with the other self-descriptors 'in tow'), produces a moment-to-moment enhancement of decision-making. Is my thinking going to sustain me? (This is an emotionally-mediated process that goes largely unremarked).**
- **However, a child's process of self-assertion is valid in determining and distinguishing self from others. But how we self-assert affects how our environment responds. Thus constructive, rewarding self-assertion comes from creating balance in relationship with others.**
- **Self-assertion is associated with the autonomy part of the autonomy/integration equation.**
- **The teacher's job is to be an enabler and source of assurance for each child's sense of self; a sense that enables constructive awareness through constructive relationship (especially with the teacher).**

## 4. Self-descriptors and group function

Beyond this 'self' application, self-descriptors can also be seen at work in group function. The group as a whole analyses, through self-descriptors, its function in relationship to externalities; often other groups. The individuals who make up the group, self-organize as a group, making decisions as to their group identity, purpose, and 'rules' of function. These are agreed upon protocols which, in most groups and certainly in the Four Communities Classroom, evolve according to the needs perceived by the group or are influenced by an individual who will attempt to prove to the group the efficacy of his/her idea of what should be. And, of course, while groups' self-organization is taking place, each group's individual members are simultaneously engaged in their own personal self–descriptor process. In the minute-to-minute life of your classroom, children's minds are engaged in the complex process of monitoring both themselves and their group. An understanding teacher and gentle guide, encouraging mutual regard and thoughtful response, helps build relationship skills that make your classroom an exciting and wonderful place to be.

Of course, children innately engage in these group functions without a lesson on group self-descriptor dynamics. Through the process of grouping and discussion, these dynamics will automatically be triggered. However, your understanding of these dynamics more readily enables your knowledgeable observation and contribution towards the environment that gives each young mind an opportunity to form responses and opinions. As the teacher, you can provide guidance to constructive group process. (See chap. 4 on group process.) Children are provided an environment where life and learning in the classroom are seamlessly engaged in processes of the mind that are ecologically-sound; self-descriptors in practice. Thus, through the life of the classroom, you provide an opportunity for ongoing positive engagement with life dynamics.

Always present, however, are the fluctuating emotional components of life that will affect the self-descriptor dynamics. But when, together, you and the children have established a classroom environment of mutual regard, with the added benefit of children's generally highly-evolved understanding of what is fair, emotions tend to be tempered with reason. Then self-correction comes into play, enabling children to bring an important life process into focus as part of their learning about self and others.

This important understanding, stemming from discussion of self-correction, (with the other self-descriptors in 'tow') enables mutual regard. And so from this one small beginning of learning about self-correction, with no need to be aware of the dynamics they are engaged in, children are enabled to become partners, with the teacher, in the learning process. As Mrs. Cummings, grade seven/eight teacher said, "Using the Four Communities Classroom makes it nice to come to work. I have such a good time." Yes, her class was full of grade seven and eight children!

But, when relationship and all associated dynamics are working constructively, does that mean everyone is going to get along well, and everyone will be best friends? Not necessarily, because within these dynamics lies the ecologically endowed infinity of the human mind; an infinity that enables, facilitates and causes difference to occur, one from another. However, with mutual regard, children more readily recognize the importance of difference and, importantly, the need to accommodate difference.

> **To summarize**
> - **Groups use self-organization. Decisions are made about group identity, purpose, and 'rules' of function.**
> - **Groups use self-descriptors in their relationship to other groups.**
> - **Groups' purpose and identity evolve according to their needs, or the influence of one or more individuals. Placing children in groups triggers these dynamics.**
> - **While groups are self-organizing, individual members are simultaneously engaged in their own personal self-descriptor process.**
> - **It is important for children that the teacher understands group process and provides guidance.** (See chap. 4 on group process)

## 5. The essential nature of difference and the ecological communication imperative

We have seen from appendix (ii) on the ecology, that boundaries are fundamental to the existence of difference and identity, and that the resulting distinct elements have their own unique job to do in concert with the whole. Think of all the individual organs and parts of your body and the job they do for you, while in ceaseless communication with each other. Communication is essential to life process, whether it is in the form of peptide communication between the cells within a person, or communication between people. Thus, it can be said that identity boundaries establish communication needs.

Identity defines distinction and makes every living thing an individual. Effective communication in the classroom is enhanced through a well established sense of identity and distinction within each child and also in group identity.

## 6. Ecological diversity and self-descriptor referencing to the surrounding environment

Diversity is the essence of life. In humans, our mind, brain and consciousness exhibit and play out the dynamics of infinite permutation. This is foundational to the existence of the differences between us. Without difference there is no need for relationship, communication, or exchange of energy. Without relationship and communication between us, self-descriptor processes have no purpose.

Diversity is the ecology's buffer against vulnerability. Vulnerability avoided produces sustainability. Sustainability is vital for life. Therefore, difference is vital for life. But it is here that we are brought to a paradox. We humans have often made difference between ourselves a basis for conflict. Thus, despite our intellectual and infinite permutation capacities; despite the fact that the ecology has gathered increasing strength and sustainability through the creation of difference over eons of change and development; and despite the fact that we are derivatives of this process and, with the endowment of conscious mind, the pinnacle of this evolution of difference, the importance of difference is marginalized, and too often removed from constructive communicative processes. Thus, through marginalizing the importance of difference we inadvertently create the profoundly anti-ecological state of vulnerability, the ecological mutuality imperative marginalized.

See chapter two, p. 110 on the 'importance-of-difference' discussion with children, where children begin to discover for themselves the importance of their own unique qualities and those of others; differences of perception, differences in what we perceive as important, differences in what attracts us and interests us most, differences in the way we learn and our speed of learning, and, of course, differences of opinion. And it is from difference that diversity arises.

Constructive life dynamics, through the use of self-correction, provide an environment in the Four Communities Classroom for learning how to understand and communicate difference as a vital part of life, rather than a source of unrest. This is a powerful process to engage as a remedy in troubled classrooms.

Often, out of these processes, expanded circles of friends result.

Charlie - grade 7 talking of grade 5.
*"It was a year for making friends - new friends. Now, even if we don't hang out with everyone, we can still go and talk with them anytime."*

While the goal is not to create a classroom of best friends, friendly interaction highlights for children the importance of difference and that difference enables engaging and interesting communication process.

## 7. Ecologically sound communication, tendency, and the process of becoming

Also factored into this mix of difference, identity and communication is the fact that we all have tendencies that contribute towards our personality and our identity. As we have seen in appendix (i) tendency is dynamic and not set, underlining that humans also are not set in absolute states; our individuality and our tendency is in a process of becoming. To a great extent, we choose what we become. But also, of course, the process of becoming is influenced by our tendencies, alongside our communication with others. So children's becoming is influenced by their tendencies alongside the environment the teacher creates for them, in which to become their best selves and become open to discovery of potential.

The process of becoming evolves and is nuanced through relationship, self-descriptors and the dynamics of living systems, including tendency. Tendency and becoming are in dynamic association. Thus, we can say tendency nuances the process of becoming, and becoming affects tendency. It is both an individual and community communicative process of becoming; each affecting the other. These elements of tendency and identity affect how children learn about themselves in relationship to others, and as they engage in self-descriptor processes.

Each child's demonstration of his or her tendencies are a mark of individuality, and a mark of difference and personality. So, for children, recognition of their difference, individuality and identity is respectful and affirming. Constructive development of these attributes in the child is enhanced through constructive relationship processes. Within the Four Communities Classroom, children are enabled to value the constructive tendencies of their personality; important building blocks in the establishment of a strong sense of self.

Any negative tendencies that a child may have tend to diminish in a positive interactive environment. This is an important consideration for teachers dealing with classroom problems.

Thus, teachers, of any grade, can think of communication as a relationship process that engages the tendencies of children. As tendency is a marker of identity, and as every child and class is different, teacher skills in communication and relationship are always in the process of being honed in the classroom.

In the Four Communities Classroom, communication is an evolving process that, combined with sensitivity to expressions of nuance, leads to a child's development. Communication and learning ability are enhanced, a stronger sense of self and self-esteem are established, and affirmation of the child follows.

Each child comes into the world as an unspoiled child of nature. As a teacher, you are honoured with the job of nurturing these young lives and enabling the expression of the transcendent ecological process that is within them and which is their birthright.

# We love school!

291   My Daughter *Can't Wait* for Monday Morning!

## (v) COMMUNICATION AND BEHAVIOUR IN THE CLASSROOM:
### The Containment Influence of Attractors Alongside Nuance, Discernment, And Learning

My reading of Briggs and Peat has been influential in the writing of this appendix.

### Introduction

In this appendix I consider how the teacher's recognition of containment influences (attractors) along with nuance and discernment can facilitate a greater understanding of children and recognition that the classroom culture acts as an external influence of containment.

As we have seen, in appendix (i) attractors are an essential dynamic in physics and also the ecology, as they are influences of containment, providing order to ecological expression. '... *nature combines influences of change with a variety of containment-influence attractors in order to maintain conditions that favour sustainability and balance in the ecology*'. (p. 239). For example, containment-influence on survival behaviour in horses creates herding, while wolves form packs.

In humans, containment-influence attractors impact tendencies, behaviours, and relationships (p. 239) functioning much like default positions, influencing many decisions and behaviours. We tend to make assumptions based on the comfort of that which is contained within the familiar. Thus the familiar can be a containment influence for our decisions and behaviour. We seek to make sense of the world and to seek positive feedback of rightness and acceptance; generally the mind seeks a comfort level.

These attractors of containment influence are also part of children's thought processes and influential in learning, development and perception in the classroom

Containment can be constructive or hinder. It is our sophistication as a specie that makes containment influences from external relationships powerful and sophisticated, e.g. the cultural influences that shape perceptions of how people think and act. However, within each of us is the power to alter, re-shape and modify containment influences with **nuance** and **discernment**. It is the thinking, questioning and discerning human mind that is better situated to sense, sift and respond to the containment influences of prevailing beliefs, benefiting from the constructive aspects of containment, alongside the ability to transcend limiting assumptions.

While attractors are having this constraining effect on relationships in dynamic systems, as Capra (ref. p. 240) says, everything is in a constant state of relationship change, making it difficult to make precise measurements of what is happening or what is about to happen. As such, a dynamic system is hard to measure and predict because it is constantly changing. With the influence of attractors, as Capra points out, we can only make predictions about the quality of how things will behave in the ecology. Thus, though we can observe children's behaviour in the classroom, reliable results cannot necessarily arise from measurement or prediction.

In children's development, learning, perception, thoughts and relationships we are enabled only to attempt to predict the quality of effect. This 'quality of effect' of attractors, the containment they provide for behaviour, thought, learning and development, perception and relationship, and our capacity to modify them, has important implications for educating children and, moreover, underlines that children's learning process is not a precise process.

> "(Our) human world centrally includes our inner world of abstract thought, concepts, symbols, mental representations, and self-awareness. To be human is to be endowed with reflective consciousness."
>
> Capra, '96, p. 282

**Communication**, as previously discussed, is also fundamental to the ecology and, since we are ecological beings, communication is also fundamental to us. However, in human communication there is increased complexity arising from nuance of thought and expression, discernment capacity, and the affect of containment influences upon perception. While containment influence affects mind process, perception and learning, its juxtaposition with nuance has a subtle yet powerful affect on communication.

Included in this appendix are thoughts on the intertwining of inner and outer aspects of mind and the possible effect upon our lives, from thought patterns to behaviours, to knowledge acquisition and response to culture and schooling.

We all respond, whether consciously or unconsciously, to nuance in body language and the most subtle voice inflection. Recognizing the power of containment influence and the importance of nuance is, I argue, essential to understanding children's behaviour in the classroom. Thus, with a view to exploring child behavioural dynamics that teachers may encounter, I consider the idea of containment influence, intertwined with our inner mind process.

In this exploration, I consider containment influence attractors as being essentially external influences on our minds (an outer aspect of mind) while nuance and discernment are essentially seen as primary elements of the inner dialogue of the mind (an inner aspect of mind).

> Our brains, with different tendencies, and different thoughts are distinct from others. We are engaged with tendencies of such complexity that nuanced thoughts arise and become the source of a further refined distinction of individualization. This is an important thought for teachers in their interactions with children.

### 1. The relevance of nuance, and tendency to the development of discernment in the classroom

Nuance can be observed in communication of personality, mood, and intent. However, nuance is also, of course, part of each child's private thought process - not necessarily to be observed. In both verbal communication and in private thought, nuance is constantly in play; an arbitrator in life process. Felt and/or expressed, nuance is linked to individual tendency.

Our thought processes make quality, pattern, movement and relationship interactively complex; we attach shades of meaning and nuance to these qualities and processes as part of our learning process. Thus, through our thought processes, we engage the subtleties of nuance and tendency, both in communication and in the learning process. Children, while developing and engaging in these processesof communication and learning, need guidance and also privacy to form their thoughts, as they discover and explore self and surroundings and strive to make sense of their world.

Since nuance is the backdrop for human questioning and also our communication exchanges, nuance can challenge containment attractors.

Say Briggs and Peat, '90 p. 194.
*"...nuances are full of the sense of missing information."*

The wondering, questioning and uncertainty of children in school, and at home, are expressions of nuance, and, it is especially important for teachers, therefore, to recognize that these elements are the beginnings of discernment evolving in a child's mind.

Briggs and Peat, p. 194, speak of nuance as being a complex of uncategorizable feelings and thoughts. This is in contrast with another tendency of mind; to use attractors as containment devices for thoughts and feelings; plateaus, perhaps, of assumptions. However, assumption contained within attractors may not necessarily concur with the nuanced thoughts of the inner mind. In fact Briggs and Peat, p. 195, regard nuance as the mind's foundation of wholeness, where shades of meaning play, sometimes beyond language and logic. *"… in nuance lies our sense of the wholeness and inseparability of experience".*

Briggs and Peat, '90 p. 195, link nuance, mind, and mental process.

*"When a germ which contains nuance falls upon mental ground sensitive to it, the result in (a) creator's mind is a disequilibrium flux of wondering, uncertainty, and wholeness which allows the material being worked with … to amplify subtleties, bifurcate to new planes of reference, and form feedback loops among different planes in a process which self-organizes a form to embody the nuance."*

These are foundational processes that lead to discernment, a valuable quality that you can foster in your classroom.

Two considerations:

1. Are the shades of meaning of nuanced thought pertinent to the life of your classroom.

> **To what extent are teachers aware that for children to translate their own nuance of thought (shade of meaning) into a verbal expression, requires careful consideration and represents an important and challenging mental process; an application of developing discernment capacity?**

2. Is an environment that is sensitive to germs of nuance pertinent to the life of your classroom?

> **To what extent, the teacher may ask, do I provide an environment conducive to openess?**

With these questions in mind, let us consider the following thoughts.

- Giving children the opportunity to voice their thoughts may allow them to think more freely.
- A classroom environment that encourages open minds encourages expressions of nuance and discernment.
- This, in turn, may lead to verbalized nuanced thoughts.
- This process tends to catch the imagination of children, giving those who engage in disruptive behaviour something more constructive to consider.

These thoughts of engagement with children have the power to shift children's minds from habitual patterns of thought, facilitating spontaneous self-organization, a point of bifurcation and a point of learning, affecting behaviour, attitudes, and perceptions. This is a process where the teacher encourages the use of nuance and discernment to constructively impact attractors.

What else would be going on?

- In isolation, our minds think what they will, but in groups, as in the classroom, children's minds engage with others in exploration of thought and assessment; self-directed learning and thought outcomes exercised in concert with the thoughts of others. Such experiences enable glimpses of self, potential and latent capacity. Such experiences supply feedback to children for the effort they have taken in responding to, considering, and expressing nuances of thought. The individual's autonomy (including their tendency) has influenced, and has been influenced through, the integrative engagement with others.
- Tendency, nuance, and attractors are all ecological attributes of the mind. Tendency and nuance are dynamics of fluctuating influence on attractors, which can cause change and evolution; a going beyond the plateaus of attractors. The process of class discussion engages these ecological elements, involving children in not only a mentally stimulating engagement, but, through their expression of questions and uncertainties,

nurturing their all-important emotions. It is important that the teacher be aware of these dynamics in the classroom.

Through nuanced response, the teacher can choose between the degree to which she allows attractors to influence developing minds, and the degree to which she accommodates nuance, in concert with individual student tendencies. It is all a matter of discernment. (The how-to of this are discussed in chapter 2.)

---

(See p. 226, 'A guide to relationship dynamics in the Four Communities Classroom', - the practical application of ecological elements engaged in the Four Communities Classroom)

---

## 2. The mind, nuance and the containment influence of curriculum learning

.Briggs and Peat, '90, p. 195, drawing on Paul LaViolette and William Gray.
*"… nuances circulate all the time from the emotional and perceptual centers of our brains only to become rapidly simplified by our cortex into thoughts that are categorical or "organizationally closed."*

The nuanced human mind shapes parameters of perception, which can develop into patterns of thought. Thought established into a pattern can then become a form of attractor (an assumption) that now exerts influence on further perceptions of the mind. Thoughts continue, but now within a self-imposed containment process.

Categorizing is one example of a parameter-setting attractor. Categorizing is an act of organization of knowledge involving containment and perhaps closure. In fact, when knowledge is compartmentalized, containment can have the effect of de-contextualizing it, making de-contextualizing also an attractor for the mind. Cartesianism, for example, is awash in such attractors, as are many cultural influences.

The emphasis often placed on knowledge-based and/or cultural attractors may explain why some people can experience disconnects between inner nuanced thoughts and accepted cultural norms.

Briggs and Peat, '90, p. 105, say,
*"Everything we regard as our knowledge of the world is organizationally closed. But our wondering, uncertainty, and questioning are full of nuance."*

Thus knowledge that is confined by its organizational structure can form an attractor for the mind; thinking contained within the parameters of a category. Simultaneously, any thinking that occurs outside the organizational parameters may be deemed marginal in relevance by self and/or others. This in itself acts as an attractor. Thus, the acquiring of knowledge may also carry the acquisition of an attractor. Incidentally, perhaps, this may have been the impetus behind the phrase, 'thinking outside of the box'.

It is important to note, however, that, despite the containment for the mind of knowledge-based attractors, we do have the nuanced capacity to wonder, to entertain uncertainty and to question.

For some, the quest for prestige, power, authority and financial reward can be an attractor outweighing wondering curiosity - if it pays, tell me what to do - if it enables acceptance, I'm in. This can be a hugely powerful attractor in restricting nuance

In school if nuance is restricted it may, over time, have a wearing effect on children's incentive for learning.

Within formalized education there exist cultural norms whereby curriculum is presented as organized and contained; in effect, attractors mandated by curriculum, and with nuanced thought seemingly constrained by curriculum requirements.

Plunkett, '99, p. 58, warns of curriculum that constrains.
*"…it is clear that a curriculum based upon rational assumptions is constrained by the scope of the assumptions made."*

Perhaps some learning opportunities in school end up being constrained by curriculum presented to children in secondary experience mode and with nuance marginalized, i.e. this is the knowledge needed - learn it.

Plunkett, again, '99, p. 58.
*"Formal models of the curriculum that rely upon rational knowledge structures cannot take account of experiential, intuitive, or creative learning. (primary learning experience) Curricula programmes determined in advance by rational calculation tend to deflect attention from individual students' needs and motivation."* [bracketed words are mine.]

Whereas it can be argued that organizing knowledge is useful and convenient for its acquisition, the concern here is that a contained emphasis can leave little room for the explorative and investigative engagement of children's emotively directed, curious and nuanced minds. I would contend that it becomes more difficult to feel ownership for knowledge and accept its acquisition through secondary experience when learning processes are separated from context and primary experiences.

However, since the sophistication of the human mind does permit choice, we are able to choose the degree to which we allow attractors to influence our minds, and the degree to which we remain open to nuance.

My intent is not to question the efficacy of subject disciplines and knowledge organization, but to examine the role of nuance and attractors, in a search for the enhancement of learning and teaching process. This enhancement includes not only the learning of curriculum, but also enabling children to constructively use their wondering, uncertainty, nuanced thought and questioning. A huge and added benefit is that such a combination feeds the development of the whole child - i.e. their autonomy nurtured in equal measure to their integration with knowledge.

I would like to continue by giving more consideration to attractors, and how they can manifest in human lives, especially those of children.

## 3. Containment influence, categorization, customary thinking, and organizational closure

Since, in the consideration of knowledge, mind is subject to attractors, customary thought patterns can arise with 'customary thinking', extending to many areas of life beyond curriculum.

Briggs and Peat, '90 p. 195.
*"Our usual patterns of thought organize themselves around their limit cycles."*

Perhaps in the need to make sense of the world the readily accessible process of organizing thought around attractors appears attractive.

Briggs and Peat, '90, p. 195.
*"(Events are) rapidly simplified by our cortex into thoughts that are categorical or "organizationally closed." Everything we regard as our knowledge of the world is organizationally closed".*

Briggs and Peat, '90, p. 193.
*"...habitual patterns of thought ... act like limit cycles."*

Thus, it appears reasonable to say that containment-influence attractors are part of customary thinking.

If attractors can affect mind processes, including opinions of culture, schools or even ourselves, these are powerful commentaries on the processes acting upon us and important when considering how to enhance children's learning experiences.

## 4. Cultural containment influence and customary thinking

If attractors form part of our cultural influences, shaping us as individuals and impacting our views, then it can be said they are an integral part of our environment and have defining influence. Perhaps many of us tend to look to the familiarity of cultural tradition with its customary patterns of thought, accepted behaviour and modes of perception. It is probably fair to say that the frontal cortex of the brain, in most instances, sifts, handles and legitimizes knowledge within culturally-influenced attractors. With the strength of the unquestioned customary thought pattern (assumptions) cultural influences can affect our worldview, our perceived options, our conclusions and our opinions (including ideology).

Moreover, individual differences will produce various interpretations of cultural influence, and span a spectrum of attractor responses, anywhere, perhaps from intransigence to open mindedness.

And, as usual, the over-riding factor cannot be ignored; that of our emotional state and the maintenance of our feelings of security and acceptance. Often feelings of security and acceptance can be found in group settings of 'mini-cultural' arrangements, i.e. the family, peer group, classroom, school, church, institution, workplace, profession, business, corporation, club, and class (as in class-consciousness), community, etc. All of these groups engage attractor parameters that can impact mental process. Such attractor parameters have the power to form the range of our thinking about ourselves and dictate 'rules' of relationship, and indeed, in some instances, the range within which authority is assumed.

Certainly each child's home will be fertile ground for an expression of attractors - those likely familiar to family members only.

One can sometimes observe children (and adults), when unfamiliar with the micro-cultural attractors of an unfamiliar place, using a variety of coping strategies, - perhaps shyness, awkwardness, politeness, or aloofness.

- **Detaching from parental containment influence - teenage exploration of self**

Children, in their teenage years, may explore alternative perceptions and alternative containment influences to those fostered in the family. This can sometimes cause uncomfortable interactions between parents and offspring, and between parents and the friends of their children. Unsettled by each other's culture, and with parental customary thinking challenged, it can be a difficult time of attractor conflict for parents and children. Mutual regard is difficult to maintain under these circumstances. Transversely, perhaps it could be said that containment influences, commonly held, can be creators of mutual regard. I think it could also be said that love is the fall-back attractor for families in search of mutual regard.

Meanwhile, within each individual, beneath the defining effect of containment influences, can lie nuance of feelings and thought which may not be legitimized by cultural attractors. The non-legitimatization of individual feelings and thoughts can create, in some young people, confusion and uncertainty.

As awareness of self grows, the teenage years, when emotions tend to run higher, are ones where peer group 'alternative' containment influences are in a state of flux, and relationship with others and the surrounding world becomes subject to greater scrutiny and, perhaps, dismissiveness.

In school, children and young adults may experience concern, confusion and frustration, as they consider a growingly complex world through culturally-induced attractors. Their immediate thoughts and conclusions may not always seem to fit with their inner thoughts of wondering, uncertainty, and questioning.

This confusion can make it difficult to both understand oneself and build and maintain constructive relationships within one's cultural environment. Thus, attractor parameters can represent obstacles for the mind (especially for the developing mind), making it also difficult to determine what constitutes sound judgment. Thus, for children, attractors can have a major impact on every aspect of classroom life, from degree of success in knowledge acquisition to sense of identity and relationship.

Culturally-induced containment influences can predispose one to primarily respond within certain parameters of communication and problem solving, whether related to subject matter, relationship, patterns of thought, customary thought, habit, or even patterns of language use, while perhaps obviating the realization of other thoughts and possibilities. Other perceptions can be denied as carrying little weight by both 'main-stream' attractors and by the attractors of teenage peer group counter-culture. In other words attractor thinking can crowd out consideration of other perceptions.

# 5. Classroom culture and its containment-influence attractors

When learning is culturally acceptable only within certain 'containment' attractor parameters ('this is the way it's done') it may mean that only the culturally acceptable bifurcation processes of the mind receive formal recognition. Selected and approved bifurcation processes, arising from 'contained' attractors of classroom culture can, therefore, have the power to limit learning process and seed diminishment of potential, (and mutual regard). This can leave little room for exploring minds.

However, discussion that is part of everyday life, as in the Four Communities Classroom, opens up an avenue for productive and positive exchange of thoughts and ideas; a place to explore, wonder, question and expand horizons, in a safe and accepting environment. This is a place where naturally occurring bifurcation is the order of the day, leading to a wider understanding of self and others and higher levels of discernment.

Class discussion that leads to awareness of difference is an important process. Bifurcation occurring in an environment of mutual regard between teacher and student is the process whereby a change in the ordered state of the 'containment' attractor can take place, taking it through chaos to a new order. Nuance, or the influence coming from another's 'containment influence' attractor, can create the impetus for this development.

Student journals that facilitate interaction between teacher and learner can become an outlet for nuance, when there is permission to go beyond 'containment influence' attractors. It is, of course, important that students feel safe in this process. To be otherwise would diminish the value of journal communication.

- **Detaching from school containment influence - when classroom protocols may contain seeds of frustration for children**

In teaching children, there is perhaps a paradox to consider. Any challenge by children to the attractors of assumed and established classroom culture may be considered off-limits by the teacher and a threat to class control and maintenance of discipline. However, attempts to maintain discipline within teacher-controlled attractors may provide no arena for expression or legitimatization of children's thoughts, questions and concerns. Children, if experiencing this disconnect, perhaps year after year, may develop a level of frustration, and perhaps resignation, where they find themselves searching for solace in self-created counter-culture peer group attractors (similar to outcomes discussed on p. 297 - 'Detaching from parental containment influence - teenage exploration of self'). Thus the attractors designed for class control can be overtaken by student-created attractors.

In other words, when seemingly without a voice and needing to make sense of his/her environment (an innate need), children may search for resolution in an attractor context of their own; perhaps a narrower context, but perceived as more controllable. Peer-created attractors could be thought by students to provide a more controllable environment, free of old restrictions, free of supervision, free of the need for legitimatization of self by adults; a peer-created sense of belonging.

Thus, it can be argued that teacher-supplied cultural attractors, which deny children expansion of perception and understanding through nuanced thought, can lead to the creation, by children, of alternative attractors of perhaps narrower perception. Unfortunately, of course, peer group attractors may isolate children from the larger reality that surrounds them, providing no effective solution in their search for making sense of themselves and their environment and, moreover, result in placing their potential on hold.

- **Can frustrations (and bullying behaviours) be abated within peer-group containment influences?**

Children's need for acceptance will cause them to form peer groups. However, with the pooled uncertainty of each individual's sense of self, children can form counter cultures based on a group-mentality of unexamined assumptions - in effect, adopted customary patterns of thought and behaviour. To belong, one must adhere to what can be a narrow set of protocols, (lingo, tonal expression, clothing, substance abuse are possible examples). Thus, attractors can be a collectively formed and self-imposed element of a young person's school life. Expression of views contrary to group attractor norms are, as in many attractor situations, not usually welcomed if they pose a threat to the group culture and the need for feelings of acceptance that initiated the group formation. If attractors include an anti-school sentiment, then classroom control becomes difficult to achieve. Thus, such attractors, which can include those that legitimize bullying, can represent major obstacles and struggles for individuals in the development of their maturity in school.

Acceptance, so needed by us all, can throw many children into these new attractor environments of peer group dynamics, even if this may not necessarily be their first choice. Internal nuance-struggles, weighing the comfort of acceptance against the price of admission, may play in many young minds.

When a peer environment pulls one way and the inner dialogue of nuance and/or school attractors another, the ensuing confusion (over resolution) may produce feelings of conflict and guilt. But do these elements of school and student necessarily have to be in opposition? It is interesting to note that the search for alternative and self-directed attractors is a phenomenon that appears more in children as they get older. This certainly is an established part of high school student experience and is often evident at younger ages, perhaps grade six onwards. Unfortunately, it seems that bullying attractors can appear at an earlier age. Is there a classroom environment that teachers can provide for children that will enable a smoother course towards maturity; the containment influences of common interest and ownership, where everyone can feel in partnership with inner and nuanced dialogue? Such a containment influence creates the assumption that all things are possible, every idea deserves consideration and every person deserves regard.

- **Teacher and children working together - learning beyond curriculum.**

In my experience, children in grades one to five do not usually notice constraining influences of classroom attractors and generally can be very amenable to, and excited by, classroom life; judgment, in a sense, suspended. This is a time of golden opportunity for teachers; opportunity, through the Four Communities Classroom, to consider and engage both with nuance and constructive use of attractors; an opportunity with lifetime implications. (See Ms. Eva's observations on p. 14.)

In the Four Communities Classroom, children are guided by the teacher towards the creation of their own classroom culture. They have a voice, a shared responsibility for outcomes and a sense of ownership. Together, they create a culture open to new ideas.

However, before widening the discussion on nuance and the constructive role of attractors in the classroom (subheadings 8, 9, and 10), I would like to consider other examples of attractor influence in the lives of children.

## 6. Containment influence of the 'neon light' face of the corporate world

In their lives beyond school, children are presented with the corporate environment of advertising, media, television, films and computer games. These are generally non-negotiable, integrative factors. Now smart phones, with a dizzying array of applications, introduce further complexity for young minds.

This increasingly dominant electronic backdrop to our towns, cities and homes is a powerful sensory environment that children, while trying to make sense of the world, find themselves obliged to factor in.

This influence of the big wide world contributes towards a child's integrative surroundings, outside of the classroom, creating an increasingly challenging environment for the child to communicate and negotiate within. This can be a lot to take on board, while trying to understand one's autonomous fit in an integrative world, complicating the development of self. Children can run into problems.

This is in contrast to a child's environment that is chiefly, and most influentially, populated by the immediate circle of adults and children in their lives; a healthy interplay created through an integrative and accepting process. This enables the development of each child's sense of autonomous well-being, within a manageable and nurturing circle.

Children, as we all do, integrate the dynamics of their autonomy with the dynamics and interplay of their surroundings. Children's peer-group is especially important in playing through the processes of negotiation and communication. This is a necessary role in the development of the constructive autonomy that is the essence of working towards autonomy and integration balance, which is nurtured in the Four Communites Classroom.

But when an environment is heavily influenced by corporate glitter, it will be an integrative one and may leave little room for the individual to shape that environment. When an environment is heavily integrative, it not a healthy environment in which to evolve and develop, during what should be, for children, a time of growing maturity within an environment referentially meaningful and of consequence to autonomous development.

While, in a sense, the corporate process is a two-way game of influence - appeal devices shaped by response - it is an uneven playing field. The giant market environment may hold sway to the detriment of the child's broader concerns and needs in life. Thus, it can be argued that an undiscerning child, operating within the parameters of a fad, be it the latest clothing or technological product, is not necessarily engaged in a productive process, when attempting the development of identity and self.

Who is there to help? The child's peer-group members are faced with the same dilemma - a corporate world that presents, to both the child and his/her peer-group, an almost overpoweringly dazzling marketplace. And here is the essential difficulty for all children. The child is attempting to negotiate and communicate with his/her peer-group in an environment heavily weighted towards one-way corporate communication. It appears that potentially meaningful child-to-child peer-group interaction is at risk of being coopted for corporate advantage. Seeking the acceptance of other children can now include demonstrating to peers tha latest product acquisition. Having the latest, coolest everything buys you in; it is a powerful way to market to children.

And so children, with the attractor of wanting to fit in, are vulnerable to corporate attractions, designed to translate, of course, into profit. On display are marketplace attractors shaped to target and appeal to the young. The imposed integration can be very persuasive and pervasive; an overweighted integration.

Thus, we may ask:
- when young people are in receipt of a seductive corporate message, telling them how to find acceptance through purchase of a product, to what extent are children able to achieve a strong sense of self, as distinct from assuming the efficacy of corporate claims and becoming a blank slate for marketing fads?
- if children are vulnerable to peer pressure, will they be able to see through the glitz and the need to belong, to the fact that someone just wants their money?

Fads/products may be fine, if accepted for what they are, and as adjuncts to life. However, if a young person adopts, without question, an all-encompassing, unexamined, kaleidoscopic life of fads and products, who are they? Perhaps they are existing more as children to be shaped to marketing attractors and corporate influence, rather than independent, nuanced, discerning, thoughtful contributors to society.

Thus we come to two questions:

> **1. How are our children equipped to resolve their sense of identity within attractor scenarios?**

> **2. To what extent do we prepare children to intelligently apply nuance and discernment, as they engage in their own lives and in their own development?**
>
> (box 5)

These questions, of course, are applicable to all attractor situations, both in and outside of the classroom.

In the Four Communities Classroom, discussion opens up opportunity for children, in a safe and caring environment, to share ideas on the world they live in and decide among their peers their preferred way of being.

## 7. Nuance, discernment, and the containment influence of texting with phones

Texting, when used constructively, can be useful for basic messaging; a tool of convenience, rather than a primary form of communication.

Communication that relies upon the inherent limitations of texting, rather than the subtle nuances of face-to-face communication, is communication where the interconnective qualities of nuance and discernment can be difficult to convey and, therefore, inhibited. Texting seems to be an especially limiting attractor.

In terms of bullying, texting would seem attractive for bullies, since it presents an attractor of particularly damaging dimension - human interaction downgraded to a hightech connectivity (to many people if so chosen) where discernment capacities can be readily short-circuited and degraded,

Discussion-based classrooms enable children to develop a sense of nuance and discernment, enabling them to see texting primarily as a high-tech transfer-of-information tool. Children with this understanding are perhaps better fortified to deal more effectively with cyber-bullying. (See 'the positive role of attractors' next page.)

## 8. Nuance and discernment viewed alongside the containment influence of attractors

Although attractors can influence minds, we do have the option of choice. Three considerations for the teacher.

1. Are there unexamined classroom attractors imposing a containment influence not necessarily conducive to mutual regard?
2. Can we use our abilities for nuance of thought and discernment to go beyond overly containing attractors?
3. Can we identify helpful attractors that enable the development of an order of mutual regard? (Perhaps thought of as 'values of mutual regard').

Since we are able, through use of the sophisticated frontal cortex of the brain, to consider discernment and nuance, individually and collectively, to determine thought, we can ask ourselves:

> **To what extent do we use, and to what extent do we submit, our minds to attractor containment influences?**

In consideration of mutuality, the question can be widened to ask:

> **What containment-influence attractors would be most enabling and encouraging for mutual regard and sustainability for the individual and community?**
>
> (box 6)

> **To what extent do we counter containment-influence attractors with deeper consideration, nuance and discernment to benefit individuals and community?**

Clearly nuance and discernment can serve as counters to attractors of the mind, but let us also consider the positive role of attractors.

- **The positive role of attractors**

Attractors in the ecology are vital for the order they provide. It is an order they also bring to the constructs of the human mind (categorization of knowledge for instance). But can we create an attractor that offers a foundation for mutuality?

In the choosing of classroom rights, the Four Communities Classroom demonstrates that such an order can be created; teachers and children, employing thought processes of nuance and discernment, choose attractors that are most likely to provide positive order; class-created constructive attractors that foster an environment of mutual regard. (See 'Classroom Rights', p. 92.)

Creating mutually-agreed-upon classroom rights is a route to constructive enriching attractors. Values that are held and encouraged in children play an important role in this process.

## 9. Seeking balance between nuance and containment-influence attractors

How does one determine what constitutes a balance between containment-influence attractors and nuance?

Into the mix go the following ecological factors.

1. Recognition that learning is an ecological imperative of life, and that children and their teacher are, therefore, engaged in life process in the classroom.
2. The purpose of learning is life enhancement.
3. Learning is of primary importance to the process of becoming.
4. Becoming is both an individual, environmental and community interconnected affair.
5. Mutuality is fundamental to the health and well-being of the process of becoming.

Since life process is subject to fluctuating influences, I believe, no one determination of attractors and nuance parameters will serve. The following may help to illustrate. In order to maintain a harmonious relationship, a couple might try to balance interactions with each other to accommodate the fluctuating influences of each person's individual development. However, success is more likely to result from striving for balance than trying to determine and maintain a set state.

So it is with the life of the classroom. Having established a positive attractor (e.g. classroom rights) as a productive foundation for good teaching and learning the class can, on an ongoing basis, discuss and resolve any issues that arise. By listening and responding to each other, teacher and children stay alert to events happenings and dynamics occurring. They monitor, react, listen, contribute, engage and participate. This is not a static process with one 'right' way of proceeding, but a fluctuating moment-to-moment life process of 'infinite permutation'; it is complex, and accentuated by the many people involved in the learning environment that teachers and children collectively and in an ongoing way create. So rather than establishing a set state in the classroom, the teacher enables a constructive environment that creates a dynamic balance of life process.

Fluctuating influences mean that balance is always in a state of becoming. Our mind's effectiveness in this process of becoming arises from our intelligence. When sensitivity, awareness, and response(ability) are engaged through a continuous flow of intelligent mutual regard interaction, then a state of balance between nuance and attractors will follow.

These dynamics, enabled by the teacher, become the currency for classroom interaction, and are held as the model that children follow as they develop sense of self in concert with others.

Thus, perhaps it is not so much a question of worrying about balance, as allowing it to happen; allowing and encouraging children to express their questions, wonderings and uncertainties in an atmosphere of acceptance and mutual learning; an atmosphere of facilitation of their ecological endowment, rather than a narrowing and restrictive containment process.

> 💡 **When the teacher understands and feels comfortable with ecologically endowed processes of nuance, discernment and tendency there is less need to try to maintain discipline and containment through attractor rules. Children are ecologically endowed. The ecological 'goods' do not have to be learned. Perhaps it is not so much a question of considering the balance between attractors and nuance, as just allowing children to express their questions, wonderings and uncertainties in an atmosphere of acceptance and mutual learning. Thus, rather than providing a narrowing and restrictive containment process, enable children to learn how to constructively use their endowment in an atmosphere of facilitation and mutuality.**

> 💡 **Creating an environment of mutual responsiveness and communicative exchange will encourage harmony between children and their externalities (children with other children, and children and the teacher).**

## 10. Maximizing learning in the classroom - engaging discernment, while seeking the balance of nuance with the containment influence of attractors

The mantra for teacher and child, in the development of balance in the classroom (of both nuance and attractors), and the development of discernment, is simple, 'Does this make sense?' Discernment and making sense of the world go hand in hand. Things have to make sense for the teacher, and for the children, both individually and collectively.

If events, happenings, processes and curriculum do not make sense to **all** lives in the classroom, then children can be adversely affected in their development of discernment. On the other hand, if context is given for events, happenings, processes and curriculum, children are more readily able to see relevance, and, therefore, sense. Development of our capacity for discernment involves the scrutiny of relevance and sense.

Intelligence in terms of sensitivity, awareness and response(ability) exercised on questions of relevance and sense can engage children in constructive wide-ranging primary thoughts; the type of thoughts from which ownership can arise, from which discussion can develop, from which the mental exercise of formulating convincing argument arises. Therefore, processes of relevance, sense-making, and discernment are processes of intellectual and mental stimulation; the stuff of learning and the stuff of classroom life. This is why discussion and experiential learning are integral to life in the Four Communities Classroom. A subject discussed or situation experienced is one more likely to be internalized and remembered.

A mind so exercised in school throughout the day, is a mind well positioned to learn all that the classroom has to offer. It is a mind well positioned to contribute intelligently to the life of the classroom, and well positioned to enable development of a discerning individual. Nuanced thoughts will be the catalyst for this development.

Such a mind can consider, with nuance, positive contributions to the sense and relevance of attractors, and develop questions to enable examination of attractors generally. This includes the attractors of curriculum knowledge which can be considered intelligently and with purpose. And, of course, minds which are mentally attuned to discern and examine containment influences (attractors) within the classroom experience are also able to extrapolate and have a better understanding and awareness of other attractor situations in the world beyond the classroom.

- **Discernment, primary experience, feedback, mutuality and the process of becoming**

Through the development of discernment, children are better able to consider what attitudes, behaviour and relationships best serve in the creation of a good atmosphere for learning. This process is helped when the classroom community of teacher and children value intelligent contributions of mutual regard. Affirmation of each individual and his/her contribution, builds the learning environment, and forms a major part of the practice of discernment capabilities.

An individual's discernment capacity, when applied to self and when seen as valued by others, makes a significant contribution to self-esteem and sense of identity.

It is a delight for teachers in the Four Communities Classroom to discover how thoughtful, nuanced and discerning children can be in the discussion process.

Mrs. Cummings, grade 7/8 teacher.
*"Using this system makes it nice to come to work. I have such a good time."*

All learning contributes to the process of becoming. What is being advocated is that as the constructive interconnection of attractors, nuance, and discernment pervade the classroom each child's process of becoming be enhanced, and be set up to be enhanced continually; a lasting legacy. Thus, children will be enabled to maintain this enhanced state indefinitely, for themselves, as they grow older. They will have learnt how. (See chap. one, p. 14, for Ms. Eva's observations of a group of grade eight children who had experienced the Four Communities Classroom during their grade five year.)

Part of the learning 'how' is modelled by the teacher in the life of the classroom in the way he/she communicates and relates when teaching curriculum or in the development of an atmosphere conducive to learning. For example, when classroom dialogue contributes to the 'making sense' process and when this dialogue causes children to engage in mentally stimulating questioning of themselves, each child is engaged in a constructive process of becoming.

The speculative question is probably the most powerful stimulus the teacher can use, and can be employed in both the teaching of curriculum and in consideration of mutual regard, e.g. "What if ...?" "What do you think of ...?" "Why do you think ...?" "How do you think that would work?" etc. Speculation can create the impetus to explore, and seed the germ that has children pursuing the excitement of discovery. Speculation, exploration and discovery enable children to apply themselves to the attractors of curriculum and knowledge, and to, simultaneously, apply nuanced questions that will lead them to make sense of what they are learning. The process of discovery also exercises discernment in assessment of the discovery. The pursuit of balance in practice.

Discovery is a powerful learning process. As nuance is applied, practiced and honed, children are enabled to explore further heights of relationship and self, and depths of knowledge.

Whether focusing on individual subject disciplines or employing a cross-curricular application of knowledge to the exploration of a topic, the teacher in the Four Communities Classroom uses an approach that makes sense to the learner. Importantly, this approach also allows knowledge attractors to be placed into context, which helps learners, considerably, in their internal ordering of knowledge. Internal ordering means knowledge remembered, as well as knowledge that can be generalized and applied, not only to other studies, but, beyond the classroom.

Children who are practiced in the nuance and discernment learning process, find that, even when they are in receipt of knowledge transmitted as a secondary experience, they are still able to order the knowledge internally by allowing their nuance and discernment of thought to come into play. (Ms. Eva's observation applies here again - p.14.)

For the child, legitimatization of their nuance, thought and discernment capacity originates from the nurture of primary experiences in the classroom. To develop this discernment, children need the freedom to practice inner thought processes, play with nuance of thought, turn them into form, and express them through discussion, questions and responses. They need to reflect on the feedback, reflect on nuances in the feedback, assess the validity of their own thoughts and ideas, and those of others. To be skilled in discernment, as is true for most things, one has to practice. The classroom, replete with opportunity for such involvement of thought, makes discernment a matter of course and daily fare for the developing mind. It is such capacities that enable children to choose constructive communications and behaviours, and be happy and productive in their lives and learning.

# CENTRAL THOUGHTS FOR TEACHERS OF THE FOUR COMMUNITIES CLASSROOM - CREATING THE HAPPY, PRODUCTIVE CLASSROOM ENVIRONMENT

An interconnected list for classroom life throughout the school day

**LIFE QUESTIONS DIRECTLY APPLICABLE TO THE CLASSROOM [arising from pp. 271 - 273 in appendix (iii) and p. 301 in appendix (v)]**

1. Does life in the classroom legitimise the child's inner dialogue? (box 1 - p. 271)

2. Does the classroom provide a non-judgemental environment for the child expression of thought processes? (box 2 - p. 271)

3. To what degree is this 'exerting control over our lives' an aspect of learning and facilitated by teachers? (box 3 - p. 272)

4. Will the ecological foundation of human emotional/neurological capacity be recognized, nurtured, cared for, and importantly, built-upon? (part of box 4 - p. 273)

5. To what extent do we prepare children to intelligently apply nuance and discernment, as they engage in their own lives and development? (box 5 - p. 301)

6. What containment-influences attractors would be most enabling and encouraging for mutual regard and sustainability, for the individual and community? (box 6 - p. 301)

**AND FIVE MAIN POINTS FOR THE CLASSROOM**

When thinking of children, think of:
- the existence of their continual inner dialogue (box 1 - p. 271) and its occasional expression (box 2 - p. 271) and their need to listen and be listened to.
- their need for control over their own lives. (box 3 - p. 272) - within a maturity-appropriate level of responsibility.
- their emotional and neurological development. (4 - p. 273)
- the importance to their development of nuance and discernment (box 5 - p. 301)
- classroom attractors (routines and protocols) that could assist development of mutual regard. (box 6 - p. 301)

**THOUGHTS THAT ENGAGE CLASSROOM-LIFE QUESTIONS**

When thinking of the child, give value to their:
- worthiness.
- constructive tendencies.
- identity.
- need to belong.
- self-esteem.
- efforts of self-assertion in balance with others.
- acceptance of self.
- acceptance of others (diversity and mutual regard).
- difference.
- need to connect to groups.
- need to make sense of the world.
- sense of fairness.
- dignity and need to protect themselves emotionally.

**ACTIONS THAT ENGAGE CLASSROOM-LIFE QUESTIONS**

As the teacher, be:
- consistent.
- the facilitator and orchestrator of the environment for good teaching and learning.
- a facilitator of the process of becoming for each child.
- a facilitator of children's self-descriptor processes.
- a facilitator of constructive feedback.
- a non-judgemental facilitator of communication.
- a partner with individuals.
- a partner with groups.
- a partner with the class.
- the guide for class and group discussions.

**AS THE TEACHER, REMEMBER:**
- the power of positive emotions and feelings for children and their learning.
- to legitimize children.
- to respect the privacy of children's inner dialogue.
- the incentive-power of the speculative question.
- the sense of journey and discovery for children.
- that context and meaning help children to learn.
- the corporate, news media, and electronic context of children's lives beyond the classroom.

# THE INTERACTIVE ENTITIES OF THE FOUR COMMUNITIES CLASSROOM THAT ENGAGE LIVING SYSTEM DYNAMICS

Striving for a balance of autonomy of self,
integrated constructively with the surrounding environment

### Teacher
The teacher is orchestrator and facilitator of balance between all entities. The teacher is the enabler of sustainable growth and learning. The teacher is the centre for communication and feedback, and constructive expediter of the living system dynamics of becoming.

### Work And Curriculum
The work and curriculum provide an avenue for interaction and effort. They form the avenue for knowledge acquisition, including knowledge of self and others in relationship, as well as curriculum.

### Child (emotions)
The child, with emotions central to sense of self, and with protection of self paramount, is likely focused equally upon the teacher and the group; analysing and assessing. Curriculum and classroom are more easily atttended to when the child is feeling settled.

### Groups
The group tends to focus mostly upon self-organization, sense of groupness and group identity. The group references itself through teacher feedback.

### Classroom
The classroom acts as a meta-system feedback process and, when all entities are coordinated and functioning effectively, exudes a happy productive atmosphere. It is the system bell-weather for everyone.

These five entities are coupled (linked) through interactions. Communication, nuance, feedback, and self-organization are the coupling agents and source and carriers of life and energy in the classroom - all are living system dynamics in the process of becoming. The quality of being and quality of potential are always in process.

Briggs and Peat, p. 197.
"... each part is coupled to, ... generated from, and is a reflection of each part."

# LIVING SYSTEMS GLOSSARY OF THE ECOLOGICAL *PROCESS OF BECOMING*

The interconnectedness of the work I have referenced and their descriptive words enables a glossary that applies to elements of living systems theory and, through the process of becoming, to learning process in classrooms.

The living systems glossary has, therefore, words that apply, simultaneously, to more than one element of living systems theory.

To offer a more ready reference for teachers, I have given an anthropocentric slant to some of the definitions of the process-of-becoming words. Living system elements and references, contribute towards understanding the process of becoming.

---

### *Autonomy*
of being individual, different. Associated with inner realms of thought and sense of self and identity.

### Attractors (of the mind)
order arising out of limits and boundaries that can bring a sense of containment/control for constructs of the mind.

### Bifurcation
a point of change, development and learning in response to externalities.

### Boundaries of identity
a mark of difference, requiring communication with other identities.

### Chaos
a process of change that breaks through previous perceptions of order.

### Chaos through to order
a process of change that coalesces and organizes to a new perception of order.

### Cognition
perception and awareness of an externality.

### Ecological core
humankind's common ecological foundation (affecting both our physical makeup and mind).

### Equilibrium
a state requiring no transaction of energy or communication.

### Emerging properties
outcomes from the interaction of many variables, the quality of which are more subject to approximation than prediction.

### Externalities
environments, people, and events that surround and exert influence upon an individual's autonomy.

### Far-from-equilibrium
a state causing engagement of transaction and communication; impetus for development, change and learning.

### Feedback -
(I) **Positive** feedback is reiterating and self-reinforcing without regard for negative feedback.

(II) **Negative** feedback is regulatory, involving, for example:
    self-regulation, self-balancing, self-maintenance, self-organizing, self-correction, self-monitoring.
    (see p. 284 for list)

**Group dynamics**

interacting elements that simultaneously engage a group and individuals within the group.

**Group self-organization**

consensus established as a requirement for group function.

**Infinite permutations**

open potential, indicative of continuous change, development, transition and becoming. Renders temporary a sense of the absolute, i.e. in outcomes there are no absolutes.

**Integrated body systems**

body system entities function in concert - identity, health and functionality depend upon integrated communication processes, from brain function to all body systems. This is illustrative of the pattern of healthy ecological interaction.

*Integration*

a communicative process for individual identities, in a healthy system, for the common good of environment for self and other constituents.

**Iteration**

repeating of an element.

**Mutuality**

interdependency - an ecological imperative that responds to the common interest, creating right conditions for life.

**Mutual regard**

a process of interaction for the common good that gives and receives regard in equal measure, maximising life process for self and for the externality made up of other people and the environment.

**Network**

mutual self-organization of communication between entities.

**Non-deterministic**

fluctuating influences mark ecological process, making precision and determination difficult if not virtually impossible.

**Nuance**

inner thoughts of wonder/speculation, and germ of possibility and creativity.

**Order**

(i) established pattern of perception/behaviour/knowledge.

(ii) can be a containment process for perception/behaviour/knowledge.

**Patterns of organization (in a healthy system)**

(agreed) communication processes designed for the common good.

**Peptides**

chemical communication processes between cells and body systems to ensure coordinated function.

**Primary experience**

individual first hand experience analysed by private inner thought - an internalized learning/knowledge process.

**Relationship dynamics**

never ceasing, non-static, fluctuating, emotion-held elements that require continuous feedback and response interaction.

**Secondary experience**

information packaged and presented by an externality.

**Self**

knowledge of the boundary that forms identity and the distinction from others.

**Self-assertion**

announcement/presentation of self as being of worth.

**Self-conducted dynamics**

the self-monitoring and other self-descriptors that guide engagement with externalities.

**Self-descriptors**

self-regulation, self-balancing, self-maintenance, self-organizing, self-correction, self-monitoring. (p. 284)

**Self-validation**

assessing of self in reference to externalities.

**Symbiosis**

a process of mutual regard interaction for the common good.

# Index

## A

absoluteness, (no absoluteness) 238, 245, 276. *See also* precision
acceptance 168, 171, 172, 174, 182, 189, 198, 202, 256, 292, 299, 300, 303, 306
attractor, attractors 193, 239-242, 254, 292-304, 306
autonomy and integration ii, vii, 12, 15, 16, 46, 56, 57, 168, 169, 170, 172, 175, 243, 251-254, 256, 261, 262, 283, 284, 286, 287, 300

## B

balance 241, 253, 261, 284, 287, 304
  balanced 253, 256, 287
  self-balancing 241, 256, 257, 287
Barlow, Connie 241, 249, 255
becoming and belonging 23-25, 169-171 *See also* process of becoming
bifurcation 46, 56, 74, 77, 79, 84, 91, 201, 237, 240, 242, 243, 246, 252, 254, 276, 283, 294
boundaries 249, 259, 289
Briggs, John and Peat, F. David 8, 56, 233, 235, 237, 238, 239, 241, 243, 274, 276, 292, 293, 294, 295, 296, 307
bullies, bully, *and* bullying 15, 106, 107, 111, 172, 175, 176, 195-198, 200-203, 286, 299, 301,

## C

Capra, Fritjof vii, viii, 9, 10, 11, 25, 51, 187, 233, 234, 235, 236, 237, 238, 239, 240, 241, 242, 243, 244, 247, 248, 249, 254, 255, 275, 292, 293
chaos 46, 50, 59, 225, 235, 237, 238, 239, 240, 242, 245, 246, 252, 254, 276, 283, 298
Chopra, Deepak, 233, 234, 235
classroom rights 71, 72, 91, 92-104, 107-109, 117, 123, 171, 183, 185-187, 194, 302. *See also* rights
cognition 251, 254-256, 259, 274
communication vii, 46, 52, 56-60, 96, 132, 140, 206, 219, 240, 242, 243, 247, 248, 250, 259, 262, 263, 264, 265, 266, 269, 270, 272, 273, 274, 276, 289, 290, 293, 301, 306, 307
community 38, 52, 170, 181, 220, 306
complexity 236, 238, 242-246, 254, 263, 266, 267, 293
containment influences *See* attractors.
context vii, 14, 213, 245, 305, 306
cooperation 16, 244, 262
coupling/coupled 251, 252, 254, 255, 267, 307
curriculum 80, 166, 213, 214, 260, 269, 279, 295, 296, 303, 304, 307

## D

Diamond, M.C., Scheibel, A.B., and Elson, L.M. 266, 267, 269, 270
difference 110, 111, 112, 117, 155, 234, 235, 248, 259, 260, 289
dignity 215-217, 286, 306
discernment 91, 96-101, 140, 160, 171, 256, 273, 275, 276, 278, 279, 280, 281, 292-295, 298, 301-306
discovery 278, 281, 290, 304
discussion 34, 40, 51-57, 59-61, 83, 84, 87, 89, 90, 95, 98, 105, 106, 109, 113, 117, 119, 176, 182, 189, 197, 205, 209, 213, 241, 246, 247
disequilibrium 237, 254, 294. *See also* far-from-equilibrium
dynamic system(s) 238-240, 292

## E

ecological classroom 12, 13, 25, 208
ecological core iv, vi, 11, 15, 17, 22, 233, 246, 255, 282
Ecological pattern (boxes) 46, 49, 51, 52, 53, 77, 84, 98, 111, 169, 208, 209, 250, 268, 269
ecological process 15, 22, 23, 84, 189, 220, 233, 237, 240, 244, 245, 246, 248, 249, 251, 253, 257, 260, 263, 290
ecology vii, 117, 232, 236, 239, 240, 244, 247, 248, 249, 252, 253, 255, 257, 260, 261, 265, 277, 282, 289, 292
emergent/emerging properties 235, 236, 238, 239, 245, 276
emotion(s) vii, 111, 262-271, 273, 274, 280, 306
environment/environmental 56, 84, 119, 132, 170, 197, 233, 236, 237, 241, 243, 244, 249, 251, 252, 257, 261, 268, 269, 271, 283, 294, 298, 299, 303, 306
exploring/exploration 35, 51, 89, 286, 294, 298
externalities/externality 27, 44, 46, 49, 50, 51, 56, 58, 59, 78, 80, 84, 105, 116, 117, 169, 174, 188, 192, 194, 250, 251, 256, 259, 262, 264, 265, 266, 267, 268, 269, 271, 272, 274, 278, 280, 283, 284, 285, 303

## F

faith in self 91, 137, 140
far-from-equilibrium 237, 239, 245. *See also* disequilibrium
feedback 50, 52, 56, 177, 203, 235, 241-244, 246, 253, 256, 283, 284, 286, 294, 307
  negative feedback 241-243, 252, 253, 283, 284
  positive feedback 241, 242, 252, 253, 283
feelings 19, 52, 56, 111, 115, 130, 131, 133, 134, 171, 200, 201, 210, 211, 214, 215, 262-265, 271, 272, 273, 282, 283, 285, 293, 297, 306
fluctuating/fluctuation/fluctuations 234, 237, 238, 242, 245, 252, 302,
freedom/task process 75, 79, 88-90
frontal cortex 189, 260, 265-272, 296, 301

## G

Goldman-Rakic, Patricia, S. 271
group discussion circles 53, 176
group dynamics 168-172, 174, 177
group function 288
group process 76, 184

## H

habitat(s) 37, 250, 251, 253
Hagelin, John, S. 275

## I

identity 248-251, 259, 288-290
individuality ii, 56, 150, 248, 249, 261, 289
infinite permutation/possibilities/potential 3, 10, 98, 235, 245, 276, 277, 281, 289, 302
inner dialogue vi, 15, 46, 89, 105, 106, 108, 111, 113, 116, 141, 157, 166, 168, 217, 219, 257, 271-275, 277, 299, 306
integration/integrative 14, 81, 84, 168-172, 174, 175, 250, 252, 253, 255, 256, 259, 261, 272, 299, 300,
iteration/iterates/iterative 242, 252, 253

## L

LeDoux, Joseph, E. 268
living systems *see* systems theory
Lovelock, James 237

## M

memory 111, 154, 163, 255, 257, 269, 271, 273
mind 270, 275, 277, 278, 279, 280, 283, 287, 288, 292, 293, 294, 295, 296, 297, 304
moments 58, 86, 111, 235, 238, 245, 254, 262, 267, 271
mutuality vii, 169, 234, 240, 241, 242, 245, 248, 251, 253, 254, 255, 257, 259, 265, 277, 278, 279, 289, 301, 302, 303, 304
mutual regard ii, 15, 18, 21, 54, 87, 96, 98-101, 106, 110, 134, 169, 170, 171, 175, 192, 196, 200, 201, 208, 209, 215, 216, 219, 236, 240, 241, 245, 248, 251, 253, 254, 272, 278, 280, 286, 297, 298, 302, 303, 304, 306

## N

network 241, 242, 245, 249, 250, 267, 269, 274
nuance 34, 92, 198, 290, 293, 294, 295, 296, 299, 302, 304, 306, 307

## O

order 46, 50, 59, 73, 79, 82, 235, 237, 238, 242, 244, 245, 246, 252, 254, 276, 282, 302, 305

## P

Pert, Candace 262, 263, 264, 267, 268, 269, 270, 271, 272, 273, 274
Pike, Graham 125
Plunkett, Dudley 295, 296
possibility 73, 234, 235, 276, 277, 281, 309
potential 165, 192, 234, 235, 242, 245, 257, 258, 271, 276, 278, 280, 281, 283, 287, 298, 307
precision 232, 238. *See also* absoluteness
primary experience 19, 24, 25, 31, 48, 57, 61, 73, 79, 84, 92, 93, 107, 175, 186, 197, 198, 207, 255, 256, 279, 285, 286
    secondary experience 19, 24, 26, 31, 48, 88, 92, 93, 175, 197, 256, 279, 280, 285, 296, 305
primary learning experience 23, 26, 75, 77, 79, 96, 123, 219, 296
primary thinking 73
Problem or Opportunity 48, 58, 109, 211, 214
process of becoming 25, 254, 259, 264, 265, 277, 279, 289, 290, 303, 304, 306, 307. *See also* becoming and belonging

## Q

quality 237, 239, 240, 245, 251, 261, 268, 274, 281, 292, 293, 307
quantum physics 10, 232-236, 241
quantum realm 234, 235, 239, 276

## R

reciprocation ii, 18, 192, 208, 209, 212, 213, 219, 250, 253
relationship 11, 12, 16, 31, 34, 41, 46, 56, 59, 96, 101, 104, 108, 116, 117, 120, 134, 168, 176, 178, 201, 202, 204, 209, 211, 216, 234-236, 239, 240, 245, 246, 248-250, 252, 259, 265, 268, 273, 275, 276, 278, 281, 282-284, 286-288, 290, 292
relationship learning 209
responsibility iv, 15-17, 19, 22, 25, 46-48, 54, 62, 65, 85, 91, 100, 102, 105, 107, 108, 116, 121, 141, 174, 176, 197-200, 208, 209, 214, 253, 255-257, 278, 283, 284, 286, 306
rights 18, 82, 86, 90-96, 102, 103, 107-109, 111, 117, 176, 177, 184-186, 209. *See also* classroom rights

## S

Sagan, Carl and Druyan, Ann 232, 255, 260, 262, 263
Selby, David 125
self-descriptors 113, 116, 256, 257, 272, 279, 282-290
Self-descriptors
  self-assertion 217, 256, 257, 287, 306
  self-correction 77, 113, 115-117, 134, 137, 170, 206, 215, 217, 219, 261, 266, 267, 284-289
  self-organization 26, 41, 43, 78, 111, 172, 177, 225, 237, 245, 246, 248, 249, 252, 256, 261, 262, 264, 265, 266-268, 272, 276, 288, 294, 307
  self-organize 14, 244, 249, 261, 267, 288
  self-organizing 14, 15, 44, 55, 111, 116, 232, 237, 238, 244, 245, 261, 263, 267, 272, 288, 308, 309
  self-regulation/regulating 49, 172, 175, 241, 242, 256, 257, 261, 272, 279
sensitivity 106, 234, 239, 245, 246, 276, 281, 290, 303
Shatz, Carla 266, 267
speculation 33, 34, 83, 204, 205, 277
Sterling, Stephen 26, 177, 178, 232, 251, 258
Sterling System for Ecologically-based Sustainable Classrooms iii, ii, vi, 227
sustainability 26, 110, 244, 246, 254, 281, 289
symbiotic 244-246, 248, 255, 259
systems theory, *including* living systems, living systems theory, *and* theory of living systems iv, 8, 10, 11, 12, 14, 19, 20, 59, 111, 232, 234, 237, 240, 245, 248, 250, 251, 256, 269, 282, 292, 308

## T

teacher's job/role/task, teacher creates, teacher's mindset, thoughts for teachers 21, 48, 56, 87, 89, 137, 176, 194, 196, 198, 203, 208, 216, 258, 269, 287, 290, 306
tendency 239, 245, 276, 289, 290, 293, 294, 303
Teske, John, A. 265, 270, 272, 273
transcendence 277, 281

## U

uncertainty 236, 239, 245, 253, 293, 294, 295, 296, 297, 299
unpredictability 17, 234, 235, 239, 245, 275, 276
unpredictable 89, 234, 235, 245, 246

## V

visiting rights 173

# Bibliography

Briggs, John and Peat, F. David, 'Turbulent Mirror: *An Illustrated Guide To Chaos Theory And The Science Of Wholeness*', Pub. Harper and Row, New York, 1990.

Barlow, Connie, Editor, 'From Gaia to Selfish Genes: Selected Writings in the Life Sciences', Pub. The MIT Press, Cambridge, Massachusetts, London, England, 1998.

Capra, Fritjof, 'The Turning Point: *Science, Society And The Rising Culture*', Pub. Bantam, Toronto, New York, London, 1983.

Capra, Fritjof, 'The Web of Life: *A New Synthesis of Mind and Matter*', Pub. Harper Collins, London, 1996.

Chopra, Deepak, 'Perfect Health: *The Complete Mind Body Guide*', Pub. Three Rivers Press, New York, 2000

Diamond, M.C, Scheibel, A.B, and Elson, L.M, 'The Human Brain Coloring Book', HarperPerennial, New York, 1985.

Goldman-Rakic, Patricia S., 'Working Memory and the Mind', The Scientific American Book of the Brain, p. 91 - 104, 1992.

Hagelin, John S., 'Is Consciousness the Unified Field? A Field Theorist's Perspective', Maharishi International University, Fairfield, Iowa.

Hagelin, John S., 'What The Bleep!? Down The Rabbbit Hole', Quantum Edition, DVD by Captured Light Industries, 2006, Twentieth Century Fox.

LeDoux, Joseph E., 'Emotion, Memory, and the Brain', The Scientific American, 1994.

Lovelock, James, 'Gaia: *A New Look At Life On Earth*', Pub. Oxford University Press, New York, 1989.

Pert, Candace, 'Molecules of Emotion: *The Science Behind Mind-Body Medicine*', Pub. Touchstone, New York, 1999.

Pike, Graham and Selby, David, 'Global Teacher, Global Learner', Pub. Hodder and Stoughton, London, 1988.

Plunkett, Dudley, 'Secular and Spiritual Values: *Grounds for Hope in Education*', Pub. Routledge, London and New York, 1990.

Ralston Saul, John, 'The Unconscious Civilization', Pub. House of Anansi Press, Toronto, 1995.

Sagan, Carl and Druyan, Ann, 'Shadows of Forgotten Ancestors,' Pub. Ballantine Books, New York, 1993.

Shatz, Carla J. 'The Developing Brain', The Scientific American Book of the Brain, p. 3 - 15, 1992.

Sterling, Stephen, 'Sustainable Education: *Re-visioning Learning and Change*', Schumacker Briefings, No. 6, Pub. Green Books for the Schumacker Society, Dartington, U.K, 2001.

Sterling, Stephen et al, Ed., Fiona Duncan, 'Linking Thinking: New perspectives on thinking and learning for sustainability', Units 1,2 and 3. A publication of the World Wildlife Fund (WWF) Scotland, 2005.

Teske, John A., 'The Neuroanthropological Fabric of Spirit'. Paper presented to the Sixth European Conference on Science and Theology - Cracow, Poland. 1996.

Made in the USA
Charleston, SC
01 June 2013